The Caste *of* Merit

The Caste *of* Merit

ENGINEERING EDUCATION IN INDIA

Ajantha Subramanian

To Preeti + Bruno,
Here's to more meetings
in Madras, NYC,
Cambridge + more!
Ajantha
2/18/23

Harvard University Press

Cambridge, Massachusetts

London, England

2019

Library of Congress Cataloging-in-Publication Data

Names: Subramanian, Ajantha, 1969– author.
Title: The caste of merit : engineering education in India /
Ajantha Subramanian.
Description: Cambridge, Massachusetts : Harvard University Press,
2019. | Includes bibliographical references and index.
Identifiers: LCCN 2019005718 | ISBN 9780674987883 (alk. paper)
Subjects: LCSH: Indian Institute of Technology (Chennai, India) |
Caste—India. | Caste-based discrimination—India. | Discrimination
in education—India. | Educational equalization—India.
Classification: LCC HT720 .S823 2019 | DDC 305.5 / 1220954—dc23
LC record available at https://lccn.loc.gov/2019005718

For my parents, V. Vasanthi Devi
and K. S. Subramanian

Contents

The Caste of Merit

Introduction

In a 2003 episode of the CBS television news show *60 Minutes*, anchor Leslie Stahl called the attention of Americans to a diasporic population in their midst. "What is America's most valuable import from India?" she asked rhetorically. "It may very well be brainpower. Hundreds of thousands of well-educated Indians have come to the U.S. in recent decades—many to work in the computer and software industries." Stahl then specified further: "The best and brainiest among them seem to share a common credential: They're graduates of the Indian Institute of Technology, better known as IIT."[1]

That same year, Stahl's laudatory assessment of the IIT system was echoed in more sardonic terms by Scott Adams, creator of the comic strip *Dilbert*. In a September 15 strip, its Indian character, Asok, announced that as a graduate of an IIT, he was "mentally superior to most people on Earth." The following day, Asok elaborated, "At the India [*sic*] Institute of Technology, I learned to use my huge brain. But I try not to frighten ordinary people with any gratuitous displays of mental superiority. For example, I no longer reheat my tea by holding it to my forehead and imagining fire."[2] With this blend of new and old racial stereotypes of the mystical Indian, the IIT was brought more firmly into American popular consciousness.

Stahl's and Adams's early twenty-first-century glorification of Indian technical knowledge contrasts sharply with attitudes in the late

I

colonial period. In nineteenth-century British India, the colonial government expressed a clear preference for engineers from England whose
minds were deemed unfettered by the bonds of tradition. Officials over-
seeing the establishment of the engineering services repeatedly lauded
the technical prowess of Europeans, at times treating technical knowledge as a form of racial property. A century later, the racial stereotypes associated with Indian technical knowledge have been inverted:
from "natives" needing to be schooled in the ways of the modern machine, Indians are now invested with an innate capacity for technical
knowledge.

Over the nineteenth and twentieth centuries, India witnessed another significant change. Technical knowledge went from being the
purview of Indian lower-caste artisans to becoming integral to state
power, economic development, and upper-caste status. This process
was intimately linked to the rise of engineering. As technological modernization became the emblem of state prowess and societal progress,
engineering emerged as a white-collar profession tied to the public display of modern power. In India, the growth of engineering education
sidelined lower castes and conscripted upper castes with no prior technical skill into the ranks of a new profession. With the postcolonial
state's fuller embrace of technologically driven development, the divergence between artisanship and engineering was further consolidated,
as was the association between technical knowledge and upper-caste
status.

The Caste of Merit chronicles the rise of engineering education in
India in the context of older forms of social and economic stratification. More specifically, it illuminates the relationship between engineering education and caste formation.[3] At the heart of the study are
the Indian Institutes of Technology. Through a historical anthropology
of Indian engineering education, the book tracks how the IITs and their
predominantly upper-caste graduates came to be seen as global exemplars of Indian technical knowledge.

A key dimension of this story is the complex relationship between
caste and merit. At first glance, the two terms appear antithetical.
Caste is the social institution most emblematic of ascriptive hierarchy,
while meritocracy is typically understood as a democratizing force that
levels inherited privileges and disadvantages. When one looks at the

uppermost echelon of higher educational institutions in India, however, caste and merit appear far more proximate, even intimate. Seventy-odd years after independence, the institutional spaces most identified as meritocratic, like the IITs, continue to be overwhelmingly upper caste in composition. Moreover, attempts at opening up these spaces to lower castes through affirmative action and other democratizing measures are consistently met with fervent opposition, not in the name of caste but in the name of preserving "merit." Part of my concern, then, is to understand how the democratic ideal of meritocracy services the reproduction of inequality. I analyze the interplay of ascription and achievement through which the collective inheritances of caste have become emblematic of individual merit. In doing so, I argue that social stratification is endemic and not anomalous to contemporary democracy.

The intimacy between caste and merit throws into question the widespread assumption that identitarianism is principally a politics of the marginalized. In the Indian context, this assumption is reflected in arguments about caste as a more salient basis of social distinction and self-definition for lower than for upper castes. More specifically, upper-caste urban professionals are thought to have transcended caste to adopt more modern forms of identification; thus, they are assumed to be casteless by virtue of their modernity. In part, this is because since the 1970s, media and scholarly attention has been far more focused on how lower-caste mobilization has transformed the contours of Indian society and politics. While attention to lower-caste politics has illuminated the transformative potential of subaltern agency, it has also produced an equation between caste politics and subaltern identitarianism. As a result, the proliferation of writing on lower castes that points to caste as a sociopolitical category operating through various registers and at different scales has not led to similarly robust engagement with upper-caste self-definition and maneuver.[4] This is where my work comes in. I look at the role of engineering education, and the IITs in particular, in producing newly consolidated forms of upper-caste affiliation. The leveraging of merit, I argue, must be seen as an expression of upper-caste identitarianism that attempts to forestall progress toward a more egalitarian society and derives its legitimacy from a larger global politics of ascription.

While this book considers the IIT system as a whole, I focus my institutional ethnography on the study of one IIT—IIT Madras, located in Chennai, the capital city of the southeastern state of Tamilnadu. Tamilnadu is a particularly illuminating context in which to look at the making of upper-caste identity because its history of caste rights politics—in particular, the Non-Brahmin and Dravidian movements—complicated the naturalization of merit and the transformation of upper castes into casteless moderns. Here, as in other regions with strong traditions of lower-caste rights, merit has long been understood as a product of historical privilege and not simply of innate ability. Moreover, Tamilnadu is the first postindependence state where upper castes challenged measures to democratize access to higher education in the name of both their caste nature and their merit. In this sense, Tamilnadu calls into question castelessness as a stable structure of postindependence upper-caste subjectivity.

While the legacy of lower-caste rights movements within Tamilnadu has been exhaustively addressed, less noted is how they have shaped a more far-reaching politics of meritocracy. This book showcases Tamilnadu as an important precedent in a proliferating politics of meritocracy. It asks how the dialectic of lower-caste claims to rights and upper-caste claims to merit in Tamilnadu might inform an analysis of caste more broadly. In foregrounding Tamilnadu as a key site for the postindependence elaboration of meritocracy, the book calls for a relational approach to merit. Claims to merit, I will argue, must be understood as responses to subaltern assertion. Analyzing meritocracy in relation to subaltern politics allows us to see the contextual specificity of such claims: at one moment, they may be articulated through the disavowal of caste; at another, through caste affiliation. As I will show throughout the book, collective belonging and claims to merit are eminently commensurable and become more so when subaltern assertion forces historical privilege into the foreground. Far from the progressive erasure of ascribed identities in favor of putatively universal ones, then, what we are witnessing today is the rearticulation of caste as an explicit basis for merit. Moreover, this rearticulation is not simply the assertion of already constituted caste identities. Rather, claims to merit generate newly consolidated forms of upper casteness that become the basis for capital accumulation.

This back-and-forth movement between the marking and un-marking of caste within claims to merit suggests the need for greater nuance in approaching the concept of meritocracy. Even the critical literature that illuminates the workings of caste, racial, or class privilege within seemingly meritocratic institutions ends up arguing for a better meritocracy where individual talent is considered over and above social identity. By contrast, my work maintains that it is precisely this gap between the social life of meritocracy and its universalistic promise that allows for the retrenchment of privilege. The hope for meritocracy as the transcendence of identity is a profoundly ahistorical aspiration that works against the actual redress of inequality.[5]

The Indian Institutes of Technology are a set of twenty-three public institutions of higher education. The original five were founded between 1951 and 1961 through bilateral cooperation with the German, American, Soviet, and British governments. The first four each occupied one corner of the new nation: IIT Kharagpur in the east, IIT Bombay in the west, IIT Madras in the south, and IIT Kanpur in the north. This distribution of IITs signaled the postcolonial state's commitment to both regional parity and national integration. Each IIT was expected to draw more students from its regional social milieu while being part of an integrated national system of education. The fifth institute, IIT Delhi, followed when the British government offered to help build a campus in the national capital in 1961. The remaining IITs were set up between 2001 and 2016, some as new institutions and others through the conversion of older institutions into IITs. The early twenty-first-century mushrooming of IITs was a state response to the gulf between the number of aspirants and the seats available in the five original institutes.

The IITs were part of a broader state commitment to technologically driven modernization as the engine of national development. From the late nineteenth century, Indian critics leveraged arguments about "underdevelopment" to point to the inadequacy and immorality of colonial rule. By the early twentieth century, such arguments had taken the form of anticolonial nationalism. Pointing both to catastrophic events, such as the colonial-era famines, and to the

longer-term immiseration of Indian peasants and workers, nationalists argued for self-rule as the only path to development. Self-rule was
to reset the terms of economic and political life by ushering in a more
robust state commitment to the linked goals of technological and social development.[6]

Part of the critique of colonial underdevelopment centered on technical education. Nationalists derided the colonial state for its meager
investment in technical training and charged it with deliberately de-
priving Indians of the kinds of modern knowledge that would allow
them to achieve economic and social progress. One particularly effective nationalist tactic was to compare Britain unfavorably with its imperial rivals and elevate the latter as better technological exemplars.
Nationalists circumvented the constraints of British imperial hegemony by seeking out other powers, most notably Germany, Japan, and
the United States, as models for a future, technologically driven
nation-state.[7]

With the transition to independence, nationalist ambitions were
made material in the large-scale state investment in technical education. While the goal of universal education accompanied universal
franchise, the process of educational expansion was highly uneven.
From the outset, the IITs were set apart as the uppermost echelon of a
stratified postcolonial structure of technical training. Deemed "institutions of national importance" by the Institutes of Technology Act of
1961, the IITs' standing was guaranteed by a set of exceptions. The institutes are directly administered and financed by the Indian central
government at far higher levels than are their regional counterparts.
They also fall outside the structure of affiliation to regional universities established in the colonial period, which gives them far greater autonomy in terms of institutional functioning, faculty hiring, and curricular development. Their autonomy was guaranteed in other ways as
well. In the name of ensuring "merit" as the only basis for admission,
they were originally exempted from policies of caste-based affirmative
action applied by regional states to their engineering colleges. These
exceptions have endowed the IITs with the aura of being *in* but not
entirely *of* the nation, an extranational orientation underwritten first
by their founding partnerships with foreign governments and subsequently by their sizable alumni diaspora. Although the IITs were

founded to produce a cadre of technical specialists to aid in nation-building, they quickly became stepping-stones to transnational mobility. As is evident in the *60 Minutes* program and the *Dilbert* comic strip, IIT graduates—or IITians, as they are popularly known—are now the global poster children of Indian education, with many joining the upper echelons of American industry and academia.

Over the postindependence period, the IITs have become the most coveted institutions of postsecondary education. The Joint Entrance Exam (JEE) to gain admission to the IITs is held every year in April and is a hotly anticipated event. Since the exam was first held in 1960, the number of candidates has grown steadily, with over a million students taking the exam in 2017 and under 3 percent earning admission to the twenty-three campuses. Every year, exam "toppers" become instant celebrities, with their faces and "All India Ranks" splashed over newspapers and billboards. The success of the IITs has also spawned a massive coaching industry to train students for the JEE. With key outposts in the states of Andhra Pradesh, Telangana, and Rajasthan, coaching centers now admit students from as early as the seventh grade, who spend up to five years mastering a single exam.

Within Indian public discourse, the IITian has become an exemplar of intellectual merit, someone seen as naturally gifted in technical knowledge. What gets occluded in such assessments of the IITian's innate intelligence and competitiveness are the forms of accumulated social and cultural capital that have enabled admission to the IITs. The majority of IITians come from upper-caste families of bureaucrats, schoolteachers, and academics, where capital has long been held in education. While arguably from middle-class backgrounds, the value of their accumulated "caste capital" has suddenly spiked due to the reorganization of late twentieth- and early twenty-first-century capitalism around the "knowledge economy."[8] At the same time, the role of caste and state in producing IITians has been obscured in favor of their portrayal as uniquely meritorious individuals.

In addition to being upper caste, the majority of IITians are also male. Unlike in regional engineering colleges, where there is more gender parity in the student body, the percentage of women has never exceeded ten on any IIT campus. Despite their being a distinct minority, I do not address the unique experience of women in this book.[9]

This is for two reasons. First and foremost, the principal axis of social differentiation and political tension when it comes to the evaluation of merit is caste. Indeed, the women students, faculty, and alumni I interviewed generally espoused similar views on meritocracy as their male caste counterparts. Second, the overwhelmingly male character of the campuses makes them ideal sites for understanding how the relationships among upper-caste men and between upper- and lower-caste men have shaped the meanings of masculinity and meritocracy. In this sense, I heed recent calls by gender theorists to move beyond the male–female binary and take into consideration other forms of relationality in the making of gender.[10]

The transformation in the status of technical knowledge and the upper-caste claim to its most elite institutional spaces prompt the following questions at the heart of this book: How does privilege become merit? What is the role of technical education in facilitating this process? How do the naturalization of the IITian's merit and the elevation of the IITs to emblems of meritocracy inform understandings of caste difference? And how have these processes shaped the possibilities and limits of democratic transformation in India?

Caste and Historicity

Technical science currently enjoys unprecedented prestige as a universal form of knowledge. At the same time, the ascendance of the technical has been associated with the cultural supremacy of particular groups and with widening social disparities. Indian engineering, which emerged within particular histories of state, caste, race, and capital, is no exception. Ideas about the role of technology in society and the place of castes and races within a hierarchical social order informed colonial state projects of technical education. The induction of Indians into a stratified structure of training generated intense debate over whether the technical was indeed a form of knowledge available to all or an expression of cultural power through which a few benefited at the expense of others. Even as this debate raged across India's transition from colony to nation-state, technical knowledge coalesced as a necessary solution for perceived social ills of economic underdevelopment and social inequality.[11] By the mid-twentieth century, it had become a veritable fetish that embodied the promise of individual, national, and global progress. In India, this process of fetishization further entrenched a stratified structure of higher education, with the IITs and their predominantly upper-caste student bodies occupying the uppermost echelon.

At one level, the adoption of technical occupations by upper castes is a surprising departure from older caste hierarchies of labor privileging the conceptual over the manual. Within the four-fold *varna* classification derived from Hindu scripture, Brahmins are the "head" of the social body, the priests and scholars who are the most removed from the "feet" of Shudra labor. Despite their continued ideological resonance, however, such scriptural typologies map poorly onto the historicity of caste practice.

The debate on the historicity of caste in South Asia has long been polarized between its treatment as a fundamentally religious phenomenon and its treatment as a product of historical and political economic power relations. For many in the first group, caste is a ritual order intrinsic to Brahminical Hinduism and defined by notions of purity and pollution. Those who subscribe to this position often assume an overlap between scriptural and lived dimensions of caste, with the latter extending from and reflecting the categories and principles of the former. Within anthropology, Louis Dumont's *Homo Hierarchicus* typified the derivation of the social from the scriptural and set the stage for the treatment of caste as a form of ritual hierarchy defined by the preeminence of the Brahmin.[12] For Dumont, the centrality of caste hierarchy as the foundational logic of Indian society marked its difference from the egalitarian West. This insistence on a categorical difference between Orient and Occident led him to disdain materialist approaches—especially Marxist class analysis—as the imposition of an alien secular framework on an essentially hierarchical, ritually ordered society.[13]

Contra Dumont's approach to caste as the cornerstone of a Hindu ritual order is a scholarly literature that approaches caste sociohistorically. This second body of work is vast; here, I take up two strands in order to specify my own approach to caste. The sociohistorical approach to caste can be divided into those who argue for caste as a traditional form of social organization that was disrupted by modernization and those who contest the assumption of such a baseline by pointing to the long historical dynamism of caste. Let me first take up the argument about the traditionalism of caste.

Authors who argue for caste as tradition typically define it as a localized form of social organization rooted in endogamy, restricted commensality, and ritual precedence, elements that give it a limited elasticity in the face of modernization. For some, the limits of caste are most evident in changing structural logics. This perspective on caste as antithetical to modernity was reflected across scholarship in the 1950s and 1960s. Anthropologist Richard Fox, for instance, argued that social changes wrought by processes of urbanization, associational life, and participatory politics, to name a few, so fundamentally transformed the workings of caste that it became something new. For Fox, when the terms of caste relationality shift to interest, competition, or voluntary association, often seen in the scaling up of caste beyond the locality, what scholars require is a theory not of resiliency but of the "functional demise of a traditional institution under the impact of modern social change."[14] Village ethnographers of the 1950s and 1960s who studied the socioeconomic life of caste also saw fundamental changes arising from the integration of a local institution into wider scales of economy and polity. While departing from Dumont's Orientalism, some—such as anthropologist M. N. Srinivas—echoed his characterization of caste as a religious institution and interpreted change as a process of secularization.[15] Whether defined as local or as religious, these accounts of caste transformation presumed its baseline traditionalism.

Other work on the breakdown of caste highlights shifts in self-definition. This position is most clearly stated by sociologist André Béteille, who argues that even when caste stratification persists as a structural characteristic of Indian society, the transformation in the terms of collective self-definition makes caste less salient. This is especially true, he maintains, when it comes to upper-caste elites who have come to think more along class than caste lines. As he puts it, "Among engineers, doctors, scientists, civil servants and managers, the obligations to one's occupation exists independently of the obligation to one's caste and to some extent displaces it. . . . Until the nineteenth century, Hindu intellectuals could argue with force and conviction about the significance and value of caste. Their counterparts of today, who are still mainly of upper caste, have lost the capacity not only to explain and justify caste, but even to describe it coherently."[16] While for Béteille "caste is no longer an institution of any great strength among the influential urban intelligentsia," he sees it as very much alive within lower-caste political mobilization. He thus concludes that "caste should be attacked for its divisive role in electoral politics rather than its active role in the reproduction of inequality which is relatively small and clearly declining."[17]

Both these positions have some virtue. The scholarship on caste from the 1950s and 1960s underscores the need to properly account for transformations in structure and practice without assuming the continuity of caste. The careful attention in this work to shifts in organizational forms and modes of association is critically important to my own research on higher education. In particular, I have found accounts of the nineteenth-century caste association as an instance of caste consolidation very helpful for thinking about how caste can scale up under new historical conditions. While I depart from seeing this shift as a movement from tradition to modernity, the larger point about attending to sociology and not just sentiment is well taken.

More problematic is Béteille's argument about caste self-definition. Reducing caste to its discursive life discounts its continued structural workings as a determinant of access and opportunity. Furthermore, seeing the social reproduction of upper-caste professionals solely in terms of class obscures the intersections of class and caste. Finally, taking at face value the terms of upper-caste self-definition disregards the fact that caste does not necessarily speak in its "own" language. Rather, to paraphrase cultural theorist Stuart Hall, it can be lived through other modalities.[18] Most striking is Béteille's unwillingness to ask why caste appears to have declined in social meaning for elites just when it has assumed a political charge for non-elites.

Béteille's insistence on parsing caste and class is echoed in a more recent book by anthropologists Chris Fuller and Haripriya Narasimhan on Tamil Brahmins, to which my work is indebted.[19] Fuller and Narasimhan offer an exhaustive and rich account of the transformation of an erstwhile rural elite into an urban middle class that argues for Tamil Brahmins as versatile strategic actors who effectively leverage their cultural capital to position themselves within shifting circumstances to ensure their economic success. All the way through, we get a nuanced understanding of caste as a dynamic social process that is irreducible to a set of traits or a worldview. This makes especially puzzling their conclusion that Tamil Brahmin professional success is best seen as a form of class reproduction. Indeed, Fuller and Narasimhan cite Béteille in arguing that "caste has ceased to play an active part in the reproduction of inequality, at least at the upper levels of the social hierarchy."[20] This begs the question of why, as they themselves underscore, Tamil Brahminness becomes synonymous with middle classness. To their credit, Fuller and Narasimhan are careful to hold at arm's length Tamil Brahmin claims to ascriptive intelligence in order to argue for a properly sociohistorical account of caste; the book is resolutely antiessentialist. However, this leads them to an insistence on the declining relevance of caste even when their own empirical material suggests otherwise.

These approaches to caste are a laudable departure from Dumont's structuralism. However, in challenging Dumont, they are too quick to reject continuities in caste sociology and sentiment that are a product not of an underlying cultural logic but of historical process. To understand caste continuities in processual terms, I have turned to scholarship on the longer history of shifting structures, forms, and meanings. Some scholars hark back to the precolonial and colonial periods to illuminate long-standing transformations of caste practice and self-definition in relation to shifts in the organization of sovereignty and political economy. Rather than a stable structure destabilized by the advent of "modernity," they argue that caste dynamics have always been informed by interest, competition, and shifting scales of consolidation. In such work, we see the various idioms through which social precedence has been established, ritual purity being only one of them.[21]

Others offer a genealogy of Dumontian structuralism itself. They illuminate the process by which, in the nineteenth century, the "field view" of caste was overtaken by a "book view." In this process, they argue, the understanding of caste as a social formation constituted by economic and political power was displaced by one that derived its essence from Sanskrit texts and Hindu religiosity. The book view not only allowed for a theological conception of caste divorced from its social life but generated a notion of cultural consensus belied by an actual history of caste struggle.[22]

The Caste of Merit builds on the latter body of work to argue for the history of caste as one of transformation, marked by significant shifts in expressions of self-definition, mechanisms of distinction, and scales of group formation. Yet this does not mean that caste has given way to some other form of social classification, such as class. While class is certainly an important form of stratification, continuities of caste affiliation, stigmatization, and ascription within the most modern institutional and social spaces reveal the irreducibility of caste to economic differences.[23] As I hope to show, such caste practices extend a long history of struggle into a contemporary politics of meritocracy, where contestation has taken new forms.

Labor and Value

B. R. Ambedkar, the Dalit leader and architect of the Indian Constitution, argued that the hegemonic power of caste lay in its operation as a form of "graded inequality" in which the gradation of status differences ensured the participation of groups lower down the ladder.[24] Caste mobility has typically taken the form of a resignification of group status through economic advancement, religious conversion, migration, or political patronage.[25] Through such strategies, caste groupings have transformed the meanings of collectivity by shifting their position relative to other groups. Despite, or perhaps because of, the nature of such claims, caste has remained a stratified structure that more often animates contestation over status than calls for a wholesale eradication of the system. While claims to higher status do not always reinstate the preeminence of the Brahmin, they do reproduce a societal structure in which enhancing one's relative standing is a more commonly conceived path to rights than achieving equality.

One enduring principle of graded inequality is the stratification of labor. Rather than simply an expression of ritual status, caste stigma has typically worked through the degradation of labor.[26] It is no accident that the sites where caste distinctions are most rigidly enforced are ones with the most oppressive labor conditions.[27] To put it differently, caste is a principle of stratification whose mechanisms are both symbolic and material. Often, groups claiming a higher status reject forms of stigmatized labor that were the basis of their subjugation. We see this, for instance, in the hope expressed by Dalits—the former untouchables who occupy the bottom rung of the caste ladder— that rural to urban migration might sever their ties to the "everyday tyranny" of agrarian caste relations and allow them the "freedom" of equal participation in labor markets.[28] We also see it in the instances of lower-caste assertion buttressed by narratives of a prelapsarian past of high birth and valued labor.[29] That these forms of aspiration and assertion are perceived as threats to caste reproduction is evident in the vigilante violence aimed at brutally suppressing Dalit and lower-caste spatial and social mobility by incarcerating them within oppressive social relations of labor.[30]

It is against this backdrop, then, that the upper caste resort to a form of labor previously associated with the low-born becomes particularly striking. As I will show in Chapter 1, this counterintuitive embrace of technical knowledge is best understood as a result of the wholesale transformation in the status of engineering during the colonial period. The rise of engineering rested on practices of distinction separating low from high, the manual from the conceptual, and artisanship from the professions. Moreover, the impact of colonialism in "racializing" caste was particularly significant for the upper-caste turn to the technical sciences.[31] Earlier, changes in practice could lead to expulsion from the caste fold. The racialization of caste under colonialism as a social form rooted in birth, heredity, and endogamy allowed for a new level of flexibility. As a result, even dramatic changes in practice, like the adoption of ritually prohibited occupations, came to be accommodated within the same caste category. Together, the distinctions that underwrote the rise of engineering and the association of caste with heredity, not practice, allowed the upper castes ease of entry into a new profession. By the mid-twentieth century, artisanship and engineering were poles apart, with engineering perceived as a coveted, high-status profession best suited to the high-born. The value of engineering as a profession was thus intimately linked to its disassociation from the "tainted" technical labor of the lower castes.

It was not just the "purification" of engineering through its association with state power and societal progress that aided its embrace by upper castes. So, too, did the promise of capital accumulation. The history of engineering is one of spatial and social mobility through which agrarian upper castes became part of an urbanized middle class. In the colonial period, upper castes were conscripted into engineering and became a class of white-collar professionals. This pattern continued under postcolonial state developmentalism. As we will see in Chapter 2, postcolonial state investment in technical education and the elevation of the engineer as nation-builder par excellence made engineering a key instrument of capitalist transformation and a particularly lucrative choice of occupation. Upper castes with histories of literacy and education flourished as salaried professionals tied to the economic engine of the developmental state. Initially, postcolonial engineers followed their colonial predecessors into public sector employment. However, the ambition of public sector careers gave way in the 1990s, when national policy shifted toward economic liberalization. The deregulation of trade and industry overlapped with the Internet technology revolution, leading to skyrocketing salaries among elite engineering graduates. These rising fortunes starkly illuminate the "payoff" of caste. While caste has always been a mechanism of both social and economic stratification, the catapulting of upper castes into the ranks of the corporate elite throws the economics of caste into sharp relief, allowing us to clearly see caste as a form of capital.

In his essay "The Forms of Capital," sociologist Pierre Bourdieu calls for more attention to the different forms of capital—economic (money), cultural (cultivation and credentials), and social (connections)—and the mechanisms through which one is converted to the other. Without such an analysis, he argues, the social world of "accumulated history" would "be reduced to a discontinuous series of instantaneous mechanical equilibria between agents who are treated as interchangeable particles."[32] Bourdieu offers a particularly insightful analysis of embodied cultural capital, those accumulated effects of family and class history that become an integral part of the person. "Because the social conditions of its transmission and acquisition are more disguised than those of economic capital," he argues, "it is predisposed to function as symbolic capital, i.e. to be unrecognized as capital and recognized as legitimate competence."[33] In this way, symbolic or embodied cultural capital "manages to combine the prestige of innate property with the merits of acquisition."[34] However, Bourdieu points out that there is an inherent instability to embodied cultural capital that is stabilized through the alchemy of institutional recognition in the form, for instance, of academic qualifications. Such institutional mediation not only stabilizes cultural capital but also endows it with greater legitimacy by appearing to be autonomous of accumulated history and social relationality. Finally, it makes cultural capital into a currency more easily traded in the marketplace.[35]

The story of the IITs is a particularly stark instance of how institutionally mediated cultural capital operates as currency. Among Indian engineers, it is the IITian who is most associated with global market success. As I show throughout the book, the IITs have underwritten the capital accumulation of upper castes by reconstituting the inheritances of family and community into a form of achievement legible in the marketplace. In the first postindependence decades, IIT alumni were still very much a part of the state's developmental ethos as professional nation-builders. The 1960s generation of Madras IITians whose stories I will chronicle in Chapter 4 derived their sense of professionalism and elite standing from a connection to state-led nation-building. At the time, the most coveted forms of employment were in public sector civil and mechanical engineering, a trend reinforced by the role of West Germany in setting up IIT Madras. For the institute's early graduates, exposure to the German model of hands-on engineering challenged caste sensibilities privileging mental over manual labor. Chapter 3 will probe this period at length to contextualize 1960s contestations over the signification of labor within long-standing debates about whether engineering was best thought of as practical or conceptual knowledge.

As with other elite engineers, IITians' link to the developmental state was short lived, but even more so. Unlike their counterparts in other engineering colleges who trained their sights on the private sector in the aftermath of Indian economic liberalization, the fortunes of IIT alumni had risen even earlier through a steady exodus from the 1970s to the United States. Their incorporation into American academia and industry and subsequent celebration as entrepreneurial successes produced an antipathy toward the developmental state and faith in the "free market," which were a bellwether for the widespread changes that would sweep Indian society from the 1990s. Not only did diasporic IITians do very well abroad, but they also began to strategize around securing their own market recognition. Chapter 7 will detail how the Silicon Valley boom set the stage for the coalescing of a new ethnic commodity: the "technological Indian" whose most visible signifier was "Brand IIT."[36] In shoring up the brand value of the IITs, diasporic alumni have done their part to suture the link between pedigree and market and ensure that caste remains a site of capital investment.

Merit and Caste

There was an added twist to the social and economic elevation of engineering and its embrace by upper castes. With the postcolonial transition, the more explicit colonial-era link between engineering and upper-caste status gave way to a different set of associations. The advent of political democracy made less evident the social relations of caste that had made engineering into a form of conceptual knowledge best suited to the high-born. Even as their position as the principle beneficiaries of engineering education consolidated, upper castes began to leverage technical knowledge as a marker not of their caste status but of their individual merit. How did this transformation of privilege into merit occur?

"Merit" is a loaded term, one that does similar political work as an earlier discourse of republican "virtues and talents." In this sense, Indian meritocracy is part of a much longer history of modern political thought and its reconciliation of universal equality and naturalized social hierarchy. As historians of the Enlightenment have shown, virtues and talents became the focus of philosophers and political writers concerned with engendering a new society based on principles of nature and reason.[37] They argued that a sociopolitical order founded on these principles would best ground the emergent notions of the republican citizen and the enlightened society. Most—like Jefferson, Rousseau, Montesquieu, and Diderot—presumed that hierarchies would necessarily remain within a democracy; now, however, they would be rooted in legitimate differences and not the legacy of family or rank. Despite the widely circulating language of equality and universal rights, they argued that the "natural superiority" of some over others—men

over women, adults over children, or Europeans over other people—
made them best suited to govern. Even for those like John Adams, who
fretted about the substitution of an aristocracy of birth with an "aristocracy of talent," there was little question that stratification would
persist as an integral part of the social order, in large part because of
differences in people's "natural" endowments. For eighteenth-century
ideologues, naturalized difference became a key alibi for the perpetuation of social hierarchy after the advent of republican democracy.[38]

As with eighteenth-century republicanism, postindependence India
witnessed heated debates over how to reconcile the formal ideal of
equal citizenship in the new republic with persistent social hierarchies.
At the same time, Indian republicanism was far more radical than its
eighteenth-century predecessor. Universal adult franchise symbolized
a radical break with colonial subjecthood. Moreover, departing from
the explicit colonial invocation of caste as the organizational basis of
society and economy, postcolonial statesmen and planners consciously
sought to overcome not just colonial "underdevelopment" but also the
purported social barriers to Indian modernity.

Caste was one of these social barriers. Unlike the colonial treatment of caste as a foundational category of Indian society, postcolonial statesmen viewed caste as antithetical to modern social life, with
no place in a democratic polity. Caste thinking, with its basis in hierarchy, stigma, and segregation, was to be rooted out in favor of civic
principles of equality and fraternity. But much like the hierarchies embedded within eighteenth-century Enlightenment thought, some Indians were thought to have achieved this enlightened consciousness
of castelessness sooner than others and were thus suited to lead. Although the material legacies of caste continued to structure postindependence life, those upper castes who were its greatest beneficiaries
were the first to proclaim their own transcendence of caste.

Sociologist Satish Deshpande has called for more analysis of how
upper castes are rendered casteless in India. He points out that the story
of how upper castes transform "their caste capital into modern capital"
is not well known because "it runs with the grain of the dominant
common sense." When it is seen and heard, it is in other guises: "It
appears to be a story about something *other than caste*, like the story
of nation-building for example, or the story of a great and ancient tra-

dition modernizing itself."[39] By contrast, Deshpande continues, the political leveraging of caste by lower castes is a recurrent, publicly debated theme. The result of this asymmetry, he maintains, is that upper castes are naturalized as the "legitimate inheritors of modernity," while lower castes are hypervisible as the illegitimate purveyors of caste.

It is undoubtedly true that non-elites have embraced caste as a vehicle of empowerment and that collective mobilization for lower-caste rights in both formal and informal political arenas has changed the contours of Indian society and politics. However, I echo Deshpande's insistence that this only underscores the need for work on how caste operates at the other end of the spectrum. There is no question that many upper-caste individuals think of themselves as modern subjects, or at least as subjects with sincere commitments to universalistic ideals of equality, democracy, and rationality. At the same time, these individuals are able to inhabit a universal worldview precisely because a history of accumulated advantages allows them a unique claim to certain forms of self-fashioning. Whereas at an earlier moment, status might have been more explicitly tied to caste, the social bases of merit continue to be constituted in ways that allow the same social groups to inhabit merit as an embodied ideal. This begs the question of how castelessness as a subjectivity is produced, and what its relationship is to caste belonging in the postcolonial, democratic present.[40]

The Caste of Merit addresses the role of the IITs in transforming caste privilege into merit. Chapter 6 will do so through a close look at affirmative action, or reservation. In postindependence India, redress for persistent social inequalities found expression in a system of caste-based affirmative action, in which reserved seats, or quotas, were set aside for the "socially and educationally backward."[41] But even as more and more ink was spilled in debating the indices of social backwardness, the inheritances that underwrote achievement slipped out of view. In contrast to lower-caste subjects, whose eligibility for reservation defined them in terms of collective histories of disadvantage, the upper-caste subject was classified as an individual citizen defined by merit. The absenting of caste from the postcolonial administrative classification of upper-caste students marked a key transition in official parlance that came to intersect in critical ways with their self-fashioning as meritocratic moderns. Moreover, the admissions categories of "general" and "reserved" generated their own caste effects within and beyond higher education by producing caste distinction and discrimination at a different scale. As a result, the antagonists of the debate over educational equality are now these consolidated caste groupings of the general and the reserved. Even when the finer gradations of inequality give way, caste stigma persists through these consolidated forms of caste.

The reconstitution of upper castes as casteless moderns was further facilitated by the modern mass examination, which funneled aspirants to higher education into different tiers of technical training. Unlike earlier processes of selection that explicitly favored the high-born elite, the mass examination was underwritten by an ideology of middle-class achievement in which labor would find its just rewards. Despite the social patterns of success and failure to which it gave rise, the mass examination appeared to exist above the political fray as an objective instrument of evaluation. Chapter 5 will delve into the role of the modern examination and its finely calibrated system of ranking in constituting merit as an index of individual achievement and an egalitarian system. In particular, it illuminates the place of the IIT entrance exam as the most fetishized measure of merit because of the presumed asocial character of technical knowledge and the sheer scale of the exam.

As previously noted, the transnational mobility of IIT graduates to the United States has added another layer of complexity to this dynamic. In Chapter 7, we will see how, in the diasporic circuits of the knowledge economy, caste privilege is consistently misrecognized as middle-class labor and racial talent. No longer beneficiaries of caste or the developmental state, IITians in the United States are seen simply as naturally gifted, if hardworking, Indians. Contributing to this aura is the rise of entrepreneurship with its ideologies of self-made success. The sizable presence of IITians in the Silicon Valley boom of the 1980s and 1990s has endowed them with a mystique as the most risk-free sites of capital investment.[42]

Constitutionalism, mass examinations, and global market success have all mediated the transformation of the IITian's caste privilege into merit. At the same time, other trends have complicated the reconsti-

tution of upper castes as casteless, meritocratic moderns. The naturalization of upper-caste merit has not gone unchallenged. Through the
twentieth century, constitutional amendments, policy initiatives, and
regional politics have variously illuminated the persistence of caste as
a structural determinant of opportunity and success. These interventions have advanced competing notions of equality that presume not
the level playing field of formal democracy but the historical accumulation of advantages and disadvantages. Attention to histories of accumulation has been particularly pointed in regions like Tamilnadu,
where a politics of lower-caste assertion has interrupted the transformation of privilege into merit by re-marking upper castes as *castes*. In
this sense, Deshpande's account seems too neat when he argues that
for upper castes, "caste-qua-caste has already yielded all that it can and
represents a ladder that can now be safely kicked away. Having encashed its traditional caste-capital and converted it into modern forms
of capital like property, higher educational credentials and strongholds
in lucrative professions, this section believes itself to be 'casteless'
today."[43] The case of Tamilnadu suggests that castelessness might be
less a fait accompli and more an aspect of upper-caste self-definition,
which has always shifted according to circumstances. Moreover, the
marking of caste is not necessarily done at the expense of claims to
merit. Rather, the commensurability of caste and merit within these
claims shows that meritocracy is not always a universalistic politics.

Ascription and Achievement

The interplay between self-marking and un-marking within upper-
caste claims to merit is most evident when we attend to the relationality of caste. Thinking of caste formation relationally not only allows
us to see caste as the product of longer historical relationships but also
illuminates the impact of democratic politics.[44] The proliferation of
rights discourses and politics, the extension of universal franchise, and
the entry of new social groups into spaces previously monopolized by
upper castes have posed real challenges to caste hierarchies. Although
in some ways formal political arenas and the broader cultural sphere
have witnessed the entry and ascendance of lower castes, elite education
and the expanding private sphere both within and beyond India have

serviced the reconstitution of caste privilege by other means. In this sense, we might think of elite and private transnational and domestic arenas as spaces of upper-caste flight, retrenchment, and accumulation away from the pressures of lower-caste politics.

When we think about strategies of upper-caste retrenchment in reaction to lower-caste rights, the role of Tamilnadu stands out as an important precedent. As the discursive target of the Non-Brahmin and Dravidian movements, Tamil Brahmins in particular came to be hypervisible and their claims to knowledge inextricably linked to caste privilege. Their explicit marking as caste subjects has in turn produced a heightened consciousness among Tamil Brahmins of their own caste belonging. For them, however, being Brahmin is an expression of both modernity and merit. Chapters 3, 4, 5, and 6 will take up different sides of this regional story. Chapter 3 addresses the impact of Non-Brahminism and Dravidianism on the regional political milieu. Chapter 4 looks more closely at how regional caste tensions shaped the first generations of students at IIT Madras. Chapter 5 considers the larger landscape of regional secondary education and exam coaching within which Tamil Brahmins in particular have shored up their claim to IIT Madras. And Chapter 6 addresses the centrality of the reservation system to the making of Tamil Brahminness.

These chapters also address a shift in the politics of meritocracy from a regional to a national scale. What was once a regional dialectic of lower-caste claims to rights and upper-caste claims to merit has assumed national proportions. Now, it is not only Tamil Brahmins who claim merit as a caste characteristic and articulate ascriptive notions of skill and intelligence. The expansion of lower-caste rights politics to the national scale—particularly the rise of Dalit and Other Backward Class (OBC) political parties in the 1990s and the expansion of reserved quotas in 1990 and 2006—has witnessed a similar expansion of an identitarian politics of meritocracy. Now, upper castes across India have embraced merit as a collective caste trait that distinguishes them from lower castes.

The return to ascription as the explicit basis of achievement is one instance of what others have identified as the neoliberal commodification of identity.[45] Whereas the explicit invocation of particularistic genealogies as a basis for social worth or market value was once discredited, we are witnessing the resurgence of claims on these grounds. Culturalist, genealogical, and even genetic claims to merit have become an increasingly common feature of the twenty-first-century global knowledge economy. Additionally, the suturing of identity and merit is generating newly consolidated forms of upper casteness.

Upper Casteness

One of my key arguments is about the impact of engineering education on the scale of caste belonging and affiliation. Since anthropologist Bernard Cohn's writings on the making of colonial knowledge, a number of scholars have elaborated on the workings of the Indian ethnographic state. Much of this work addresses the social life of state administrative categories by tracking how enumeration and classification travel beyond the worlds of law and policy to shape forms of collective self-definition. As a result, we better understand both the dynamism of identity and the intimacy between state and society. When it comes to caste, the bulk of this scholarship has looked at how governmental practices have shaped the contours of subaltern self-definition and collective expression, giving rise to lower-caste rights movements and political parties.[46] Much less has been written about the traffic between state classification and upper-caste politics. To the extent that upper-caste identitarianism has been addressed, it has generally been through analyses of Hindu nationalism.[47] Most accounts of caste consolidation as a sociopolitical process have been limited to lower castes and Dalits. By contrast, my concern is with how both the tracking of social groups into different tiers of technical training, and constitutional measures to redress caste inequality through reserved quotas in higher education, have produced consolidation among upper castes.

To understand upper-caste consolidation, I have turned to scholarship on the production of whiteness in the United States. This also helps explain my choice of the awkward neologism "upper casteness." Historian Matthew Frye Jacobson's work on the incorporation of various European immigrants—Irish, Italians, Poles, Ashkenazi Jews—into the category of "white" speaks eloquently to a new order of distinction that emerged in the United States over the course of the twentieth century.[48] Through this period, Jacobson argues, the assimilation of Europeans into the category of white replaced all earlier racial divisions among them with the result that the distinction between black and white became the paramount racial division. The now common-sense, phenotypical understanding of white thus emerged out of two associated processes: the consolidation of Europeans into one unified racial category and that category's distinction from blackness. The production of whiteness as a consolidated category has also been taken up by others, who argue that its assimilationist logic extended certain privileges of race to marginalized European immigrants while precluding cross-race solidarities.[49] This logic was resolutely material and structural: racial privilege was reproduced through legally authorized practices of housing, policing, and schooling, among others, through which the "possessive investment in whiteness" was solidified as a form of property.

As with twentieth-century whiteness, upper casteness has been forged through both state and private sector initiatives and in opposition to lower castes. These consolidated categories of upper and lower caste have acquired an outsized importance in the political life of caste that in many ways overshadows the salience of caste at a smaller scale. Moreover, upper casteness has an incorporative logic that allows for the accommodation of nonideal upper-caste subjects and even some lower-caste subjects. However, this flexibility—its basis in the interplay of incorporation and exclusion—generates an incessant politics of evaluation and distinction that speaks to the anxieties of privilege and the uncertainties of its reproduction.

We see both the incorporative and exclusionary logics of upper casteness around the IIT admissions process. The general category of admissions is putatively open to anyone with "merit" even while it is underwritten by the assumption that upper castes are uniquely meritorious. Since the 1990s, the expansion of the JEE coaching industry and the implementation of new quotas for lower castes has produced the need to police the boundaries of merit like never before. The result has been a relentless effort to match bodies to meanings in order to distinguish the "true" IITian from various "imposters." These diagnostic rituals convey understandings of caste qualities that are assumed to attach to particular meritorious and nonmeritorious bodies.

They capture the qualitative dimensions of being upper caste—those meanings of caste read off the body—that are so key to the quotidian life of affinity and stigmatization. They also point to the nonfungibility of the general category. In Chapter 6, we will see that when Dalit and lower-caste students lay claim to merit by pointing to their admission through the general category—which several of them do consistently and vocally—they are legible only as exceptions. Moreover, these students are routinely compelled to erase the complexity of their own history and participate in producing a phantasmatic imaginary of backwardness that collapses a dense field of signification into a binary opposition.

It is not only backwardness that is flattened in order to produce merit as exclusively upper caste. So, too, is upper casteness. We see this most clearly in Chapter 5 with the case of students from coaching centers whose presence is unsettling because they are the wrong kind of upper caste. These are upper-caste students whose family histories are at odds with the IITian norm of urban professionalism. Their unfamiliarity with English and open embrace of regionalism run counter to the cosmopolitanism that is supposed to distinguish upper from lower. The discomfort their presence produces speaks to the phantasmatic quality not only of backwardness but of upper casteness. In these micronegotiations over who is a "true" IITian, we see the centrality of caste consolidation to the contemporary meanings of meritocracy. Meritocracy is constituted through the very interaction between caste and castelessness and between ascription and achievement.

Ultimately, this book argues that meritocracy offers a window on the relationship between capitalism and democracy. As historians and anthropologists of Africa, Asia, and the Caribbean have long argued, capitalism works through social differentiation. Rather than producing abstract labor, capitalist processes have always been elaborated through ascriptive understandings of race, gender, ethnicity, and sexuality. To put it differently, capitalism is a culturalist as well as an economic epistemology that builds on and generates inequality. What, then, is its relationship to democracy? As with capitalism, democracy embodies a tension between individuated and collective conceptions of the social body. The formal conception of individual rights is in tension with the inherited privileges and disadvantages that underwrite democratic social stratification. In different contexts and depending on the political pressures in play, law and policy are more or less able and willing to address such contradictions between the inheritances of history and formal equality.

Their overlapping structures and ideologies have led many to dismiss democracy as a mere tool of capitalism. However, the Indian context calls for a more nuanced understanding of the relationship between the two. Rather than simply service capitalist accumulation, what we see in the politics of meritocracy is a battle over the very terms of democratic membership and transformation. Democracy—as ideology and a set of structures for making political claims—does provide leverage for subaltern politics that challenge the status quo. As a result, structures of inequality do not seamlessly reproduce themselves. Rather, upper-caste claims to merit are emblematic of an ongoing "war of maneuver" in reaction against lower-caste assertion.[50] Upper-caste maneuvers—universalistic on the one hand, identitarian on the other—are part of a broader dialectic of caste contestation elaborated on a transnational scale. The story of merit at the IITs thus illuminates caste hegemony, not as a stable structure of Indian life but as a process and a politics.

1

The Colonial Career
of Technical Knowledge

To UNDERSTAND THE elevated status of engineering in India today requires a foray into the pre-independence past. The career of technical knowledge from the mid-nineteenth to the mid-twentieth century is one of shifts from guild to state, shopfloor to classroom, and lower to upper caste. These shifts were conditioned by processes at an imperial scale: the transfer of power from the East India Company to the British Crown in 1857, inter-imperial industrial competition over the latter half of the nineteenth century, efforts to minimize the cost of colonial rule, and nationalist critiques of underdevelopment. Over a century, technical knowledge went from being the purview of lower-caste artisans to becoming integral to state power, economic development, and upper-caste status. With the postcolonial transition and a fuller embrace of technologically driven development, the divergence between artisanship and engineering was further consolidated.

What does this account add to our understanding of colonial South Asia? The scholarship on South Asia has extensively covered the relationship between technology and power. Scholars have addressed how British technological dominance reinforced colonial racial hierarchies, consolidated state administrative authority, and advanced the project of human mastery over nature.[1] Less considered, however, is how these interventions interacted with a preexisting landscape of hierarchically ordered, caste-based forms of knowledge and skill. Similarly, the vast literature on continuities and shifts from colonial-era political economy to Indian developmentalism does not directly address the influence of a caste worldview on development imaginaries and practices. This is also the case for the much more limited social scientific scholarship on engineering. While the stratified structure of the colonial engineering corps has been referred to as a "quasi-caste" or even a "caste" system, the actual role of Indian caste differences in the making of colonial technical education is unclear.[2] Consequently, we know little about how caste assumptions and practices shaped technological development in general, and technical education more specifically, and the impact of these processes on meanings and practices of caste.[3]

Here I take up one piece of this larger story: the evolution of Indian technical education in a context of imperial transformation, and the centrality of caste imaginaries to that process. We will see how, in the early nineteenth century, the political terrain shifted to allow for the development of modern education in British India. This new arena witnessed key debates around engineering education, with different constituencies arguing over race, caste, technical aptitude, and the proper balance of mental and manual skill. Gradually, engineering came to be associated with classroom-based theoretical knowledge and professional service to the state and disassociated from an earlier British orientation around guild apprenticeship and private industry. The professionalization of engineering was part and parcel of the entrenchment of the colonial state as an infrastructural and administrative apparatus. The shift from shopfloor to classroom also clinched the identity of the British Indian engineer as a member of a colonial elite who was to embody the hierarchies of the colony. Initially, this meant racial exclusivity. But dual pressures—from England to do colonialism "on the cheap" and from nationalists charging Britain with underdevelopment—led to a lifting of the racial glass ceiling and entry of upper castes into the engineering service.

We will also consider the other side of technical training: industrial schooling for lower castes. While first intended as a response to the embattled status of artisanal castes under colonial free trade, industrial schooling eventually shifted toward an emphasis on producing labor for new industries. By the transition to independence, the engineering profession had effectively displaced lower castes with histories of technical skill and knowledge in favor of upper castes who previously disdained hands-on labor. Overall, the chapter will track how the divergence between professional engineering and industrial schooling both deepened the penetration of the colonial state and economy, and sutured the link between caste status and technical knowledge.

Modernizing Education

In British India, the question of whether and how to promote technical education was repeatedly raised beginning in the mid-nineteenth century. Both colonial and nationalist advocates of Indian modernization pointed to the predominance of classical literary education and the need to cultivate other "practical" fields of study in the colony. The debate over the approach and scope of technical education revealed a range of positions on preferred forms of tutelage, what kinds of knowledge were perceived as most beneficial or transformative, and who was best suited to acquire this knowledge.

Before 1857, the colonial government moved slowly on provisions for modern education, primarily because of the powerful Orientalist lobby and an overall conservatism toward the existing status quo. Clause 43 of the East India Company Act of 1813 spelled out two goals: "The encouragement of the learned natives of India and the revival and improvement of literature; secondly, the promotion of a knowledge of the sciences amongst the inhabitants of that country." The company's Court of Directors determined that the existing institutional structures of formal education for social elites would remain, as the more extensive spread of modern public education would be incompatible with "the customs and mentality of the people."[4]

Criticism of Orientalist approaches to education arose early. In 1823, Bengali modernizer Rammohan Roy wrote to Lord Amherst, the governor-general of Bengal, criticizing the proposal for establishing a Sanskrit college in Calcutta and urging the government to instead "promote a more liberal and enlightened system of instruction." Roy felt that "the establishment of Sanskrit schools specializing in metaphysical niceties was regression to a pre-Baconian universe" and destroyed "the sanguine hopes of the native intelligentsia for courses in mathematics, philosophy, chemistry, and anatomy."[5] But his argument fell on deaf ears. In 1824, the colonial government opened a Sanskrit college in Calcutta and another in Delhi for "instruction in the three classical languages of India."

The critique of colonial education policy leveled by Indian modernizers like Roy resonated with the position adopted by utilitarians within the East India Company directorship. In an 1824 despatch, they stated that the government's original approach to education was "fundamentally erroneous. The great end should not have been to teach Hindu learning, but useful learning. . . . In professing, on the other hand, to establish seminaries for the purpose of teaching mere Hindu or mere Mohamadan literature, you bound yourselves to teach a great deal of what was frivolous, not a little of what was purely mischievous, a small remained indeed in which utility was in any way concerned." Thomas Macaulay's 1835 "Minute on Education," which argued for a shift from classical Indian to modern European knowledge, tipped the scales and initiated a broader reorientation of Indian education. Inspired by Macaulay, Lord Auckland in 1840 called for education "through the medium of English and the Vernaculars, in accordance with modern ideas." This modernizing vision was encapsulated in an 1854 despatch sent by Charles Wood, the President of the Board of Control of the East India Company, to Governor Lord Dalhousie, which advanced a new approach to Indian education as the general diffusion of European knowledge. Known as "Wood's Despatch," it highlighted the limitations of the dominant literary approach and urged professional training in law, medicine, and civil engineering through the establishment of vocational colleges and schools of industry. A noteworthy section attributed by some to John Stuart Mill argued the need for "useful and practical knowledge suited to every station in life" and underscored the critical role of the state in disseminating this form of knowledge "to the great mass of the people who are utterly incapable of obtaining an education worthy of the name by their own unaided efforts."[6] The point was clear: unlike in the metropole, the state in the colony would be integral to the advancement of modern education.

Before the 1854 despatch, there was already one engineering college in operation: the Thomason College of Civil Engineering at Roorkee.

The college was founded in 1847 in response to the demand for civil engineers to aid the construction of the Ganges Canal in the North-west Provinces.[7] After the despatch, three more engineering colleges followed in quick succession: the Poona College of Engineering in 1859, the Madras Civil Engineering College in 1862, and the Sibpur College of Engineering in 1880. All four colleges were tied to employment in the Department of Public Works, which expanded rapidly after the Indian Rebellion of 1857–1858 as part of the shift in authority from the East India Company to the British Crown. The promotion of engineering as useful knowledge was thus intimately linked to the goal of expanding the presence and power of the colonial state.

After the 1880s, the colonial government made a more concerted effort to extend technical training beyond the collegiate level through industrial schooling. Industrial schooling was intended to mitigate the effects of colonial free trade by retraining and channeling displaced artisans into new industries. Unlike engineering, it targeted a very different segment of the native population: not disaffected elites but dispossessed subalterns who, as missive after missive stated, were "destined for industrial and commercial pursuits."

Colonial technical education policy thus advanced in two directions: the first toward building a native cadre of college-educated engineers, and the second toward equipping artisans for modern industries. Policy, however, was not practice. Both college engineering and industrial schooling advanced in fits and starts. Engineering was stymied by the enduring English suspicion of the classroom as an appropriate site for training engineers and by an institutional investment in maintaining a racial hierarchy within the colonial engineering corps. Industrial schooling, on the other hand, suffered setbacks because of the tug of war between interventionism and laissez-faire and because of indecision over whether to promote small- or large-scale industry.

Despite the slow growth of technical education, there were some clear outcomes of the process. Most importantly, the development of technical training along two tracks was informed by and, in turn, reinforced caste differences. By the advent of independence, the status of technical knowledge had transformed; while engineering was now an upper-caste intellectual aspiration intimately tied to nation-building, artisanship had been demoted to a form of unskilled labor seen as far less instrumental to economic development.

Engineering Education: Defining the Professional

In advocating for the growth of professional engineering in India, colonial statesmen typically invoked the metropolitan engineer as forerunner and model. But in nineteenth-century England, there was little scope for technical training as a process of formal education. The pioneers of industry were workingmen trained by apprenticeship and self-taught in industrial science, and the leading engineers were products of the old system of guild pupilage. There was widespread conviction that factories, offices, and workshops were the nation's "true technical schools."[8] This older vocational approach to engineering as a form of shopfloor learning persisted into the twentieth century, long after engineering had become an academic discipline in other parts of Europe. In 1901, Edward Buck, who was commissioned by the colonial government to conduct a study of technical education in India, offered a scathing critique of this English conviction: "In England people are still content to repeat that trades cannot be taught in a school. The Austrians and Germans have discovered that trades cannot be efficiently taught *without* a school. In many towns, employers are required to send their apprentices to a technical school for a certain number of days a week, and a breach of the law is followed by fine or imprisonment. Nor are the schools confined to a few large towns. In Austria, in particular, a great point is made of carrying technical training to the small towns and even to the villages."[9] But even Buck's criticism of outmoded English ways was ultimately less about technical education as a path to professionalization and more as a necessary supplement to the existing set of trades. It was this argument for a more robust and systematic investment in the trades that he took from the Austrians and Germans and recommended for India.

In India, opposition to bringing technical training under the auspices of the Department of Education lasted into the early twentieth century. In 1908, John Wallace, the editor of the *Indian Textile Journal*, submitted this opinion to the Industrial Conference held at Ootacamund:

The cause of the present state of technical education in India is traceable to the constitution of the Educational Department which is controlled by University men, whose ideas of education are so built upon reading and writing as a foundation that they have overlooked the true relation of technique to science in a country whose industrial training is still in a very backward condition. In every other country, which has reached any industrial eminence, the knowledge of handicraft preceded by many generations, that of reading and writing. India has yet to recover from an educational impulse in the wrong direction. Reading and writing, which have been of incalculable value for certain classes, are not of use at all, and they become positively pernicious when they entice young men away from a sure living by handicraft to the overcrowded ranks of clerical labor.[10]

Wallace's statement is striking for its social and developmental advocacy. His was a call for building technical education from the foundation of India's handicraft traditions. As he saw it, technical education had been usurped by those who, with their faith in book learning, had little understanding of "technique." In attempting to make technical education a mirror of what they knew, these "University men" were on shaky ground and sure to fail. Instead, Wallace urged a resuscitation of technical education as embodied technique through which India could advance more surely along the path to industrialization.

This sentiment in favor of "technique" as the appropriate form of knowledge for the majority of Indians was echoed time and again in government commissions and resolutions from the mid-nineteenth century. Initially, even those closely associated with the development of professional engineering institutions expressed this conviction. In 1857, Lieutenant Winscom, the first principal of the Madras College of Engineering, stated his preference for those with experience in hands-on work in this missive to the director of public instruction:

My own idea would lead me very much to prefer a rough steady man with good constitution and with strong natural good sense to a weakly bookworm. It is from men of the former stamp that the great English Engineers have sprung with very few exceptions. . . . I conceive therefore that men to be taught to excel in the Engineering profession in this country are not those who have all their lives been engaged in study, but rather fresh clever lads from the country, sons of overseers, Maistries, etc. who have seen and taken interest in works in progress.[11]

Winscom's preference was shared by Major Richard Strachey, who averred that "no amount of college teaching will make the Engineer. It will merely fit young men to become Engineers when they have the opportunity afforded them of acquiring practical knowledge."[12]

As indicative of the dominant British view of engineering as an endeavor of "the practical man," only three of the first ten presidents of the Institution of Civil Engineers (founded in 1818) were university trained men. As late as 1869, Colonel Chesney of the Corps of Royal Engineers retorted that "the very name of a college for engineering would be utterly abhorrent to the ideas of most civil engineers," as "a college to them conveys the notion of a place where students are to be crammed with mathematics and theory and are to learn nothing else."[13] It was only in 1903 that the Institution of Civil Engineers placed the sanction of the profession behind the system of higher education in engineering.

It is curious that so much of the resistance to the classroom came from military men, since the military was the exception to the rule of workshop learning. The formal training of officers for the Corps of Royal Engineers, the engineering arm of the British army, has a history dating back to 1741 with the establishment of the Royal Military Academy at Woolwich. Subsequently, the directors of the East India Company founded a military academy of their own at Addiscombe in 1809 to train officers, first for the engineer and artillery corps, and later for the cavalry and infantry. Until it closed in 1860, the academy at Addiscombe produced the engineer officers of the British Indian Army. Ironically, the same military officers produced by this academic training resisted the development of engineering as classroom knowledge in India. It took a change from military to civilian oversight of engineering to more effectively tie it to the classroom.

The colonial state's shift toward civilian technical education in the classroom occurred virtually in tandem with similar changes in England. Imperial rivalries were key to this change. As Home Secretary A. P. MacDonnell noted in July 1886, the policy shift followed from the great industrial exhibitions of the 1850s. At the first one in London in 1851, metropolitan policy makers recognized the "deficiencies as regards art of the English workman, and as regards science of the English manufacturer."[14] This concern was affirmed during the fourth exhibition in Paris in 1857, after which the British Commission of Inquiry admitted that "the English workman is gradually losing the race, through the superior intelligence which the foreign governments are carefully developing in their artisans. The education of Germany is the result of national organization which compels every peasant to send his children to school, and afterwards affords the opportunity of acquiring such technical skill as may be useful in the department of industry to which they are destined."[15] Beginning in 1853, but more so after the 1857 industrial exhibition, in which Britain was shown up by France, Germany, and America, a more concerted effort was made to bring technical training within the purview of formal education. England began to introduce technical courses under the auspices of the Department of Education. Even after this point, however, prejudices against classroom learning of technical skills persisted, and universities that opened engineering facilities saw very low student numbers.

The 1854 despatch, which advocated a scheme of technical and industrial education for India, followed a mere three years after the 1851 exhibition. In this sense, the introduction of formal engineering education in India can hardly be seen as an instance of a temporal lag between metropole and colony. In many ways, India was quicker to move ahead with the institutionalization of engineering as part of a modern system of classroom education.

The greater speed with which engineering was institutionalized as part of Indian higher education was largely due to its being a state project. The difference from the prevailing model in England, where engineering was a private sector practice, was stated early on by commissioners of the Public Works Department of Madras, who argued that "education, and more emphatically this species of education, is not at such a point in this country, that the Government need merely to fix a standard of qualification, and invite candidates to compete for admission into the service; it must itself provide all the training machinery."[16] This argument for a kind of colonial "affirmative action" gave the government of India a far more central role in the promotion of engineering than England. Even after Governor-General Dalhousie delinked engineering from the Military Board in 1855, it remained under the auspices of the newly created Department of Public Works.

The institutionalization of engineering as classroom education shifted the model of training away from England and toward other industrialized states. In his writings on his days as a student at Roorkee's Thomason College of Civil Engineering in the early 1870s, William Willcocks, a leading irrigation engineer of the late nineteenth century, observed that they "were taught on the sound lines of the Ecole Polytechnique in Paris, and not on the ridiculous lines generally in vogue in England at the time." One key dimension of the shift in training from shopfloor to classroom was the elevation of mathematics. Technical education planners felt that the status of engineering could only be secured through "a sense of shared expertise drawn from a common body of 'theoretical' (i.e., mathematical) published research. The increasing prestige and professionalism of irrigation engineers in India in the late nineteenth century was thus rooted particularly in the conjoining of the prestige of mathematics to the prestige of service to the state."[17] This was a far cry from Winscom's midcentury argument for an engineering corps composed of the "sons of overseers [and] Maistries." In the colony, engineering had come to serve a very different purpose. Instead of hands-on learning, it was becoming an elite persuasion associated with conceptual knowledge and state power.

By the 1940s, the earlier, more pragmatic approach to engineering was regarded as something of an embarrassment. Emblematic of this sentiment was the observation in a Punjab Irrigation Department manual from 1943 that despite the "amazing courage and resources" of mid-nineteenth-century military engineers, "their knowledge of irrigation and hydraulics was nil." In retrospect, they were seen as working largely by trial and error. While the Punjab's Bari Doab and Sirhind canals had been built with "beautifully drawn and skillfully colored plans," they had "shocking mistakes of design."[18] It was only now, armed with the science of engineering and its mathematical formulas, that the true professional was thought to come into his own.

By the mid-twentieth century, then, technique had morphed from being a basis for engineering into a barrier to its true expression.

Race, Caste, and Class in the Making of the Indian Engineer

Alongside the concern over the suitability of engineering for the classroom, there was another repeatedly raised question: the suitability of the Indian for engineering. Although technical skill was more clearly evident among artisans, the emerging consensus over engineering as classroom learning and its link to the prestige of the state made literate upper castes the principal targets of this new knowledge. To paraphrase John Wallace, in elevating the classroom as the new site of technical knowledge, education planners marginalized those who had technique in favor of those schooled in reading and writing.

There were also other reasons to push for engineering as a new focus of upper-caste education. Its proponents saw engineering as an answer to the saturation of elite employment in law and government. The imbalance between fields of knowledge was evident in the distribution of colleges. When Lord Curzon arrived in India in 1899 to assume the viceroyalty, there were 191 colleges, of which 145 were arts colleges and the rest professional colleges, including law (30), teaching (5), agriculture (3), medicine (4), and engineering (4).[19] For colonial officials like Lord George Hamilton, the secretary of state, there was an immediate political reason to direct Indians away from literature and philosophy. As he put it peevishly, literary education, "joy of the Babu and anglicized Brahmin . . . produces a wholesale mass of discontented individuals who, if they cannot find government employment spend their time in abusing the government which has educated them."[20]

Despite the expansion of colonial public works from the 1850s, the consolidation of a civilian classroom orientation to engineering by the late nineteenth century, and its promotion as an antidote to nationalist sentiment, the growth of a professional cadre of Indian engineers moved in fits and starts. This was largely due to the existence of a racial glass ceiling expressed in British assumptions about Indian technical incompetence. Indians were prevented from getting the training they needed to rise up the ranks of the colonial engineering service because of built-in prejudices against native technical capacity.[21] Sweeping generalizations about Indians were commonplace. W.T. Thornton, secretary of the Public Works Department, for instance, maintained that the poor output of the existing engineering colleges was not due to any failing on the part of the government but simply that "the taste for civil engineering is likely to be of slow growth among the people of India." He predicted that Indians would "take the place of European engineers but very gradually."[22] Even those who came to support arguments in favor of increased Indian representation in the colonial services, such as Alfred Chatterton of the Indian Industrial Commission, questioned Indians' capacity for technical knowledge. "The subtle mind of the Hindu," Chatterton observed, "delights in philosophic speculations and in unraveling the intricacies of legal enactments; it is possible that the same qualities applied to scientific investigation would afford their possessors equal gratification in probing the hidden mysteries of natural phenomena. That the practical aspects of such inquiries would appeal to them is less certain."[23] For Chatterton, it was this lack of practical sense, the fact that Indians "do not possess in any very large measure the grit and common sense which mark the engineer," that ultimately kept colonialism in place. "It is fairly certain that if they did possess these qualities," he opined, "they would not want our assistance to maintain peace and order." Chatterton singled out engineering in particular as the cornerstone of self-rule. As he put it, "when India can do her own engineering work and carry on her own industries, then, and then only, she will be able to govern herself, and our dominion, in its existing form at any rate, will come to an end." For Chatterton, engineering and democracy proceeded apace. "With the gradual development of local self-government," he argued, "there will assuredly be a corresponding development of engineering skill and a gradually decreasing demand for external assistance. The progress in one direction will measure the progress in the other."[24]

While the racial overtones of such judgments are difficult to deny, there was also a caste sociology in play. With the shift to classroom education, the "Indians" who were the object of official scrutiny were the upper castes, not the artisans whose practical orientation and technical capacity were evident. While regarded as well suited for higher education, upper castes were also seen to be singularly lacking in practical skills.

In 1911, Edwin Atkinson and Tom Dawson, authors of a report on technical education in India, opined that "the general disinclination for hard physical labor on the part of the average educated Indian is the chief cause of failure in the technical education of the India of today."[25] They went on to valorize the British ideal of on-the-job training: "Every technically trained student must be prepared to start on the lowest rung of the ladder, show his superiority by hard work and technical knowledge, and having made himself indispensable and a commercial asset to his employer, he will then rise by the natural laws of supply and demand."[26] Another official report on education explained that "individual bhadralog (upper caste people) do not, in fact, wish their sons to be mistris (carpenters). Each thinks that the sons of others, not his own son, may be diverted from the competition for employment in the clerical and professional market."[27] A member of the Indian Industrial Commission echoed this characterization in more oblique terms: "Our trouble in India is that the practical side of industry is not at present considered an honorable calling by any but a fraction of the section of the Indian community who should be attracted to our large industries, and until there is more inclination on the part of the Indian student to 'take his coat off,' the advantages of technical education are bound to be to a great extent nullified.'"[28]

Even when British officials were willing to grant Indians technical proficiency, they found other ways to point to the problem of caste sentiment. One repeated trope was how caste affinity and social embeddedness undermined the professionalism of Indian engineers. For instance, one British engineer expressed discomfort with Indian colleagues and superiors by complaining that they "would listen to the grievances only of fellow caste men when on inspection tours."[29] Sir Charles Harrison, chief engineer of the large-scale Sukkur Barrage project in Sindh Province, told the Simon Commission deputized to assess the effects of the Montagu-Chelmsford Reforms of 1919 that Indian engineers, "though often technically efficient, were subject to outside influences pressing on them to make a partial distribution of water, influences which often made it difficult for them to carry out their duties as efficiently and impartially as they would wish to do."[30]

Such commentary on the predilections of Indian engineers expressed several things at once: that the Indian engineer was expected to be drawn from among the educated upper castes; that Indian hierarchies of caste were set in stone; that elite diffidence was the principal reason for the absence of industrialization; and that English society, by contrast, was a meritocracy where hard work paid off. In effect, the simultaneous shift to the classroom and the enduring influence of an older model of hands-on skill produced a double exclusion. On one side were lower castes whose social standing made them ill-suited for the classroom. On the other side were upper castes whose intellectual and social orientation made them unfit for the practicalities of technical work and, by extension, for the higher ranks of engineering. Who, then, was left to populate colonial engineering?

In short, the English. But it was not only Indians who were subject to critical scrutiny; so, too, were the English.[31] The British engineer in India was expected to fit a social mold suited to the racial hierarchies of empire. Two successive schemes to supply metropolitan expertise for the Indian engineering service clearly illustrate this expectation. With the expansion of colonial public works in the 1850s, the newly opened India Office in London turned to England for technical experts. In 1858, Lord Stanley, the secretary of state for India, started a new scheme for the recruitment of British engineers for Indian public works. These recruits came to be known as "the Stanley engineers." They were expected to take the Indian civil service exam, supplemented by a short "conversion course" at one of the four Indian engineering colleges.

These Stanley engineers proved to be disappointing to men like Colonel Chesney, who found them poorly educated and unable "to pass an examination involving any knowledge of the principles of mathematics or theoretical mechanics."[32] More significantly, they were lower class, a concern that was articulated by the Public Works Department (PWD) in an 1870 resolution expressing concern that "the class of men asked for are not such as is expedient to introduce in large numbers into India, where, in the intercourse between Europeans and Natives, more consideration for the feelings and prejudices of the latter is desirable than such of the former as have not had their manners softened by education are much in the habit of showing.[33] Chesney and others worried that metropolitan recruitment done without care to ensure an appropriately elite cadre would upset British India's balance of social classes.

What they desired were English engineers who were both gentlemen and workers and who could fulfill the demand for technical labor without destabilizing the racial and class hierarchies of the colony. Moreover, as is evident in the stated sensitivity to Indian "feelings and prejudices," they repeatedly used native prejudice as an alibi for pursuing conservative policies that belied British claims to enlightened government.

When the Stanley scheme failed, the British made a second attempt to preserve the racial character of colonial engineering. In 1870, Chesney was appointed by the secretary of state to found the Royal Indian Engineering College at Cooper's Hill near London to train students for the Indian engineering service. In addition to being "of sound constitution and of good moral character," applicants had to pass a test covering mathematics; natural science; Latin; Greek; French; German; the works of Shakespeare, Milton, Johnson, Scott, and Byron; and English history from 1688 to 1756. In effect, it was a test of gentlemanliness.

For all their talk of technical competence, then, when colonial policy makers pictured the ideal public works engineer, they thought not only of a man with practical skill but also of an Englishman with a particular class bearing. These racial and class requirements for admission into the colonial civil services, ones that were reflected more broadly across the British Empire, appear to have satisfied the supporters of Cooper's Hill in India. In 1878, a military officer on the North Bengal State Railway crowed that "a better, abler and more gentlemanly set of men than the recently joined men from Cooper's Hill could not have been sent out to India."[34]

Despite such exalted opinions of Cooper's Hill graduates, by the 1880s, this scheme had failed to produce the desired results. As a final attempt to preserve the racial hierarchy within colonial public works, the Aitchison Commission of 1886–1887 recommended that the civil service be divided into an upper imperial and several lower provincial services, with only the latter open to Indians. However, none of these initiatives arrested the decline in the metropolitan hold on Indian engineering. Cooper's Hill was finally closed in 1907, although its graduates dominated the upper echelons of colonial engineering until the 1930s, when the last batch of alumni came to the end of their careers.[35]

The exorbitant cost of staffing British Indian services with Europeans generated opposition not just from nationalists but from the British themselves. In 1880, Viscount Cranbrook, the secretary of state, insisted in a strongly worded letter to the viceroy that "all reasonable facilities for entering on a career as Civil Engineers in the service of Government should be offered to Natives." His opinion, however, remained in the minority for decades after, despite the fact that the 1917 report of the PWD Reorganization Committee also underscored the need to recruit Indian engineers to all levels of the public works bureaucracy. Only with the Morley-Minto Reforms of 1919 did a commitment to participatory governance through "Indianization" begin in earnest.

These repeated exhortations to open the services to Indians make clear that there were significant racial barriers to access and advancement within engineering. British officials and engineers found creative ways to discredit Indians and prevent their entry and advancement within the engineering profession. It is also the case that caste and religion were tropes deployed by British officials to disqualify Indians whom they perceived as being unable to transcend their social affiliations to embody the supposed integrity and impartiality of colonial officialdom. All sorts of contradictory rationales—practicality on the one hand, gentlemanliness on the other—served to justify a sense of English progressivism and competence while maintaining a racial glass ceiling in the colonial services.

Still, throughout the early twentieth century, upper-caste Indians did enter engineering in increasing numbers. As previously mentioned, the British were keen to meet the need for technical expertise without rocking the boat socially. This was the reason for withdrawing the Stanley engineers, whose lower-class backgrounds were seen as socially destabilizing. It was also why upper castes were identified as best suited—socially, if not technically—to the engineering profession. It is in their approach to Indian students that we most clearly see British accommodation of upper-caste "feelings and prejudices" and the need to preserve existing forms of social distinction.

By all accounts, Indian upper castes did eschew programs such as the vocational and industrial schools set up by European missionaries and government officials, a tendency that European observers attributed to "a much older tradition of Brahmin intellectualism."[36] On the other hand, as noted by S. F. Downing, the first principal of Sibpur College of Engineering, upper-caste inhibitions about technical labor fell away once such work was associated with high-status institutions:

> I have learnt from conversation with respectable educated natives that the fact of the department belonging to the Presidency College gives it a certain status in the eyes of native society; consequently a superior class is attracted to it than would be the case were a school attached to large Government workshops in which the students would have to work daily, such manual labor being, unfortunately, considered derogatory by upper class Bengalis. This appears to me to be an important point, because native Assistant Engineers, Public Works Department, have to associate officially with English gentlemen, and consequently the former ought, if possible, to be recruited from the upper middle class community.[37]

Downing's statement betrays the consistent effort on the part of the British to attribute the elite character of colonial engineering to indigenous cultural barriers while at the same time doing their part to accommodate and reinforce these "unfortunate" prejudices. As a result, by the early twentieth century, public works had become a gentlemanly affair conducted between white and brown elites.

Even a cursory look at the membership rolls of the two main professional engineering bodies in the British Empire—the Institute of Civil Engineers and the Institute of Mechanical Engineers—reveals that the few Indian members were all upper caste and mostly Brahmin. This was equally the case with the Institution of Engineers (India), which was set up in Calcutta in 1920 as the Indian counterpart to the professional bodies in London. Although some of its first presidents were European, most thereafter were Brahmin members of the Madras and Bengal Public Works and Railways departments.

Official testimonies to the Indian Industrial Commission of 1916–1918 show that Indians made the choice to enter engineering education with full regard for existing social distinctions. Arguments made by both British and Indian witnesses reflect two key concerns: that technical work was socially devalued, and that the way to enhance the value of the technical was to connect it to upper castes. At times, we see the role of caste in comparisons drawn between engineering colleges. In his testimony, B. Heaton, successor to Downing as principal of the Sibpur College of Engineering, contrasted Sibpur's difficulties with recruiting upper-caste students with the relative ease experienced by the College of Civil Engineering at Roorkee. The problem, as he diagnosed it, was with the structure of Sibpur, which provided three tiers of training: one for officers; one for supervisors; and one for carpenters, blacksmiths, and tinsmiths from affiliated technical schools. Heaton observed that the fact of such social heterogeneity "would make gentlemen who are capitalists . . . chary of sending their sons to the college."[38] Besides, he could not "give them the kind of accommodation they are accustomed to at home." Commensality came in for special comment. Heaton contrasted the situation at Sibpur with that at Roorkee, "where the students live entirely separate lives . . . were expected to live in a good style, to dress for dinner. My students have a joint mess with sub-overseers and overseers." The institutional practice of co-dining across social divides was inimical to the effort to recruit Indian upper castes, who opted instead for institutions where caste practices of purity and pollution were maintained. Not only did maintaining status through practices of distinction vary across colleges, but their graduates were also treated differently. Heaton observed that every person who graduated from Roorkee was guaranteed a job at the level of an assistant engineer, "while only one of my thirteen students was assured a guaranteed post."[39] Alfred Chatterton of the Madras College of Civil Engineering commiserated with Heaton but suggested that the problem lay with the university as the sole path to high-status government employment. The "PWD State," he opined, had created a structure of expectations where a university degree in law and humanities was a passport to a job in the revenue service.[40] This assumption prejudiced upper castes in favor of the university over the engineering college.

The solution put forward by Chatterton and Heaton was to elevate the status of engineering to make it attractive to Indian elites. They proposed several routes to achieving this outcome. First, the state could establish an autonomous technological institution modeled on the Osborne Naval College in England. This would require "cutting off the lower classes," recruiting from the early age of fourteen, wooing potential technical students away from the university while still providing them with elements of a liberal education, and assuring employment up to the executive engineers' grade.[41] Second, they suggested the establishment of an imperial college of engineering as an umbrella encompassing all the branches of engineering or, as a compromise option, the federation of the four existing colleges of engineering. The creation of a pan-Indian body would enhance the status of engineering by linking it more definitively with the imperial rather than the regional scale of government.

While upper-caste Indians and British policy makers were preoccupied with enhancing the status of engineering by severing it from other forms of technical training, others argued against this move. One question posed by the Indian Industrial Commission was whether technical schools should fall under the Department of Education or under the Department of Industries. Hanumantha Rao, the head of the economic nationalist Andhra Jateeya Kalasala, answered definitively. Manual work was already socially devalued, and locating technical training under the Department of Industries would only diminish its value further. Rao instead proposed that technical training as a whole be actively promoted as both an educational and a cultural ideal. He argued that to alter the cultural perception of technical skill required that "the whole power of the educational ideal must be directed to awaken in the popular mind an inclination and a passion for industrial enterprise."[42] This awakening would only happen by "introducing into the scheme of general education in the country a course of manual training such as would help to give early enough in life a bias towards work involving skill and efficiency of muscular power."[43] Only such a far-reaching scheme would induce a wholesale shift in the value of technical labor. In addition to rethinking hierarchies of value, Rao also argued against an instrumental approach to learning, "for otherwise the Indian youth would instinctively turn away from training which holds out not the ideal of culture, but of purely professional training."[44]

Rao's critique was leveled against both the denigration of the technical and its elevation solely through its link to professionalism. Rao proposed a wholesale transformation in cultural worldview to recognize the value of technical labor as a source of knowledge that should be foundational to both education and nation-building. This was a far more radical stance than the solutions proposed by Chatterton and Heaton, who were principally concerned with making engineering professionally attractive to upper castes.

Rao's advocacy for a necessary cultural revolution in perception and practice was partly echoed by attorney B. N. Basu, who offered this wry observation:

> I am told that when the first Hindu student in the Calcutta Medical College was induced to perform an operation upon a dead body, guns were fired from Fort William in recognition of the fact that a Hindu got over the prejudice of touching a dead body. . . . In the course of twenty or thirty years we got a very fine class of Indian surgeons and physicians, and so I do not see why if we fire a gun when the first Brahmin begins to make a shoe now we should not get in thirty years quite as satisfactory results.[45]

Although Basu still saw the conversion to modernity of upper castes as a necessary stepping-stone to advancing the cause of technical education, he nonetheless shared Rao's conviction that this had to involve a broader transformation of cultural prejudices against embodied labor.

Despite the eloquence of their testimonies, Rao and Basu were unable to effectively challenge the widespread assumption that the only way to elevate the technical was by disassociating it from lower-caste technique and associating it with upper-caste knowledge. That technical education policy reinforced existing caste divisions is evident in another set of testimonies given to the Indian Industrial Commission by manual workers in artisanal industries. Daivasikhamani Achari, secretary of the Kumbakonam Visvakarma Mahajana Conference Committee, came before the commission to speak on behalf of "the artisans of the South" and to express his concern that technical education was marginalizing those very groups who came from histories of skilled manual labor. Although artisans were "the industrial backbone of the country," he attested, "they were not going to be the beneficiaries of the new policy regarding technical schools." Achari singled out the state technical scholarships that sponsored students to go abroad for technical training as indicative of a larger problem: the prerequisite of formal education barred most artisans from accessing these scholarships. Rather than cultivate those who historically bore the weight of industry, "the mistake lay in the very first steps taken, viz., in the selection of students to go to foreign countries for training, from communities other than industrial or artisan classes who possess the initial aptitude for manual labor, born of an inherited capacity and instinctive professional skill which a University graduate of any other class despised as a derogation of his caste dignity or literary merit."[46] To drive home his point about the injustice of favoring upper castes at the expense of artisans, Achari cited the 1911 census report on "the complete dissociation of the intellectual class in the country from its industries. . . . Manual work of any kind was looked upon as degrading and the higher castes treated with contempt the artisans and craftsmen who carried on the industrial work of the country."[47] Achari's criticism could not have been more pointed; still, his testimony met the same fate as those of Rao and Basu.

It is evident from all these statements that technical education was propagated in a context thick with assumptions about the value of labor and expectations that existing social distinctions of caste not be blurred with the advent of the new knowledge. British testimonies before the Indian Industrial Commission addressed the need to expand the scope of technical education by targeting upper-caste groups who, for social and professional reasons, would have opted instead for the law or humanities. They were clear that the appeal of technical education could not simply be assumed; in a context where the hierarchies of value worked against the hands-on character of engineering, its status had to be cultivated through active association with high-status groups. As with Christian missionizing in the nineteenth century, an upper-caste convert to the technical professions was highly prized.

Catering to upper castes did see results. While they did not go for anything that smacked of manual labor, upper castes were more enthusiastic about entering professional engineering programs that promised social status and well-paying careers. Indeed, the stratification of technical training was perfectly well suited to the upper-caste desire to maintain social distinctions within native society while entering new, modern fields of knowledge and bridging the racial gap in professional employment within the state. For their part, colonial officials were happy to accommodate caste prejudices in order to enhance the status and growth of engineering. In effect, upper-caste prejudice and colonial policy dovetailed to consign those social groups with a history of technical skill to the margins of the growing field of engineering.

Industrial Schooling: Defining the Artisan

Marginalizing artisans did not mean that they were ignored. Just as there was considerable ink spilled in determining the appropriate bearing and orientation of the engineer, much was written about the artisan's place within a modernizing society. And just as there was little consensus over whether the engineer was best taught on the shop-floor or the classroom, the jury was out on how to deal with the threat posed to the artisan by industrialization and free trade.

Artisanship occupied an ambivalent place within colonial and nationalist imaginaries of India. There were those who believed in the artisan's inevitable obsolescence. This faith in the technological timeline was echoed by state officials such as the Punjab government's industrial expert, who predicted the "ultimate ruin of the native tanner" and advised that it "is merely a question of time, and the Government can do nothing, nor is it in the public interest to do anything, directly to save him. The only course to follow is . . . to offer every reasonable encouragement to large tanners, and in particular to subsidize a suitable factory."[48]

In contrast, others saw the principal function of industrial policy as the defense of artisanal traditions against the rise of factories. Those who sought to rehabilitate the arts and crafts of India included Luddites like John Ruskin and William Morris and the principals of the schools of art set up in the 1880s. For them, Indian artisanal traditions represented the prelapsarian past, which could still be protected from the predations of industrial capitalism.

Often, the defense of the artisan within colonial officialdom was a way of discrediting the Swadeshi movement to boycott British goods, revive indigenous products, and push for protected industrialization. For colonial critics, Swadeshi was Indian in name but not in content. Rather, it was the British colonial and not the Indian nationalist who was the true patron of Indian traditions. As the principal of the Madras School of Art put it in 1910:

It is doubtless the easier way for Indians to throw aside all their artistic traditions as obsolete, to accept blindly the teaching of European commercial experts, to multiply factories and join in the mad
scramble for markets which Europe calls civilization. . . . Will India
be freer, happier and wiser when, instead of lacs of village craftsmen,
every town has its "swadeshi" cotton mills . . . and . . . "swadeshi"
music halls and gin palaces . . . ? Nowhere in India—not even in the
direst time of famine and pestilence—is there such utter depravity,
such hopeless physical, moral and spiritual degradation as that which
exists in the great cities of Europe.[49]

Even those at the heights of colonial administration, like Viceroy
Curzon, expressed an ambivalence toward industrialization because of
its anticipated effect on Indian art and craft. For him, modern industry
could only be an impoverished form of Western mimicry in a country
whose authenticity lay in its hereditary traditions:

The expansion of [factory] industries would be valuable insofar as
they would give increased employment to an increasing number of
workmen and would therefore swell the number of those who are not
compelled to depend on agriculture. From this point of view the introduction of factories and mills is equally laudable. But then comes
the other or artistic point of view, which appeals, at any rate to me,
much more forcibly. I would sooner attempt to revive the rapidly perishing art industries of India, perishing not because a market is not
forthcoming for them, but because the already existing market is
being lost by shortsighted parsimony and by the indulgence in vulgar
and semi-Europeanized designs.[50]

These critics of Swadeshi insisted that only colonial rule could be a
bulwark against the ills of modern industrial society. For them, India's
artisanal traditions represented forms of indigenous "art and craft" antithetical to modernization. But like their opponents who favored
rapid industrialization, they were unable to envision an approach to
technological change with artisanship at its center. Rather, artisans
were survivals of another age that needed to be cherished and protected
against the inexorable force of industrial modernity.

There were others, however, who argued for the significance of artisanship, not to a vanishing past but for an alternate future. Alfred

Chatterton, who became famous for his "pioneering factories" to make artisanship commercially viable, was one such person. But even Chatterton opposed the Swadeshi call for protectionism, which he saw as being driven primarily by political rather than economic considerations. "In lieu of protective duties," he argued, "I am strongly in favor of an energetic educational and industrial policy having for its object the fostering of industrial enterprise and the diversion of a fair proportion of the intellect of the country from non-productive to directly productive occupations."[51] Chatterton approached indigenous industrial development largely as a technical endeavor. Although he appreciated the role played by the Swadeshi movement in highlighting the destruction of indigenous industry under foreign competition, he disparaged the impulse to attribute to such issues "a political character." He thought politics an unnecessary distraction from the real business of growing and innovating with local industries.

In the end, and despite differences in emphasis, such arguments in favor of indigenous industry fed the broader opposition to the rising tide of economic nationalism. For all these advocates, regardless of whether they believed in preserving or developing artisanship, the artisan had to be a ward of the colonial state, because Indians were not equipped with the aesthetic or technical skills necessary to properly induct an artisan into the modern world.

Education "Destined for Industrial and Commercial Pursuits"

Chatterton was among those concerned with the side of technical education dealing with groups "destined for industrial and commercial pursuits." This was training intended not for the disgruntled "Babu or anglicized Brahmin" facing unemployment after a degree in law or medicine, but for youth from families specializing in handicraft and other traditions of manual labor. In contrast to the civil engineer's mix of mental acuity and practical know-how, students of industrial schools were expected to be primarily practically oriented.

At the same time, what a practical education should consist of and toward what end remained ill-defined despite ongoing debate from the 1880s to the 1930s. In 1883, the Hunter Education Commission underscored the "real need in India for some corresponding course which shall fit boys for industrial or commercial pursuits." In 1884, the Government of India followed with a resolution to implement the commission's recommended bifurcation of high school education into two divisions: one intended to lead to the entrance examination of the universities, and the other, of a more practical character, designed to "direct the attention of native youth to industrial and commercial pursuits." Despite these pronouncements, nothing much was done by way of implementation. In 1886, when Home Secretary A. P. MacDonnell examined the conditions of industrial schooling in the various provinces, he noted with dismay that only the Madras Presidency under Chatterton had taken steps to implement the 1884 order.[52]

Another resolution followed in 1888, which distinguished two kinds of technical training corresponding to different levels of industry. First, there was technical education "of a preliminary character including the study of natural science and the cultivation of the faculty of observing and reasoning from experiment." Second was technical training "proper," which was "the preparation of a man to take part in producing effectively some special article of commercial demand." The latter was identified as "an auxiliary of manufacture and industrial capital" and, as such, was to be promoted at the centers of industrial development. The government proposed that local administrations conduct a survey of important local industries in collaboration with a committee of educational experts and professional men. This would ensure the coordinated development of industrial and educational policy.[53]

The mantra of "industrial and commercial pursuits" signaled a different orientation for industrial schooling. Unlike engineering, which led graduates to professional careers in the civil services, industrial schooling was tied to industrialization. This opened it up to a different set of debates. Most importantly, as an "auxiliary of manufacture and industrial capital," industrial schooling was drawn into the battle between free marketers and state interventionists over the proper path to industrialization in India.

To advance industrial schooling, the government requested Sir Edward Buck in 1901 to submit a report on the position and progress of practical education in each province. Buck's chart of the different types of primary and technical schools indicated the prevalence of industrial schools following the model established by Christian missionaries in their promotion of native industry. Typically, such schools offered literary education alongside the teaching of minor trades, particularly carpentry and smithy work, with the sale of articles made in the school contributing to its maintenance. Buck offered the following criticisms of the existing paradigm: general and technical education were combined to the disservice of both, instruction was not adequately differentiated for different classes, there was disproportionate attention given to carpentry and smithy work, trades that were taught were not pursued, and attempts at working for a market ended in failure.[54]

The government had a mixed response to Buck's report. Some officials agreed that instruction should be differentiated for different classes. Others argued for the need to break the caste domination of particular trades by following the example set by missionaries in providing opportunities for Christian converts to learn trades that were socially closed to them. There was also disagreement over Buck's recommendation to distinguish general and technical education because general education was "so little advanced among the population at large and more especially among the classes and castes who were likely to adopt an industrial life."[55]

In 1904, the government passed a resolution echoing the 1883 Hunter Commission report. It noted the "too literary" character of secondary schools and called for alternative courses to meet the needs of "boys destined for industrial or commercial pursuits." While the government did not expect a sudden increase in the existing number of industrial schools—123 schools, with 8,405 pupils and 48 different trades—it did underscore the need to "confine their institutions to boys belonging to the specialized caste or occupational groups who were likely to practice the crafts taught in the schools."[56]

Official documents show that caste defined both the past and the future of students in industrial schools. Just as engineering education was targeted at upper castes with particular family and educational profiles, so, too, was industrial schooling channeled toward lower castes from families with very different occupational histories. There was some acknowledgment that those "destined" for industrial labor should still receive a general education, and that missionary attempts to break caste barriers were important. Nevertheless, the stratification of technical education did ultimately reproduce caste differences.

As with engineering education, those advocating industrial schooling instrumentalized caste in policy. We see this, for instance, in testimony given before the Industrial Commission by W. W. Hornell, the director of public instruction. It was difficult to recruit students to industrial schools, he explained, because "no scholarship can compensate the boy or his parent for the loss of wages." Speculating about alternative avenues to recruitment, Hornell wondered whether caste groups could serve as functional equivalents of trade unions. "Had caste been adopted as an educational unit in the first instance the result might have been different," he suggested. "It is in many ways a valuable social organization of which use might have been made." Even while insisting that caste was un-British and unnatural and that "there never was a possibility of a constructive attitude toward it," Hornell regretted that "a democratic outlook in sociology has emphasized its worst features."[57]

Despite the disavowal and disparaging of caste as antithetical to British culture and universal morality, its structuring role in administrative sociology and practice persisted. As we have already seen, the combined discursive disavowal and practical use of caste was most often justified with reference to native sentiment. At the same time, colonial technical education only reinforced caste differences by tracking social groups into their "destined" occupational niches.

Advocating State Intervention

In the 1910s, the recurring debate over whether industrial schooling was primarily an educational or an industrial endeavor began to shift more decisively toward the latter because of a new focus on industrialization. In their 1911 report, Atkinson and Dawson underwrote this reorientation. As pointed out by K. T. B. Tressler, Madras Presidency's superintendent of industrial education, Atkinson and Dawson's investigation was essentially an inquiry into what was needed to produce a class of workers for modern industry. Tressler also added his own opinion that however excellent industrial schooling was in imparting the principles of various trades, graduates still needed to be employed. As far as he was concerned, the real solution to both the elusive purpose of industrial schooling and the impediments to industrialization was the more effective integration of the employers of labor into both processes.[58]

Even with the policy shift toward industrialization, it was not until World War I that the question of how to push it forward was seriously addressed. The war lent a new urgency to what was previously a desultory engagement with Indian industrial growth. It exposed India's dependence on the import of essential commodities and the need to avert future shortages in the supply of dyes, medicines, and other chemicals. Moreover, it was now thought necessary for the state to aid private enterprise in ensuring that India was war ready. Finally, as detailed in Chapter 2, the spread of anticolonial nationalism, particularly the accusation that Britain was "underdeveloping" India, forced the hand of the colonial state. As a consequence, the Government of India resolved to push harder for a new industrial policy.

The clearest expression of the new commitment to industrialization was the report of the Indian Industrial Commission. The report represents what science studies scholar Shiv Visvanathan calls "the translation of Swadeshism into the grammar of official technological discourse."[59] Put more simply, it is a sustained argument for state-led industrialization. Foreign precedent was important here, particularly the experiences of Germany and Japan. Debate over their economic miracles, and the role of their states in industrialization, strengthened the hands of the interventionists and put the advocates of laissez-faire on the defensive.

In advancing state intervention, the example of Chatterton in Madras became crucially important. Chatterton first arrived in India to be a professor in the Madras College of Engineering, was subsequently appointed superintendent of the Madras School of the Arts in 1897, and finally moved to work as the director of industries and commerce in the princely state of Mysore. While working in Mysore, he was appointed a member of the Indian Industrial Commission.

Visvanathan refers to Chatterton as an "ethno-technologist" whose admiration for the history of technological innovation in India—for instance, he remarked on the outstanding quality of Mughal canals and Dravidian tanks—made him an anomaly in British officialdom. However, Chatterton was most controversial because of his "pioneer factories." His experience with the decline of handicrafts and indigenous industry in Madras Presidency, as well as the underemployment of students from industrial schools, had led him to the conviction that more needed to be done. Chatterton came up with the novel scheme of starting pioneer factories run on commercial lines that would educate the manufacturers of Madras about innovations in practice, jump-start indigenous industry, and employ the graduates of industrial schools.[60] The success of his factories, which were running at a profit by 1899, led to the creation of the first provincial Department of Industries in 1908 under his leadership.

Chatterton's work created a furor over the proper role of government in the economy. The business houses of Madras lobbied hard through the Madras Chamber of Commerce against what they perceived as the unfair participation of government in economic development. Eventually, laissez-faire opposition won out. In 1910, the secretary of state abolished the Department of Industries, shifted Chatterton to the Education Department, and made him the superintendent of industrial education. It was only after repeated protests by Indians in the Madras Legislative Council that the Department of Industries was reinstated in 1914.

Chatterton's scheme also came in for strong criticism from England. As one member of the Council of India put it, "I regard it as a waste of money and wrong in principle. I don't believe as a rule in attempts to create industries . . . and the probabilities are that the lethargy of . . . Madras . . . is due to causes beyond the reach of State effort."[61] Even more strongly worded was the rebuke of Sir James Mackay, representative of commerce on the India Council, who characterized Chatterton as a man "who can have no business or practical experience of factories, [is on] a salary of £1,200 p.a. with a lot of highly paid assistants to fool about with model childish factories which will never earn a sixpence. . . . This is how money is frittered away in India."[62] Despite sustained opposition, Chatterton was given time to prove the success of his intervention, which he managed to do. Nonetheless, the damage was done, and the Government of India was instructed to abide by the "natural laws" of the free market and limit its intervention to "industrial instruction."

Even among those advocating state-led economic change, there were other, irresolvable differences. The proper scale of industry, the proper economic sectors for state intervention, and the proper path of development—all these were left open to debate. While some stood by the protection and promotion of handicrafts and small-scale industry, others pushed for large-scale industrialization along the lines of Germany and Japan. Chatterton's factories continued to draw positive and negative attention as examples of what was right or wrong about state intervention. The Governments of India and Madras remained loyal to him, and his work occupied pride of place at the Simla Education Conference of 1900, when the provincial departments of industries were being established between 1905 and 1912, and during the work of the Indian Industrial Commission.

As a member of the Indian Industrial Commission, Chatterton had a second shot at advancing his arguments for state-led industrialization and its alignment with industrial schooling. In its recommendations on education, the commission proposed that authority over industrial education should remain with provincial departments of industries, with the government reserving the right to decide whether particular schools should be controlled by the education or industries department. The commission also proposed the constitution of an imperial department of industries as a centralized authority that would rely on visiting experts to advise provincial governments on the conduct of industrial and technical education.

On paper, the Indian Industrial Commission report was a sea change in colonial economic policy. However, its timing was off because it was published around the same time as the Montagu-Chelmsford report on constitutional reforms. While both reports emphasized the need for rapid industrialization of the economy with active state participation, they differed on the process. The Indian Industrial Commission's report emphasized the need to centralize direction in the Government of India. By contrast, the Montagu-Chelmsford Reforms Committee promoted decentralization to the provincial level. Provincial autonomy was accompanied by financial stringency, which was exacerbated in the years after the Great Depression. This slowed industrial development to a near standstill until the advent of independence. All of these false starts to state-led industrialization undercut the possibility of employing those lower-caste students who were "destined for industrial and commercial pursuits." Industrial schooling was a dead end because of the strident opposition to initiatives such as Chatterton's, which might have mitigated the deleterious effects of imperial trade.

On the whole, the two tracks of industrial schooling and college engineering diverged but without significant developments to either. Regardless, their respective association with industrial labor and the professions was clinched. As we will see in Chapter 2, the transition to independence and an emerging consensus in favor of industrialization only reinforced the government's commitment to the two tracks. For independent India's engineers, the association with state developmentalism enhanced their status as nation-builders, while those trained to populate the industrial workplace assumed their structural position on the lower rungs of an industrializing society. While engineers in general benefited from their link to the developmental state, their institutional location mattered. We will now turn to the founding of the IITs as the uppermost tier of postcolonial technical education and look more fully into their role in consolidating the caste basis of professional engineering.

2

Building the IITs

SECRETARY OF STATE Hamilton's critique of India's ingrate Babus and Brahmins highlighted the broader context in which debates over the scale, scope, and object of colonial technical education were unfolding. As we saw in Chapter 1, the push for a more scientific approach to education emerged as early as the 1830s in elite Indian circles. While initially geared toward professional employment in government services, the demand for technical education was eventually brought within the framework of anticolonial nationalism. By the 1930s, nationalists linked technical education to the emerging consensus around the need for an independent state, which would be the prime engine of economic growth.

How did the push for political independence shape the trajectory of technical education? This chapter explores the place of technical education within Indian nationalism and early postindependence nation-building. We will look in particular at the rationale behind the founding of the IITs and arguments for and against this tier of engineering education. Why was it thought necessary to add a new set of institutions to the existing ones? And how did India's statesmen envision the place of the IITs within an existing social and institutional landscape?

Beginning in the late nineteenth century, a series of nationalist writings underscored the link between technical education and the need for self-governance. In the 1880s, the *Mahratta*, the newspaper started by nationalist and social reformer Bal Gangadhar Tilak, focused its attentions on the demand for technical education and the associated need to look beyond Britain to the United States and Germany for inspiration and instruction. In 1886, geologist P. N. Bose's pamphlet *Technical and Scientific Education in Bengal* decried the lack of training within British India for industrial development. In 1887, the Indian National Congress passed a resolution demanding that the government "be moved to elaborate a system of technical education."[1] The "imperative need for technical education" was echoed in subsequent years by a number of prominent nationalists: W. C. Banerjee in 1892, Anandamohan Bose in 1898, N. G. Chandarvarkar in 1900, and Madan Mohan Malaviya in 1909. Over this period, the demand was also picked up by other Indian newspapers. By 1918, when the Indian Industrial Commission wrapped up its work, the demand for technical education had been coupled with concerns over representation. Srinivasa Sastri, a member of the Imperial Legislative Council, called for a democratization of expertise by reserving the technical and scientific services for Indians.[2]

While anticolonial critiques of underdevelopment arose in the 1860s, it was only in the aftermath of World War I that they were tied to the prospect of industrial development under a sovereign nation-state. This was also a moment for influencing policy. The hegemony of laissez-faire had weakened, and there was more room for alternatives both within and beyond imperial administration. The broader institutional context had also changed with the proliferation of formal economic associations, such as local chambers of commerce, trade associations, and industrialist groups. And beginning in 1905, the annual Indian Industrial Conference—held in the same town and time frame as the meetings of the Indian National Congress—provided a national platform. Nationalist opinion echoed in the conferences at Naini Tal, Ootacamund, Dacca, and Lahore. Provincial governments organized their own campaigns to lobby the India Office for a new, interventionist industrial policy and to get support for new departments of industries. Legislative councils passed resolutions in favor of intervention, government presses put out official publications lauding existing industrial departments, and efforts were made to win over business leaders.[3]

Alongside pressuring the colonial government to grow technical education, nationalists began their own initiatives. In 1904, they formed an association in Calcutta for the advancement of Indian scientific and technical education, which supported the studies of Indian students in Japan, the United States, and Europe. In 1905, Indian industrialists and the Indian National Congress sponsored an industrial conference in Banaras, where a recommendation to establish a national poly-technic institution and at least one technical college in each province was forwarded to the government. When no response was forthcoming, conference leaders founded a college of engineering and technology at Jadavpur, Calcutta, in 1907.[4]

Although the politics of Indian engineers varied, the rise of eco-nomic nationalism shaped even the perspectives of those operating within colonial state institutions. They began to echo the argument that industrialization was a necessary cornerstone not of a colonial India but of a self-reliant one. Even those who held prominent positions within the colonial engineering establishment—such as C. V. Krish-nasawami Chetty, chairman of the South India Centre of the Institu-tion of Engineers, and M. Visvesvaraya, the most influential and cele-brated south Indian engineer—began to reorient themselves around the prospect of national independence. Chetty argued that World War I had made Indians aware "of their utter dependence on other countries for most of their daily wants" and of "the urgent necessity for starting various industries." The Institute of Engineers, he declared, must offer its support to the National Planning Committee: "Our Institution must place at the disposal of the National Planning Committee all the technical assistance it can give. Our Institution must play an impor-tant part in the industrialization of the country. . . . Time has come for engineers to evince greater interest and take part in the political life of the country."[5]

Visvesvaraya's memoirs are even more illuminating. His profes-sional tenure was remarkable for the sheer diversity of positions he held and the range of places he worked. Visvesvaraya was deputed to work on project sites as far-flung as Bombay, Hyderabad, Mysore, and Aden. He received his engineering degree in 1883 from the Poona Col-lege of Engineering, which was affiliated with Bombay University. As the university's top engineering student, he was appointed to the Bombay Public Works Department as assistant engineer. Unlike many who faced racial hurdles to entry and advancement, he was remarkably successful in securing coveted positions in the engineering service. Moreover, his move from the colonial service to the service of the princely state of Mysore gave him an interesting comparative perspective on the relationship between engineering, state, and society under conditions of direct versus indirect rule.

In his memoirs, Visvesvaraya narrates his identity as a technical man, as an intermediary between state and society, and as a member of a modernizing high caste destined to lead. Much of the narrative consists of extended accounts of his work on projects and his ingenuity in the face of technical challenges. There are also several instances where he recounts his handling of social protest in the face of project implementation. It is in his leveraging of social hierarchies to meet his desired goals that we see most clearly his self-appointed role as an expert intermediary between state and society as well as his unshakable faith in reason and procedure in the face of social opposition. He was convinced that the right information delivered in the right manner would necessarily produce consent. Rarely did Visvesvaraya betray doubts about the necessity or virtue of his expert knowledge or its ability to transform the world. Even in his support for nationalism, Visvesvaraya expressed an understanding of the engineer as a bearer of universal knowledge whose contribution to nationalism was primarily technical. Engineers were not the rabble-rousers of anticolonial nationalism or the statesmen of postcolonial politics. As he saw it, they were first and foremost technical men whose mastery of mechanical systems equipped them to engineer society.[6]

Visvesvaraya's affiliation with social elites and his sense of himself as an enlightened Indian destined to lead comes through palpably in his descriptions of his social world. Here we see his identification not just as a professional state engineer who prized efficiency and procedure but as part of a set of modernizing high castes. His memoir lists a number of prominent nationalists as close friends, including M. G. Ranade and G. K. Gokhale, whom he described as "guides of the enlightened public of Poona and Maharashtra" and as liberals and moderates who had one foot in government and one in politics. Unlike leaders such as B. G. Tilak, who, as Visvesvaraya saw it, "took up an uncompromising attitude in criticizing British policies and methods of administration," Visvesvaraya's inner circle consisted of those who understood how to straddle the two worlds. They were also Hindu reformers who increasingly saw themselves as distinct from their more orthodox caste fellows. Visvesvaraya aligned himself with these liberal proponents of Hindu reform and kept at a distance from both political "radicals" and the Brahmin orthodoxy of Poona, whom he saw as intransigent in their attitudes. History, as he understood it, was on the side of progress, which increasingly pointed in a liberal nationalist direction.

The welling up of nationalist sentiment even among the colonial administration's most celebrated successes demanded a response. As we saw in Chapter 1, some members of the Government of India pushed for a new industrial policy as "a great sedative of political unrest." Others, however, argued the opposite. Even those who actively advocated for industrialization were concerned that it would generate new tensions. T. H. Holland, the president of the Indian Industrial Commission, warned that "neither the capitalists nor the educated employees will thereby become more contented and loyal; on the contrary, they will soon forget that the industrial impetus came from Government; they will imagine that the prosperity is due to themselves entirely, and that therefore they are capable of managing their own affairs." Another commission member agreed by pointing to Russia, which, he argued, "has shown that industrial development with the consequent assemblage of bodies of workers in factories, tends to promote political agitation, agitators and seditionists taking the opportunity of exploiting the workers' . . . grievances for political ends."[7]

Despite such differences of opinion, the new industrial policy did move forward as a program of state aid to industry without protectionism. But as we saw earlier, it was stymied by the Depression and by the decentralization of power to the provinces. It was only with the postcolonial transition that the state commitment to industrialization became a reality. So, too, did public investment in engineering education become a linchpin of technologically driven development.

The Comparative Methodology of Indian Economic Nationalism

One repeated strategy in Indian nationalist arguments for industrialization was the use of the comparative method to gauge the value of Britain as a model. And time and again, Britain came up short. Sometimes such comparative analyses were used to debate the appropriate relationship between science and technology in India. One point of contention was whether the Indian Association for the Cultivation of Science should be for science alone or also for technical education and entrepreneurship. On one side was Bengali doctor and social reformer Mahender Lal Sircar, who argued for the priority of science over technology by comparing Britain and Germany. Sircar maintained that it was the enthusiasm of Germany's wealthy classes for science and the anti-science spirit of the British that allowed Germany to leapfrog over England in the development of industry. On the other side was the Indian League, which insisted on privileging technical education and vigorous entrepreneurship to stem the growing unemployment among university graduates. The league also used Germany as an example and proposed the establishment of a series of technical schools modeled on the German *Technischen Hochschulen*.[8]

At other times, comparisons were used to advance an argument for the intimacy between state and school. Indian National Congress president Madan Mohan Malaviya's dissenting note on the Indian Industrial Commission report is an example of how a comparative methodology ended up elevating the school as the primary pedagogical instrument of the industrializing state. Malaviya argued that the British factory was an instrument not of industrialization but of deindustrialization. British factories were about domination and coercion. If India was to industrialize, it would have to look for other models, such as those of Germany and France, where industry had moved from domination to discipline, and where the school rather than the factory was the paradigmatic organizational entity.[9]

Malaviya pointed to the industrial exhibitions of the 1850s to make the case for the centrality of schooling to industrialism. At the first exhibition in London in 1851, he argued, the Germans realized their inferiority in industry to England. In response, they established a network

of schools in every major town and center of industry to create an industrial cadre extending from professionals to workers. By the fourth
industrial exhibition in Paris in 1857, even England's own inquiry
commission concluded that "the English workman is gradually losing
the race, through the superior intelligence which the foreign governments are carefully developing in their artisans." Malaviya insisted
that "the education of Germany is the result of national organization
which compels every peasant to send his children to school, and afterwards affords the opportunity of acquiring such technical skill as
may be useful in the department of industry to which they are destined."[10] Britain's defeat in these surrogate wars between imperial
powers, he concluded, had effectively dismantled the myth that its
command of coal and industrial skill rendered it superior to the
"unironed, uncoaled and unengineered nations of the world."[11]

Other Swadeshi nationalists, including attorney B. N. Basu, also argued for the irrelevance of Britain as a model of industrial education.
The inadequacies of Indian colonial education, Basu suggested, were
nothing but a reflection of outmoded metropolitan theories. Since the
idea of a formal applied science was new to England, and Oxford and
Cambridge had "not got over the feeling that humanistic studies should
predominate in the Universities," one could hardly expect anything
different in India.[12] In the place of Britain, Basu and Malaviya proposed
Germany and Japan—the "Asian Germany"—as appropriate models for
a modern industrial society based on applied science.

From Nationalism to the Technocratic State

The Indian Industrial Commission was a staging ground for the debate
between commission members, other colonial officials, and nationalists over the various models of industrial society. For some colonial officers, it was occasion to reiterate the conviction that Indian technological incompetence was a reflection of cultural backwardness or
moral temper and the necessity of British tutelage. For nationalists, it
was an opportunity to challenge Britain's claim to a monopoly over
industrial expertise as a justification of rule. By pointing to other
models, both Western and Eastern, they rejected British tutelage and

claimed the right to independent interactions and collaborations outside the imperial fold.

But these nationalist arguments were not just about the illegitimacy and constraints of colonialism. They also articulated a particular vision of the modern industrial state and of the role of the school within it. Shiv Visvanathan points to Malaviya's note on the Indian Industrial Commission report as the clearest articulation of this argument for a technocratic, pedagogical state. I quote him here at length:

> Malaviya's note has been embedded for too long in the archival monuments of nationalism. . . . At one level he is the nationalist arguing against colonial duplicity. But in the submerged archeology of the modern industrial state, the Pandit outclasses Holland as the technocrat. . . . Implicit in the structure of the . . . text are three arguments which Malaviya elicits and elaborates. First, modern technology necessitates as a discipline a new linking of knowledge and power. It is the logic of this technology which eventually reconstitutes in a new fashion the state and the school. Both exist in order to ensure an economy in the reproduction of industrial norms. The intersection of knowledge and power is further embodied in the isomorphy between the pedagogic state and the compulsory school. The link between knowledge and power is also revealed in the special status given to the notion of intelligence. It is no longer regarded as hereditary but as an input to be fed in by the agency of the state. Intelligence becomes industrialized, standardized and productivity-linked in the new notion of personnel. It is the state which assumes responsibility for it through the school.[13]

This connection between state, industry, and school captured in Malaviya's advocacy was never fully realized under colonial rule. Even while engineering was developed under the auspices of the colonial state, it grew in fits and starts for the reasons detailed earlier. Only after the transition to self-rule did the "isomorphy" between state and school become an integral aspect of a planned economy and a nationalized citizenry. One can see the link between schooling and industrialization in the postindependence expansion of engineering education and the many programmatic statements about the centrality of engineering to nation-building.

Still, there was a disconnect between the purported goal of industrialization and the vision of education advanced by the postcolonial state. Unlike in Germany, where technical schools were more clearly tied to industrial development and valorized on these grounds, the Indian investment in maintaining a distinction between the mental and the manual undercut this possibility. Moreover, the upper echelons of engineering education soon became delinked from the state development project altogether and repurposed for private sector growth in India and beyond. As we will see, the privatization and transnationalization of professional engineering transformed the relationship between state and economy and gave "nation-building" a very different meaning. Finally, the reconstitution of intelligence from a hereditary quality into a state "input" was never complete. Even as technical expertise was more decisively yoked to state developmentalism, there were clear continuities in assumptions about the innate and inherited capacities of particular castes. In all these ways, Malaviya's vision of an all-encompassing state with its ideological apparatuses was only a partial premonition. The postindependence Indian state was certainly both interventionist and transformative. But as we will see, it was also profoundly shaped by older hierarchies of skills and persons.

The Sarkar Committee Report

On the eve of independence in 1945, the Government of India appointed a committee under N. R. Sarkar to review the state of technical education in India in anticipation of the need for personnel to assist with postindependence industrial development. In 1948, the committee submitted an interim report that underscored "the extreme urgency of the situation." The report pointed out that self-sufficiency was the need of the hour because "the calls of reconstruction in Europe and elsewhere, and the enormous industrial and Government undertaking contemplated in Europe and America to provide full employment, will make it difficult, if not impossible, to secure from abroad, the services of the right type of engineers, architects, technologists and planners, etc. to carry out India's post-war projects." Therefore, "a programme of higher technical education and research in India should . . . be pushed forward with utmost speed and determination."[14]

The committee argued for the need to establish new institutions that would "integrate mathematics, science, and humanities with the specialized professional subjects." This, it was felt, would distinguish them from existing engineering colleges, whose purpose "was limited to supplying recruits to government departments responsible for the maintenance of civil works located in the provinces." By contrast, the new institutions would educate engineers who were also well-rounded scientists and would-be leaders in India's technological development.

While the committee acknowledged that a more systematic survey could better assess the "relation of each new institution to those which already exist," it contended that "the needs of the present situation are so apparent and urgent that a solution cannot be deferred pending such a survey which would necessarily take a considerable time." However, it suggested that such a survey be conducted "before a final decision was reached as to the organization and structures of Higher Technical Education in the country as a whole."[15]

The committee recommended the establishment of one higher technical institution in each of the four regions of the country. This distribution of institutions would "conform with the geographical position of industrial areas as well as with location of the great majority of existing technical institutions and would be the most equitable and effective in the interest of India as a whole." While these higher technical institutions were to be centrally administered, the committee emphasized the need to coordinate each institution's teaching and research so as to be "of use to the region which it is designed to serve" and "after careful consideration of the contribution which can be made by existing institutions (including Universities) in the region." The committee's assessment of regional needs led to a proposed sequencing of institutions, beginning with the east and followed by the west, the north, and finally the south. The committee envisioned each of these regional institutions in "a large industrial Centre." It was only by privileging larger centers for the new institutions, it felt, that the "right relationship between the public, industry and education should be established and maintained."[16]

The committee received representations from both military and civil authorities on how to increase the supply of trained engineers and, in response, invited several of them to a discussion.[17] A key question raised was about timing: Would the lag in turning out technical graduates from these new institutions retard industrial growth? And if so, would not the needs of these industries be more immediately served by institutions designed to cater to them? The other question was about the fit between these proposed institutions and the needs of industrialization. Would these college graduates really have the requisite skills to service industry?

The lack of fit between the proposed institutions and industrial development was addressed most extensively by Brigadier Woolfe, comptroller general of inspection, and one of the committee's external invitees. In a letter to Dr. John Sargent, educational adviser to the Government of India, Woolfe expressed his unhappiness with the committee's approach. In particular, he doubted whether the proposed institutions would fulfill their purported purpose of "ensur[ing] an adequate supply of technical personnel for post war industrial development." To illustrate his point, Woolfe provided a list of industries— textiles, fibers, vegetable drugs, dyes and chemicals, lumber, detergents and edible oils, coal tar, fuel, tanning, ceramics and glass, mining—and noted that most of their needs would not be met by the kind of basic undergraduate training to be offered. What was needed, he opined, was far more specialized training "along the lines of the Manchester Institute of Technology," which catered to specific industries and was ideally conducted by them. What was not needed was "to flood the market with B.Sc.s whom no one will employ. Give me a Fuel technologist or a Dye Chemist and I know what to do with him but difficulties arise at once when I am asked to employ a B.Sc. with chemistry or physics as his special subject." As did his predecessors a half century before, Woolfe recycled concerns about the irrelevance of book learning to the practicalities of industry.

Despite concerns raised by Woolfe and others, the committee concluded that "the probable demands of industries for High Grade Technical personnel (Executives, research workers, maintenance engineers, and teachers) . . . have to be met through the proposed Higher Technical Institutions, while the demands for lower grade Technicians could be met by the Junior Technical Institutions of the less advanced type that would be linked to the Higher Technical Institutions."[18] The committee's report makes clear that these new institutions were to be set apart, not only from industrial schools for artisans and workers but also from the regional engineering colleges established in the colonial period to train an emerging professional class. This was a vision of further institutional stratification, with the higher technical institutions occupying the topmost echelon. And even while they insisted on India achieving self-sufficiency in technical expertise, foreign models continued to provide guidance. In particular, the committee identified the Massachusetts Institute of Technology (MIT) as the most desirable model, with its mix of practical and theoretical sciences, mathematics, and the humanities.[19] Like MIT, these institutions would have a dual purpose: undergraduate instruction to produce technical graduates "for post-war industrial and Governmental projects" and postgraduate study and research "to produce research workers and technical teachers."

The report proposed "a combination of a fundamental scientific training with a broad human outlook, which will afford the students the type of collegiate education endorsed by leading engineers." As the authors saw it, this would be an ideal middle ground that avoided both "the narrowness common among students in technical colleges" and "the superficiality and lack of purpose noticeable in many of those taking academic college courses."[20] The imagined graduate would thus be the perfect combination of mind and hand: a useful citizen, a qualified engineer capable of exercising initiative and thought, and a professional enabled and motivated to apply engineering principles in practice. When it came to practical training, the report attempted to address the debates of the past and find a compromise. The engineer, it stated, "is not a craftsman nor is expected to possess the same degree of manual skill as an artisan." Still, the authors expressed a strong conviction that "he must have an intimate knowledge of workshop processes and methods."[21] For this reason, facilities for instruction in elementary workshop processes and methods were deemed essential to academic instruction.

There appears to have been some disagreement on the terms of the admissions process. The report notes that "selection for admission should be made purely on merit and no provincial quotas should be allotted, but some proportion of the seats should be reserved for the educationally backward classes so that in due course the general level of education throughout may be raised." However, this recommendation was footnoted with the following: "This is only a tentative view not unanimously subscribed to by the members of the Committee and will receive further consideration."[22]

While the disagreement over admissions is not further explained, what we do have is Nazir Ahmed's dissenting note on the more elemental question of whether new institutions were at all necessary. Ahmed objected strongly to the precipitous decision to recommend wholly new institutions without adequately assessing whether the country's existing facilities could be further developed. Ahmed drew on comparative instances to make his case: "In real planning for the future, we must take into account the existing resources and must try to build upon them. This process has always been followed in Europe and America, where, whenever the need has arisen, the possibility of developing the existing institutions has first been explored before putting up new institutions." He warned that if the Sarkar Committee took its current course, "the existing institutions are likely to stagnate and decay while the newer institutions will work in an atmosphere of isolation." Ahmed opined further that the benefits of establishing a few new institutions "would be extremely limited leaving vast regions of the country out of the scope of their utility." Their necessarily uneven impact "would be avoided if the existing institutions in the various provinces were developed and expanded so as to be within easy reach of the people of all parts of India." In the event that these new institutions were founded, "quotas should be assigned to different provinces so that the inhabitants of all the provinces may be in a position to share their benefits." It was only "logical," Ahmed concluded, that relying as they would on public funds, "the people of the country as a whole should have an equal share in the facilities provided in these institutions."[23]

Ahmed's arguments about the potential for institutional isolation, limited impact, and undemocratic limits to access went largely unheeded. The Sarkar Committee's recommendations were implemented after independence as part of the ruling Congress Party's First (1951–1956) and Second (1956–1961) Five Year Plans. The plans conceived of a strong industrial base as a precondition for development. The Second Five Year Plan in particular invested heavily in industry, dam construction, metallurgy, and the railways, with expertise in civil and mechanical engineering identified as an urgent need. Beginning in the

1950s, the Indian government began to set up massive steel industries with foreign collaboration. An added dimension of these partnerships was the transfer of technical knowledge. The foreign partners had insisted that this transfer of know-how should occur within autonomous technical institutions where freedom from the bureaucratic structure of the existing university system would foster the spirit of research. This was a perfect storm. Older forms of institutional stratification based on hierarchies of skill and persons, the Sarkar Committee's recommendations for the creation of a top echelon of technical education, and the demand for autonomy as a condition of foreign support produced the IITs.

The Original Five

On the recommendations of the Sarkar Committee, the Indian government moved ahead with establishing a technological institute in each of the four regions of the country. While the committee report provided the basic template for the IITs, later committees refined its recommendations. In 1950, the All India Council for Technical Education and the Inter-University Board decided that the IITs should grant bachelor of technology degrees in four kinds of engineering: civil, mechanical, electrical, and telecommunications. In their first two years, all students would take the same courses, and in their third and fourth years, they would concentrate on their chosen field. The committee also recommended that the institutes offer a master's degree in each of the four kinds of engineering. While these recommendations provided the overarching structure for curricular development, the academic and administrative autonomy granted to the institutes meant that they were more able than most other Indian universities to try out new ideas.

The first IIT was established in 1951 at Kharagpur, near Calcutta. IIT Kharagpur received support from a variety of sources, including the United States, the United Kingdom, the Soviet Union, and UNESCO. Following this, the Government of India arranged for each subsequent IIT to receive most of its support from one international collaborator: IIT Bombay was opened in 1958 through collaboration with the Soviet Union, IIT Madras in 1959 with West Germany, and IIT Kanpur in 1960 with the United States. These were the four institutes envisioned by the Sarkar Committee: Kanpur in the north, Madras in the south, Kharagpur in the east, and Bombay in the west. A fifth followed in Delhi due to the unexpected help of Great Britain, which contributed £400,000 to transform Delhi University's College of Engineering into IIT Delhi in 1961. Altogether, the Soviet Union, West Germany, the United States, and the United Kingdom supplied over $17 million worth of equipment to the IITs and sent over 150 full-time visiting staff and 300 short-term consultants to India. In addition, more than 230 Indian professors from the IITs received fellowships to study in sponsor nations. The technical assistance programs ended in the 1970s, but the IITs continued to have strong ties with Western institutions.

Professor V. Indiresan, IIT Madras director from 1979 to 1984, opined that the real contribution of the foreign partners "was in creating a world-class academic ambience, in terms of the autonomy of the teachers, the freedom to design your own courses, the credit system, examination reforms, the tutorial system and so on."[24] The IITs were indeed founded on the premise of autonomy. In terms of governmental oversight, this placed them wholly within the purview of the central and not the regional state governments. Second, they fell outside the structure of affiliation to universities, giving them greater say in institutional functioning, faculty hiring, and curricular development. Third, their place outside regional education allowed the IITs to take students from all over India through a centralized examination. As we will see in Chapter 5, the examination would quickly become the central symbol of the autonomy, integrity, and excellence of the IIT system.

Democracy versus Excellence

The first IIT at Kharagpur stands on the site of the former British prison of Hijli. In the institute's first convocation address, Prime Minister Jawaharlal Nehru spoke of the location's symbolic value. "Here in the place of that Hijli detention camp stands this fine monument of India," he pointed out. "This picture seems to me symbolic of changes that are coming to India." Nehru went on to laud the engineer as the world's new nation-builder. "Now you are Engineers," he proclaimed, "and this world today . . . takes shape more and more under the hands of Engineers." For Nehru, it was appropriate that the engineer had superseded the administrator as the primary agent of governance and development. Administrators had always played an important role, he admitted. However, "the time has now come when the Engineer plays an infinitely greater role than anybody else." In fact, he predicted, the division between administrator and engineer would gradually fade away "because the major work of the country today deals with . . . engineering schemes of various types. We are building up a new India and the administrator who is completely ignorant of engineering does not help much in administering." This was already true of more technologically developed countries, where "engineers and scientists play a far more important role even outside their sphere of engineering and science." Given the precedent they had set, Nehru concluded, "that is bound to happen in India."[25]

Nehru's pronouncement of engineering as the new technology of nation-building heralded its importance in the project of postindependence developmentalism. The engineer was to be the linchpin of the developmental state, with his technical feats putting the prowess of the state on display. But Nehru did not bestow the same level of recognition and responsibility on all of independent India's engineering colleges. His convocation address at the first IIT indicated the exceptional status of the IIT system. As beneficiaries of bilateral relations with the world's industrial powers, the IITs were elevated as institutions that would best realize the promise of technological development.

Institutional stratification was not limited to the field of technical education. In science too, a similar process had produced the Indian Institute of Science (IIS) as the most esteemed of scientific institutions. Both the IITs and the IIS were founded to distinguish effort from expertise. Indeed, this was quite explicitly stated in the government's review committee report on scientific institutions, which defined scientific expertise as the work of a "few men of high calibre" and emphasized the constitutive link between excellence and selectivity.[26] The report tied the success of the IIS directly to uneven investment.[27] The IIS's excellence "required the judicious investment of resources in 'the development of fewer establishments for advanced training and research,' since a more expansive approach would mean that 'the general level of technical education and research would be lowered.'" In other words, democratizing access to training would be antithetical to excellence. Nehru concurred. "I am all for democracy," he opined, "but democracy normally means mediocrity too. It is a well-known thing, you put up with it in a democracy because, well, it is better to have democracy than having something worse. But the fact is that numbers lead to mediocrity."[28]

Scientific and technological expertise was thus set apart from "the manpower mandate" through the development of a parallel institutional structure of higher education in techno-scientific fields with separate budgetary allocations, entrance examinations, fee structures, and curricular frameworks. The exclusivity of institutions such as the IITs and the IIS was ensured despite the dissenting opinions of a few scientists, such as Nazir Ahmed and Meghnad Saha, "who argued for a closer alignment between scientific and technological research and education and the existing network of national universities."[29] Saha, the son of a lower-caste shopkeeper from East Bengal, was also an outlier when it came to the upper-caste social backgrounds of most prominent scientists and technologists.

Exclusivity and excellence were to be maintained by insulating such institutions from politics, commerce, and bureaucracy. Scientific and technological policy was formulated by Nehru's handpicked group of scientific advisers without much parliamentary debate. This did not mean that scientists and technologists were removed from the work of government; indeed, they were intimately tied to it. As political scientist Srirupa Roy puts it, "The inauguration of each laboratory was the site as well as the means for the material representation of the science-state-nation triad that structured social relations in Nehruvian India. The joint presence of state officials and scientists at these events attested to the partnership between science and the state."[30] At the same time, the repeated contrast between the creative labors of experts and the unimaginative labors of bureaucrats sustained the idea of an autonomous, insulated intellectual universe.

Significantly, caste serviced these distinctions both as social reality and as metaphor. Although the Nehruvian government was officially committed to democratization and against the use of caste in educa-

tion policy, insulating these institutions from the ferment of democratic politics ensured their role in the social reproduction of caste.
Furthermore, caste operated as a metaphor for merit. Nehru, for instance, characterized nationally oriented science and technology as
infused with "the Brahminic spirit of service." This idea of the elite
scientist-technologist as Brahmin "conveyed both the ability of an elite
caste to disengage from the quotidian and material concerns that preoccupied those less privileged, and the unique qualities of creative
thought that emanated from the 'head' of the social body."[31]

IITian Exceptionalism

The Indian state underwrote the exceptionalism of the IITs in many
ways. First, it did so through their founding as institutions distinct
from the existing educational ecosystem. Second, the patronage of foreign partners set them apart as "world-class" institutions that would
act as forerunners in developing India. The state indexed its intimate
association with this class of institutions through routine rituals of
recognition. The presence of prime ministers, presidents, ministers,
and foreign diplomats at IIT convocation ceremonies was commonplace, putting on visual display the institutes' standing at the highest
echelon of Indian education. This did not go unnoticed by the institutions' students. As one 1963 alumnus of IIT Madras put it, "Within a
couple of days of our joining, IITM held its first convocation with President S. Radhakrishnan as the chief guest. For many of us, I think that
grand ceremony was a momentous introduction to the status of our
new home for the next five years."[32]

IITians have internalized this sense of status all too well. One recent account of the IIT system is *The IITians*, a 2004 book by alumnus-
journalist Sandipan Deb. Deb's approach is historical and ethnographic. The book's subtitle—*The Story of a Remarkable Indian
Institution and How Its Alumni Are Reshaping the World*—makes
clear that it is also hagiographic. In this sense, it is a valuable primary
text for understanding the IITian worldview. Deb ends the book by recounting a conversation with Jairam Ramesh, another alumnus who
took the now unusual step of entering the civil services and went on

to serve in different capacities under various Congress Party governments. Deb runs into Ramesh in the Delhi airport, where they are catching the same flight to the IITs' fiftieth anniversary celebrations in Bangalore. After hearing about the book, Ramesh asks, "Why don't you call it Midnight's Brahmins? Because that's what IITians are, aren't they? The first educational institute was set up by India after its tryst with destiny at midnight on 15 August 1947. And created with the specific purpose of creating a new elite, the new Brahmins, except that they wouldn't be reading the scriptures, they would be technocrats."[33]

The sense of exceptionalism expressed by Ramesh runs deep. He, like Nehru, uses caste as a metaphor. At the same time, the self-consciousness of being a breed apart—an intellectual elite—expresses a pervasive form of caste sentiment. Deb's book is peppered with examples of how IITians are "the Chosen Ones." Exceptionalism is also a recurring trope in the interviews I did with IITians from across the generations. There are many ways IITians underscore their own status. While a minority do so by explicitly invoking caste, most prefer more democratic indices, such as merit and autonomy. As we will see throughout this book, the tacking back and forth between caste and non-caste markers of excellence signals a transformation in the languages of distinction, which nonetheless keeps in place older patterns of differentiation.

However, there is also a perceptible shift between how earlier and later IITians articulate their relationship to the state. For earlier generations, being an engineer meant a strong association with the state and its developmental projects that was very much in continuity with the late colonial period. Those inducted into the colonial engineering services experienced a new public identity fostered through association with the state and with scientific expertise. Through his training, the professional engineer was brought within the framework of colonial administration and bureaucracy and was predisposed to identify with the imperial state.[34] This was equally the case with the first generations of IITians.

By contrast, the link to the state has more recently become an indication not of excellence but of its opposite. This shift even extends to minimizing the role of Nehru, now demoted as a socialist, in favor of other agents in the IIT origin story. Deb, for instance, argues that rather than see the IITs as "Nehru's dream," they are most aptly characterized as "the brainchild of Sir Ardeshir Dalal, an aristocratic Parsi technocrat of extraordinary dynamism."[35]

The meaning of autonomy, too, has shifted from indicating an association with the central government to conveying a general antipathy toward the state, this despite the IITs being among the most well-funded public educational institutions in India. IITians routinely disparage state actors as drags on the system by contrasting their own institutes with other regional engineering colleges. A professor who shifted from one such college to an IIT makes the comparison in Deb's book: "In the government engineering colleges, when they want to buy an oscilloscope, they have to go through a tendering process, get three quotations and send them to some *babu* in a government department. By the time the *babu* clears the file and sends it back, the prices are no longer valid, the technology has possibly changed, and they have to start the whole cycle again."[36]

For many, this disdain for regional engineering colleges extends to Indian education more generally. Most IITians see their institutes as islands of excellence in a sea of mediocrity. This sentiment is perfectly captured by the statement of another alumnus in Deb's book: "It's like the Calcutta Metro. It's as if it's something iconic. Everything in the city is crumbling. But the Bengali *bhadralok* is proud of his Metro and takes impeccable care of it, and keeps it neat, clean and smoothly functional. Every society or nation wants to create a beacon, to remind the world and themselves what they were capable of but couldn't achieve. IIT is that in Indian education."[37]

Autonomy at the IITs, then, is both structural and discursive. The IITs' status as institutions of national importance hinged on their structural position outside and above the wider educational system. IITians themselves have come to see the schism between the IITs and other educational institutions as that between excellence and mediocrity and, increasingly, between nonstate and state spaces. These distinctions underwrite a claim to meritocracy that has only sharpened over time alongside growing challenges to the IITs' exclusivity.

Internal Criticisms

Nazir Ahmed's dissent on the Sarkar Committee report, in which he warned against the strong possibility of institutional isolation, limited impact, and undemocratic limits to access, turned out to be quite prescient. As early as 1969, critical reviews of the IITs began to circulate. Some of these critical voices echoed Ahmed's concern with the elitism of the IITs and their inability to catalyze wider processes of social transformation. A case in point is the 1968 study of one unnamed IIT—most likely IIT Delhi—by sociologists C. Rajagopalan and Jaspal Singh. The sociologists looked into the caste and class backgrounds of students to determine whether, as top-tier institutions, the IITs were contributing to social mobility. The authors concluded their study with the observation that the IITs' goal of producing what they call a "potential elite" had made "only a limited contribution to social mobility."[38] The production of this new elite, as they saw it, was a process of social reproduction, not transformation.

Others were less concerned with elitism and more with the failure of the project to realize its own ambition of producing an elite corps of engineers who would help with nation-building. Critics, such as Professors S. P. Sukhatme and I. Mahadevan of IIT Bombay, pointed to the developmental impact of the "brain drain" from the IITs as more and more graduates opted to go abroad rather than work in India.[39] Others characterized this outward flow in terms of a diminished tax base, noting that "although the emigrant population can represent a small fraction of the total population, the fiscal effects are considerable nonetheless."[40]

IITians themselves have diverging opinions of the success of the IIT project, although very few object to the idea of an elite stratum of institutions where excellence is fostered. Deb, for instance, dispenses with the charge of elitism by using an anecdote. He narrates an interaction between Ashok Jhunjhunwala, IIT Kanpur alumnus and professor at IIT Madras, and his Gandhian grandfather. After receiving admission to the IITs, Jhunjhunwala traveled to Lakhi Sarai, a small town in Bihar, to meet his grandfather. "'So, you are joining this Brahmin institute?' the old man asked his grandson. 'I was taken aback, I didn't understand what he was talking about,' says Jhunjhunwala. 'But then I went to IIT and forgot all about it.'"[41] Deb goes on to recount a later encounter with the grandfather after Jhunjhunwala came back to India from the United States. Returning to Lakhi Sarai, he asked his grandfather what he had meant by his comment years before. His grandfather admitted that initially, most Gandhians had found the IITs elitist. After much debate, however, "they agreed that it was a good thing. India had a tradition of elite educational institutes, exemplified by the ancient Buddhist university at Nalanda. The idea was to pick the best people and train them. So you gave these institutes tremendous resources, even in times of war or famine. The aim was to train leaders for the country."[42] Through the invocation of the Gandhian grandfather, Deb naturalizes the IITs as in continuity with "Indian tradition" and justifies the social exclusions of the system. In one sense, the invocation of tradition acknowledges the continuities in social status underwriting the IITs. At the same time, Deb obfuscates caste and class structures through recourse to a cultural notion of excellence. Lost in this recourse to the ancient past is any question of how public investment in the perpetuation of exclusionary excellence is to be reconciled with democratic transformation. Even while Deb decenters Nehru the socialist in favor of Dalal the technocrat in his version of the IIT story, his assessment of the IITs is very much in tune with Nehru's valorizing of excellence over democracy.

While most IITians echo Deb in insisting on the need for a separate stratum of institutions in which excellence is not sacrificed to other considerations, there are those who criticize the IITs for not fully developing their capacity for primary research. Even here, the concern seems to be more with the IITs' noncompetitiveness in the sphere of scientific discovery—several alumni bemoaned the absence of a single Nobel prize winner among IITians—and less with how such an emphasis might shape the intellectual development of students or the social and economic welfare of the country. Instead, excellence is gauged in terms of global competitiveness and recognition as goals in their own right. As we will see in Chapter 7, this emphasis on global legibility has assumed a more strictly market character with the rise of Brand IIT.

Lost too in Deb's invocation of the IITs' continuity with the ancient past is the question of whether the IITs do in fact "train leaders for the country." While he does address debates over diasporic mobility, Deb ultimately endorses the presence of a successful diaspora as a net good for India. Other alumni admit that IITians have not contributed as much to the nation-building project as they could have but insist that the problem is with India and not the IITs. Professors Indiresan and N. C. Nigam of IIT Delhi, for instance, argue that if Indian industry had developed, "IIT graduates would have formed the core of creative scientist-engineers required for such an effort." They also maintain that IITians will no doubt do so in the future "provided the goals of excellence are preserved and supported."[43]

While internal criticisms are typically muted, other perspectives call into question the IITs' claim to excellence by focusing on the caste contours of meritocracy and the curricular orientation of the institutes. Such arguments typically vary by region and speak to the particularities of regional history and of the institutes' founding charters. They speak as well to the tensions generated by the presence of elite central government institutions within regions with their own social hierarchies and political proclivities. In Chapter 3, we will delve deeper into how the history of caste, education, and employment in the southeastern region shaped the founding and reception of IIT Madras. This discussion will set the stage for the book's key argument about the role of Tamilnadu as a precedent for the making of upper casteness nationally and transnationally.

3

Challenging Hierarchies of Value in Madras

ALL THE INSTITUTIONS within the IIT system had certain unifying characteristics: they fell under the jurisdiction of the Indian central government, they drew students from across India, they were established through collaboration with a foreign partner, and they were funded at far higher levels than other engineering colleges. There were also differences between them. The greater numbers of students from the immediate vicinity gave each IIT a regional cultural flavor. The founding partnership was also a key factor in shaping the training students received.

These distinguishing characteristics shaped the making of IIT Madras. IIT Madras was set up with the active collaboration of the Federal Republic of Germany, a relationship that continued a long history of transnational exchanges between Indians and Germans from the period of British imperial hegemony. One of the unique features of West German engineering was the privileging of technique over theory; Germans located skill in the hands, not the head, and the engineer was regarded first and foremost as a skilled technician. Moreover, Germans associated the technical labor of engineering with the production not just of objects but of selves. The engineer became an expert and a person through hands-on labor. In terms of training, these ideas translated into an emphasis on the practical dimensions of engineering.

The regional political context also shaped the founding of IIT Madras. As we saw in Chapter 1, the vast majority of colonial-era engineers were from upper-caste backgrounds. Although many disdained manual labor, they embraced engineering because it was a white-collar profession whose status was enhanced by its relationship to conceptual knowledge and the colonial state. In many ways, Madras Presidency was an extreme case of technical education reinforcing existing social hierarchies. Unlike other regions, where a wider spectrum of upper castes entered engineering, Madras's cadre of Indian engineers had a disproportionate number of Brahmins. The predominance of Brahmins in the modern professions—not just in engineering but also in law and the bureaucracy—was a lightning rod for political opposition. The Non-Brahmin and Dravidian movements of the twentieth century articulated a critique of Brahmin dominance and offered an alternative vision of political society oriented around two key categories: the Hindu scriptural category of the Shudra, and the racial-linguistic category of the Dravidian. In a more limited sense, they also advanced arguments about caste hierarchies of knowledge and the need to rethink the privileging of the cerebral over the embodied.

Both the German approach to engineering and the political currents that swept Madras sat uneasily with the forms of colonial and postcolonial institutional stratification we explored in Chapters 1 and 2. How, then, did the German emphasis on self-fashioning through bodily technique and the Non-Brahmin and Dravidian critiques of Brahmin dominance intersect with prevailing caste ideologies? Let us turn now to the southeastern region and consider the founding of IIT Madras in relation to a longer regional history of caste and technical education. Our exploration here of broader political trends will lead us to Chapter 4's closer look at the life histories of the 1960s generation of Madras IITians. Across both chapters, we will explore how the tensions over the founding and orientation of the institute shaped the perspectives of IIT Madras's first cohorts.

Technical Education in Madras Presidency

Madras Presidency was one of the earliest regions where technical education was launched in various forms. It housed the first survey school, it had a concentration of Christian missionary trade schools offering vocational training for lower-caste converts, and it witnessed some of the most innovative experiments in industrialization. Before the founding of IIT Madras, the premier engineering institution in the region was the Madras College of Engineering, previously named the Madras Civil Engineering College and later renamed the College of Engineering, Guindy. The college was first started in 1794 as a school to train surveyors from the colony and reduce the cost of metropolitan personnel in the East India Company's Surveyor's Department. Its students were mainly trainees from among the destitute European and Eurasian children in Madras Presidency's schools. In the early 1820s, the school was transferred to the Madras Revenue Department, and training in leveling, drafting, and hydraulics was added to its roster. In 1842, the government of Madras proposed a college where civil engineering could be taught. The East India Company's Court of Directors rejected the proposal because the level of general education in the colony was thought too low for candidates to absorb advanced training in mathematical and technical sciences.

After the establishment of the Madras Public Works Department in the 1850s, there were more consistent arguments for technical personnel. This time, the government was more amenable. In 1854, Governor General Dalhousie proposed that "a complete system of instruction" be provided to "every class belonging to the Department of Public Works, Europeans, East Indians or Natives, whether Artificers, Foreman Overseers, Surveyors or Civil Engineers."[1] In September 1859, the new Madras Civil Engineering College opened with approximately one hundred students. By 1887, the diploma structure had stabilized to offer three grades of training: four years for engineers; three and a half years for engineer subordinates; and two years for sub-overseers, surveyors, and draftsmen.

There are some noteworthy aspects of the progression of engineering education in Madras Presidency that are relevant for understanding its attraction to regional upper castes. First, the Madras Civil Engineering College changed from a trade school in 1859 to an advanced teaching institution in 1931, in the process expanding its range of subjects to include mathematics, science, and engineering. The mathematics curriculum in particular expanded significantly to become a prominent part of the engineering curriculum as a whole. Second, between 1857 and 1907, the college changed from a military to a civilian institution, a shift symbolized by its affiliation to Madras University in 1859. This was a mere two years after Cooper's Hill College opened in England to train engineers for exclusive service in India. To maintain the racial hierarchy in the engineering services, the government ordered the Madras Civil Engineering College to limit its instruction to the lower grades. However, the director of public instruction vehemently opposed the government's decision and forcefully argued that "it would be a retrograde and impolitic measure to abolish the Senior Department of the Civil Engineering College, as such a move would practically debar the natives of the Presidency, and the European and Eurasians permanently settled in it, from admission to the higher ranks of the Public Works Department."[2] As a result, the training of all grades continued apace, and the college even enhanced its status through university affiliation. Finally, the college curriculum was aligned with the requirements for the civil service so that graduates were automatically eligible for civil service employment. All of these factors—the elevation of mathematics, the continuity in higher grades of training, and enhancement of the opportunity for civil service employment—significantly shaped the regional status of engineering and its attraction for upper castes. But what about the relationship between the theoretical and practical dimensions of engineering education?

As in other parts of British India, Madras too witnessed a lively debate over the appropriate balance of theoretical and practical training in engineering education. From the outset, Public Works commissioners felt that the earlier survey school had not prepared students theoretically, resulting in "a desultory mode of study, the effects of which may be traced in the afterlife of the Surveyors."[3] Senior policy makers envisaged a college to train scientifically qualified engineers who would be managers and not just technicians. In Chapter 1, we encountered Lieutenant George Winscom, the first principal of the Madras Civil Engineering College, who believed that engineers needed a "knowledge in Engineering science and intellectual vigor."[4] At the same time, Winscom had carried over from England and from the military a preference for the practical man. These clashing opinions resulted in a college with a dual emphasis on theoretical and practical training.

The theoretical orientation of the college came in for criticism by employers frustrated by the lack of practical knowledge of the first generations of students entering the colonial engineering service. In response, the director of public instruction issued a fervent defense of the college in 1869. It was unreasonable, he argued, "to express surprise that students fresh from the College are not experienced Overseers" and to expect an engineering graduate, "without guidance, to build a barrack, drain a Cantonment, or carry out an Irrigation project with as much rapidity and confidence as if he had done it all before."[5] Still, he granted that the purpose of the college was "to prepare its students in the most efficient manner practicable for entering on the duties connected with the Engineering and Survey works of the country, with a groundwork of such knowledge as is most essential to qualify for undertaking these duties, and such practical training as a place of instruction of this nature can afford."[6] For the most part, the Madras college continued its theoretically oriented approach to engineering. However, the criticisms of excessive book learning continued, prompting a revision of the curriculum in 1881. From 1886, in addition to a three-year course in theory, every student would spend a year undergoing practical training. The added emphasis on practical training and more priority given to the physical sciences, workshops, and laboratories met with the approval of the Public Works Department.

Despite the ongoing insistence that practical training was foundational to engineering, the trend in Madras, as elsewhere, was toward privileging the theoretical over the practical. As engineering became established as a profession rooted in mathematical science, it was increasingly distinguished from the practical vocations of industrial life. The professionalization of engineering was crucial to its appeal to upper castes, who saw it as a means to be modern, affiliated with the colonial state, and endowed with rational, systemic forms of knowledge. Reports of the engineering college between 1884 and 1905 note the preponderance of Brahmins over students from the "artisan classes [which] should have the greatest natural aptitude" for engineering.[7] By 1921, Brahmins made up approximately 74 percent of engineering college students, despite being only 3 percent of the enumerated regional population.[8] In the Public Works Department, Brahmins were the first Indians to gain prominence and take up senior positions. In 1900, across all grades, there were 67 engineers, of whom 58 (86.5 percent) were Europeans, 8 (12 percent) were Brahmins, and 1 (1.5 percent) was a non-Brahmin.[9] By 1919, of a total 535 employees, Brahmins numbered 398. This included posts for superintendent engineers and 10 out of 14 posts for executive engineers.[10] Even after 1920, when non-Brahmin numbers rose, Brahmins continued to be overrepresented in the engineering profession, just as they were in administration and law.[11] Even compared with other regions, then, Madras's engineering profession was an upper-caste stronghold.

When it came to industrial schooling, Madras Presidency stood out once again. It was here that Alfred Chatterton embarked on his "pioneer factories" to build up the industrial and commercial strengths of artisans. While Chatterton is best known as a British administrator who advocated for artisanal entrepreneurship and state-led industrialization, his role in instrumentalizing caste as the basis of industrial development is less so. This comes through in his work in Madras. Chatterton had an understanding of Tamil society, particularly Tamil industrial life, as rooted in caste. It followed that industrial schooling and development should similarly be structured around caste. "For the indigenous industries," he argued, "it seems inevitable that we must have recourse to industrial schools, but I would suggest that instruction in each industry should be confined to the sons and relatives of those actually engaged in the industry at the present time: that is to say, we should carry on the industrial schools on a caste basis." Only then would those who depend on indigenous industries for a livelihood be benefited and not "have added to their difficulties the competition of locally trained people belonging to the non-artisan castes."[12] This did not mean that Chatterton subscribed to prevalent caste hierarchies of value in disparaging artisanship and other forms of manual production. On the contrary, he greatly admired the artisans he worked with and expressed faith in their capacity for critical scrutiny and innovation. In speaking of farmers, weavers, and wood and metalworkers, he argued that "the reputation that Indians are averse to all change and are obstinately wedded to the antiquated ways of their forefathers is not justly deserved. They are conservative but they know their own business fairly well and many of the so-called improvements they rejected were really unsuitable innovations."[13]

Unlike the sidelining of artisans in other regions, Chatterton's pioneer factories attempted to enhance and channel their skills in order to make them commercially viable. But while Chatterton's primary concern was to build up indigenous industry, and to do so without displacing an existing artisanal population, his proposals further strengthened and naturalized the link between caste and occupation. His insistence that industrial schooling be housed with the Department of Industries rather than the Department of Education more clearly distinguished industrial workers from those headed to professional occupations. Although Chatterton's effort to revalorize industrial work was laudable, colonial hierarchies of caste ultimately worked against its resignification as a form of labor on par with the occupations of the high-born.

State Technical Scholarships

In Chapter 1, we encountered Daivasikhamani Achari, secretary of the Kumbakonam Visvakarma Mahajana Conference Committee, who testified before the Indian Industrial Commission about the sidelining of artisans in the selection process for state technical scholarships. Let us now look more closely at the regional selection process to see how expectations were weighted in favor of the high-born even when it came to nonprofessional tracks of technical training. To compensate for the lack of practical training afforded to Indian graduates, the Conference on Technical Education held at Simla in 1901 recommended the institution of state technical scholarships to encourage Indian students to pursue further studies abroad. Ten scholarships were established a year: two each for Bombay, Bengal, and Madras, and the remaining four for other local governments and administrations. The stated purpose of the scholarship program was to encourage Indians to take up further studies in the higher branches of technical education and apply them to industrial development. The program was specifically not for the study of engineering but for cultivating other forms of technical training in industries that were important to their regions.

In Madras, eleven scholarships were given between 1906 and 1915. The application files offer insight into the practices of evaluation that informed colonial officialdom. Despite the stated requirements of educational accomplishments and practical experience, family background and social networks were of utmost importance in determining the success or failure of applicants. Even evidence of industry connections, which would have facilitated the application of new skills to industrial development—the very purpose of the scholarships—was ultimately less important than who someone was socially.

The year the program was started, four applicants submitted their requests for support, and none were awarded scholarships. One application was from Mr. Pothery Koran, a clerk in the District Munsiff's Court in Cannanore, who applied "to go to America or to England and learn all arts in connection with the industry of weaving." He described himself as "a Hindu and Tiya by caste" who had "passed Matriculation Examination and Handwriting Test examination" and had a "fair knowledge of English and Mathematics." Moreover, one of his brothers was "a merchant and a partner in a Weaving Company on a small scale at Chova in Cannanore." If granted the scholarship, Pothery Koran promised to "try my best to benefit all the Indians and especially the people in my locality with the knowledge I acquire in this enterprise of mine." In his rejection of the application, E. W. Middlemarch, the director of public instruction, merely stated that "the candidate seems to me to be quite unsuitable. I would suggest that Mr. Chatterton be commissioned to try and find a suitable candidate."[14]

There is no further explanation for why Pothery Koran was unsuitable. What we do know is that he, a lower-caste weaver, was rejected despite having the basic educational requirements and family connections in weaving that would have allowed him to apply his new skills to the further development of a regional industry.

At times, applications were rejected despite testimonials of support provided by community associations. This was the case with the application of M. Duraiswami, a textile student at the Victoria Jubilee Technical Institute, who was a Sourashtrian native of Madura. Duraiswami stated in his application that the Sourashtrian community "rightly deserves all sorts of encouragement at the hands of the Government, being classed as backward in education." Moreover, he states that "this community shared nowadays in all kinds of industry and is thoroughly industrial. They now come the foremost in trade in Southern India next only to the Nattukottai Chetties. If therefore industrial education is freely imparted to a poor scholar of this community, it is sure to improve the present status of industry of his own people, who now form the bulk of the population of Madura which is a great centre of trade, and the people at large." Duraiswami further underscored that his community "has a greater inclination to an industrial life than to any other pursuit of life and the only great bar to any further development in industry is want of education in a great majority of the population and I am sure that the only way in which Government can help them is to give them chance though a little out of turn."[15]

Duraiswami's letter was accompanied by a resolution by the councilors of the Sourashtra Sabha. The councilors pointed out that their role in industrial development had been recognized by none other than Lord Curzon, who, "during his visit to this city of historic fame as the viceroy of India," observed that their "immigration from Gujarat (the ancient kingdom of Sourashtra) into this city was . . . responsible for the propagation of the Industries of Weaving and Dyeing in Southern India." They then provided a narrative of decline: "This law-abiding and peaceful community of weavers and dyers which received a severe shock from the competition of the machine-made fabrics is slowly bettering its industrial condition by the spread of English Education which several of its members were enabled to receive by means of scholarships bestowed upon them by the Government as members of a community classed as backward in education." The councilors ended their letter with the conviction that "the prosperity of the industrial population purely depends upon the fact that they should be educated in the improved methods of industries" and that Duraiswami, "who, as a member of the Sourashtra Community, has a natural aptitude for this kind of study[,] . . . is pre-eminently fitted to receive instructions in a Technical subject."[16] Despite the council's masterful rhetorical framing and evidence that Duraiswami was an ideal candidate who was well positioned to use the scholarship to buttress his technical skill and contribute to his city's industrial life, his application was rejected with but a single word of explanation: "unsuitable."

Most of the applications were rejected on the basis of unsuitability. This begs the question of who was deemed suitable. In Madras Presidency, the overwhelming number of successful applicants were men from the Nair caste. While none of them had any history of technical skill, they came from well-connected families with a history of education and government employment. Along with Tamil Brahmins, Nairs were among the earliest southerners to take advantage of the opportunities afforded by modern education and the professions and become part of the colonial bureaucracy.[17] This placed them in a very different position from the majority of applicants from artisanal and trading castes who had a wealth of technical knowledge, along with family and community histories in small- and large-scale industry, but were of lower social status.

The first successful applicant was V. G. Nair, a clerk in the Pusa Agricultural Research Institute, who applied to study textile chemistry. In response to his application, the Madras Educational Department wrote to the director of Pusa to request his opinion on "whether V. G. Nair is a suitable candidate for a scholarship and particularly whether he is a man of good physique and to what family in Malabar he belongs."[18] The family history provided allowed him to pass muster.

Another successful applicant was K. Krishna Menon, who was vouched for by none other than Ravi Varma, the sixth prince of Cochin. The prince attested not only to Menon's educational credentials but to the standing of his family. "His father, who held several responsible posts in Cochin State with credit to himself and advantage to the State, is a member of one of the most respectable Nair Tarwads (families) in Cochin. Mr. Krishna Menon is my brother's brother-in-law. I have known him from his cradle. He is an amiable young man full of energy and bears an excellent character." Ravi Varma concluded with the opinion that, if granted a scholarship, Menon would "prove himself worthy of such trust, of the Education he has received and of his respectable parentage and his connections." Varma's personal assessment was buttressed by a letter bearing the seal of the Cochin Durbar that certified "that Mr. K. Krishna Menon belongs to a respectable family in Ernakulam. He is an intelligent, honest, hardworking and well-behaved young man."[19]

Finally, we have Ramunni Panikkar, who was awarded a two-year scholarship in 1907 to study tanning. Mr. H. D. Taylor, acting secretary of the Educational Department, laid out his social standing thus: "M. A. Ramunni Panikkar is a native of Malabar and a Nayar by caste. He comes from a well-to-do family of good social position. His father,

V. Damodara Panikkar, is a retired Sub-Registrar and is now a Bench Magistrate at Palghat; and one of his brothers is the adikari or headman of a village in one of the taluks of South Malabar."[20] Panikkar was in competition with another applicant, Abraham B. Salem, who applied to study fisheries and fish curing. Salem was a clerk to fisheries director Frederick Nicholson. Nicholson's favorable recommendation noted the following about Salem:

> [He is a] Jew by nationality and religion, smart, well educated, and pushing; belonging to the West Coast, he is acquainted with the merchants and trades of the coast, and he is strongly desirous of working at the fishery business and especially at the curing branch of the industry. He has acquired a good deal of fishery knowledge while in my office, having been on tour with me and independently; he will do much better as a practical man than at mere office work and I can rely on him not to waste his time or opportunities; his energy is shown by his attaining his B.A. and B.L. degrees in the face of much difficulty; and he is the first Jew to obtain a degree.[21]

Despite Salem's qualifications and experience in the fishing industry, and the considerable doubt cast on whether Panikkar would even continue in the tanning field, the latter was chosen. Even those who recommended advancing both applicants used the occasion to express their anti-Semitism in less than subtle terms: "I submit that the names both of Panikkar and Salem may be submitted, preference being given to the former. Mr. Panikkar informed me that he had private means. Nothing is known in this respect of Mr. Abraham B. Salem except that he is a Jew, and that with him 'time is money.'"[22]

Alfred Chatterton, who was on the board reviewing applications for the scholarship, was frustrated by the mismatch between experience, prospects for future employment, and selection. He pointed out that of those selected, "few have any knowledge of or connection with the industry in India which they propose to take up." As a result, apart from "the rare case where the technical student belongs to a family already engaged in manufacturing work," foreign returnees typically languished without a professional career.[23] Still, the scholarships continued to be granted to applicants who had the desired social, not technical, qualifications. In the process, they reinforced the upward mobility of high-status groups while doing little to support those applicants who came from histories of technical skill.

Non-Brahminism and Dravidianism

The social profile of engineering students and the fate of most applicants for state technical scholarships make clear that Madras Presidency was a particularly striking instance of the pan-Indian tracking of castes into different tiers of training. However, there was an added form of classification that lent a different texture to regional caste distinction. Consider this quote from the director of public instruction's report for 1906–1907: "Out of the large population of this Presidency, less than three thousand children were receiving technical instruction in the various handicrafts and of these less than nine hundred were *non-Brahmin Hindus,* the class of the community to which the bulk of hereditary workers in wood and metal and textile fabrics belong. There is as yet little demand for technical education, and the little advance that has been made has practically left unaffected the great mass of the industrial population."[24] Here we see not only the emphasis on enhancing "hereditary" occupations, a code for caste labor, but also how the expansion of technical education in Madras increasingly hinged on the distinction between Brahmin and non-Brahmin populations.

In Madras Presidency, the category of the "non-Brahmin" had accrued salience over the late nineteenth and early twentieth centuries. The distinction between non-Brahmin and Brahmin entailed the ideological reduction of the region's remarkable social diversity and complex forms of stratification into two consolidated, opposed groupings. This process was precipitated by a variety of factors, including Orientalist scholarship, Anglo-Indian law, and bureaucratic centralization. Here I offer a broad-brush history of the social and political transformations that precipitated the polarization of Brahmin and non-Brahmin and set the stage for subsequent Tamil Brahmin claims to meritocracy.

From the fourteenth to the eighteenth century, the regional landscape of social power and political authority was characterized by heterogeneity. The south was highly decentralized, with no central governmental mechanism capable of redistributing resources or maintaining an army. Political decentralization was also mirrored in commercial networks that were never consolidated in urban centers. Even when it came to conceptions of morality, there was no regional consensus. Rather, there were discontinuities and tensions between upper castes, with their Vedic ritual traditions, and the larger mass of people, who participated in localized, non-Vedic forms of worship. All of these factors contributed to a remarkable diversity of social arrangements of power and forms of stratification across subregions and ecological zones.[25]

To the extent that there were structuring forms of power that applied regionally, they were encapsulated in three institutions: *kaniachi*, kingship, and religion. The *kaniachi* system, which allocated shares in property based on prior settlement, allowed corporate groups to make genealogical claims to land ownership. Kingly power was accessible to many warrior castes, which would lay claim to legitimacy through military force and lineage organization, and often involved the mediation of priestly authority. In terms of control over resources, kingship was typically expressed through the symbolic incorporation of river valley *kaniachikarar* communities and the disbursement of land grants to Brahmins in the uplands. The third source of power was the temple, where honor and status derived from services performed for the gods. By donating lands, money, and products to temples, social groups would accrue rights to participate in ceremonies and receive gifts from the gods that underwrote their local status. Kings, too, were major donors to temples, a practice through which they ritually incorporated the social order of their domains and established their authority. This tripartite structure of *kaniachi*, kingly, and divine authority fostered competition for honors and status through which groups could elevate and transform their standing in regional society.

The existence of multiple avenues of mobility made precolonial claims to status variable and dynamic. The occupations, ritual practices, and social groups associated with high status varied across context. The rules of social precedence were similarly dynamic. Donations to temples could bring honor and the means to redefine status. Caste boundaries were commonly reset through participation in religious sects associated with influential seers. New claims to status were also

made through emulation. Landowning groups such as the Vellalas, for
instance, emulated Brahmins by being purity conscious and developing
Brahminical qualities of vegetarianism, scholarship, and conspicuous
piety. However, even this varied across ecological zones. While emulation of Brahmins was more prevalent in the agricultural zones, groups
in the uplands paid little attention to the culture of purity and rested
their claims to privilege on kingly attributes of power and martial tradition. Furthermore, because of the way endogamy was localized and
status was tied to the achievement of royal and temple honors, the same
caste could have a very different standing in different localities.

The defining characteristic of regional caste society, then, was ongoing contestation. Between them, *kaniachikarars*, kings, and Brahmins distributed rights and privileges and allowed social groups to vie
for relative status. This is not to say that the region was nonhierar-
chical. Although status was fluid, it entailed jostling for position
within a hierarchically ordered society. However, there was an external
limit to these forms of maneuver. Unlike all other groups—Hindu,
Muslim, and Christian alike, who by the eighteenth century participated in competitions over precedence and honors—untouchable castes
were explicitly excluded from access to the three institutions that mediated claims-making. This rigidity of status beyond the bounds of
"clean" caste society was seen most clearly in the Thanjavur delta,
where untouchable castes constituted the mass of agricultural laborers
whose bonded servitude was an inherited condition.

Colonial rule brought far-reaching transformations to South Indian
society. In the agrarian economy, the colonial state instituted a system
of private property, which broke up the *kaniachi* system of corporate
rights and vested ownership in individuals. Private property undercut
the forms of reciprocity that had structured the relationship between
kaniachikarars, tenants, and landless laborers, allowing the landed to
accumulate wealth with no regard for the customary rights of non-
elites or for maintaining the infrastructure of agrarian production. At
the same time, colonial rule in the south did not lead to the establishment of a *zamindari* class of landowners. Rather, the revenue system
that developed over the nineteenth century was based on the direct
taxation of peasant households. Although capitalist transformation
made the peasant economy more unequal during this period, there was

no associated loss of land rights and expansion of proletarian labor. Furthermore, the exodus of landowners to the towns in the early twentieth century opened up new land for purchase, leading to the proliferation of petty landownership and the conscription of family rather than wage labor.[26]

The fragmentation of agrarian landholdings resulted in a decline in productivity and precipitated an exodus from villages to towns, whose rapid growth made them the new centers of economic development. Between 1921 and 1961, the urban population grew almost three times as fast as the rest of the state. These shifts in population transferred power from the river valleys and coasts to the upland plains. As in the rural economy, urban economic development did not lead to the concentration of wealth and the expansion of an urban proletariat. While a small segment of the urban population was employed in modern factories, the sectors of the economy that expanded most rapidly were petty commerce, informal trading, and government employment. Between 1901 and 1951, approximately one-third of the total increase in urban population was in white-collar employment, and it was in this sector that Brahmin dominance was most apparent. Brahmins' early exposure to English literacy and modern education, in part through the efforts of Christian missionary societies, became a significant advantage with urbanization. Despite being only 3 percent of the regional population, Brahmins were overrepresented in higher education and government service, where they constituted 70–80 percent of graduates and native employees. Even with the introduction in the 1910s of communal awards, or reserved quotas for non-Brahmin candidates, there were few who had the literacy and education to take up the posts, with the result that the proportion of Brahmins in government employment was even higher in 1927 than it had been in 1900.[27]

Apart from economic changes, colonial rule ushered in administrative and legal changes that transformed the status claims of the precolonial period. By making courts of law the sole rights-defining authority, the colonial state undercut the more dispersed and varied forms of political authority, which had underwritten localized customary rights and community identities. The centralization of authority came with new bureaucratic mechanisms, such as the census that transformed what had been a dynamic process of status contestation into a static form of caste ascription. In addition, Anglo-Indian law enshrined a notion of tradition heavily influenced by an understanding of Sanskritic Hinduism, which was at odds with the variability in local forms of worship. The extension of Sanskritic conceptions of rank, or *varnashramadharma*, elevated Brahmins above their erstwhile competitors for status, who were now classified as Shudra, the groups occupying the fourth rung of the *varna* hierarchy.[28]

The new fixity accorded to caste status involved a reconceptualization of caste as a form of collectivity rooted in blood and birth, not practice. In effect, colonial rule racialized caste as heredity, a shift that was profoundly consequential for understandings of caste continuity and change. Instead of caste membership being tied to both birth and codes of conduct, "birth and behavior became separated in people's minds such that birth alone came to define group membership."[29] When it came to Brahmins, Maratha Brahmins were the first to pioneer the model of the modern Brahmin as one who could take on new practices outside the bounds of ritual prescription without losing caste.[30] When this colonial-era model of Brahminness circulated to Tamil Brahmins, they took it up by embracing new professions while remaining firmly invested in their caste identity. This new understanding of caste as rooted primarily in heredity facilitated the entry of Brahmins into fields such as medicine and engineering in high numbers, despite this being a radical shift in caste practice.[31]

The racialization of caste came with certain presumptions about the innate propensities of distinct groups. The British approach to caste as heredity, combined with the active role of Brahmin intermediaries in the making of colonial knowledge, produced the notion of the Brahmin as innately intelligent and destined to lead. Molony, a British civil servant in Madras, was representative of this outlook. Writing about the success of Brahmins in colonial Madras, Molony drew on eugenics to opine that their "refusal of intermarriage seems understandable. The higher race sought to preserve the purity of its blood." It was this purity, he added, that had allowed the Brahmin to take "the lead in South Indian politics in virtue of his intellectual superiority; for the same reason, he enjoyed a practical monopoly of lucrative employment under the foreign government which he professed to detest."[32] Such opinions were echoed by the Tamil Brahmin intelligentsia.

R. Swaminatha Aiyar, a retired deputy collector, insisted that "the Brahmans constitute a type superior to other castes." Intercaste marriage, he opined, "must inevitably lead to further deterioration of the Brahmans, physically, mentally, and spiritually."[33]

Alongside the legal codification of Sanskritic Hinduism, the colonial state transformed temples from institutions intimately linked to the patronage of mercantile and agrarian elites into public trusts with absolute power over managing the resources at their disposal. In the process, it undercut the long-standing reciprocity between priests and worshippers and the role of the deity as a redistributive authority through which honors were bestowed on donors from a wide range of social groups. This newfound institutional autonomy made Brahmin priests and their gods far less beholden to donors and significantly circumscribed social claims on the temple. Moreover, the rigidification of caste undercut the claims of those who were now regarded as too lowly for participation in the honors system.[34]

These changes loosened the ties of Brahmins to other social groups, especially those who were most proximate in status. The fracturing of the *kaniachi* system, the codification of Brahminical norms in Anglo-Indian law, the severing of ties between the temple and its erstwhile patrons, and their near monopoly of education and government employment granted Brahmins a newly fixed position as social superiors. This discrepancy between the precolonial fluidity of status and the fixity of caste hierarchy, which accorded Brahmins a permanent status written by colonial law and governance, was a key catalyst for Non-Brahminism.

Non-Brahminism began in the 1910s as a politics spearheaded by elite non-Brahmins. Their reduction to the *varna* category of Shudra within Anglo-Indian law grated against such groups, who had been competitors with Brahmins for status and were now placed on par with those they considered social inferiors. The Justice Party, formed in 1916 as one of the earliest non-Brahmin political organizations, counted among its patrons many merchants and landowners, who used their social and economic power to challenge the rising status of Brahmins in the colonial public sphere.[35]

The party announced its political arrival through the publication of the "Non-Brahmin Manifesto," which laid out a case against Brahmin hegemony in the nationalist movement, modern education, and the professions. The manifesto called for greater non-Brahmin representation in the emerging political and economic arenas of South Indian society and challenged colonial assumptions of the Brahmin's innate intellectual superiority and leadership. In part, it did so by transforming Brahmin intelligence from nature to history. Justice Party ideologues advanced an argument about caste expropriation by making Brahmin social and cultural capital the product of expropriated non-Brahmin labor. As T. M. Nair, one of the party's founders, argued, "The Brahmins toiled not, neither did they spin. The sweated slaves supplied them with everything, and they in turn cultivated 'spirituality.'" Nair and others advanced their own labor theory of value, which elevated non-Brahmin productivity over Brahmin non-productivity. Non-Brahmins were recast as "the toilers, the producing communities" whose work "made possible the riches of Indian civilization."[36] In equating manual labor with the production of value, Non-Brahminists reconstituted Brahmin intellectualism as nonproductive and parasitic. While the Justice Party was largely supportive of British rule—a position that gained it notoriety—its leaders did charge colonialism with expanding the possibilities of Brahmin expropriation of non-Brahmin labor and wealth through the extension of caste power from the otherworldly domain of religion to the worldly domains of law and politics.

One manifestation of the Justice Party's emphasis on productive labor was its endorsement of technical education. Justice Party leaders called for a comprehensive educational model, with mass primary education as a foundation. This was necessary, they argued, to address "the hiatus that existed between the demands of formal literacy," which many non-Brahmins could not meet, "and a certain kind of experiential and 'guild' knowledge which they knew they possessed."[37] It was only with formal literacy that non-Brahmin producers could avail themselves of the technical education offered by the colonial government and enhance their standing in the worlds of industry and commerce. As with the comparative methodology of anticolonial nationalism, Justice Party ideologue Theagoraya Chetti compared India's paltry advance in technical training unfavorably to Japan's: "In British India, with a population of 255 millions, the universities have 36,000 students pursuing a literary course, while only 12,000 study in technical schools, which teach mostly type-writing, book-keeping, short-hand, etc. Japan on the other hand with a population of 51 millions has only 7500 students pursuing a literary course in its universities whereas 2,900,000 pupils attend technical schools."[38] Only an educational model prioritizing the technical, Chetti argued, would lead the way out of the existing system, which produced only "automatic quill-drivers, indifferent school masters and pettifogging lawyers rather than competent agriculturists, technicians and tradesmen."[39] Instead, the *Non-Brahman*, the Justice Party's English paper, valorized forms of productive and commercial labor. "The greatest demand for our community at the present time," it argued, "is a Commercial and an Industrial university. . . . We still carry the martial spirit in us that rebels against crams and mocks at the worthless examinations of the Madras University."[40] The paper called for the empowerment of non-Brahmin youth as "merchants, skilled laborers and mechanics who can earn a hundred rupees a month by striking the hammer with their sinewy hands on iron and steel."[41] Following the 1919 Montagu-Chelmsford Reforms, which instituted a system of limited representative government at the provincial level, the Justice Party came to power in Madras and promoted industrial development through physical and educational infrastructure as a key policy goal.

Non-Brahminist arguments for rethinking the hierarchies of labor were rhetorically powerful. However, they were in tension with and ultimately far less consequential than the demand for reservation in professional and political spheres of Brahmin dominance. During the Justice Party's rule in Madras from 1921 to 1926, and again in 1930, it institutionalized the reservation of government jobs for different categories of non-Brahmins. In a display of rhetorical prowess, Justice Party ideologues likened these modern, putatively caste-free spaces to the rural *agraharam*, or Brahmin quarter, and argued that government employment needed to be both desacralized and desegregated.[42] The *Dravidan*, the Tamil newspaper of the Justice Party, quipped that the Madras Presidency's All-India Congress Committee, in which thirteen out of fifteen members were Brahmins, should be called the "All-India Agraharam Committee."[43] Similarly, the Madras High Court Vakil's Association (an association of lawyers) was likened to a caste body because of its overwhelmingly Brahmin membership. By extending the metaphor of the *agraharam* in this way, Non-Brahminists deliberately conflated rural and urban, sacred and secular, and nonmodern and modern to show how suffused modern political and professional spaces were by logics of caste. But rather than pushing for an end to caste-based recruitment in government jobs and the professions, they argued that the application of communal quotas would make the composition of these spaces better reflect regional demography.

The demand for quotas also pointed to another key argument of Non-Brahminism: the self-interestedness or non-universality of Brahmin leadership. The Justice Party rejected the idea that Brahmins could represent the greater social good. Instead, its ideologues argued that Brahmins were incapable of political neutrality because their primary concern was to protect caste privilege, as seen in the sustained opposition within the nationalist movement to democratizing party and professional spaces through communal quotas. In this way, they refuted the Brahmin claim to political modernity and identified non-Brahmins instead as the true moderns motivated by concerns of justice and equality.[44]

While the Justice Party remained an elite formation, the Self Respect Association that followed in 1926 was more able to tap the roots of mass discontent. The association was founded by E. V. Ramasami Naicker, or Periyar, who later renamed it the Dravida Kazhagam (Party of the Dravidians, or DK). The term "Dravidian" drew inspiration from the scholarship of philologist Max Mueller and linguist Robert Caldwell, whose racial-linguistic theories posited a divide between an autochthonous Dravidian–non-Brahmin population and Aryan-Brahmin settlers.[45] The son of an affluent merchant from the artisanal Balija Naidu caste, whose father was the patron of a temple, Periyar aligned himself with those who experienced the downside of colonial modernization. His message of reviving a communal economy of distributed rights struck a chord with urban artisans, rural migrants, and others who were shut out of the most coveted arenas of urban employment. Periyar's critique of Sanskritic religion also resonated with those who experienced as alien and denigrating the forms of caste religiosity underwritten by Anglo-Indian law that were increasingly prevalent in upland towns. The DK under Periyar lent Dravidian politics a more iconoclastic and subaltern flavor and extended its reach beyond the elite public sphere. His public rituals—burning Hindu sacred texts and breaking idols; holding events at inauspicious times; organizing beef-eating ceremonies; and wearing black and celebrating the antagonists of Hindu epics, like the demon-king Ravana of the Ramayana—took Dravidianism into the sphere of everyday cultural practice. Periyar's use of bawdy language in popular journals; his antireligious, rationalist rhetoric; his sensationalized performances; and his choice of public meetings to convey his messages were all tactics intended to constitute a subaltern public.[46]

Periyar placed the blame for the elevation of the Brahmin over the non-Brahmin on the ideology of *varnashramadharma* and argued that it was this structure of value that deprived the Shudra of self-respect. Contra Mohandas Gandhi's idealized version of caste as a system of interdependent complementarity, he insisted that caste-based occupations would ensure the perpetuation of existing patterns of social dominance. At the same time, Periyar had an ambivalent relationship with the category of Shudra. Even as he located the Shudra at the core of his conception of the Dravidian community, he was indignant about the demotion of groups like his own to Shudra status. Moreover, his valorization of the Shudra maintained the outsider status of Scheduled Castes (SCs). While there were certainly times when Periyar aligned himself with the struggles of SCs, his preoccupation with the relative status of the Shudra kept in place the graded inequalities of caste. Ultimately, Dravidian politics was unwilling to fully address the disabilities of caste experienced most palpably by SCs. The legacies of this preoccupation with status is still evident in today's intractable conflicts between Backward Castes and Dalits.[47]

From the 1930s to the 1960s, Dravidian politics gained momentum through a sharper focus on opposing the Indian National Congress. The Congress in Tamilnadu was led by the elite beneficiaries of colonial modernization: Brahmins, educated professionals, wealthy landowners, and businessmen. Three Congress policies in particular became pivots of Dravidianist critique and mobilization. First, Brahmin leaders in the Congress pushed for greater legal and state control over the affairs of temples, a step that was interpreted by Dravidianists and their sympathizers as advancing the further consolidation of Brahmin caste power over religious life. Second, the Congress argued against the application of communal quotas in recruitment to government jobs, which threatened the already tenuous hold of non-Brahmin groups in this most dynamic and coveted employment sector. Third, the party passed a resolution to make Hindi the national language, a move that antagonized aspirants to government jobs, who feared that these jobs would now be claimed by northern migrants. The Hindi Resolution catalyzed the DK's most successful mobilization. By equating the imposition of Hindi with the hegemony of three "alien" forces—Aryanism, Brahminism, and Hinduism—Periyar constituted the Dravidian community, or Kudi Arasu (Republic of the Popular Community), as a non-Brahmin Tamil collective.[48]

While Periyar's message reached groups well beyond the elite core of the Justice Party, it was the formation of the Dravida Munnetra Kazhagam (DMK, or Party of Dravidian Uplift) in 1949 that gave Dravidianism a truly mass character. The DMK built on certain aspects of the DK's platform and departed from others that limited the latter's appeal. Under its first two leaders, C. N. Annadurai and M. Karunanidhi, the DMK held on to the idea of the Shudra, or Backward Caste core of the Dravidian community. The DMK also reinforced Periyar's critique of the cultural and caste bases of Indian nationalism but added the alleged economic neglect of South India. Despite clear evidence that the south was rapidly industrializing, the DMK advanced its critique of underdevelopment by arguing that the Nehruvian focus on large-scale enterprises was contrary to the property regime rooted in Tamil tradition.[49] In expanding the conception of Dravidianism to foreground Tamil language and regional territory as unifying ingredients, the DMK also departed from the DK's anti-Brahmin, antireligious rhetoric. Instead, the party framed the Dravidian not as a racialized caste collective but as an ethnic territory defined by linguistic and cultural commonality, a shift that allowed for the symbolic reincorporation of Tamil Brahmins. The opposition to Hindi as a national language was a particularly powerful ingredient of the DMK's growth in the 1950s and 1960s. Although the Congress in Madras did advance language policies favoring Tamil, such as the publishing of scientific and technical textbooks in Tamil, introducing the Tamil typewriter, and making Tamil the language of administration in many government departments, the party was outpaced by the DMK when it came to linking language to Tamil mytho-history.[50]

The use of cinema was particularly effective in communicating Dravidianist conceptions of culture and history to a mass audience. Annadurai and Karunanidhi were both film scriptwriters who recruited a raft of stars for their politically charged films and, through these appeals, dramatically expanded the electorate to include small farmers and laborers who had never voted before or had simply gone along with the Congress's machine politics.[51] Through these various strategies, the DMK more definitively shifted the class affiliation of Dravidianism from the Justice Party's original base of elite non-Brahmins to lower-class groups and small property owners. This was no longer just a politics of elite resentment; it had become one of subaltern assertion.

The DMK's ability to capture a broad base of popular support led to its unseating of the Congress in 1967. The DMK has since experienced a number of internal schisms, most significantly the defection in 1972 of the charismatic actor-turned-politician M. G. Ramachandran (MGR), whose breakaway party, the Anna-DMK (ADMK), emerged as the main alternative to the DMK. MGR is credited with using his film personalities and paternalistic appeals to woo the Tamil poor away from the Congress and the DMK. As the DMK had done with the Congress, MGR charged the DMK with elitism and projected his own ADMK as the party of the Tamil poor. In a five-year campaign that carried him to victory, MGR branded the DMK a middle-class party that had consolidated its base among socially powerful Tamils and was unconcerned about the plight of the masses. By the time the ADMK came to power in 1977, MGR's rhetoric had split the meaning of Dravidianism, with the DMK as the vehicle of middle-class self-assertion and the ADMK as the party of the poor, centered on the figure of a benevolent leader.[52] Despite such political flux, however, Tamilnadu's formal political arena has been controlled by Dravidianist parties since the late 1960s, with power alternating between the DMK and the ADMK.

The legacy of Non-Brahminism and Dravidianism is evident in a Tamil "structure of feeling."[53] Although Brahmin privilege relative to other high-status non-Brahmins was more of a colonial phenomenon and one largely concentrated in education and the professions, the two movements projected Brahmin dominance and non-Brahmin subjugation into the distant past as enduring features of Tamil society. By the mid-twentieth century, the understanding of Brahmins as uniquely privileged and of non-Brahmins as long subjugated had acquired broad acceptance in Madras Presidency. Later Dravidianist emphases on regional sovereignty, linguistic identity, and the technical professions have also become key ingredients of postcolonial Tamil life.

In terms of policies too, the continuities are clear. It was not only the Justice Party and the DK who pushed for quotas. By the time of independence, the argument for non-Brahmin quotas echoed across the regional political spectrum. In 1951, Madras's Congress government under K. Kamaraj, the party's first lower-caste chief minister, introduced a 25 percent quota for Backward Castes in educational institutions and state government jobs. Unlike in other parts of India, the Congress in Madras based the quotas exclusively on caste criteria and included a much higher 51 percent of the population in the list of Backward Castes. With this move, Kamaraj received the blessing of Periyar, who called him a *pachchai Tamizhan* (pure Tamil) and proclaimed that such preferential policies, even under a Congress government, could still be a counterweight to Brahmin social power.[54]

The continuing valorization of the technical is evident in the pace of change in postcolonial Tamilnadu, which rapidly became one of the most industrialized states in the Indian Union. It is also reflected in the proliferation of institutions of technical education across the state. Despite the ideological work done by Non-Brahminism to unsettle hierarchies of labor and value, what has carried through most effectively to the postcolonial period is the demand for democratizing access to the professions. If anything, the stratification of technical training has hardened non-Brahmin opposition to occupations associated with lower-caste labor and claims to more valorized pursuits. To put it differently, technical education has been more a vehicle for advancing status claims than for transforming the caste bases of value. A clear instance of this occurred in 1953, when the government of Congress chief minister, C. Rajagopalachari, introduced a scheme for part-time craft education during school hours to train students for non-white-collar careers. The first session would involve regular teaching, whereas the second would have students being sent home to learn the occupations of their parents. Criticism arose immediately and was spearheaded by the DMK, which dubbed the scheme the *kula kalvi thittam*, or "hereditary education policy," that would perpetuate caste barriers to occupational mobility. Rajagopalachari's Brahmin identity was also deployed to discredit the scheme. Despite the government's decision to defer the scheme, public opposition built and, in combination with hostility toward other policies—especially the effort to impose Hindi as a national language—eventually forced the resignation of Rajagopalachari. His successor, K. Kamaraj, dropped the scheme in 1954 in a public show of his allegiance to Non-Brahminism. Today, the desire for professional technical education as a means to lower-caste uplift and assertion is evident in the proliferation of engineering colleges in Tamilnadu. By the late 1990s, the state had outpaced all others in the number of such colleges. As we will see in the following chapters, the mushrooming of regional public and private engineering colleges has thrown the presence of IIT Madras into sharper relief and made it a lightning rod for caste critiques that recycle the terms of Dravidianism.

To what extent has Dravidian rule transformed the political economy of caste in Tamilnadu? The arenas in which its impact is most palpable are public education and government employment, where reservation for lower castes has increased their share of seats and jobs. However, such steps have not addressed the rapidly expanding business and commercial sectors, which since as early as the 1960s became the new focus of wealth accumulation and elite aspiration. Moreover, to the extent that upper castes pursued government careers after the 1960s, they tended to be in the central government, where quotas were limited to members of SCs and Scheduled Tribes. In this sense, even lower-caste quotas have not had as significant an impact on the redistribution of wealth as might be assumed. The patronage politics of Dravidian parties expressed through handouts to the poor have been supported not by progressive taxation but by sales taxes, government borrowing, and other initiatives that have not adversely affected the wealthy. In addition, state support for entrepreneurialism deepened networks of private capital that disproportionately favored caste and class elites. These trends were reinforced in the 1970s and 1980s under

MGR. His ADMK government further entrenched the economic conservatism of the DMK, which he offset in popular perception through highly visible ventures—such as a Midday Meals Scheme to feed the poor—that were linked to his own heroic imagery in films as a benevolent patron. The post-1990 period of economic liberalization has witnessed the rapid rise in private sector accumulation by upper castes and the consolidation of political power by dominant Other Backward Class (OBC) groups tied to networks of Dravidianist party patronage. The latter trend has been particularly inimical to Dalits, who have borne the brunt of OBC vigilante violence aimed at checking their economic and political aspirations. In all these ways, socioeconomic inequality has grown under Dravidianist rule even as the rhetoric of caste rights suffused Tamilnadu.[55]

How have Tamil Brahmins responded to these currents of change? As we shall see in the following chapters, despite their economic power in the domestic and transnational private sectors and in certain cultural spaces, there is a palpable sense among Tamil Brahmins of their own victimization by a non-Brahmin majority and resort to notions of caste-based intellectual merit to reclaim their standing.[56] A crucial part of this defense in the name of meritocracy is a claim to middle classness. Class has become a critical alibi that makes possible a reconciliation between caste inheritances and the democratic principle of meritocracy. While Tamil Brahmins are an early instance of this use of middle classness as identity and alibi, it has become a much more widespread ingredient in an expanding politics of meritocracy. Another part of the Tamil Brahmin defense against Non-Brahminism has involved the resort to bodily metaphors that recycle the caste essentialisms of the colonial period. We see an early instance of this in 1919. In response to non-Brahmin opposition, Brahmin nationalists sought to reclaim the mantle of leadership by throwing into question non-Brahmin political capacity. Writing in the nationalist newspaper *New India* in 1919, lawyer G. Annaji Rao warned that such challenges would lead to political decline. The Brahmin was best suited to lead, he argued, because of "his religion, training, and tradition." By contrast, Rao warned, non-Brahmin rule through which "the common soldier, the man in the street, the man with perhaps more sinews than brains," would assume leadership would bring about "rebellion" and "war."[57]

This distinction between sinews and brains, or the manual and the mental, has become a common feature of a defensive Tamil Brahmin and upper-caste politics.

German Tutelage

It was in the context of sharpening Brahmin–non-Brahmin tensions that IIT Madras was founded. In 1956, Prime Minister Jawaharlal Nehru, while on an official visit to West Germany, was offered assistance to establish a higher technological institute in India. West German chancellor Konrad Adenauer also promised one hundred scholarships for Indian students wanting to study in Germany. During their interaction, Nehru gave Adenauer a copy of India's second Five Year Plan, in response to which Adenauer cautioned that "while undoubtedly it was good to have gigantic plants, concentration on these alone would leave a vacuum." Adenauer pointed out that "fifty percent of German technicians were drawn from small-scale industries and even handicrafts" and "offered German technical help to India not only in the field of big and medium scale industries, but also in that of small-scale industries."[58]

The first Indo-German Agreement was signed in Bonn in 1959 for the establishment of an Indian Institute of Technology at Madras. As part of the deal, the Government of Madras granted 633 acres of reserve forestland to the Government of India on which to site the new institute. The agreement provided for the services of German professors and foremen, training facilities for Indian faculty members, and a supply of scientific and technical equipment for the establishment of the central workshop and laboratories. The first batch of German professors and technical experts arrived in 1959. In the late 1960s, there were still twenty German professors and five experts remaining at the institute. In addition to their role in teaching and curriculum development, laboratory development, workshop training, and joint seminars, a large number of German experts visited the institute individually and in delegations to exchange ideas, establish research cooperation, and conduct seminars. A number of faculty, technical staff, and students from the institute also visited German universities for practical training and career development. German involvement formally ended in 1973.

The early collaboration with West Germany continues to be actively commemorated as a key part of the institute's history. IIT Madras opened its Heritage Center in March 2006 to showcase the institute's founding and work. Here, the Indo-German partnership is on graphic display in photographs and newspaper articles. Many of the articles are from the two main English-language newspapers in the region, *The Hindu* and *The Indian Express,* which followed the Indo-German collaboration with avid interest. The year before the institute's founding, *The Hindu* carried an article noting that "for several years German industry has, to a considerable extent, been called upon for the realization of the great Indian development projects and that it is ready to continue to take a share in them."[59] *The Indian Express* also did its part in publicizing West Germany's contribution to establishing a "center of excellence" in Madras and its generous offer of scholarships to travel to Germany for study.[60] Between them, the two papers kept in circulation information that they deemed most newsworthy to their anglophone readers.

The photographs and quotations speak to the significance of the collaboration for both sides. German president Heinrich Luebke laid the institute's foundation stone and unveiled a tablet symbolizing Indo-German cooperation in 1962. Quoting Mohandas Gandhi, Luebke announced the ambition of the partnership as one of making knowledge "the common property of the people." Not to be left out, former West German president Theodor Heuss, who visited the institute in 1960, chimed in from a distance that the collaboration "should certainly bring about a development and revival of the technical abilities of the Indian people."[61] Herr von Heyden, West German chargé d'affaires at New Delhi, offered a more pointed observation about "the engineer," who, he noted, "was a responsible person and every professional action of his had human and social consequences because he was instrumental in creating a new society and evolving a new economic order and new physical environment."[62]

Indian dignitaries, too, offered accolades. S. Radhakrishnan, president of India, appreciated the institute as "a visible demonstration of German friendship for India." Humayun Kabir, union minister for scientific research and cultural affairs, described it as "one of the finest examples of co-operation among the nations of the world in the pursuit of science and technology" and registered his confidence that "the German professors and experts would lay down the traditions of the institution on sound and progressive lines and give it the thoroughness and efficiency, which characterized scientific and technical education in Germany." Kabir pointedly expressed his hope that the German experts "in giving practical training to students would help in raising the standard of the cultivation of manual skill of the students, which was almost neglected in their education."[63]

This chorus of appreciation from Indian and German dignitaries signaled the status of IIT Madras as an emblem of the new India, where world-class expertise would be developed in the service of nation-building. German tutelage was deemed necessary but only as a catalyst to jump-start technological and social development. Indian officials like Kabir were clear about the contributions of German expertise: it was the practical orientation of German engineering that India needed most. For their part, West Germans were eager to participate in this endeavor as a way of leveraging development expertise in the service of Cold War diplomacy. It helped that unlike with Britain, Indo-German relations were not bogged down by a shared imperial past. It was easier to present this collaboration as an equal partnership of two nations that harked back to German-Indian interactions before World War II.

Germany has long occupied a unique place in the Indian developmental imagination. From the late nineteenth century, intellectual collaborations between Indians and Germans shaped a sphere of exchange extending beyond the boundaries of the British Empire. German economic nationalism, particularly the work of Friedrich List, had a profound influence on Indian anticolonial thought. From the 1880s, List's critique of classical political economy informed Indian nationalist critiques of British rule and imaginaries of development.[64] Indo-German intellectual exchanges also extended into physics, philosophy, psychology, and art. The life histories of Indians who went to Germany to study beginning in the 1920s illuminate the fuzzy boundary between academics and politics. Engineering students were no exception. A case in point are the stories of Brajesh Singh and Tayab Shaikh, two engineering students in Berlin, who "soon abandoned their studies completely in order to work exclusively in M. N. Roy's communist group."[65]

Many of the Indian students who went to study science and technology in Germany in the 1920s and 1930s drew inspiration from German understandings of the relationship between science, state, and society. They developed their model of a nationalist science from the Germans, combining fundamental research with industrial development. Within British India, Germany rose in prominence as nationalist advocacy for science shifted from a 1920s emphasis on theoretical research to an increasing focus by the 1940s on applied and industrial science.

Elevating a German scientific model for national uplift was not simply an Indian inclination. Germans, too, made science a central plank of national self-definition and international relations. In the early twentieth century, German cultural diplomacy was self-consciously oriented around the spread of intellectual institutions. This was even more the case between the world wars. Just days after signing the armistice that ended World War I, Max Planck addressed the plenary session of the Prussian Academy of Sciences with these words: "If the enemy has taken from our fatherland all defense and power, . . . there is one thing which no foreign or domestic enemy has yet taken from us: that is the position which German science occupies in the world."[66] This sense of comparative advantage was echoed by Fritz Haber of the Kaiser Wilhelm Institutes in Berlin, who argued that although the war meant that Germans "no longer sit on the board of directors of the world . . . scientifically we believe we can still be numbered with those peoples which have a claim to be reckoned among the leading nations."[67] Especially in the context of a League of Nations boycott of German scholars between 1919 and 1924, science became the stage for demonstrating German leadership. During this period and until 1934, Germany showcased its "scientific internationalism" by going out of its way to invite visitors from the United States, Eastern Europe, and Asia. The intellectual and political traffic between India and Germany was arrested only with the rise of Adolf Hitler, although it lived on in part through Nazi support for Subhas Chandra Bose's Indian National Army.[68]

German involvement in India resumed more fully in the early 1950s. Scholars have argued that the Cold War in the Third World can be understood as a competition over the best model of modernization.[69]

American modernization theory crafted in the 1950s offered a combination of anticommunism, liberal notions of progress, and development aid to decolonizing countries. West Germany's version highlighted its own recent experience with war and reconstruction. It was living proof that development assistance from the capitalist world could rapidly take a society from devastation to economic and social health.

West Germany's developmental work in the Third World was also very much a part of its own postwar self-fashioning as a peaceful, altruistic nation. Moreover, foregrounding the technical aspects of development assistance helped West Germany define itself as "an independent nation despite its strategic dependence on the United States." Through a focus on "'hard and honest' work, on achievement and efficiency, and on high quality," West Germany promoted its developmental diplomacy as a nonpolitical, nonideological "Third Way," distinct from both U.S. and Soviet agendas. The demonstration of technical prowess, it was hoped, would help the country "[claim] a spot among the former colonial powers in the postcolonial scramble for markets and influence."[70]

West German involvement in India's post-independence development dovetailed with India's own emerging focus on rapid industrialization. During the period of India's Second Five Year Plan (1956–1961), India received 14 percent of all West German development aid. Two West German projects in India—the Rourkela Steel Plant and the cooperative district project in Mandi—represented distinct models of top-down industrialization and bottom-up agrarian reform, respectively.[71]

IIT Madras was the third. How did this third project unfold, and what were its effects? Indian scientists and planners in the 1950s continuously raised the question of how to balance the need for foreign collaboration with the aspiration to national self-sufficiency. Significantly, many of them were themselves trained in Western countries, which only reinforced their conviction that this balance was possible. A case in point was Meghnad Saha, who did part of his training in Germany in the 1920s. In his work on the Indian Planning Commission, Saha underscored the danger of international collaboration leading to technological dependence. Speaking to the Indian Parliament about the work of German engineers at the Rourkela Steel Plant in the 1950s, he argued in favor of "engag[ing] a number of Indians of promise and ability to act as assistants to these Germans, in every phase of their work, so that when we wish to go for our next million ton iron and steel plant, we can do the planning and designing entirely with our own men, and we do not have to depend upon foreign technicians any further."[72] The "Indianization" of science needed to be a priority to ensure a future "technical autonomy."[73]

When he inaugurated IIT Madras in 1959, Humayun Kabir explicitly compared it with Rourkela. Even more valuable than the help given by West Germany in the erection of the Rourkela Steel Plant, Kabir argued, was the assistance in establishing IIT Madras, "because it would enable India to train successive generations of technologists and scientists, who would constitute the country's man-power, which was its greatest asset." As did West German developmental outreach, Kabir singled out the country for its postwar recovery. The Germans, he stated, were "known for their genius," as seen in the rebuilding of their economy to the point where "West Germany today was among the leading countries of the world in science, technology, industry, and in every field of human activity."[74]

West Germany's technical advocacy is evident in IIT Madras's early approach to pedagogy. More so than at the other IITs, German influence resulted in a curriculum "heavily focused on practical training in manual skills such as blacksmithing and woodworking."[75] On a 1961 visit to the campus, a group of MIT professors noted the German insistence "that six months of the first year and three months of the second year of undergraduate training be devoted to workshop practice."[76] The showcasing of technique as a unique West German talent is in clear evidence in the IIT Madras Heritage Center, where a number of displays depict the importance of workshop learning in the early years of the institute. One display in particular is worthy of further description. Under the heading "Workshops" appears the following summary:

> The report of the Prof. August Ruker Technical Mission (23rd November 1956) observed: "Since a broad introduction to practical work in India was of great importance in a country yet to get industrialized, the Institute should provide compulsory workshop training to the students in special workshops to be set up for the purpose." Accordingly, the visiting German experts left no stone unturned to

equip the workshops, which were one of the very first buildings to come up in the campus with the latest and the best machines, instruments and other experimental facilities. A large number of Indian experts and technicians collaborated in this task of establishing a "hands-on" culture among the students in their learning process. The Central Workshop, both from the points of view of its training programme and its potentiality for fabricating sophisticated engineering equipment, was acclaimed as the best of its kind in the country.

To drive home the importance of this "'hands-on' culture," a photograph appears below the text of Walter Scheel, minister of economic cooperation of the FRG, demonstrating his carpentry skills to then IIT Madras director B. Sengupto, who looks on with a somewhat bemused smile.

How did West Germans perceive Indian responses to technical training? We know from work on German involvement in Rourkela that the West German technologists sent to set up the steel plant found much at fault with Indian attitudes. They saw many of Rourkela's problems as the result of "the lack of a modern work ethic among the Indians."[77] They complained that "Indian workers were unwilling to take charge and neither understood the value of labor per se nor showed the required professional ambition." The West Germans reached the conclusion that if Indians "did not internalize the value of industrial work, Rourkela's production would never reach the projected output and India's industrialization would remain a dream."[78]

At times, these criticisms took on a more blatantly colonial, even civilizational tone. West Germans perceived their tutelage not simply as technical but as an education in values. The FRG's development aid policies in 1957 argued for a focus on "educational tasks in the widest sense," especially on "education toward sensible economic conduct."[79] This was echoed by a 1961 expert advisory board, which maintained that "if one wants economic development aid to succeed, one has to remodel those people's thinking through patient, tedious training." One of the most pointed remarks came from Walter Scheel, the carpenter-diplomat we met earlier, who expressed his conviction that foreign capital investment would only bear fruit if Third World societies internalized "the importance of work and craftwork, the value of the individual . . . and dynamic thinking instead of static-feudalistic ways of living."[80]

These West German perceptions of their Indian trainees echo earlier British colonial rhetoric on Indian technical capacity. Like the British before them, the West Germans were frustrated by dismissiveness toward "craftwork," but interpreted this as an Indian rather than a caste-specific characteristic. Unlike the British who reinforced caste in practice even as they decried it rhetorically, the Germans were more insistent on the need to link the industrialization of society to the modernization of the individual. In this they echoed the expectations of 1950s and 1960s modernization theory that, with exposure to the modern workplace, traditional identities and practices would give way to individuated subjects making rational choices. For the Germans, the modern workplace was transformative not just because of its social dynamics. As a space of modern techniques, it would reorient the individual mentally by remaking his body.

Non-Brahminism and Dravidianism, together with German tutelage, issued multiple challenges to the role of modern technical education in entrenching caste hierarchies. While the former suffused the Tamil public sphere, the latter was contained within an institutional setting consciously set apart from the wider universe of regional education. Non-Brahminism and Dravidianism elevated the standing of the non-Brahmin collective. German tutelage emphasized the modern individual as the site of embodied technical knowledge. Both sat uneasily with existing hierarchies of value that placed upper over lower caste. Chapter 4 turns to the reception of these frameworks by the first cohorts of IIT Madras. As we will see there and in subsequent chapters, the terms of debate set in play by Non-Brahminism, Dravidianism, and German tutelage—region versus nation, mental versus manual, lower caste versus upper caste—have lived on in IITian narratives and claims to merit. We will also see the reverberations across national and transnational arenas of a defensive Tamil Brahmin politics of meritocracy. Let us turn now from the broader currents of social transformation we have explored in this chapter to the life histories of IIT Madras's earliest alumni.

4

IIT Madras's 1960s Generation

WE HAVE SEEN that the vast majority of colonial-era engineers were from upper-caste backgrounds. Although many disdained manual labor, they embraced engineering because it was a white-collar profession whose status was enhanced by its relationship to conceptual knowledge and the colonial state. In Madras Presidency, upper castes, and Brahmins especially, were all the more amenable to engineering because the Madras College of Engineering curriculum was weighted in favor of theoretical knowledge and because the college offered a fast track to the civil services, a privileged site of professional belonging.

The founding of the IITs reinforced the institutional stratification set in place during the colonial period. They were intended to be the cream of Indian higher education, set apart from both industrial schools and regional engineering colleges. Caste served as both social structure and metaphor to render future IITians exceptional. As upper castes, they were meant to embody the Brahminical spirit of learning and be the builders of the new nation.

These trends were called into question by Non-Brahminism, Dravidianism, and German tutelage. Non-Brahminism challenged the hierarchies of value that placed Brahmin over non-Brahmin. German tutelage elevated practical knowledge as foundational to industrial society and the modern individual. How did these competing frameworks inform the making of Madras IITians? How did they come to see themselves as engineers, as nation-builders, and as upper castes?

The Institute's 1960s Alumni

The story of John Abraham, a 1969 alumnus who was an avid chronicler of IIT life, best exemplifies West German influence on the making of the 1960s IITian.[1] The trajectory of Abraham's life also illuminates the shifting ambitions of the IITs and of IITians. From being emblematic of the German-trained IITian in the 1960s, he soon became an anomaly. Abraham's shift in status is intimately linked to the changing fortunes of the German model as the early emphasis on practical training and jobs in "core engineering" was supplanted by a turn to more "conceptual" branches, such as computer science, and to careers in management, finance, and information technology. As a lifelong mechanical engineer in India, Abraham thus represents a path not taken, one oriented around the leveraging of technical expertise for national development.

In other ways, however, Abraham had much in common with other IITians. He was from an elite Syrian Christian family of English-educated professionals. Syrian Christians are a high-status Christian community in Kerala, considered to be on par with Hindu Nairs in the caste hierarchy. In the eighteenth and nineteenth centuries, they followed strict caste rules of purity and pollution and were part of the court culture of the native state of Travancore. Not only was Abraham from a high-status and affluent family, growing up in the 1960s, but he thought of himself as a nationalist subject whose technical training at the IITs placed him in an elite category of engineers called to a higher purpose. Moreover, he identified and continues to identify strongly as an IITian, an expression of institutional kinship that is the basis of both affective and material investment.

Despite these commonalities, Abraham diverged from other IITians in his sustained investment in the German model of nation- and self-making through hands-on engineering. He was also critical of the caste sensibilities of his peers, which he saw as inimical to productive labor. Abraham's similarities to and differences from his peers help to mark

shifts in career trajectories and sensibilities in a particularly illuminating way.

Here I use Abraham's story to frame the narratives of 1960s IIT
Madras alumni. I showcase the life histories of twenty alumni, including Abraham, who attended the institute over the decade. Some are
life histories that I recorded; others come from the 2008 volume *Reflections by IITians,* compiled by Ram Krishnaswamy, an IIT Madras 1970
alumnus. These are supplemented by contemporaneous documents
from the 1960s collected in a volume titled *Campaschimes: IITM
through IITian eyes.* All the life histories are retrospective construc-
tions of personal and professional lives that are mediated by the events
and experiences of the intervening forty-odd years. As a combination of
memory and reinvention, they offer a window onto life history as a narrative process of subject formation. In my analysis, I treat these accounts
as true memories that speak both to the past and to the context of their
enunciation in the late 2000s. They are also practices of self-fashioning
through which IITians narrate themselves in relation to gender, caste,
nation, and state.

The chapter begins with an account of the caste backgrounds of
early IITians. Most came from urbanized, professional families. Many
followed family members into engineering. In this sense, the IITs were
spaces of caste and class homogeneity as well as professional reproduction. These narratives point to a discrepancy between alumni from
families in the national civil services, who had an early awareness of
the IITs, and those more firmly embedded within a regional milieu.
But as I go on to show, for all 1960s IITians, the time at the institute
was one of nationalization. No matter their background, most came
to understand themselves as exceptional because of their link to state
and nation. At the same time, to be the cream of national education
was to also be world-class, an orientation that soon led to paths beyond
both public sector and nation and beyond hands-on engineering. Despite German influence, the conceptual gradually emerged once again
as distinct from, and superior to, the practical, and more fitting for
those inhabiting the highest tier of technical training. Now, however,
it was expressed through a disavowal of the state and an embrace of
diasporic and private sector trajectories.

Significantly, there is also an active disavowal of caste across most of the narratives. Unlike during the colonial period, when caste was openly embraced as the basis of modern national identity and leadership, 1960s IITians almost uniformly claim a form of post-caste subjectivity. Some even contrast the 1960s as a time of castelessness to the 2000s, when they perceive caste as having resurged and infiltrated the IITs. By contrast to this otherwise shared account, Tamil Brahmins stand out for their explicit self-marking as a caste and for their portrayal of IIT Madras as a national refuge in a context of regional caste hostilities. This, I will show, is due to the regional political milieu in which their marking as caste subjects foreclosed the claim to castelessness. As I elaborate in later chapters, the willingness of Tamil Brahmins to mark themselves in caste terms and to read their own and the institute's exceptional standing in relation to caste politics was an important precursor to what would become a more widespread national and transnational politics of meritocracy.

This chapter is a bridge between the preceding analyses of colonial and early postcolonial institutional and political histories and the following ethnographic accounts of making merit at the IITs. In looking at the experiences and perspectives of the 1960s generation of Madras IITians, I hope to throw into sharper relief the changes that followed with the expansion of the reservation system, exam coaching, and diasporic mobility.

Region and Nation

Abraham attended IIT Madras (IITM) from 1964 to 1969. His schooling was representative of the elite anglophone social profile of many early alumni. He was a graduate of La Martiniere Boys' College in Lucknow, one of India's oldest and most elite schools. He finished his schooling with the Senior Cambridge examination and then took the IIT entrance examination in Kerala. In this, he followed in the footsteps of his brother, an alumnus of IIT Kharagpur's second cohort. At the time, the IIT exam and admissions were conducted on a regional, or zonal, basis, and Abraham emerged as a front-runner for the southern zone. He admitted to having an "unfair advantage" taking the exam in Kerala, where the "pre-university standards were so miserably low that nobody who studied in Kerala could ever possibly dream of getting into IIT. . . .

The only Malayalis who would get into the system were those who studied in convent schools in Madras or in even more elite institutions like La Martiniere." By laying out the landscape of regional education in these terms, Abraham set himself apart as both socially elite and supraregional in orientation.[2]

Like Abraham, most students admitted to IIT Madras in the 1960s came from upper-caste backgrounds and went to one of two kinds of schools: private, English-medium schools, most often run by Catholic orders, or central government schools catering to the children of central government services personnel. For the first group, the discovery of IIT Madras was somewhat accidental. Although they were from professional families with histories of education, they were also firmly rooted in the wider southern region. The choice of IIT Madras over one of the other regional engineering colleges was by no means a given. As we saw in Chapter 3, the College of Engineering, Guindy was the southern region's premier technical institution and would have been the better-known choice for an engineering degree.

Balachandran, a 1969 alumnus, was in this first category of students. A Keralite from Chennai, he attended St. Mary's school and got to know about the IITs after getting into Madras's Loyola College for his pre-university course. He told me that it was a "bit of a default" that he attended IIT Madras at all.[3] "In '63, '64, IITs were not all that well known," he explained. "It was because of a couple of friends of mine who were writing the exam that I got to know about IIT. Otherwise the option generally was Guindy. And there were a few other options, like the PSG College at Coimbatore and Coimbatore Institute of Technology."

A number of alumni had fathers or other family members who had studied engineering at Guindy. Paul, a 1966 alumnus, had attended St. Bede's school for boys in Chennai and had a close connection to both engineering and Guindy. Paul's father and two elder brothers were mechanical engineers. In addition, his father was a graduate and then principal of Guindy. For Paul, the choice of engineering was a no-brainer. Like his brothers before him, his idea "was to enter a good engineering institution—either Guindy or one of the big three in Coimbatore (PSG, CIT, or GCT) and to follow my engineering dream." But his plans to attend a regional engineering college were derailed by a friend who alerted him to "the existence of the IITs and also that there was one IIT literally on our doorstep." The friend told Paul that the chances of admission were slim, since "approximately 100,000 youngsters were expected to sit for the 1st Joint Entrance Exam." This challenge appealed to him, and he decided to try his hand at the exam. When word came of his admission and selection for the Mechanical Engineering branch, he found himself at a crossroads. Because of its exalted status in his family, Paul accepted the invitation to appear for an interview at Guindy but ended up deciding on IIT Madras just a few days before the interview. It was a difficult decision because at the time, he "did not realize the numbers of doors and opportunities that would open due to that one decision."[4]

Similarly, Rajesh Vedula, a Telugu Brahmin from the very first IITM cohort, came from a family of engineers. His three brothers are engineers with lifelong careers in academia. One is the director of technical education in Andhra Pradesh, another is a professor of electronics at the Madras Institute of Technology, and the third is a professor and head of the Department of Aeronautics at the Indian Institute of Science. Engineering was a veritable family business. But Vedula's fate was sealed even more decisively by a family tragedy. His eldest brother had been a gold medalist from Guindy, where he studied from 1937 to 1941. However, a bright future was cut short by his sudden death in August 1941. When Vedula was born just over a year later, in December 1942, he was given his brother's name. As his namesake, he felt morally obliged to continue his legacy. Even so, Vedula ultimately decided to attend IIT Madras and not Guindy, his brother's alma mater. When I asked him why, he paused and then recalled feeling "excitement about getting into these new institutes of higher technology that were supposed to have high standing compared to even Guindy."[5]

For some, choosing the IITs over Guindy provoked intergenerational battles. Krishnaswamy, a 1970 alumnus from the Andaman Islands, found himself in the favorable position of having gotten admission into both IIT Madras and Guindy. Although his choice was the IIT, he had to fight his father, whose verdict was "Good: No IIT, BIT, CIT and no hostel life, just go to Guindy Engineering College." His father "believed IIT was the same as CPT—Central Poly Technique or MIT [Madras Institute of Technology]," which gave an "AMIE [associate member of the Institution of Engineers] Diploma in Engineering."[6] It took a visit to IIT Madras's impressive campus and conversations with students and faculty to convince him otherwise.

For Mathew, a 1969 Syrian Christian alumnus, the intergenerational battle was with his mother. His father, "a qualified Industrial Chemist, had told [him] about the IITs and given [him] a booklet with five years' entrance exam question papers."[7] Mathew took the IIT entrance examination in 1964 at St. Joseph's College in Tiruchirapally, "where generations of [his] family had studied before [him]." Much to his mother's chagrin, Mathew got admission. She implored him not to go away "when there [was] an ITI [industrial training institute]" right there in their town. Mathew ended his narrative with the wry observation that "'Brand IIT' may now be a universally recognized one, but obviously was not known so well among the denizens of this backwater region in those days!"[8]

The relative obscurity of "institutions of national importance" and preeminence of regional institutions was a common tale for the first group of 1960s alumni embedded within the southern educational ecosystem. However, this did not apply to the second set: the children of employees in the central government services. These were students who were already extraregional in outlook and experience. They spoke other languages, had pan-Indian itineraries as a result of parental employment, and studied in central government schools or national private schools. As a result of this national orientation, they were among the first to hear about the IITs and avail themselves of the opportunity to study there.

An example was Vijayaraj, a 1969 alumnus. Vijayaraj went to one of the Sainik Schools, which were administered by and for the Indian Army. His father was an army man and principal of his school. Much of Vijayaraj's mobile social world—he had spent his life moving across northern cities—consisted of other families in the central services. In fact, it was one of his father's engineer friends in the central services who told him about the IITs.[9]

Similarly, Baliga, another 1969 alumnus, came to know about the IITs through his father's networks. His father was about as entrenched in the national engineering service as one could be. He had been the first chief engineer at All-India Radio, then chairman and managing director of Bharat Electronics Ltd., and finally founder of the Institute of Telecommunications Engineers. This was a family with a social network and a worldview that was more attuned to the IITs as fledgling national institutions than to the regionally based system of education.[10]

Among these students with parents in the central government services, many were diasporic Tamil Brahmins from northern metropolises like Delhi and Bombay, whose families had been part of colonial and postcolonial bureaucracies. Several from Delhi had attended the Delhi Tamil Education Association higher secondary schools. Popularly known as Madrasi schools, these are private, government-aided schools that cater specifically to the Tamil diaspora. As upper castes whose families had sought employment elsewhere to escape the politics of Non-Brahminism, many of them were also resolutely antiregional. One Madrasi alumnus, Thyagarajan, narrated a life history that fit a typical pattern of Tamil Brahmin mobility. His grandfather was a landlord and *kanakkupillai,* or revenue collector, in a village in Madras Presidency's Thanjavur district. Over the course of a generation, four of his five male children migrated to Delhi, and the remaining son took on the role of *kanakkupillai.* In Delhi, the four sons "followed the family tradition" and finished college degrees in accounting. Thyagarajan's father went on to government jobs in the postal service and then in the Indian Agricultural Research Institute. He described his Delhi world as a mini-Madras of Tamil Brahmins with a Tamil Sangam (Society), a Carnatic music association, and a Bhajan Sangam. It was also one that became intimately linked to the IITs; from Thyagarajan's school cohort alone, fourteen students were admitted to IIT Madras.[11]

Madrasi schools were among the most highly regarded in Delhi, where word of the IITs caught on especially early. Sri Kumar, a 1968 IITM alumnus, recalled forty years hence that "everyone" from his Madrasi school was taking the JEE. Madrasi students did not lack in self-regard derived from a sense of urban cosmopolitanism as Delhiites. Iswaran, another Madrasi school product and 1969 IITM alumnus, conveyed this in self-mocking terms. "When I first came to IIT Madras," he confessed, "I was full of myself. After all, I was the graduate of the prestigious DTEA (Madrasi) Higher Secondary School . . . and

I was moving from the cosmopolitan capital of India to a relatively hick town in South India."[12]

We see from these early accounts that, in the 1960s, alumni came with different senses of belonging. While most were upper-caste Hindus or Christians from family histories of higher education, only a minority had a pan-Indian sensibility that came from being members of an internal diaspora of civil servants. Still, IIT Madras had a leavening effect that produced an overall reorientation from region to nation. It was an education not just in engineering but in a new hierarchy of value, in which the region and its institutions paled in comparison. Being an elite engineer with an IIT pedigree meant being a national one. The growing divide between regional and national education confirmed Nazir Ahmed's fears about the IIT system's exclusivity and isolation from the wider world of Indian engineering. As we will see in subsequent chapters, this divide further widened in later decades with IITians' departure both from engineering and from India.

It was no accident that students became national subjects over their years on campus. As we saw in Chapter 2, the IITs were established with this specific purpose in mind. The exceptionalism of the IIT system was embodied in its transcendence of regional education and its ambition of producing a national cadre of engineers. This sense of collective purpose—even destiny—was consciously cultivated through official annual rituals of commencement and matriculation, at which visiting dignitaries reinforced the IITs' hallowed standing. The nationalism of the time was also intimately linked to science and socialism. As Mathew put it, "In those idealistic times the first flush of independence still lingered and most educated Indians were inspired by Gandhian thought and Nehruvian socialism. Like them, I was eager to acquire 'the scientific temper.'"[13] The affective link to the state and its projects was by no means limited to IIT Madras. Sandipan Deb notes that before weekly film screenings at IIT Kharagpur, students had to watch a government-sponsored documentary that proclaimed the IITs to be "Nehru's dream."[14]

In alumni memories of campus life, national affiliation comes through powerfully as a defining feature of the IIT experience. Hardly anyone failed to mention the melting pot experience of IIT Madras, where one met students "from Kanyakumari to Kashmir."[15] Vedula attributed this sense of cohesiveness to the first of IITM's directors, B. Sengupto. "The director really promoted the national integration of all the students," he recalled. "He essentially wanted to make IIT Madras the technological Shantiniketan."[16] Others, like Iswaran, put it in less hallowed terms that perfectly captures the propensity for regional stereotyping: "I had never laid eyes on a Jew before, nor had I ever met a Sardarji who spoke English fluently. Add to this, a Sindhi who spoke better Tamil than I did and a sprinkling of UP walas (whom I had always thought of as dumber than a bag of rocks) who knew more mathematics than I did. Finally throw in a Golti who carried his own toilet paper! I was totally flabbergasted and humbled within a matter of days."[17]

The resort to poetry was a common one in those days and reflected the enduring influence of British-style education in elite anglophone schools. One 1962 poet encapsulated regional diversity in a poem titled "Impressions," which ended with a lament about the workload at IIT Madras:

> Delhi: Concrete structures, bustling streets.
> Kerala: Communists and calm retreats.
> Gujarat: Gandhi caps and millionaires.
> Maharashtra: Marine drive and Western airs.
> Orissa: Gushing Mahanadi, floods and blushing belles.
> Nagaland: Recesses, Ravines and Rowdy Rebels.
> Andhra: Mangoes, Mica, Charminar.
> Punjab: Akali Dal and Chandigarh.
> Mysore: Coffee, spices, Chamundi Hills.
> Bengal: Classicists and mundane mills.
> Jammu & Kashmir: Lakes, houseboats, eternal snow.
> Assam: Oil rigs and the rare rhino.
> Uttar Pradesh: The moonlit Taj Mahal and the laughing hyena.
> Madras: Gopurams, natyams, the famed Marina.
> Rajasthan: Pseudo tiger-hunts, deserts, durbars.
> Bihar: Unsung source of fragrant cigars.
> Madhya Pradesh: Desperate dacoits and manganese.
> IIT: Periodicals and constant 'D's.[18]

Caste and Class

Much of the commentary on social differences faithfully echoed statist discourse about unity in diversity. Even when pushed to consider other differences, most alumni only flagged them in the most anodyne terms. "There were some variations," Balachandran admitted. "Maybe some could speak English more fluently, others could not speak English that fluently. That would have been the only difference. Some people might have known how to eat with a fork and a spoon, some people would not have known how to eat with a fork, but they picked up in no time. Some people liked fish curry and rice, some people liked sambar and payasam."

Sometimes the denial of meaningful differences was more vehement. "There were no social divisions," Balachandran insisted emphatically. "Nobody said, for example, that you are a Keralite, or that you are a north Indian, and you are a Brahmin, you are a . . . no, nobody looked at whether you are a Brahmin or a Scheduled Caste or whatever. I mean, it was immaterial. People ate from the same plate, they drank from the same glass, they would sleep in the same bed sometimes." Significantly, he contrasted what he experienced as a more egalitarian time with the 2000s. There had been a "societal change" in caste consciousness, he brooded, that had even "infected" IIT Madras. "In 1996, 32 years later, my son got into IIT Madras," Balachandran continued,

> The dormitories were overcrowded so they were placing two students to a room. My son had to share it with another Keralite, and when we went in and put in his baggage, the parent and the other boy also came. My wife and I were quite surprised. We don't carry a, what you might call a family name. We don't say we are a Menon or we are an Iyengar or Parmar. We had dropped all that by that time. The other family was quite worried, and finally they couldn't contain themselves, and they asked my wife, "Are you all Scheduled Caste?" because the other boy was a Brahmin.

Balachandran and his wife proceeded to tell the other parents that his wife's parents were from the royal family of Cochin, "and that kind of seemed to reassure them." The whole exchange made him "very sad because that was a question we never would have asked." When I asked to what he attributed this change, he replied, "I would say to a large extent it could be awareness, but the political direction that it took and the political climate, with more emphasis on reservations . . . and of course some people are just hung up about these things."

Balachandran's perception of caste divisions as evidence of a more recent politicization of caste, and his emphasis on reservation as the root cause, is a common upper-caste tale. It speaks to the comfortable inhabitation of an unmarked upper-caste category in the early postindependence years, especially within elite spaces like the IITs. At IIT Madras, the insulation from regional caste politics offered by central government education added to this feeling of castelessness. For Balachandran, being an IITian in the 1960s simply meant being a modern national subject who had transcended the unseemly social divisions of Indian life. This was made possible by the near absence of anyone who was explicitly marked as lower caste. In contrast to the anxious query by his son's roommate's parent, the unthinking assumption in his day was that your peers were all upper castes like you. It was such a naturalized fact of inhabiting an institution of national excellence that it hardly needed stating.

While Balachandran denied the salience of caste in his day, he did acknowledge class differences, although he insisted that even these ultimately did not matter. "I knew many boys who were from middle class families or lower middle class families who got in," he recalled, "and they were living on scholarships." He continued:

> Many of them have done exceptionally well. They were bright, very bright, and it had nothing to do with your father's standing, or the earning capacity of your parents or wealth in your family. That may have given you better exposure at that point of time. To that extent, yes, when you came in you did have an advantage. In terms of the exposure that you had already had, you could participate in things like debates, you could speak English more fluently, so to that extent. . . . But as far as the curriculum was concerned, you had to just have the brains. That's all.

With this distinction between "exposure" and "brains," or nurture and nature, Balachandran insisted that the 1960s IITian was best defined by natural talent and not social background.

For others, however, wealth differences weren't quite so inconsequential to either academic ability or social standing on campus. Several 1960s alumni mentioned classmates from industrialist and other well-to-do families who stood out because of their wealth and sophistication. Several were also "toppers" in classes. I asked Vijayaraj whether there was a way of describing the toppers sociologically, to which he replied without hesitation, "Yeah, they were mostly from rich families." The most common indicators of wealth were facility with English and access to luxury goods. Of such goods, the most conspicuous was the car. Vijayaraj made a point of mentioning that his two wealthiest classmates both had fancy cars. One from Chennai would spend his weekends at home. "Every weekend, a Mercedes used to come and pick him up," he recollected. The other was also from a local family. "IIT is a big campus," Vijayaraj explained, "so to go from the hostel, we had bicycles. But this guy, first he had a motorbike, and soon, by the second year he had a Mazda car, one of those small matchbox cars. Mazda car, a Japanese car, in those days he had a Mazda car! And he had a stereo, so his room was always full of friends because all these goodies were there." Such luxuries, especially a foreign car, were rare at that time of protectionist tariffs and became notable markers of status.

Even for IITians who regarded wealth differences as consequential, class was a form of social hierarchy that effaced rather than provoked considerations of caste. In part, this was because caste differences were largely absent or hidden at IIT Madras, with its overwhelmingly upper-caste faculty and student body. Even after the implementation of reservation for Scheduled Castes and Scheduled Tribes (SCs and STs)—those occupying the lowest rung of the governmental schedule of castes—in 1973, the demographic weight of upper castes and the extreme marginalization of SC and ST students translated as the nonconsideration of the caste question.

The illegibility of caste was further reinforced by IITians from lower middle class and rural backgrounds, whose stories worked to neutralize caste as a form of capital. Dasigi, a 1966 Brahmin alumnus from Orissa, is an example of someone who described himself as an outlier in class terms. His father had joined the Bengal-Nagpur Railway as a railway guard on a monthly salary of sixty rupees. However, this did not prevent him from living his dream through his sons. Even before Dasigi started school, his father was telling him about IIT Kharagpur. It is only when recounting the admission interview that the father's social network comes into view. At the interview to determine his campus and field, his father "met one of his contemporaries from college days. They recognized each other and exchanged pleasantries." The friend turned out to be a professor at IIT Madras, who advised Dasigi to choose metallurgical engineering, "since the steel industry was offering great employment opportunities."[19] This was a new beginning for the family. "Once I was in IITM with financial support, the entire family learned more about getting into IITs. Three years later my younger brother got into IITM (Aeronautical Engineering) and he got his scholarship based on his performance at the entrance examination itself. In 1967, a cousin of mine got into IITM (Mechanical Engineering). In 1982 another cousin joined IITM (Computer Science) and the greatest pleasure was when my brother's son got into IITM (Civil Engineering) in 1997!"[20]

Dasigi's narrative is revealing both for what it says and for what it does not say. By his account, his family succeeded against the odds in producing five IITians. What are mentioned, but in terms that do not unsettle the dominant narrative of class disadvantages, are the structural conditions for this favorable outcome: the fact that his father was an upper-caste college graduate who had a government job and professional friends. Unlike paternal perseverance and individual grit, these forms of caste capital are presented as mere happenstance and not attributed real causal force.

There is a similar absence of caste in the story of Shenoy, a 1965 Brahmin alumnus. Like Dasigi, Shenoy was raised outside India's major metropolitan centers in Bantwal, "a minor trading town on the banks of Netravati, 25 km from Mangalore." He recounted "boyhood thrills of seeing our roads asphalted for the first time (1953) and the coming of electricity (1957)."[21] As with Dasigi, Shenoy talked of his arrival at IIT Madras as a minor miracle. He had studied in the regional language, Kannada, until he completed his School Leaving Certificate examination, at which point he moved to St. Aloysius College, where English was the medium of instruction. The move was profoundly unsettling. At Aloysius College, he "found it difficult to ask a question, because of [his] inability and shyness to speak in English."[22] He had to master a new language, learn new subjects, and get accustomed to a new environment after having been schooled in a village. The adjustments were so overwhelming that he almost dropped out and returned home, but he ended up staying and getting ranked ninth statewide in the Pre-University Exam. This was his ticket to IIT Madras, which he had heard about from his "classmate Janardhan Baliga from Bantwal, who knew a little more about the outside world than [he] did." Shenoy came away from this experience with an appreciation for the power of English education. When he became an employee of Conoco, the American oil and gas company, he started Bantwal's first English medium school. Despite this, he notes regretfully, "for the next 46 years there have been none from this town who went to IITs."[23]

In these narratives, we see a foregrounding of personal and professional ambition—one might even call it an ideology of individual destiny. Class is a form of social disability that is heroically overcome by a combination of family support and individual intellect. These are stories of self-actualization. What is much less apparent is the relationship between individual achievement and caste networks. This is even more striking given how much families *do* figure in the narratives. The combination of presence and absence conveys an impression of family and community as interpersonal but not structural, which is reinforced by the silence around caste. The vast majority of IITians privileged nation and sometimes class as forms of collectivity while vociferously disavowing caste and casteism. Their sense of themselves as technical moderns whose merit was earned and deserved simply did not allow for the possibility that caste was a factor either structurally or affectively.

There was, however, one set of students who *were* willing to talk about caste: Tamil Brahmins. However, they did so not to mark their own inherited capital but for the opposite purpose. They had opted to take the IIT exam to bypass a set of educational barriers: regional quotas for lower castes. At IIT Madras, these were mostly less affluent Tamil Brahmins who came from histories of education but were not part of the nationally oriented set of central government employees. Kalyanaraman, a 1966 Tamil Brahmin alumnus, conveyed this perspective most clearly. He made a point of distinguishing himself from his more urbane, non-Brahmin classmates. "I didn't study in any of the convent schools or other schools," he emphasized. "Up to SSLC, I studied in Tamil medium."²⁴ His father had been an electrical engineer with the Tamilnadu Electricity Board, and he had done most of his schooling outside Chennai in Vellore's Sri Venkateswara High School and Madurai's American College. "Most of the people that you see here today, from my generation at least, are all ordinary, middle class people from educated families," he noted. "That was the only criterion: we thought education was important."

The "we" Kalyanaraman was referring to were Tamil Brahmins. When I asked him whether people knew about the IITs in the 1960s, he replied, "People at large did not, but my father was an engineer, he's from an engineering college. He got a gold medal from a government engineering college."

"Guindy?" I asked.

"Yes, Guindy Engineering College," Kalyanaraman replied.

"So, why did he send you to IIT? Why not Guindy?" I persisted.

"Because Guindy wouldn't give me a seat, because I'm Brahmin. So, IIT was the only avenue for us all."

Despite the fact that many of his Tamil Brahmin counterparts were more affluent urbanites, like the students of Madrasi schools, Kalyanaraman chose to group himself with them and in contradistinction to other non-Brahmin elites. For him, Tamil Brahmins were by definition "ordinary, middle-class people" who prioritized education but were unfairly denied access to regional institutions. Moreover, Kalyanaraman faulted Dravidian politics for this recent change, which affected his generation in a way that it had not affected his father's.

As mentioned in the Introduction, anthropologists Chris Fuller and Haripriya Narasimhan offer a sustained analysis of the mutual constitution of Tamil Brahminness and middle classness.²⁵ In their 2014 book *Tamil Brahmans: The Making of a Middle-Class Caste,* they show in exhaustive detail that the Tamil Brahmin transformation into a middle class has everything to do with the forms of caste-based capital—land ownership, ritual purity, literacy—that they are able to leverage. They also point out that Tamil Brahmins express a sense of being middle class in two key ways. First, by transmuting "their caste's traditional value of ascetical self-restraint—symbolized by vegetarianism . . . into the modern, middle-class virtues of self-discipline and moderation."²⁶ Second, through a claim to intellectual superiority and educational attainment, which marks a departure from older claims to ritual purity as the basis of elevated status. Despite such evidence, Fuller and Narasimhan come to the conclusion that Tamil Brahmin "social stability is not primarily caused by persisting caste privilege, but by class reproduction operating within a modern society and economy."[27]

My own analysis builds on theirs but shows that rather than class supplanting caste as the primary mechanism of social reproduction, the two are inextricably linked.[28] The distinction between class and caste is belied by their structural and affective entanglements. For instance, Dasigi's and Shenoy's stories show how prevalent avenues into the middle class are for Brahmins because of the institutional and social caste networks that allow for mobility. Moreover, the powerful discursive trope of Brahmin intellectual superiority continues to suffuse the most lucrative sectors of the Indian economy—most clearly information technology—and creates unique opportunities for less affluent upper castes. For instance, Super 30 at the Ramanujan School of Mathematics, an IIT-JEE coaching institute, aims to discover the next Srinivasa Ramanujan, a poor Tamil Brahmin autodidact reputed to be one of the greatest mathematical minds of all time. Caste continues to be a powerful index of value that channels affective and material investment to shape class formation. Finally, as we see from Kalyanaraman's account, the intimacy between class and caste is a pervasive theme in Tamil Brahmin self-representation. For him, class is an identity that works discursively to efface the advantages of caste and transform Tamil Brahminness from the product of accumulated literacy, education, and professional advancement into a disability. In the process, lower-caste politics is faulted for denying Tamil Brahmins their rights, while upper casteness is made into a power-neutral form of identity.

What is less clear is whether this claim to a middle-class identity through the effacing of historical advantages is a retrospective move on Kalyanaraman's part or one that had equal resonance in the 1960s. It may well have been the case that Kalyanaraman opted for the IITs to bypass the regional reservation system; this does not mean that he had *then* the strong sense of being middle class that he has *now*. As we will see in Chapter 7, this sense of Tamil Brahminness as a middle-class identity firmly associated with meritocracy has only strengthened over time. Not only has it gotten stronger for Tamil Brahmins,

but it has informed an expanded politics through which IITians as a
whole have come to define themselves in more explicitly identitarian
terms in opposition to lower-caste rights.

The Mental and the Manual

Whereas Tamil Brahmin alumni were the most explicit about their
caste identities, others echoed ideologies of caste through remarks
about intelligence. This is where the distinction between the mental
and the manual and the assumption that conceptual ability is the true
measure of merit come back into view. Even before the JEE coalesced
into a nationally celebrated examination, with its fetishized ranking
system, IITians had an obsessive need to rank one another. Before the
JEE began in 1961, students were selected on the basis of their standing
in high school as toppers. The advent of the exam only reinforced this
sense of intellectual worth.

When they arrived on campus, however, many students found their
sense of self-worth upended by the presence of "genius." They were
"now in a different league." Across cohorts, the stories of peer brilliance abound. "Here, there were geniuses," Vijayaraj told me. "They
didn't study for the exam. They'd just come, and before the exam they
spent time teaching others. This was unbelievable. You wouldn't believe it unless you experienced it. That's the kind of people who were
there. And in every class, there were three or four."

Very often, alumni compared these peer geniuses and their in-born
capability with the mediocre faculty. As Vijayaraj put it, "Most of the
lecturers were just ordinary. It was the brilliance of your classmates
that made the experience so special." Some faculty came in for stronger
derision. Nageshwar, a 1964 alumnus, noted that "Mr. V. S. Kumar (Humanities) reminisced at the reunion (35th) that before his first lecture
to us, he was gripped by fear and awe at facing the assemblage of brains
in front of him!"[29]

There is a near consensus across cohorts that they learned more
outside the classroom through interaction with their brilliant peers
than from teachers in the classroom. Kalyanaraman drew this comparison most sharply by referring to an incident with his Tamil Brahmin
classmate, Shankar. "In one of the physics classes when he started
asking some questions the lecturer said, Shankar, I think you know

more than me. Can you take the class? He just challenged him. And Shankar came and took the class." Significantly, none of the stories of "genius" had to do with technical prowess. Almost all featured forms of conceptual or theoretical mastery long associated with being upper caste. How did these evaluations of relative intelligence intersect with the German insistence on hands-on technique?

All the IITs had a workshop requirement for practical training. Sandipan Deb points to the workshop as a key distinction between the IITs and MIT. "The IIT student was also to spend far more time on practical training than at MIT," he writes. Unlike at MIT, IITians "would actually have to file, forge and weld metal" and "sweat through hundreds of hours of this."[30]

At IIT Madras, the German connection further enhanced this emphasis on the practical dimensions of engineering. Abraham recalled that all the laboratories were headed by Germans, who tried to instill in their students the value of practical work. Not just the students, they also insisted that professors and faculty associated with a lab should have their offices on the premises rather than in a separate academic building. This, Abraham remarked wryly, "was in contrast to our traditional attitude of isolating practical work which is typically perceived as inferior to intellectual activity!"

Like his German mentors, Abraham relished lab work. "Contrary to the opinion of a great majority of my contemporaries," he attested, "my verdict is that we had a damn good curriculum, provided one was seeking a career in hardcore engineering. Since that was true in my case, I took my workshop and drawing and lab exercises quite seriously, and of course my final year project. I think the facilities we had with regard to lab equipment, library, classrooms, hostels and so on were excellent, at least for our country at the time. I doubt whether any single German university had the full range of facilities and departments which we enjoyed." Abraham's aspiration to be a "hardcore" engineer made him an outlier. His focus on the content of an IIT education rather than on the status of the IITs as "institutions of national importance" came out of what he characterized as his "natural affinity" for mechanical engineering. "Right from childhood days," he recalled, "I worked with mechanics and was fascinated by it, by building things . . . opening up alarm clocks, that type of thing."

Thinking back to his choice of vocation, he noted, "It must have been the sight of a steam locomotive puffing steam and spewing smoke that first triggered my fascination for the career path which I ultimately followed." He also attributed it to the historical moment. "A small boy growing up in the 1950s was likely to encounter a variety of mechanical devices and contraptions ranging from clocks to road rollers to exercise his curiosity," he pointed out. This was a very different time from the present, when external stimulus for children "may be quite substantially restricted to pixel arrays on a display screen of some kind."

When I asked him why he chose IIT Madras, he said it was because his brother's experience at IIT Kharagpur had attracted him to German training. "Even in Kharagpur there were some German professors," he explained, "and my brother got a scholarship to go to Germany." His brother's positive experience with Germans sealed the deal for Abraham. He opted for IIT Madras because, as he saw it, West German influence meant a stronger mechanical engineering curriculum.

Abraham singled out his German professors as particularly inspirational. "One German professor," he recollected, "taught me turbo machines. . . . I think I picked up half my engineering knowledge in . . . those lectures. The way he expressed things, the way he drew diagrams, I found absolutely fascinating. Although he had a funny accent and mostly the students would make fun of him, I made it a point to really take him very seriously. And that influenced me a lot. . . . Even among the Indian professors, those who had the Indian industrial experience, I could notice the difference in their approach." Abraham's time in the IIT classroom eventually led him out of academia. This was because, as he put it, "those [faculty] who had industrial experience, they made the subject come alive." Those who "possessed only textbook knowledge . . . their lectures lacked life and liveliness."

But by all accounts, the German emphasis on valuing practical knowledge had mixed results. Most students experienced workshop activity as an encounter with the unknown. A 1970 graduate who became the additional director-general of police and the chairman and managing director of Karnataka State Police Housing Corporation recounted to Deb "the shock of the first metal workshop." In their very first week, they were taken to the tooling workshop and told to file down an iron cube. "Most of us filed away the rust and took the piece to the instructor who laughed at us," he recalled. "He told us what we were in for: we had to file a full three inches off! It was raw physical work in extremely hot and humid conditions. Those tender hands that all of us had come to IIT with turned callused and tough overnight."[31] Another alumnus was more pointed about the cultural dissonance that the workshop requirement produced. "The rigorous workshop training," he explained, "was naturally a sore point with most of the students, for obvious reasons rooted in the traditional structure of Indian society."[32] While some rationalized their aversion to practical training through oblique references to caste, others defended this side of their education— not through caste critique but by invoking the conception of the engineer as a combination of the mental and the manual. As one alumnus put it,

> Some die-hards, the forever unsatisfied set of wise-guys, indignantly point out the absolutely impractical point of view involved in having a rigid workshop programme, devoid of almost all engineering values for the ever suffering first year students. They insist we aren't going to become workmen and vehemently condemn anything that calls for a test of brawns coupled with brains. They would rather specialize in the brains department—of course, whether they *can* or *cannot* is quite immaterial. And here's where they make their biggest slip. For after all, a workman knows *how*, a theoretical man knows *why*, but a good engineer should know the How *and* the Why.[33]

During the first year, students were divided into four groups—A, B, C, and D—with A and B and C and D alternating between weeks devoted to theory and workshop. Abraham, who was in group A, recalled how "over the hostel mess tables, C and D listened to our horror tales of what was in store for them [in the workshop]. . . . The half-day on Saturday was a blessed relief, just three hours of drawing preceded by Maths. . . . I think most of the students deeply resented the emphasis on workshop skills." By Abraham's assessment, he was one of a small minority that saw practical training as integral to the process of becoming an engineer. In an essay for the IIT alumni magazine, he staged a debate with another 1960s Madras IITian, who expressed his strong objection to the required amount of practical training. "When I reflect on our extraordinary emphasis on 'practical training' in terms of fitting, carpentry etc.," he wrote, "I seriously question the usefulness of that type of practical training. When there is so much to learn in such a limited time, our time would have been better utilized in learning about the theories underlying engineering principles. Since the practical training emphasis was suggested, and perhaps even imposed by the Germans, it was never even questioned."[34] Abraham responded with the following: "This is probably the most prevalent view among IITM alumni, and seems to reflect the 'brahminical' attitude of our educated elite towards practical skills, whichever community we may belong to. I hold a diametrically opposite view, because in my experience, those who get into IIT are mostly from the privileged or affluent sections, whose motivation is not to take up engineering but to make it good in life by any means."[35]

How did Abraham arrive at this heterodox stance? His time in Germany, where he spent a year on an internship, was formative. He was struck by how German diploma programs to train engineers for industry were valued equally with university research programs for future academics. He was also highly impressed by the pace of postwar reconstruction, which he attributed to German grit and technical efficiency. Abraham received his training at the head office of one of the biggest mechanical engineering companies in Germany. "Socially also, I found it very interesting," he recalled, "because it was a factory which had been absolutely flattened at the end of the Second World War. Because they were making armaments, like all the big concerns, of course, were doing. So, they had built it back brick by brick and then a lot of people, handicapped people, with one arm missing, one leg missing . . . they brought this thing back, and the kind of pride it took . . . that old generation was still there."

German appreciation for practical knowledge was most visibly on display in the workshops. So, too, was the pejorative assessment of Indians. "They were used to Indians coming occasionally as trainees from other organizations," Abraham pointed out, "so, I found that there was already a bias against Indians, in the sense that they had already got the impression that Indians are people who don't like to do any work. So, I had to prove myself. Once I showed that I was interested, then I found that they really opened up. Because, otherwise they said that, you people have this lofty attitude, and that we don't lift our fingers."

Abraham dwelt at length on one episode that captured for him the difference between German and elite Indian attitudes toward physical labor. "A couple of times, you know, I was ashamed," he confessed.

> I was in the workshops, I used to wear overalls and I would be put with a team of people, assembling things. . . . I had to go to different stations, assembling these big diesel engines. . . . I was there just as a trainee. [The trainer] asked me to pick up something that was under a workbench with a lot of things piled up underneath. It was a fairly heavy item. I tried to reach it; I couldn't get it. So I told him I can't get it. He didn't say a word. He just got down on the floor, crawled underneath the bench and pulled it out and I felt really ashamed of myself. He set an example for me like that, because I was supposed to be taking instructions from him. He never said a word.

For Abraham, this wasn't simply a one-off; it was emblematic of racial difference. "I started observing the disciplined way in which the bulk of them work," he said emphatically.

> By and large the attitude to work, how carefully you assemble a whole series of things. You finish one by one. They would line it up neatly at the end of the table. Our tendency is, you know, okay you finish one you throw it there, you throw it there. . . . But, you know, the sense of discipline, which was inculcated probably due to the war, the period of war, after the war, whatever it is, but basically they are a disciplined race. I could see those things. And that goes into all their thinking, in their design, in the systematic way they do it. All these things fascinated me.

Abraham's sense of shame in the face of German competence and his desire to emulate what he saw as national racial discipline demands further analysis. On the one hand, he leveraged German technique to advance a critique of Indian upper-caste assumptions about the superiority of intellectual over manual labor. On the other hand, he was in thrall to the civilizational logic that elevates Western industry over Eastern indolence. Paradoxically, Abraham rejected caste hierarchy only to back into an acceptance of racial hierarchy. Significantly, his admiration for German technique was not even tempered by the politics of the war; not once in all of Abraham's appreciative remarks about Germany did Nazism receive any mention. Even as he reflected on German technique as national racial talent, the political did not intrude.

Abraham may have been a minority, but he was not alone in his frustrations with the prevalent attitude in the IITs toward practical training. Raghavan, a 1960s alumnus, was also exasperated with the privileging of theory by many of the faculty. He had "always been very 'hands-on' and had spent the previous years in high school making and flying model airplanes." Getting into the Aeronautical Engineering branch at IIT Madras was "the ultimate dream." But, he recalled, it was a "huge letdown" from the very first lecture. "The instructor walked into the classroom, went straight to the blackboard and started drawing curly brackets with i, j, and k sprinkled here and there." Raghavan waited to be told "what all this had to do with Aircraft Design."[36] He never found out because the course was limited to Set Theory. By the third year, Raghavan was fed up and decided to start a rocket club with some classmates, but their "grandiose plans for a multi-stage rocket" were thwarted by the faculty discovering their secret lab.[37]

Raghavan went on to a job with the Oil and Natural Gas Corporation's Bombay Offshore project. "There was no way this was going to be theoretical," he remembers thinking. On his first assignment, he was put in charge of maintenance on an offshore oil drilling rig. "I was literally 'At Sea!'" he bemoaned. "They assumed I knew everything just because of my engineering degrees! This was a job for a Real Engineer, not me. My mechanic essentially told me how to do my job."[38] Raghavan returned to academia a year later for an advanced degree in the United States at the Georgia Institute of Technology. At an interview with his future adviser, he was complimented on his level of analytical competence and asked if he had "ever worked on something practical and actually built any piece of hardware." When Raghavan admitted that he had, his adviser "burst out with a spontaneous response, 'Aha! A Practical Hindu!'" and then went on to explain that "he had met numerous Indians who were very good at theory but had no good practical feel for things."[39] We see here an echo of the pejorative colonial assessment of upper-caste practical skill, although in the U.S. diaspora the specificity of caste is obscured by a generic conception of the impractical Hindu.

Masculinity

We might think of the privileging of theory and intellectual one-upmanship that pervades the IITs in terms of a culture of upper-caste, homosocial masculinity. The IITs are overwhelmingly male campuses; the percentage of women has never exceeded ten. On campus, students experience an extended period of intense male sociality, a four-year ritual of collective bonding out of which they emerge as IITians. It even comes with a soundtrack, a specific IIT slang through which these in-group, fraternal relations are expressed and cemented.[40]

But the forms of male bonding forged on campus are predated by another key set of male relationships within the family. As mentioned earlier, many alumni had male engineers in their families, whether these were fathers, brothers, or uncles. Even for those who did not personally choose engineering as a desirable field, going into the technical sciences was a by-product of male example and pressure.

The relationship between sons and fathers is a thread that runs through all the narratives. Many alumni whose fathers were engineers recounted their choice of the IITs as an extension of these relationships. For some, entering the IITs was the realization of paternal aspirations. For others, it was simply the only choice imaginable. For all of them, fathers were a critical point of reference in forging their own paths as men and as professionals.

Dasigi's is the story with the most reverential attitude to "the father," who is the all-sacrificing elder deferring his dreams to the next generation. For some, like Paul, the order is reversed. His father is an example to emulate but one that remains beyond reach. He refers to his father as "a born engineer" who "enjoyed getting involved with engineering issues of all types." By contrast, Paul confesses, he was "not a born engineer," but "being brought up in a home like ours, one couldn't think of any other profession as a future career."[41]

Baliga's father also looms large but in a slightly different way. Unlike Paul, for whom engineering was a default option, Baliga shared his father's passion for electrical engineering and wanted to follow in his footsteps. But he wanted to do so without using his father's "considerable influence." The IIT exam was a way to prove that he could gain admission to a prestigious institution without his father having to pull strings. Because he was ranked in the top fifty on the JEE exam, Baliga was able to choose any branch at any campus. Instead of exercising an independent choice, he "dutifully" consulted his father, who, "to [his] chagrin . . . promptly stated 'Mechanical Engineering.'" What followed was a mixed blessing. Baliga recounts that "fortunately, during my entrance interview at IIT-M, the panel chairman stated 'You must want to join the Electrical Engineering curriculum because of your father's background,' to which I immediately replied 'yes.'"[42] Despite his initial gesture of independence, then, Baliga was only able to follow his chosen track because of his father.

For Vijayaraj, the son of an army man, engineering was a kind of masculine middle ground. His younger brother was his father's heir: he had gone to the National Defense Academy and become a decorated lieutenant general. "But I was not so well on the physical side," Vijayaraj told me, and so he was unable to continue the patrilineal tradition of army service. In any case, his heart was in teaching mathematics. However, his father's derision when told about his choice—"You want to become just a *vathiyar* [teacher]?"—made him opt for engineering, which, even if not sufficiently "manly," was at least more lucrative.

Through these narratives, we see the father as the exemplar, the dreamer, the motivator, or the authoritarian. By contrast to the sometimes adversarial but always motivating relationship with fathers, mothers—when they appear at all—play quite a different role. They are nurturers but ones that inadvertently inhibit ambition. Mathew's story about his mother, who preferred that he attend an industrial school at home than move away to IIT Madras, is a case in point. Similarly, Krishnaswamy talked about his mother expecting the worst from the IIT exam and "quietly preparing me for the rude shock and sweet talking me into studying B.Sc. Physics at Vivekananda College; closer to home in Mylapore was the appeal."[43] When considered together, these narratives convey the sense that if left up to mothers, those who are destined for excellence would sink into mediocrity.

These early, formative relationships with fathers set the stage for the peer relationships that followed at IIT Madras. Almost to a person, alumni idealize these campus friendships. It is clear that for many, these bonds of institutional kinship lasted a lifetime. The innumerable tales of quirky personalities, slapstick escapades, and mutual support both while at IIT and after are suffused with admiration and competition in equal measure. In some ways, this combative intimacy is a predictable outcome of campus life. But for IITians, there is the added dimension of feeling like the chosen ones. The ties that bind are not simply personal; they shore up a sense of collective destiny.

State and Public Sector

For 1960s alumni, this sense of upper-caste, masculine destiny was reinforced by a link to the state. It is easy to forget from today's vantage point, after economic liberalization and the information technology boom, that the IITs began as institutions more aligned with the older, late colonial model of producing technical expertise for public sector engineering. While they were always endowed with an exceptional world-class status that arguably oriented them more outward than inward, this did not mean a total disavowal of the state. The experiences of IIT Madras alumni from the first decade of the institute's history reveal an identification with the state that has fractured in the decades since.

Sometimes the connection to the state was fostered through militarism. The first two cohorts of IIT Madras students graduated together in 1964 because the 1962 Sino-Indian border conflict had made war preparedness a new state imperative. The Indian government wanted to quickly produce more engineers who could be pressed into military-related technical work. As the institute's 1962–1963 annual report states, "The unprovoked aggression by China on our Northern borders posed a grim challenge to the country and institutions like the IIT Madras. We are happy to record that the Institute, in its own humble way, rose to the occasion gamely. National Cadet Corps training was made compulsory for certain years of the B. Tech degree course so as to ensure disciplined military training to the youth in the context of the Chinese menace. The Five Year Degree course was accelerated in order to turn out more engineers in response to the call of the country."[44]

K. Narayanan, an alumnus from the second cohort, noted in a newspaper interview that their syllabus "was rushed through and the final examinations were conducted in December 1964." N. R. Dave, one of Narayanan's batch-mates, added that "due to this, we were called the 'emergency' batch."[45]

For some, the relationship to military service continued after graduation. Narayanan, who graduated as a chemical engineer, joined Indian Oil's Guwahati Refinery in 1965, when the Indo-Pakistan War was just beginning. "The engineers at the refinery had to go on night patrolling," he recalled. "During the day, we received military training. They wanted to train us to be able to defend the refinery."[46] Others like Ramiah, a 1967 alumnus, signed up for military service. Although "many companies like English Electric, Larson and Toubro, Tata etc. came for selection," he with his "patriotic ardor" was "captivated by the terrific lecture given by Squadron Leader Thambi and especially when he referred to the heroic deed of the IAF [Indian Air Force] pilot who smashed his burning plane into the Sargodha radar station in the '65 Ops." Swayed by Thambi's tales of daredevil patriotism, Ramiah ended up enlisting with the Indian Air Force.[47]

For the most part, however, IIT alumni from the 1960s sustained their link to the state through civilian rather than military service. Over their college years, students were sent for training to public sector enterprises, like the Durgapur, Rourkela, and Bhilai steel plants and National Metallurgical Laboratories. Some went to public-private partnerships, such as Tata Steel, that were most emblematic of nationalist development. These periods of training often led to job offers, as it did for Dasigi, who "was offered a scholarship of Rs. 150 per month and a job at Rourkela Steel Plant after graduation."[48] Other Madras IITians began their professional lives in public sector enterprises where engineering as nation-building was a core dimension of their work. And many of them did so after a period of practical training in West Germany.

In this sense, Abraham was very much aligned with his peers. Although his time in Germany gave him a lasting appreciation for all things German, it only motivated his return to India. When he returned after his year's sojourn, he chose a position in Utkal Machineries, one of the Larson & Toubro group of companies, because of its German partners. Utkal Machineries was in Orissa, and it supplied heavy machinery for steel plants, mining, and paper industries, including for the nearby Rourkela Steel Plant. "It was really my cup of tea," Abraham remembered. "I mean, I really got into it, because I not only knew German, I knew German standards. I still have most of my textbooks in German. I found them more systematic than the British and American textbooks. So I found that quite fascinating. I was there for ten years at that first job."

Despite this early orientation around the developmental state and its public sector enterprises, reinforced by German training, many alumni still conveyed their sense of being a unique breed of employee. To the extent that they entertained the option of government services, only the central, not the regional, government tier was deemed worthy. For several, like Sri Kumar and Raghavan, this amounted to following in their fathers' footsteps. Sri Kumar, who joined the Indian Police Service, characterized this choice as inevitable because he was "the son of a Central Government servant who spent over three decades of government service in the Union Public Service Commission." Similarly, Raghavan followed his father into the Indian Administrative Service (IAS). His characterization of the IAS echoed the colonial understanding of the state as an enlightened bureaucracy governing a divided people: "The IAS is the Steel Frame that has to meet the challenge of holding our nation together. Without this Steel Frame, India will be like Iraq and Afghanistan, with warring factions taking over control and terrorizing the people."[49]

For most, however, the initial commitment to the public sector quickly wore thin. Dasigi found the job at Rourkela "not fulfilling" and got out "soon after completing the 'bond' (get trained for one and a half years and work for a further period of five years or pay Rupees 10,000 back)."[50] Balachandran put his antipathy toward the public sector most bluntly: "Because it's a bureaucracy . . . as a technical person there is only so far that you could go. You're one of so many, so you get lost in that ocean. Unless you have a godfather in those places you really can't move." For him, the very scale of bureaucracy bred anonymity. Moreover, it worked against the recognition of the IITian's innate excellence.

Balachandran compared his summer training in the Bhilai Steel Plant "where [his] uncle was" with another stint at Union Carbide. He experienced Bhilai as utterly unmotivating and so stopped going after ten days. By contrast, he was far more engaged with his work at Union Carbide. "They took the life out of me," he said cheerfully. "They made me work day and night, and gave me a project, made sure that the project was completed. . . . Every day there was a review. . . . That impressed me. There was some accountability, you know." It was striking that Balachandran had not rethought his impression of Union Carbide even in light of the gas disaster of 1984. The disaster was a case of corporate malfeasance that led to the deaths of thousands and to ongoing intergenerational harm from the effects of toxicity. Despite glaring evidence that Union Carbide was far from "accountable," the contrast with the public sector remained salient for Balachandran well into the 2000s.

Some, however, chose to stay on in the public sector. Vijayaraj worked at MECON for fourteen years. The reason was telling. He admitted that the only thing that made working there worthwhile was his boss, who was an IIT Kharagpur graduate. "We got along very well," he told me. "He was the only guy who gave me [a] promotion in time. You see, all the idiots, they thought I didn't deserve it. I used to always feel I'm in the wrong, I'm a misfit. I was frustrated. But this guy taught me, he would encourage me. That's why I stayed for 14 years. But he was another IIT guy. I mean, it required that."

In many little ways, then, even those IITians who worked in the civil services or in public sector enterprises managed to convey the impression that they were *in* but not *of* the state. In addition to an understanding of their own incorruptibility, diligence, and conceptual prowess, IITians' sense of exceptionalism derived from an understanding of temporality. Across the interviews, there was a repeated refrain of the IITs being temporally out of step with the nation. As Iswaran put it, "It was the right thing at the wrong time. . . . In creating the IITs, we intended to have top quality people serving in quality jobs in India. Of course that did not happen because we lacked the economic and industrial infrastructure to offer these graduates handsome jobs. They fled to foreign lands and became shining beacons elevating India's status in the eyes of the world."[51]

It did not help that the pickings were slim at the time for ambitious engineers. Several alumni characterized the 1960s as a barren time with few job prospects. Drawing a contrast with later generations, Mathew remarked that "a large number of B. Tech grads of those times, even if they did not want to, had to enroll for postgraduate courses— M. Techs in IITs, MBA in the fledgling IIMs [Indian Institutes of Management]—or go abroad. Difficult as it may be to believe now, there were no readymade jobs waiting for the triple distilled IIT products of 1969!"[52] Vijayaraj put it more bitterly: "When we graduated in 1969, life was a bed of thorns. Many did not get any jobs under Pundit Nehru's socialist economy and there was a great mismatch in supply and demand in every aspect of the Indian Economy."

One option was to go for an MBA at the newly founded Indian Institute of Management in Ahmedabad. Established in 1961, the IIM quickly emerged as an attractive alternative to a career in core engineering. It allowed IITians to leapfrog over the hands-on labor and lower pay scales of the engineering profession and into the ranks of management. A manager was less a practitioner than an overseer; he was the brains and not the brawn behind the operation.

Characteristically, Abraham's take on management was iconoclastic. "In my view, what killed the engineering profession as I knew it," he stated, "was first of all the management industry, represented by the Harvard Business School and its clones the world over. It became lucrative for people with engineering qualifications to take up this new option, and avoid the responsibilities involved in taking technical decisions. This culture was entrenched in our country even in the 1960s. If you joined an organization as a 'management trainee' you started on a higher salary and rose much faster compared to those who were 'engineer trainees' and had limited horizons." Abraham admitted that the problem is structural. "The justification, no doubt, is that nobody pays an engineer," he lamented, "and we are effectively considered as little more than skilled workers. That is a failing in our society and our culture, but nobody likes to talk about it, still less try to do anything about it." We see here the beginnings of a shift in the political economy of value as a result of which public sector engineering, the coveted ambition of the colonial era, was starting to be overshadowed by the specter of managerialism. Although still a minority trend, by the 1980s, this turn to management and away from even professional engineering would become a defining feature of the IIT system.

Beyond the Nation

A more common trend was to go abroad, something that I take up at more length in Chapter 7. Although the numbers who left India rose steadily after the 1960s, even at that time there were some who headed out for training, jobs, or higher degrees. Typically, those from IIT Madras who chose the route of practical training and core engineering work in the public sector headed to West Germany. Those who sought postgraduate degrees and a move beyond hands-on work went to the United States. Over time, traffic to West Germany slowed to a trickle and then petered out almost entirely while the U.S. diaspora kept increasing in size. These trends were hugely significant in reorienting IITians away from core engineering and the state sector toward private "knowledge work."

Usually, the IITians who went to the United States were those who had the grades to secure university admissions and scholarships. From 1960s alumni accounts, it appears that the IIT name had yet to catch on across U.S. academia. This is made clear in the comparative experiences of two 1969 alumni. Baliga, who graduated at the top of his class, "applied to only the top tier universities in the US." He had disappointing results. Unfortunately, he recalled, "IITM had not yet established a reputation among these universities and my request for financial aid was declined." In July 1969, he opted instead for the Indian Institute of Science. By a stroke of luck, however, he "received an offer with financial aid from Prof. Gandhi at Rensselaer Polytechnic Institute in August 1969 because one of the other applicants was unable to join his group." By the first week in September 1969, he was on a plane to Troy, New York, to do his MS and PhD "under one of the pioneers in the semiconductor field."[53] Giri, also a 1969 alumnus, had a somewhat different account. He joined an engineering graduate program at the State University of New York along with three other classmates, "thanks in part to Gursharan Singh Sidhu's outstanding IITM alumni legacy he left at SUNY few years earlier."[54]

Although these two accounts of the IIT's reputation in the 1960s United States vary, both convey a clear sense that, from the outset, alumni understood name recognition as hugely consequential in the admissions process. As they saw it, institutional reputation mattered

equally if not more than the strength of any one candidate, and therefore needed to be secured and protected. This was well before the emergence of "Brand IIT" as a term. Nonetheless, the cachet of the pedigree was already very much in view.

Among 1960s alumni, there is another matter that generates more
serious differences of opinion: the impact of the U.S. diaspora on India.
The perspectives of Shenoy, Iswaran, and Abraham capture the range
of positions within this debate.

Shenoy lamented the flow of IITians abroad as "development aid
by a poor country to a rich country." "It is true," he admitted, "that
occasionally some billionaire IITian will donate a princely sum of 5
to 10 million back to their IIT and we all rejoice. But how many of us
stop to think that if only these IITians had stayed back like Nandan
Nilekani, how many Infosys (not just in IT sectors but also in energy,
steel, petrochemical, Banking etc.) we would have been able to develop?
Even more important, what kind of revolution we could have had to
overthrow today's unscrupulous political class?"[55] This early twenty-
first-century fantasy of India as a smoothly functioning technocracy
manned by IITians is a far cry from the strong state affiliations of the
late colonial and early postcolonial periods. Even while it remains concerned with questions of national development and the privileged role
of the enlightened technocrat, it shows the distance traveled by IITians
in their imaginaries of the state and their relationship to it.

Shenoy also tracked a shift from an earlier concern about the "IIT
brain drain" to its acceptance and even embrace. "After Rajiv Gandhi's
much quoted statement—a brain drain is better than the brain in the
drain," he opined, "the continuing exit of knowledge capital did not
worry any planners or politicians. Some even referred to them as brain
banks. They were implying that those who remained could not really
contribute, because of the pathetic conditions in India."[56] Shenoy, who
did stay behind, was affronted by the assumption that to realize the
true value of an IIT education, the IITian had to go abroad. For him,
this was indicative of the outward orientation of IITians that was there
from the outset. As an alumnus from rural Mangalore who was the
object of urban paternalism, he experienced the closeted existence of
campus life as a kind of suffocating, willful ignorance. "We were iso-
lated from the outside world," he recalled with some bitterness. "We

led a sheltered life, comfortable in its own way. We even had movies during the weekends." This self-enclosed bliss, he continued, produced bizarre forms of identification and disidentification:

> We never knew about people living in abject poverty in the nearby village of Taramani, right next to our comfortable quarters. But when we heard about the suicide of Marilyn Monroe, many of my class-mates were devastated. Being a villager myself, I never could under-stand why they were mourning the death of a movie star in a distant land. I had never heard of her till that time. We knew even less about the grinding poverty of a significant population of India. Rarely did we discuss the problem of India's poverty. The politics of governing India did not capture one's imagination. We were more eager to know about the luxurious life in the U.S. or Germany than the appalling living conditions in nearby Velachery.[57]

Shenoy's caustic assessment resonates with Nazir Ahmed's warning about the isolation of the IITs from their social environments. Ahmed was principally concerned about the IITs standing apart from other engineering colleges. By the time of Shenoy's reflections in the 2000s, there was the additional hierarchy of the diasporic over the homeland IITian. Now, even the homeland IITian was not at the pinnacle of edu-cational stratification. In Chapter 7, we will return to the tensions among alumni produced by this newer hierarchy of value and ask whether these have significantly fractured institutional kinship.

A second perspective was Iswaran's, who, contra Shenoy, expressed what is now the most popular position on the U.S. IIT diaspora. For him, "this so-called brain drain worked in India's favor. The thousands of IIT alumni who fled to greener pastures outside India were a living billboard for the superior intellect cultivated and honed by their IIT education."[58] Iswaran's idea of the diasporic IITian as "a living bill-board" anticipates the concerted effort that followed in later years at producing Brand IIT. In Chapter 7, we will explore diasporic migration and its relationship to branding at more length to showcase continu-ities and shifts in the operations of institutional kinship. What is important to note here is that the forms of upper casteness and branding that became more pronounced and defensive were already present in a nascent form in the very first decade of the institute's functioning.

Even then, IITians had a clear sense of themselves as marked by an institutional pedigree with potential international cachet.

Finally, there is Abraham, for whom the exodus of IITians violated an implicit social contract with the Indian public. "I think it is only from some of the early Kharagpur batches that a significant number actually contributed to Indian industry," he noted bitterly, "but by my time the best of the lot—in terms of rank—sought greener pastures abroad with no qualms of conscience at all. The fees we paid were so low that we effectively got a free education at the tax-payers' expense." As did Shenoy, Abraham saw the aspiration to foreign careers as indicative of a skewed hierarchy of value. For him, this privileging of the United States over India was an expression of the IITs' growing distance from the German model of industrial engineering. Moreover, it was a betrayal of the public trust and the duties of citizenship. He took strong issue with the notion that the symbolic value of Indian success stories abroad was adequate compensation for the loss of material value at home.

Of all the alumni I interviewed, Abraham was the most stridently critical in his assessments of the IITs. For him, engineering colleges should produce engineers who had expertise in the most tangible, hands-on forms of labor. Abraham's sense of the continuities and shifts in the IITs came both out of his own ethical and intellectual mooring, and out of his enduring link to IIT Madras. In 1984, he returned to IIT Madras for a master's degree in science and found the changes in the institute thoroughly unsettling. "I sort of got put off the whole idea of technical education altogether," he confessed, "because the students weren't interested in engineering. For most of them, engineering was a stepping-stone to a good career, not in engineering."

He was also unsatisfied by the teaching. "Some of the people who were teaching me, at the M. Tech. level, some of them, you could see, were really third rate," he said. Once again, Germany figured prominently in his assessment. "Some of them were simply bluffing because they knew they could get away with it," Abraham continued. "There were people who had good reputations among the students, were considered knowledgeable, but because I knew German . . . the fellow takes a textbook and he shows a figure and he says that this is something, and I can read the caption in German, I know it's not what he is talking about, but he can get away with it."

The decline of standards, as Abraham saw it, had to do with the decline more broadly of the value of engineering. As a result, the IITs had lost their sense of purpose. He tracked this decline through the shifting hierarchy of branches within IIT Madras. When the first IITs were founded in the 1950s, civil engineering was the most coveted branch. "Those days," he told me, "engineer really meant civil engineer." With the decline in the aura of the Public Works Department, mechanical engineering got the edge, with IIT Madras seen as particularly strong in this branch. By the time Abraham arrived at IIT Madras in 1964, mechanical engineering had also been supplanted by electrical and electronical engineering, with civil engineering lagging even further behind. Chemical engineering too was coming up, as was metallurgy, and these were followed in the 1980s by aeronautical engineering, naval architecture, and finally computer science. When Abraham returned in 1984 for his master's degree, "computer science was the in thing. The top rankers in the JEE would invariably opt for it."

He told me a story that was in circulation at the time. "There was this one chap, the JEE topper. When he came for his interview, he asked for civil [engineering branch,] and the panel was absolutely shocked. 'Are you sure you want civil? Why do you want civil?' and they questioned him for quite some time. But he was influenced by his father and he was very sure that he wanted civil. And they were quite taken aback by that."

Across my interviews with successive cohorts, I heard echoes of the shifting pecking order of branches from the more practical to the more conceptual. While most accepted the changing hierarchy of branches as a natural progression correlating to changes in market value, Abraham remained doggedly opposed to the eclipsing of older fields by newer ones. Market value, he insisted, was not the same as intellectual value. A case in point was the rise of computer science. "The final nail in the engineering coffin was the computer industry!" he claimed in an exasperated tone. "As long as computers actually computed—think Fortran—there was still some hope as the developments were in the hands of practical people. But after the Computer Science theoreticians took over the field and introduced C and its successors, computers started doing everything other than computing—presumably under pressure from the business and management world for 'manipulating information' which seems to be the primary activity today."

Ultimately, for Abraham, the root of the problem was money:

> Whereas at one time many engineering organizations were led by real engineers, today it is mostly people with a finance background, often with a B. Tech. or similar qualification serving as a decoration. They can only talk about the bottom line and related jargon, have no patience with failures or delays in this imperfect world, and do not understand that technical skills need to be nurtured and incentivized. The attitude is that if there is a technical problem one can throw some money at it and get it solved. . . . The other big area is sales and marketing, where ethics is given the go-by. Someone who can sell an oversized or unsuitable product to an ill-informed customer gets credit for a job well done. Maybe that is inevitable in our consumerist society which thrives on promoting waste of all kinds.

At the end of Chapter 2, we looked in passing at the 1968 study by sociologists C. Rajagopalan and Jaspal Singh, which analyzed the caste and class backgrounds of students at a northern IIT to determine whether the institutions were contributing to social mobility.[59] The authors interviewed 86.5 percent of students admitted in 1966 and found that as many as 88 percent were from urban areas. Even most of the 8 percent who indicated a rural background were now urban residents. In terms of caste, most were from Brahmin or trading castes and had fathers who had gone through some form of higher education, ranging from college to doctoral and professional degrees. Mothers, too, while consistently educated at lower levels than their spouses, were nevertheless pedigreed. Another significant finding was about engineering itself: the study showed that, on average, students had at least two relatives within the wider family circle who were engineers. Last but not least, the vast majority of students came from the most elite urban schools that offered English medium instruction.

Rajagopalan and Singh's study resonates strongly with my own, more qualitative account. Madras IIT's 1960s alumni largely shared the social profile of their northern counterparts. They, too, tended to be urban and English-educated upper castes with professional fathers and relatives who are engineers. What Rajagopalan and Singh could not have anticipated, however, were the caste and class challenges to the exclusivity of the IITs, the influx of groups from lower-caste and lower-class backgrounds, and the responses from upper castes to the changing social composition of student bodies.

The next three chapters will consider these transformations and the maneuvers made to shore up upper-caste exceptionalism. Chapter 5 on the examination, Chapter 6 on reservation, and Chapter 7 on diasporic mobility all address the dialectic of lower-caste claims to rights and upper-caste claims to merit through which a consolidated form of upper casteness has emerged. As I have already gestured to, we will see how being middle class became central not only to Tamil Brahmins but increasingly to other upper castes. Arguments about class became a way to reconcile their ascriptive identities as members of caste groupings with claims to achievement. With the expansion of quotas for lower castes, upper-caste IITians coupled assertions of middle-class identity with arguments about the need to defend formal equality. Alongside these strategies, diasporic mobility became an important mechanism of retrenchment away from the pressures of democratic change. Through these maneuvers, IITians constituted upper casteness as the very embodiment of meritocracy. Let us now turn to the first instrument for the making of upper-caste meritocracy: the mass examination.

5

Testing Merit

BY THE 1970s, the decline of the German model of hands-on engineering was under way at IIT Madras. The exodus of IITians to the United States only reinforced this trend. As Germany faded in symbolic value and the United States took its place as a desired destination for education and employment, IITians shifted away from core engineering jobs in the Indian public sector toward academia, management, and private sector industry. The expansion of engineering education from the 1980s, along with the spread of private schools and colleges in the 1990s, as part of the liberalization of the Indian economy, contributed to the preference for private sector jobs. As new colleges opened across India and more and more students entered the ranks of engineering, the IITs worked to distinguish themselves as the most conceptual and rigorous of B.Tech programs whose alumni were better suited to the managerial class and to the most coveted technical fields, such as computer science.

The labor of distinction owed much to the IITs' Joint Entrance Examination (JEE), which, as noted in the Introduction, has become the single most important emblem of the system's excellence and exclusivity. Held every year in April, the JEE is a hotly anticipated event. Since the first exam in 1961, the number of candidates has grown steadily, from 12,771 in 1969 to 79,559 in 1990. By 2001, it had reached 147,775, and by 2006, it was 299,087. In 2011, a total of 468,280 students took the exam, with under 3 percent winning admission to the then fifteen IITs.[1] These dramatically low percentages only reinforce the prestige of the examination, setting in motion a vicious cycle of attracting ever more candidates who, by failing, contribute to its aura of selectivity. Despite evidence that the vast majority of aspirants fail to pass the JEE, increasing numbers of families send their children to coaching centers to train them for the test. Although the cost of coaching centers can put middle-class and lower-middle-class families into debt, the JEE as a stepping-stone to financial success and social mobility makes this investment seem worthwhile.

As with other examinations, IIT aspirants often turn to spiritual intercession for securing a passing mark. The stories of family *pujas* and pilgrimages leading up to the JEE echo accounts of the de-secularization of examinations in East Asia. It is clear from such accounts that the competitive examination is by no means a rationalized exercise. Rather, it is a key collective ritual where the role of the sacred in determining outcomes persists.[2]

It is not just belief in divine intervention that has survived the rise of the modern examination. So, too, have understandings of innate intelligence. The scale of a test like the JEE elicits a world of social commentary around who is destined to succeed or fail. In these evaluations of success and failure, caste as an index of intellectual merit is very much in play. This raises the question of what the relationship is between ascription and achievement in the dynamics of the modern examination. How does the IIT-JEE stage this relationship? And how is caste reconstituted through this process?

Ascription and Achievement

The competitive examination is commonly taken as an index of modern meritocracy. Unlike older forms of patronage, which rest on networks of power and affiliation, the modern examination is thought to create a level playing field where any and all can participate. The only form of capital deemed necessary is one's ability; other forms of inherited social and cultural capital are supposed to be irrelevant. It is through this purported shift from ascription to achievement that the modern examination comes to symbolize meritocracy.[3]

When looking at the history of examinations, however, we see that indices of evaluation are more often cumulative. Examinations are not culturally or socially neutral. Rather than the end of ascription, examinations mark the layering of seemingly objective, socially neutral criteria on top of older evaluations of relative social worth. As filtering mechanisms, they favor those who come from histories of education and have a facility with this technical instrument. They also work to reproduce existing social hierarchies in a post facto way: examination results are typically read to reinforce rather than unsettle commonsense understandings of relative merit.

Pierre Bourdieu and Jean-Claude Passeron have written exhaustively about how the prestigious examination and elite higher education guarantee the reproduction of older social hierarchies. Examinations and elite institutions do so, they argue, by "concealing social selection under the guise of technical selection and legitimating the reproduction of social hierarchies by transmuting them into academic hierarchies."[4] In the process, older hierarchies and affinities are reproduced, but now in the name of objectivity, egalitarianism, and meritocracy.

But, they continue, examinations do not do this all on their own. As "downstream events," they rely on other aspects of social structure to regulate access. As they put it, "In every country, the inequalities between the classes are incomparably greater when measured by the *probabilities of candidature* . . . than when measured by the *probabilities of passing*."[5] While the examination does perform a gatekeeping function by passing some and failing others, Bourdieu and Passeron maintain that this result is actually preempted by the broader structure of social and economic relations, which eliminate most even from candidacy.

They also make the point that highly valued formal qualifications, such as the passing of prestigious exams and attendance at elite educational institutions, do more than they claim. While they formally certify technical competence, their real value is in the attestation of cultural competence. In other words, examinations and degrees appear to be formal markers of achievement when they in fact "act as proxies for ascription."[6] In acting as proxies for ascription, examinations blur the distinction between innate and learned ability. Success or failure seems to point to something innate in the candidate that the examination merely illustrates. Achievement is thus glossed not as the outcome of a set of learned practices but as a reflection of ascriptive qualities. In this sense, the examination contributes to the naturalization of talent. Moreover, as a seemingly absolute measure of intellectual ability— even social worth—the examination reinforces the relative merit of the successful.

Finally, in addition to determining success and failure, the examination also generates gradations of rank among the successful. These gradations produce the effect of individuation, where the social and intellectual worth of the individual becomes an extension of the rank. As a more fine-grained outcome, ranking also contributes to the sense of the examination as a fine-tuned technical instrument whose efficacy in gauging relative worth is beyond question.

Together, these three aspects of the modern examination— gatekeeping, cultural certification, and ranking—set in motion the dialectic between ascription and achievement. The scale and technical dimensions of the examination seem to depart from older models of selection through patronage and affiliation. However, the promise of open access and equal opportunity embodied in the examination as a rationalized instrument is belied by the structuring force of economic and social relations and the ideological power of cultural assumptions. Success in examination is by no means merely a measure of individual competence. It is made possible by the accumulated advantages of unequal opportunity, and it reinforces prejudices about who is or who is not innately talented. In other words, it is profoundly social and cultural in its structure and its effects. The success or failure of an individual is commonly understood as an index of "culture," or of the essential traits of the person's social group and milieu.

The history of mass examinations in India illuminates this dialectic between ascription and achievement. From as early as the mid-nineteenth century, we see efforts to promote the examination as the actualization of modern meritocracy while ensuring its function as a gatekeeping, certifying, and ranking device sustaining existing social hierarchies. But we also see interventions in the examination process, which seek to correct for the structuring force of accumulated privileges and cultural assumptions. As I will show, such redistributive measures often had the unintended effect of reinforcing rather than loosening the link between ascription and achievement. They set in motion a more strident politics of meritocracy through which ascriptive status became a more explicit basis for claims to meritocratic achievement.

Imperial Liberalism and the Examination

Within the British Empire, the Indian Civil Service (ICS) was the first instance where recruitment shifted from patronage to competitive examinations. Earlier, the East India Company had founded its own college at Haileybury in England, from which the company's directors nominated candidates for the ICS. Until 1860, the directors of the East India Company and the ICS were recruited almost entirely from London's banking and commercial families, and from landed groups in Scotland and the southeast of England. Not only did they share class backgrounds, but their cultural and economic ties were also buttressed by ties of descent and affinity. From 1840 to 1860, "fifty or sixty interconnected extended families contributed the vast majority of the civil servants who governed India."[7] Among the top reasons given for the appointment of civil servants by the East India Company's Court of Directors were, in descending order, friendship, kinship, business relationships, company service, political recommendation, and recommendation of board of control.

In the 1850s, members of the Liberal Party challenged this model of appointment by patronage as outmoded. Instead, they argued for the institution of a competitive examination as a way to preempt more radical, unmanageable popular demands. Such reforms would entail a "voluntary renunciation of patronage" in accordance with changing standards of political morality. To echo John Adams, the competitive examination was instituted at a time when "an old aristocracy of birth concluded an alliance with a new aristocracy of intellect."[8]

The institution of competitive examinations for the civil services in both England and India dovetailed with pressures on the university system. Throughout the early nineteenth century, Britain's universities suffered a crisis of identity, most clearly seen in rising rates of graduate unemployment. As the numbers of graduates rose, there was no parallel growth in their traditional areas of employment: education, the clergy, and the bar. The introduction of recruitment by competitive examination allowed the universities to repurpose themselves in a more utilitarian mold. Not everyone agreed, and a sizable opposition argued for university reform along German lines to make them centers of research and scholarship for "training scholars, not rulers." India offered a space for compromise: as part of training for the civil service, teaching in the field of Oriental languages and in Indian geography and history also expanded. As Thomas Macaulay opined, this would provide "fresh incentives for the middle and lower classes to attain high educational standards."[9]

Ultimately, the competitive examination won cabinet approval—not on educational or political grounds but as a means to enhance administrative efficiency. Liberals and conservatives alike agreed that drawing from a much larger pool of talent was necessary at a time when administrative responsibilities weighed ever more heavily on civil servants. In both England and India, "a new type of civil service seemed necessary; a civil service selected for competence, not connection, and promoted for ability, not seniority."[10]

Although the Home Service was actually considered to be in worse shape, it was the ICS that was the object of most reformist concern. This was partly because the East India Company administration had become synonymous with entrenched, corrupt patronage, but it was also because of the perceived relationship between colonial administrators and Indians. The Indian civil servant was thought to "exercise a power for good or evil which no English civil servant—perhaps no functionary in the world—possessed." Macaulay made the most strident argument for the scholar-gentleman as the most appropriate choice for such responsibility. "Has it not always been the case," he argued, "that the men who were first in the competition of the schools have been first in the competition of life?" For Macaulay, examination success correlated not just with career success but with "character."[11]

Initially, Macaulay's ambition was fulfilled. In the first year of the open examination in 1855, 70 percent of successful candidates were Oxbridge educated, and the average for the next four years was almost 60 percent. But this was followed by a precipitous decline, and by 1864, only 10 percent of recruits were from Oxbridge. Moreover, the proportion of successful candidates of all universities also fell.

The culprit was "the crammer." ICS aspirants sidestepped universities and went straight to crammers, institutions that were opened in response to market demand for a new examination for which students were given intense preparation in a short period of time. This was due to the structure of the examination itself. Although Macaulay had envisioned the Oxbridge graduate as the ideal candidate, there was little overlap between university curricula, with their early specialization in mathematics and the classics, and the general intelligence tested by the ICS examination. Moreover, the age ceiling of nineteen for ICS candidature meant that aspirants had to choose between years spent at university and going straight to India. As a result, the ICS was quickly taken over by graduates of the crammers and not of Oxbridge.

This was an unanticipated outcome. The point of the examination was to transfer the education of India's civil servants to the universities, not to crammers. An inquiry in 1874 by the Duke of Argyll, then secretary of state for India, produced an indictment of the crammer as the negation of the liberal education envisioned by the 1854 reforms. The crammer also induced anxieties around colonial rule, which historian Clive Dewey captures in trenchant prose:

> Cramming was intellectually superficial; worse—in an era of muscular Christianity, it neglected morality and physique. Its prevalence aggravated existing doubts about the quality of the competition-wallah. The competition-wallah—the product of cramming—might be more intelligent than his Haileybury-educated predecessors, more prolific and agile with a pen; but was he also a gentleman? Was not his physique so weakened by excessive concentration on the book work needed to succeed in the open examination that his health broke down in India? Of sedentary disposition, could he ride? Could he inspire the same respect in the natives?[12]

These concerns led to further proposals for reforming the process of ICS recruitment. First, Argyll proposed a revived Haileybury housed within one of the universities. This was shot down and replaced with a suggestion from the universities that examination candidates follow with a two-year probationary course at Oxbridge. This would ensure additional filtering after the crammers without putting the full burden for training on the universities. But even this proved unsatisfactory, and eventually, in 1892, a further set of reforms raised the maximum age limit from nineteen to twenty-three and aligned aspects of the examination more closely with Oxbridge honors courses. With this, Macaulay's dream finally came to pass: the proportion of non-university recruits fell to 6 percent, and Oxbridge graduates climbed back up to 78 percent.

Though all these shifts, we see that arguments in favor of the open examination and against patronage were not really about democratizing access. There was always an envisioned ideal candidate: the Oxbridge graduate. Official hostility to the crammer expressed anxieties around the entry of those who did not fit the liberal imaginary of the colonial civil servant. As Macaulay and others saw it, the crammer undercut the ability of the examination to filter out socially and intellectually undesirable aspirants. The reforms instituted in 1874 and 1892 were corrective measures intended to allow the examination to perform its gatekeeping function and produce the desired selection of civil servants with the appropriate cultural credentials.

Much of this negotiation was around the ideal *metropolitan* candidate for the ICS. But what about expatriate British candidates from the colony? The increase in the maximum age of applicants came about through opposition not from within England but from India. The previous ceiling of nineteen years had effectively cut out expatriate competitors altogether because it did not allow time for them to come to England, attend a crammer, and prepare for the examination. Such opposition from India found an advocate in Viceroy Ripon, who viewed the ICS examination as a critical tool for inducting expatriates into metropolitan political culture. This unification of the Home Service and the Indian Civil Service under a common cultural umbrella, he believed, was the best bulwark against Indian nationalism. It was this that led Ripon to endorse the increased maximum age of recruits so that colonials would have time to imbibe metropolitan norms. Such norms, he hoped, would equip the expatriate with the necessary tools to withstand the pressures of colonial politics and remain true to the imperial mission.

Once again we see here that the examination was by no means simply an acultural, objective tool of testing. It was a process of cultivation through which those who fit a desired cultural mold were favored and those who did not were disciplined into new ways of thinking and being. As we saw in Chapter 1 with the engineering service, the examination as a form of discipline was applied to the British themselves in order to address differences in class and context and to identify the ideal gentleman-generalist for service in India.[13]

Recall Bourdieu and Passeron's argument about exams concealing social selection under the guise of technical selection. What was the social selection that the ICS examination legitimated? Significantly, "neither extreme of the social spectrum was represented in the Indian civil service."[14] Of the 1,600 or so recruits selected at forty examinations between 1858 and 1897, only one was the son of a manual worker, and the number of aristocrats was equally negligible. For the most part, recruits came from three middle-class groups in the following order: the sons of professionals, the sons of businessmen, and the sons of farmers or lesser gentry. While there was some fluctuation in representation within these categories, the ICS was a solidly middle-class cadre.

It is this class character of the modern examination that most contributes to its popular perception as the linchpin of meritocracy. Unlike erstwhile forms of patronage through which candidates were nominated on the basis of elite social networks, the examination connotes the dawn of individual ability and achievement as the basis for selection. It is emblematic of a shift from an older model of patronage to liberal governance. Of course, this was not about unlimited opportunity. Rather, to quote Bourdieu and Passeron again, "the probabilities of candidature" were already limited to those endowed with certain forms of educational and cultural capital.[15] Sons of manual workers were not included in the shift from rule by patronage to rule by examination.

What this suggests is an amendment to Bourdieu and Passeron's argument: the ICS examination was not simply a reproduction of the status quo. It also occasioned a shift in the relative weight of particular social constituencies in the project of rule and thus points to the need to attend to both the reproductive and the transformative role of the competitive examination.

Indian Recruitment to the Civil Services

All of this wrangling over ICS recruitment occurred before the Indianization of the services. As we saw in Chapter 1, in the early twentieth century, Indians began to level strident criticisms against the

racial glass ceiling in the civil services. How did this criticism relate
to the rise of the competitive examination?

While the recruitment of officers in England to the ICS and the
Indian Police Service was carried out through competitive examinations, recruitment remained by nomination in other services. In the
engineering service, the secretary of state would call for applications,
a committee would be appointed to assess candidate qualifications,
and, on the basis of an interview at the India Office, a selection would
be made. Candidates also had to pass a medical examination and a
riding test before they could be confirmed.

In India, too, nomination was the norm in recruiting officers. No
competitive examinations were held before the end of World War I
because the country's education system was considered insufficiently
developed and too unevenly distributed for examinations to yield the
required type and mix of officers. The result of recruitment by nomination was a preponderance of Anglo-Indians and domiciled Europeans in
those branches of government services for which officers were recruited
in India. This favoritism was compounded by the disparity in the educational requirements stipulated for candidates of different categories.
To be eligible for certain subordinate posts, Anglo-Indians and domiciled Europeans, who were usually educated in schools meant exclusively for them, were only required to complete the "European schools"
curriculum, whereas "native" Indians had to be university graduates.[16]

Opposition to nomination as a racially weighted process resulted
in a set of reforms. The Islington Commission, instituted to look into
recruitment reform, suggested measures to improve the nomination
process toward increasing the proportion of Indians in the services.
These included creating selection committees with Indian members,
advertising openings systematically, and starting new technical institutions. As part of the reforms, an ICS exam was instituted in India in
1922, but it was held after the London exam each year, which limited
its importance as a leveling instrument.[17]

We see here that when it came to Indian recruitment, the examination was seen as too risky a technology to ensure the appropriate results. The racial parameters of rule could not be guaranteed with such
a process. Instead, recruitment by nomination remained the norm in
the colony. For nationalists, the discrepancy between examination in
England and nomination in the colony took on huge significance. Uni-

versalizing the examination as a technology of selection became the silver bullet that would solve the intractable problems of racial bias and exclusion. With the transition to self-rule, the examination came into its own as the measure of merit par excellence. Over the postindependence period, examinations have proliferated across the subcontinent, their scale continuously expanding with the growth in education. The most competitive of these—the Union Public Service Commission (UPSC) exam, which was the postcolonial iteration of the ICS exam; the Institute of Chartered Accountants of India exam; and the IIT-JEE—are also the ones that are most associated with upper-caste intelligence and competitiveness. As we will see with the IIT-JEE, the dialectic between ascription and achievement has become a crucial part of the selection process and of charged public debate.

Examinations in Independent India and the IIT-JEE

It is strange to look back to the late colonial debate over the viability of the competitive examination as a technology of selection in India. From the vantage point of contemporary India's examination fever, it seems surreal that this was ever a question. The mass examination is now an integral organizing principle of Indian education and, indeed, of Indian social life. It is an annual ritual that has become as naturalized as the monsoons. How has the postindependence spread of examinations shaped the dialectic between ascription and achievement?

Sociologist of education Krishna Kumar addresses this question in his discussion of "early selection" and "mass examination," two structuring mechanisms of India's educational system. Early selection tracks elite students into separate tiers of training through which they effectively exit the general pool of applicants. The stratification of educational institutions into elite and non-elite, private and public, underwrites this early selection process and offers the children of the elite "safe routes towards status professions." It is in effect a mechanism of reproduction in which ascriptive characteristics of family, caste, and class are transmuted into indices of merit and secured through a parallel educational track.[18]

In this context where institutional stratification and privatization undercuts the possibility of a truly mass education system, the examination holds out the promise of parity. The rituals of the mass examination—paper-setting shrouded in secrecy, strict invigilation during the exam, and the public declaration of results—carry the symbolic message that all individuals have an equal chance. It stands in for open competition and equal opportunity. In this sense, Kumar argues, the practice of mass examinations acts as a symbolic corrective to institutional stratification and elite reproduction.[19] It does so by foregrounding the universality of achievement over the particularity of ascription.

What about the internal mechanisms of the examination? Sociologist Satish Deshpande points to two types of examinations in India—exit and entrance—each with its specific characteristics. Exit exams advance students from one stage to another of the educational hierarchy. Significantly, the expanding educational opportunities in postcolonial India have been accompanied by lowering rates of failure; the pass percentages for exit examinations tend to be very high. Nevertheless, the assumption that this means increasingly higher levels of education for the population as a whole is belied by the pyramidal structure of enrollment, with the numbers of those who advance dropping steadily from primary school to secondary, higher secondary, and college.

In this sense, factors other than the exit examination itself are important for explaining the increasing exclusivity of higher levels of education. Bourdieu and Passeron's analysis of "self-elimination" is salient here. As they point out, non-elite students are more likely to "eliminate themselves" from higher levels of education because of the social expectation of failure. In other words, ascription—who is destined for certain paths and not others—delimits the field of competition in such a way that achievement is always a greater possibility for those social groups who enjoy inherited privilege.

What about the entrance examination? Deshpande points to a striking contrast between the pass percentages of exit and entrance examinations in India. Whereas the pass percentages of exit examinations are typically in the 70–90 percent range, those for entrance examinations are dramatically lower. The three examinations with the highest number of applicants—the UPSC exam, the Institute of Chartered Accountants of India exam, and the IIT-JEE—tend to have pass percentages between 2.6 and 2.8. Deshpande argues that these low rates of admission are "an artefact of the very status of the examination itself."[20] Because these examinations symbolize stepping-stones to social mobility, they attract a large number of aspirants who have no realistic chance of passing. In this sense, "the prestige of the examination . . . tautologically reaffirms itself by attracting a large number of candidates who are essentially cannon fodder and contribute to the aura of selectivity that surrounds the examination."[21]

Deshpande also points to another crucial aspect of entrance examinations: their conflation of eligibility and excellence. He argues that exams like the JEE need to push the ideology of excellence to obscure the long-standing inequalities, especially in access to higher education, that have structured a society like India. Excellence becomes a crucial rationale for justifying the concentration of opportunities and resources that underwrites the reproduction of privilege. Deshpande notes that "the typical competitive exam claims to measure excellence or 'maximum merit'" rather than the more modest claim of establishing a threshold of competence.[22] He adds that this ideology of excellence is very difficult to shake. Once the examination is established on these grounds, any suggestion that what might be at stake is not excellence "appears as an insult to the exalted ethical-intellectual status of the already-sacralised examination."[23]

The overinvestment in notions of excellence has generated an obsession with ranking. The JEE is a particularly good example of how the minute rank ordering of candidates comes to stand in for differential intelligence. It is also a clear indication of the absurd limits to which ranking can extend. Deshpande offers the example of the 2009 JEE, in which "the 501st rank had an aggregate mark of 302 (out of 489), while the 5,501st rank had an aggregate of exactly 200 marks."[24] There were as many as 5,000 ranks within a mere 102-mark range, or "an average difference of 0.02 marks per candidate."[25] These minuscule differences in scores acquire far more weight when they are translated into neatly distinguished ranks as the objective truth of relative intelligence. Deshpande goes further, calling the ranking system "a moral-ethical ordering" that allows "the most vocal and resource-rich groups in society . . . to maximize their advantage over the rest of society."[26]

When it comes to the JEE, the rigidly ranked results do not just ensure entry into the IITs; they also limit the degree to which successful candidates can choose their institute and branch of engineering. Here, other hierarchies come into play. As we saw in Chapter 4, the pecking order of branches has shifted over time from civil engineering to computer science on top. Since most IITians faithfully follow the hierarchy of branches in vogue, the status of the JEE rank is further reinforced by the status of the branch one chooses.

At the IITs, ranking does not end with the JEE. The preoccupation with ranks persists all the way through campus life. The acronym "RG" refers to the system of relative grading through which students are made acutely aware of where they stand in relation to their peers. Udhay, a 1990s alumnus of IIT Madras, put it this way: "Your entire focus is on a good rank. It's not just that you get a pass or fail on an examination. It's actually your rank that matters, which means that how well you do relative to others is more important than what you have learned. That thought is sort of ingrained in your preparation for IIT and it continues through into IIT also."[27]

The rank also follows students on their way out of the institution. In the job selection process, recruiters almost always inquire after the candidate's JEE rank, which matters as much if not more than the cumulative grade point average over the years in the institute. The JEE rank with which one enters remains the ultimate signifier of intellectual merit. Let us now turn to IIT Madras for a more in-depth look at the social meanings associated with the JEE.

The Social Meanings of the JEE

The IIT-JEE represents the fullest realization of India's examination fetish. When IIT Madras opened in 1959, the all India entrance examination was not yet in place. In the first two years, students were chosen based on their performance in school board examinations. Even after the institution of the JEE in 1961, the selection process was first administered regionally, or zonally, with a certain percentage of seats allotted to each zone. The all India selection that now exists began in 1962, but it was only in the 1970s that the number of applicants started to steadily rise. By the late 1990s, the JEE had acquired a mythical status as the stepping-stone to private sector financial success.

The expanding scope of the exam had a significant effect on the perception of its outcomes. As an all India exam, it came to be seen as a national arbiter of merit. The sheer scale of the JEE and its finely calibrated results reinforced its standing as an objective measure of individual intellectual worth and made the student's All India Rank, or AIR, into an indisputable index of innate abilities. The AIR acquired a talismanic quality that marked the individual for life. Throughout the 1980s and 1990s, engineering education was a growth industry, particularly in southern India. During this period, the JEE sealed its reputation as the ultimate test of conceptual prowess and the stepping-stone to economic mobility, attracting increasing numbers of students who wanted to try their hand in a national competition.

In terms of its national scale, the JEE was the direct descendant of the UPSC exam. The increasing scale of the JEE also changed the social profile of applicants to be more aligned with the UPSC. Unlike in the 1960s, when the number of applicants was smaller and the social composition of IIT Madras cohorts included both the wealthy and some poor students, the JEE's expansion was largely due to its growing attraction for aspirants from upper-caste professional families. These were the students whose parents were typically employed in the central government services, where they had been acculturated into the intense competitiveness of the UPSC exam. As participants in another all India ritual, these parents made a point of training their children to successfully pass the JEE, making caste and class history key to exam success. At the same time, the generational shift from the UPSC to the JEE reinforced a sense of middle-class status, since both exams were understood to be objective filters of individual ability dissociated from other structural factors. After the 1970s, this class sensibility was further enhanced by the growing exodus of IITians to the United States, where they encountered another national myth of middle-class, meritocratic individualism. All these factors—the expanding scale of the JEE, its tightening association with an educated middle class, and the influence of diasporic experiences—had a significant impact on the perception of caste, which increasingly came to be foregrounded as a cultural identity and obscured as a form of inherited advantage. To put it in the terms we have been considering thus far, ascription was reconciled with achievement by delinking caste from capital.

In this sense, IITians as a whole came increasingly into line with what was previously characteristic of a Tamil Brahmin worldview.

As we will see, this had a significant impact on attitudes toward JEE coaching—the contemporary version of the colonial crammer—and caste-based reservation. Both came to be perceived as illegitimate impediments to the smooth operation of the JEE, which prevented the exam from selecting those it was meant to select.

Innate Intelligence

In Chapter 4, we saw how prevalent the idea of innate intelligence was among 1960s alumni. Still, there was at least some recognition that wealth and family histories of education were contributing factors in shaping academic success. Although very few addressed caste openly, inequalities were referenced through the rural–urban divide, facility with English, and access to consumer goods.

For alumni from the 1970s and 1980s, the growing status of the IITs, the scope of the JEE, and its ever more finely calibrated results seemed to eradicate any consideration of inherited caste capital in shaping testing outcomes. Rather, the attribution of success to "raw talent" without any reference to structural factors was far more common. One's raw talent was thought to be objectified in the JEE rank.

Nearly all the 1970s and 1980s alumni I spoke with remarked on their single-minded aspiration to pass the JEE. In fact, passing the exam with a good AIR was a greater ambition for most than studying engineering. The exam did not just symbolize merit; it was the very essence of the IIT system. This sense of the JEE was conveyed to me by three Tamil Brahmin IITians who graduated in the 1970s and 1980s. Swaminathan, a 1978 alumnus, told me that the JEE "is the only reason why the quality of the institution didn't diminish."[28] Subramaniam, a 1986 alumnus, added that, to him, "what made IIT, if I think back about it, is one thing: it's the entrance exam."[29] Another 1989 alumnus, Venkat, referred to the JEE as a "filtration system that created a concentrated gene pool."[30]

The JEE rank is common currency at the IITs. Everyone knows one another's rank, and this knowledge is part of everyday discourse. The rank is an indication not just of one-time performance in an examination but of future success or failure. Alumni would commonly reference a peer's JEE rank as a shorthand explanation of that person's career trajectory. Those instances in which the rank was not an accurate predictor of the future came in for much commentary. There were numerous stories I heard of JEE toppers who had defied expectations by not being particularly successful in their careers or by not being big earners. These stories were rendered with a mix of intrigue and bafflement, as if a life trajectory in defiance of the examination's evaluation was difficult to comprehend.

One story in particular was repeated by several IIT Madras alumni. It was of Madhavan, a Tamil Brahmin All India 4th, who earned his PhD in electronics and communications in the United States in the record time of three years and then decided to forgo high-paying corporate jobs in order to work in the Indian nongovernmental sector. The story took on the aspect of a parable that alumni used to point to life's inexplicable contingencies. Others made sense of this unorthodox trajectory by folding it back into Hindu scriptural orthodoxy. Madhavan's choice, they maintained, was that of a sannyasi who had renounced worldly gain for a more spiritual path.

Often, ranking would affect dynamics not just between classmates but among family members. Madhavan himself remarked on how much pressure his All India 4th put on his siblings. "It set a very high bar for my brothers," he recollected. "My middle brother got an All India rank of 180 which is objectively very, very good, but in our family it was seen as below par. What was terrible was my youngest brother who didn't get into the IIT and was devastated by it. I tried to talk to him but he was inconsolable for a very long time."[31]

Beyond their exam ranks, the understanding of intelligence as innate followed students into their time on campus. Sometimes this meant that they learned to feign a lack of effort. "You have to do well but never let on that you study," explained Swaminathan. "You have to act like it all somehow just comes to you." He went on to characterize this attitude as inherently contradictory. "On the one hand you say that it is very much by the dint of my effort that I passed the JEE but, on the other hand, once you get in, you have to say, no, it just came to me." Swaminathan did not reflect further on this IITian propensity. Rather, the sociological contours of this attitude of moving between claims to what we might call natural intelligence and learned intelligence—or simply nature and labor—were left unexamined. Interestingly, Swaminathan contrasted this IITian attitude to that prevalent in the United States. "In the U.S., it's the opposite," he mused. "I came to graduate school and saw that people were very proud of saying, 'I pulled five all-nighters in a row.' You would never let that on [at IIT]. In fact, if anything, you would study when everybody else was asleep. I kid you not. And then when people are awake you go around saying, 'What are you wasting your time for?'" Here we have yet another instance of the dialectic between ascription and achievement. While IITian exceptionalism invariably references the JEE, which appears to provide objective proof of intellectual standing through individual achievement, there is a discourse of ascription, of innate abilities, that is always close at hand.

This ideology of innateness is also evident among the JEE's test setters: IIT faculty. In the labor of organizing the JEE, we see efforts to shore up its ability to filter out the unmeritorious. IIT faculty tried to stay one step ahead of the increasing pressure on the evaluation process through continuously reforming its structure and content. Key to this process was striking the right balance between objective and subjective questions, with the former seen as a test of learning and the latter of innate conceptual ability. The notion of true merit as innate ability was manifest in the creation of a two-tier exam involving a first tier of a fully objective screening exam and a second tier of conceptual problems in physics, chemistry, and mathematics. The two-tier process was not simply a technical solution to the practical impossibility of subjective grading at the growing scale of the JEE; rather, it was "an expression of particular values: the 'merit' of a candidate is seen in his innate talent; the years of coaching a candidate goes through to succeed are distrusted and seen only as a measure of his endurance."[32] The JEE reforms are reminiscent of the reforms of the colonial ICS exam. Now, as then, the tension between the putative universality of access and the highly particular vision of the ideal candidate set in play an endless process of adjustment aimed at producing the "correct" outcome. The exam had to do what it was supposed to do: select those with innate talent, or true merit.

Being Middle Class

What is the form of merit that the JEE tacitly certifies and that Swaminathan referenced through the claim to natural intelligence? Many alumni spoke of the examination in terms that illuminated another aspect of the JEE: its perception as a vehicle of middle-class mobility. For them, this is what makes the JEE—and, by extension the IITs—truly meritocratic.

In some ways, IITian understandings of being middle class are very much in keeping with definitions elsewhere. One key aspect is fairness. Almost all the alumni I spoke with highlighted the impartiality of the JEE. In a country whose educational system is thought to be corrupted by nepotism and money power, the JEE has come to represent a shining example of the incorruptibility of the IITs. Sandipan Deb captures this sentiment with a rhetorical question: "How did this Third World nation manage to invent an entrance examination system that is the toughest and fairest of its kind in the world, and maintain the integrity of that system through half a century, so that even an Indian President's son stands as much (or, to be more precise, as little) chance of getting through?"[33] For Deb, the JEE is what symbolizes the IITs' transcendence of Indian conditions to be on par with First World meritocracy. It is what allows the middle class equal opportunity for admission. Here he is again: "The only way, the salaried middle class has always believed, that its children could get a fair chance to earn an honest living was to excel academically, do so well in their examinations that 'pull' did not matter." The contrast between "pull" and "fairness" rests on a well-worn binary between politics and virtue that underwrites the story of the middle class as representative of democratic modernity. "Once you had the 'IIT stamp' on your biodata," Deb avers, "the lack of 'pull' was not something to be bothered about at all."[34]

As with Deb, most IITians foreground the JEE's imperviousness to political corruption as its signal characteristic. Across interviews, I heard versions of this refrain: "Here, not even a powerful politician can use his influence to get his child admitted." The inordinate amount of labor that goes into developing the examination papers each year and guarding against leaks that might compromise the integrity of the exam speaks to the faith IIT faculty and administrators have in its role as a near-perfect arbiter of intellectual worth. That applicants are admitted solely on the basis of their performance on the exam is taken as proof of the system's integrity. In singling out overt *political* influence as the only threat to fairness, what such assessments of the JEE sidestep is the question of *societal* influence. They obscure the ways in which the JEE as a test of "excellence" builds on and extends histories of unequal caste capital.[35]

IITians go beyond lauding the JEE for its imperviousness to political influences. For them, its socially blind process of evaluation actually makes the examination a social equalizer. Swaminathan put this most succinctly and in comparative terms: "I still think it is truly egalitarian," he maintained.

> You go in for 6 hours on one day and 6 hours on the next day. You take an exam in mathematics and physics and chemistry and English . . . and that's it. That's what matters. Your school grades don't matter, who wrote letters for you doesn't matter, which I think is a good thing. And the closest I can see to that—certainly nothing in the U.S.—but in France there is the *grandes écoles*, I'm sure you are aware. Napoleon did that for them, because there was a university system which was very good but it wasn't a system that allowed people to come in from all walks of life. It wasn't a mixer, it wasn't an equalizer. The *grandes écoles* started to play that role.

It is striking that Swaminathan draws a parallel between the examinations for the IITs and those for the *grandes écoles*—the two most elite tiers of higher education in their respective national contexts—as social equalizers. As with the IITs, the *grandes écoles* were deliberately set apart from the national university system as a distinct and superior stratum for which the competition for admission was far more intense and the selection process far more exclusionary. Another similarity is in how they model meritocracy through their examination process but end up being technologies of social reproduction in their examination outcomes. The *grandes écoles,* like the IITs, stage the dialectic between achievement and ascription in such a way that achievers come from a very narrow social segment.

However, unlike the forms of distinction operating at the *grandes écoles,* IITians have an acute sense of themselves as non-elites, which derives from the complex relationship between class and caste.[36] We see this complexity in Swaminathan's remarks about class and labor. He noted that IITians' performance of innate intelligence and disdain toward hard work was reminiscent of "the upper-class, English aristocracy. . . . Things have to be ingrained. . . . That's very much the landed-gentry attitude. Why would I do something which would actually require me to work? It should just come to me." Swaminathan's effort to explain the IITian by recourse to both notions of egalitarianism and aristocratic culture gives us some sense of this blend of self-definitions, economically non-elite on the one hand and culturally elite on the other.

The understanding of education is key here. The primacy of education was a ubiquitous refrain across interviews with 1970s and 1980s alumni. This was reinforced by their own trajectories after graduation. Most went on to get higher degrees in engineering or related fields. Among these, some went on in academia and others shifted to industry. Those who stayed in India tended to supplement their engineering degrees with MBAs. The vast majority of alumni from these decades underscored their difference from those who came from industrial or commercial wealth. They, by contrast, had "only" educational capital. Chatterjee, a Bengali Brahmin 1982 alumnus, put it this way:

> All the kids I knew and all their parents viewed that there were two ways, roughly speaking, for their kids to make a living if they were not families that owned businesses and stores. If that's not what you were but part of the professional class of people in India—they were educated certainly but they were not owners of businesses and so forth—for these people they felt that their kids had to go in one of two routes in order to succeed, which was either to become a doctor or to become an engineer. . . . If you like mathematics, you were destined to become an engineer and try to get into the IITs, and if you like biology, you were destined to try to get into one of the premier medical colleges. That was the bifurcation.[37]

Such remarks by IITians about educational achievement point to their varied treatment of different forms of capital. Chatterjee's characterization of the professions effaces education not only as a form of capital but, more specifically, as a form of caste capital. Unlike land and business, alumni treat education not as inherited capital tied to histories of caste but as individual achievement. Moreover, by dissociating education from caste histories of privilege, upper-caste IITians deny that it is an index of inequality. This fungibility is a function of

the place of modern education—and, more so, technical education—
within democratic society. As a purported leveler of opportunity, it
stands in for individual, meritocratic achievement and not the social
reproduction of privilege. Modern education allows its beneficiaries to
obscure continuities with forms of putatively "nonmodern" capital
that make education a collective inheritance.

The JEE is key to this fungibility through which caste inheritance
is equated with individual merit. To build on Bourdieu and Passeron,
the JEE worked at two levels: it formally certified individual achievement, and it tacitly endorsed ascriptive forms of caste belonging as the
basis of intellectual ability.[38] This relationship between the formal and
the tacit is crucial: in order for caste claims to merit to appear as legiti-
mately modern and consistent with democratic principles, it is important that ascription remain an implicit assumption. For the examination to enact the transition from patronage and ascription to meritocracy
and achievement, caste had to be the unspoken basis of merit.

While IITians define achievement mostly in terms of being middle
class, they also smuggle in notions of ascriptive intelligence that index
caste belonging in less overt ways. Swaminathan, for instance, gestured
to caste in his characterization of the IITs' intellectual culture. After
saying that it was an investment in education that really set IITians
apart, he pointed to what he perceived as our shared Tamil Brahmin
identity: "In the society that I grew up in . . . very middle class . . . I
mean from your name I gather you were probably in the same kind of
society that I grew up [in] . . . education is everything." With this
oblique reference to being Tamil Brahmin, Swaminathan characterized
the middle-class culture of education as a caste phenomenon. Significantly, even when a propensity to educational achievement is attributed to caste culture, its treatment as nature and not history allows
for a simultaneous claim to individual merit. In Chapter 6 we will see
how opposition to reservation produces a far more overt claim to a caste
culture of education as a way of naturalizing intelligence and defending
against perceived threats to the IITs' exclusivity.

As with earlier moments around the ICS exam, the relationship between ascription and achievement in the evaluation of merit is most
apparent in the face of changes that disrupt settled expectations. IIT-
JEE coaching was one of those changes. With the growing prestige of

the exam, the coaching industry flourished and chalked up many successes. As this postcolonial version of the crammer brought in new groups from rural areas and small towns, it also brought demands for reform in its wake. The idea that one could cram for the JEE challenged its status as a test of rarefied conceptual ability. It was an indication that the exam was tilting too far away from its desired social outcomes. As we will see, once the JEE no longer served as an effective barrier to entry, the claims to merit became more overt in naming the ascriptive bases of achievement. Let us turn now to an in-depth look at the impact of coaching on the relationship between caste and merit.

The Coaching Industry

Initially, coaching for the JEE was a much smaller-scale operation, involving either private tutors or one of two coaching companies: Agrawal Classes and Brilliant Tutorials. By the mid-2010s, JEE coaching had become a veritable industry. One 2008 estimate by India's Associated Chambers of Commerce and Industry values the industry at over $2 billion.[39]

There is a whole spectrum of institutions that fall under the umbrella of JEE coaching. On one end are the classes that cater to specific subsets of IIT aspirants either explicitly, through their admissions process, or as a de facto outcome of their location and pedagogical orientation. Some of these are "boutique" classes in metropolitan centers run by "star teachers," many of whom are themselves IIT alumni.[40] They tend to attract students who fit the dominant mold of the upper-caste urbanite IITian, with a family history of education and central government employment. Then there are projects like Super 30 at the Ramanujan School of Mathematics, which I mentioned briefly in Chapter 4. Super 30 is a coaching institution established in 2003 for the express purpose of offering free training to thirty economically disadvantaged students each year, so that they can "crack" the JEE and gain admission to the IITs. This is a very specific intervention in the IIT system that foregrounds the untapped brilliance of the poor and seeks to identify and cultivate this promise. As noted earlier, the institute's name gestures to the unlikely life history of Srinivasa Ramanujan, a poor Brahmin who became one of the world's foremost mathematical minds.

At the other end of the spectrum from these more specialized centers is coaching at an industrial scale. The two sites that have become most emblematic of this scale of coaching are the cities of Kota in Rajasthan and Hyderabad in Andhra Pradesh. Beginning in the 1990s, Kota transformed into a coaching hub, with more than 150 centers that admit students from as early as the seventh grade and drill them for years in JEE preparation. This is a major money-making operation. Approximately 160,000 teenagers attend Kota's coaching institutes every year, paying between 50,000 and 100,000 rupees (approximately US$740 to $1,480) as annual tuition. In a few institutes, they are taught by IIT alumni, who claim salaries of 15 million–20 million rupees (approximately US$220,000 to $296,000) for their expertise. Neither coaching centers nor their affiliated hostels have exit policies or refunds, so for students from poorer families who borrow money to come to Kota, the stakes are even higher. Similarly, Hyderabad has transformed into a second coaching hub with an ever-expanding student constituency. We will look at coaching in Hyderabad at more length at the end of the chapter through an in-depth account of one student's experiences.

The competition between Kota and Hyderabad was showcased in a sensationalist 2011 essay in the *Times of India*, which tracked the intense rivalry between the two cities to secure top rankers in JEE admissions. The article begins by announcing that "Coaching institutes headquartered in Hyderabad have outdone Kota as the preparatory mecca for IIT-JEE" and then offers a blow-by-blow account of the "race":

> If JEE-2010 results are pored over, the maximum number of candidates to clear the exam was from Andhra Pradesh (AP). The state dominated the merit list. Seven of the top ten rankers were from there, the share of Kota starting only after rank 15. While in 2006, 938 candidates from AP and 1,004 from Rajasthan made it to the IITs, a year later the tables had turned, with 1,384 from AP clearing JEE and 1,344 from Rajasthan. It has been a close race since. In 2009, for example, 1,862 students from AP and 1,898 from Rajasthan cleared JEE. But just a year later, AP went for the kill, dominating the merit list like a hungry wolf having a succulent supper after years. AP's success has been like a rising tide. Last year, it sealed its superb showing by snatching the top rank.[41]

The need to publicly showcase JEE results produces intense ranking within these coaching institutes. When students are admitted to an institute, they start at the same level but are quickly grouped into batches based on their performance on frequent review tests. Because JEE top rankers enhance the reputation of coaching centers, students with "top rank potential" are rapidly nosed out and given special treatment.[42]

Students are kept constantly aware of their relative standing. There is now an online platform for students called C-SAT (Systematic Analysis of Test for Classroom Students), which generates a detailed analysis of their performance that is accessible by both students and their parents. There is also a section where student scores are compared with those of previous JEE toppers. An android app with the tagline "To aim is not enough—you must hit" is now available for this purpose on the Google Play Store.[43]

Institutes have mechanisms of self-monitoring, such as mandatory diaries in which students are supposed to detail their day-to-day activities. According to a 2015 article in *India Today*, the diary required by Kota's Allen Career Institute is titled "Mera Sach" (My truth), and it contains columns such as "Did I wake up prior to sunrise?" "Did I complete my daily routine, exercise and prayer timely?" "Remembered my parents, mentors and the career goal," and "Took completely balanced and nutritious meal[s]."[44] The institute's walls also offer motivational messages, such as "If you can dream it, you can do it," "Hard work beats talent when talent doesn't work hard," and quotes from previous IIT-JEE toppers.[45]

Not only are students within the institutes ranked, but some of the institutes have started their own schools to identify and train students early. For instance, one of Kota's institutes, Career Point, started a residential school called Career Point Gurukul, which covers grades six through twelve and focuses mostly on coaching for various competitive examinations, including the JEE.[46] The school has on-campus apartments where families—usually just mothers—can live with their children, take care of them, and ensure that there are no distractions, such as access to social media.[47]

The industry is now so lucrative that people leave corporate jobs to work in coaching institutes. The 2015 *India Today* article cites the example of a man who secured an all India rank of 41 in the 2006 IIT-JEE, graduated from IIT Bombay in 2010, got placed with Goldman Sachs, and quit after three years to come to Kota and teach physics at Allen Career Institute, where his father, A. K. Gupta—an IIT Kanpur alumnus—heads the IIT division. The article also points out that coaching institutes routinely poach faculty from one another.[48]

The coaching industry has revolutionized the IIT admissions process. Across the institutes, there are growing numbers of students who come through the coaching centers of Hyderabad or Kota and arrive at the IITs after years of JEE drilling. The percentage of these students—the majority of whom are from nonprofessional, often rural family backgrounds—receiving financial aid is steadily on the rise. These students mark a significant departure from the institutional norm of the upper-caste, English-speaking urbanite that coalesced over the 1970s, 1980s, and 1990s.

The JEE Crisis and Calls for Reform

The coaching centers of Kota and Hyderabad have come in for critical scrutiny as the source of indebtedness and student suicides. Called "coaching factories," their grueling routines are likened to the industrial shopfloor, with students as grist for the mill of company profits. In Kota alone, the number of suicides reached a high of thirty in 2015 and prompted calls for reform. In response, some companies have established helplines for students to call for support. However, very little has changed in the daily routines of twelve-hour nonstop study.

For IIT managers, the coaching industry has been cause for different concerns. In a 2008 newspaper interview about the proliferation of coaching classes, IIT Madras's then director M. S. Ananth clarified that he was "looking for students with raw intelligence and not those with a mind prepared by coaching class tutors. The coaching classes only help students in mastering pattern recognition skills. With this, you cannot get students with raw intelligence."[49] This notion of "raw intelligence" places the ideal IITian outside institutional, or even social, formation as a naturally gifted individual with a native capacity for technical knowledge. Raw intelligence is supposed to be an innate characteristic that cannot be acquired through training. In conversations with Ananth and other IIT administrators, I heard their concerns that the coaching industry undermined the ability of the exam to test for those who were truly worthy.

To put it in Bourdieu's terms, what IIT administrators fear is that the exam is now proving unable to distinguish between what candidates *are* from what they have *learned to do*. The exam is failing to capture "raw intelligence" and has instead succumbed to the sustained onslaught of coaching centers that drill students in successful performances. As these centers trumpet their successes in producing JEE top rankers, the dialectic of ascription and achievement on which the examination rests appears to be in peril.

Just as with the colonial-era crammers, the perceived crisis of exceptionalism produced by the marketization of the JEE has generated calls for examination reform. The hope is that reforms might reinstate the exam as a measure of merit instead of just a measure of a student's ability to endure years of coaching. Some, like P. V. Indiresan, another former director of IIT Madras, have argued that given different circumstances, they would do away with the exam altogether. "If I had my way, I would scrap the JEE in its present form, because it has become a trainable exam," opined Indiresan. "As long as one has the stamina, and does not get bored, you can get through the JEE. . . . To some extent, the coaching class syndrome and the willingness of the middle-class student to devote four or five years of his life to this entrance examination is turning the JEE into more a test of endurance than of intelligence or talent for science." But, Indiresan qualified, "if the JEE is scrapped entirely, there could be political interference in IIT admissions, and that would be disastrous."[50]

This sense of being trapped between a rock and a hard place, with politics on one side and the market on the other, pervades IITian concerns about the transformation of the JEE. In June 2010, a panel set up to recommend reforms announced that the JEE was to be renamed an "aptitude test" and would constitute only 30 percent of the admissions evaluation, with the school board exam results making up the remaining 70 percent. (The relevance of the school board exam is discussed later in this chapter.) The move was highly controversial, fiercely debated, and ultimately not implemented.

What is particularly significant about this sense of crisis around the JEE is that coaching is nothing new. In fact, it is as old as the exam itself. As early as 1962, Bombay's Agrawal Classes made news when one of its students bagged the All India 1st rank in the JEE, making its centers the top destination for IIT aspirants. By the early 1980s, over 55 percent of students entering the IITs were Agrawal students. In the 1984 JEE, 84 Agrawal students secured ranks within the first All India 100. After Agrawal, a number of other coaching centers also came up, most importantly its close competitor, Brilliant Tutorials, in 1970.

IIT alumni from previous decades attested to the ubiquity of coaching. Swaminathan recalled that in his 1974 cohort, "the number of people who got in with low preparation was very low. Very, very few people got in, and all of them were in the low ranks. The top rankers, not one of them came in without a lot of preparation." Jayaram, a 1980s alumnus, concurred that "everyone attended coaching classes," although many, like him, opted to do so through correspondence courses.[51]

But Jayaram's "everyone" did not actually include all IITians. Pandiarajan, a 1970s Backward Caste alumnus from the town of Dindigul in southern Tamilnadu, contradicted this assumption on the part of his peers from Chennai. He studied for the JEE on his own because there were no coaching classes where he lived. To give me a sense of the unevenness of coaching in his day, he laid out the channels into IIT Madras from different parts of Tamilnadu: compared to five students from all the four southern districts, there were eighty just from the city of Chennai. In other words, coaching in the 1970s was largely a metropolitan phenomenon. Pandiarajan further characterized this discrepancy in caste terms: coaching was largely the monopoly of urban upper castes, with Tamil Brahmins being the best represented group.[52]

What is new, then, is not coaching itself but the recent geographical and social expansion of the phenomenon. Now, more and more students who might previously have thought the IITs out of their reach have turned to Kota and Hyderabad in hopes of admission. The mass marketing of coaching has rendered more permeable a social barrier to entry and generated acute anxieties among IITians about their claim to meritocratic exceptionalism.

While calls for examination reform are one way that these anxieties are processed, there are others. Within Chennai, the rise of boutique coaching reinstates the distinction between upper and lower caste through differentiations of various sorts. By contrast to assessments of "coaching factory" students as instrumental and mechanistic, "bou-tique" students are characterized as cerebral and oriented toward the lofty ambition of mastering conceptual knowledge. While some of these distinctions in approaches to JEE coaching do hold, the contrast between the conceptual and the rote does much more than differen-tiate training. This difference in *kind* translates into a difference in *status*. Within IIT Madras, the distinction between the gifted and the coached is reproduced in everyday negotiations. Through talk about training, students and alumni reference notions of caste and class dif-ference that call into question the claim to a generic middle classness on the part of more culturally elite, upper-caste IITians. Moreover, such arguments about the conceptual versus the rote once again reprise older colonial distinctions between mental and manual labor on the basis of which technical education was first stratified.

Inside Chennai's Boutique Coaching Classes

It is in reaction to the scaling up of the JEE industry and the perceived crisis in mechanisms of distinction that a new breed of boutique coaching has arisen. These classes revert to an older model of small-scale private coaching that existed alongside the two earliest coaching companies, Agrawal and Brilliant. However, they are now a conscious departure from the model exemplified by Kota and Hyderabad and seek to recuperate a more conceptual approach to the JEE. Within Chennai, boutique coaching reinstates a distinction between the gifted and the coached along recognizable axes of differentiation. It mobilizes the cleavages of the Non-Brahmin movement by associating the "concep-tual" with Tamil Brahmins and the "rote" with non-Brahmins.

Madhavan, the "All India 4th" we met earlier, runs a nongovern-mental organization working to enhance the quality of public primary education in Tamilnadu. On the side, he coaches JEE classes in Chennai. He has come to be known as a "star teacher," whose classes are highly sought after by students from Chennai, most of whom are Brahmins and other upper castes. Madhavan recalled that even when he took the JEE in 1990, JEE coaching was set apart from other tuition classes. "Generally, you'd go for tuitions if you were not doing well in school," he explained. "It was insulting if you went to a tuition class. But JEE coaching was seen differently." This was in part because of the admissions criteria set by coaching class teachers. "They would say, I will only take people who have got above 90 [as their school marks percentage]." Ironically, Madhavan's tenth-grade marks did not qualify him for admission to a coaching class, and so he ended up studying on his own for the JEE, with some weekly help from a relative who had been an IIT professor. For the most part, he scoured secondhand bookshops for mathematics and physics books and trained himself "on concepts." Additionally, he did the Agrawal correspondence course and participated in the practice testing administered by the center.

Then, Madhavan was catapulted to stardom with his JEE rank. "There was a lot of hype," he told me. "Agrawal put my photo in the newspaper. Within Chennai, there was a lot of noise. A lot of people called, people congratulated. So, I was very happy. People told me if I had gone to Brilliant they would have given me some 30–40,000 rupees in hand." The hype followed him into IIT Madras as the "south zone topper," an achievement compounded by the fact that no one from Chennai had gotten within the first ten JEE ranks for quite some time. Madhavan was even asked by the IIT Madras director to give the opening speech at his commencement ceremony.

Unlike most other toppers, Madhavan chose the unorthodox route of finishing his PhD in the United States and returning to India to work in rural popular science education in the nonprofit sector. To make extra money, he decided to turn to JEE coaching, where he found a ready-made audience because of his reputation as a JEE All India 4th.

I asked Madhavan whether he had any qualms about teaching at the two extreme ends of the education spectrum: rural science education on the one hand, and JEE coaching on the other. Was he not just contributing to the JEE rat race? No, he told me, because what he offers "is not just teaching to the test." In fact, he "wrote a book on why we should not worry about exams." What, then, are his coaching classes for, I puzzled? "It is not that people actually go to IIT coaching to get into IIT," Madhavan clarified. "They know full well they're not going to get into IIT. Just look at the percentages. 15 lakh [1.5 million] people write it, a few thousand people get in. . . . The number of seats increase, the number of people attempting increases. So why do they try? Because there are a lot of side benefits to it. . . . Science education isn't happening in schools today. So, there's an alternate stream for science education. It's called IIT coaching." Although he granted that his di-

gressions from more tailored exam coaching did elicit student and parental complaints, he insisted that his classes functioned as a catch-all
space for intellectually ambitious students who were broadly interested
in conceptual training.

What was the social composition of Madhavan's classes? Most, he
told me, were middle-class Brahmin students, the "traditional IIT profile." Scheduled Caste students were nonexistent, and while Backward
Caste students were a small minority until the early 2000s, their numbers had increased since the extension of the Backward Caste quota to
the IITs in 2008. Madhavan also pointed to significant class differences.
"The Backward Caste students are actually far richer compared to the
upper caste students," he said. "For them it is a matter of pride and prestige to get in. One guy's father is actually running a private engineering
college. Why would he try for the IITs? He can join that college, right?
He always has a college."

In Chapter 6 we will explore in depth this prevalent sense among
Tamil Brahmins of their narrowed educational horizons in Tamilnadu,
especially in contrast to that of wealthier Backward Castes. Madhavan
himself did not endorse a notion of Brahmin victimhood, although he
did link the Tamil Brahmin aspiration to join the IITs to Tamilnadu's
educational milieu, with its expansive quotas for Backward and Scheduled Castes. This IIT aspiration, he told me, had dovetailed with "a
Brahmin culture of coaching." I quote him here at length:

> I feel that paying for classes is a culture. IIT coaching—the idea that
> you have to pay money to get in, and that it is valuable whether or
> not you get into IIT—has sunk into the Brahmin community because
> they've been doing this for very long. Many students—their parents
> have gone for UPSC classes and now they go to IIT classes, so it is
> almost a no-brainer for them. They will go. For the Backward Caste
> students, this is the first time they are even thinking along these
> lines. Should I invest so much—I will invest in ten other things, but
> should we invest in this or not—is more a cultural question than a
> utility question. The richer sections [of the Backward Castes] are
> more in tune with that. I don't think the culture has yet set in across
> the Backward Caste community. It will take time.

Madhavan's insight into this "caste culture" illuminates a long-
standing Tamil Brahmin orientation around examinations and coaching
that extends back to the heyday of the UPSC exam to enter the central

government services. Just as many parents attended coaching classes to prepare for the UPSC exam, now their children do so with the JEE. Indeed, this was the pattern in Madhavan's own family. His parents entered the central government services by passing the UPSC exam, as a result of which Madhavan studied in Central Board of Secondary Education (CBSE) schools, where the vast majority of students were Tamil Brahmins like himself.

Not only did Madhavan attribute the greater propensity of Brahmins to attend JEE coaching classes to a "caste culture," but he has responded by making sure that his classes are relevant to both the JEE and the CBSE examination. In fact, he refers to his classes as "CBSE-plus-IIT training." Why, I asked him, did he single out the CBSE? Because, he told me, the vast majority of IIT aspirants in Chennai were from CBSE schools. By way of example, he gestured to his own schooling in Chennai's DAV Boys Senior Secondary School, a CBSE institute where a sizable percentage of students are Tamil Brahmins. "I would say about three-fourths of my class would go for JEE coaching," he told me, "and those who didn't still studied for the JEE at home. We had about 50 students or so in my class section at that time and, except for 10 students, everyone else studied for and took the JEE. And out of 80 students, out of those seriously writing the JEE, 40 of us got into IIT." Given these numbers, it made sense to Madhavan to cater to this constituency. Besides, he told me, his classes tended to attract a self-selecting type of student, one who was more concerned with "learning concepts and not just doing problems." Although over the years he has capitulated to the demand that he teach more to the test and now regularly assigns worksheets, his constituency has remained fairly consistent.

What was the cost of his coaching classes? Madhavan charged what he told me was the standard rate for boutique classes: 20,000 rupees (approximately US$300) for one subject for eleventh and twelfth graders; 15,000 rupees (US$222) for tenth graders; and 11,000 rupees (US$163) for ninth graders. Most took physics, chemistry, and mathematics, the three subjects tested in the JEE, which added up to between 33,000 and 60,000 rupees (US$490–$900) per year. These rates, while high, are much lower than some of the corporate coaching centers that charge up to 400,000 rupees (US$6,000) per year.

Although Madhavan caters to a distinct constituency and charges relatively affordable rates for coaching, he admitted that the scaling up of coaching has had an effect. "Many of these coaching classes, particularly the Kota/Andhra model, shifted what we were doing," he told me. "I felt the pressure, a lot of other teachers felt the pressure. For me, it was okay for a long time not to worry about it, but now I have a lot more worksheets, and practice, and—*ithai maadhuri problem four poddu* [do problem 4 like this]. We have more and more classes which are making kids do pattern recognition." He bemoaned this shift from "first understanding the philosophy and then doing the practice" but acknowledged that it was the natural result of a "hyped up system." With any system that acquires this kind of hype, he rationalized, "people will figure out a way of breaking it. Do you need to really understand concepts to crack the JEE? No. That's what these coaching classes have proved. Now the teachers who were earlier saying, let me understand and help, they started finding that their students weren't doing any better than the Kota/Andhra students. So, they thought, why should I waste all this time trying to make them understand? Let me also start shifting."

This sense of a decline in standards—a kind of downward spiral from the conceptual to the rote—has permeated the field of boutique coaching. Even as "star teachers" like Madhavan adjust their methods, they try to maintain distinctions between their own students and those of the "coaching factories." While distinctions in training are undeniable, the discourse around them is also an exercise in social boundary making, intended to reinforce the meritocratic value of the exceptional "boutique" student over the generic "factory" student. As we see from the social profile of students in Chennai's boutique classes, this exercise in boundary making is also very much one of caste distinction, which reproduces the Brahmin–non-Brahmin binary.

JEE Coaching and the Politics of School Boards in Tamilnadu

What about Madhavan's students? How do they position themselves within the universe of JEE coaching? Speaking with his coaching class students, it became evident that the distinction between "the gifted" and "the coached" predates arrival at the IITs. As we heard from Madhavan, most of his students are from schools that fall under the

CBSE. This is not just an institutional designation. In Tamilnadu, and more specifically in Chennai, the difference between schools that administer the central and state board examinations carries a powerful symbolic charge, as it maps quite explicitly onto upper and lower caste. For most of Madhavan's students, being a CBSE student was a collective identity and a point of pride. It was a way of marking themselves as more conceptually oriented and, by extension, more suited for the IITs.

Tamil Brahmin affinity with the CBSE and with IIT Madras is in part a response to the politics of Non-Brahminism and to the expanding scope of Tamilnadu's reservation system, something that I consider at length in Chapter 6. It also comes out of a longer history of pan-Indian mobility and national education. Since the nineteenth century, Tamil Brahmins leveraged their cultural capital as knowledge bearers to move from the countryside to the city and outside the region for employment. Tamil Brahmin exodus from rural to urban areas, and beyond Madras Presidency, was accelerated by a sense of victimization by the Non-Brahmin and Dravidian movements, especially their role in advancing communal quotas for non-Brahmins in public education and regional government jobs. For the vast majority of Tamil Brahmins, the UPSC exam was their ticket out of regional and into central government employment. As a result of their conscription into the central government bureaucracy, Tamil Brahmins are overrepresented in schools that follow the curriculum set by the CBSE, rather than state or regional boards. Many attend government-run CBSE schools that cater to children of the national civil services, guaranteeing them a seat regardless of frequent interregional transfers.[53] Others send their children to private schools, which also offer the CBSE exam. These schools state as one of their key missions "to develop the spirit of national integration and create a sense of 'Indianness' among children."[54] The notion of "Indianness" gestures to a cosmopolitan subjectivity that is supraregional and supracaste. At the same time, in the Tamil context, the distinction between the regional/state board and the national/central board maps discursively onto low and upper caste and has become the basis for claims to intellectual merit.

The assumption that the CBSE curriculum produces "thinking students" who are better suited to intellectual life in general and the

IITs in particular was conveyed to me across a wide swathe of interviews with CBSE teachers, administrators, and students. Person after person distinguished the CBSE's "conceptual training" from the "rote learning" in the state boards. It was this training, they argued, that made their students a natural fit for the IITs. One principal told me that his school sends an average of fifteen to eighteen students each year to IIT Madras. It was not merely the affinity between the CBSE and the JEE that made these feeder schools for the IITs. The schools specifically tailor their CBSE exam preparation in such a way that it dovetails with the JEE curriculum. As we heard from Madhavan, the more exclusive coaching classes in Chennai also follow suit.

CBSE schools are not only set apart as conceptually oriented. Like IIT Madras, they are also marked as upper-caste enclaves in the city. Udhay, another 1990s IIT Madras alumnus who now conducts JEE coaching classes, told me about his experience of moving from a state to a CBSE school. "I could see a huge shift when I went to Padma Seshadri," he told me. "Everybody talked about IIT, breathed IIT." Plus, the social composition of the student body was strikingly different. "I can't think of too many non-Brahmins who were there," Udhay recalled. "It was very homogenous that way. Clearly upper caste, plus it's a more Hindu school. So the prayers and everything were Hindu prayers and all that. And you wouldn't find many Christians. Of course, Muslims were unheard of." Madhavan had a similar description of his alma mater, the DAV Boys Senior Secondary School. That, too, was predominantly Brahmin and oriented around IIT aspiration. The school even held a Hindu *puja* before the annual JEE.

I conducted group interviews with students in some of Madhavan's JEE coaching classes in Chennai. The overwhelming majority were Tamil Brahmins who went to CBSE schools where there was a commonsense assumption that they would take the JEE and gain admission to the IITs. Many conveyed a strong conviction of the natural fit between CBSE schools and the IITs because of their shared commitment to "conceptual training." Many also contrasted their own intellectual formation to the inferior training received at state board schools, from which far fewer students went to the IITs.

Let us look at a set of curated comments by Madhavan's coaching class students about the two school boards.

AS: What schools do students in your coaching class come from?
STUDENT 1: Shankara, DAV, Padma Seshadri, Kendriya Vidyalaya.
AS: Are these all Central Board schools?
STUDENT 1: Yeah. From any metric [state board] school, we'll have maximum of one student per class. Even IIT Madras, you'll have maximum of one or two students, not more than that. Everybody else will be from CBSE only.
AS: What's the difference between the training in the state and central boards?
STUDENT 2: In metric, the exam paper and the textbook are exactly the same. You just have to mug up [memorize] and take the exam. But in the Central Board, you have to concentrate in classes because the teachers tell you more than what's in the books. In metric, you can pass and get good marks without the help of teachers because the books are more than enough.
AS: Do you think that the Central Board prepares you better for the JEE?
STUDENT 3: Yeah, it does, definitely. Up to tenth standard we were all studying together and in the eleventh, a few guys went to metric. Now, they're coming and saying, why did we go there?
STUDENT 4: I was going to take metric, but then I spoke to the seniors and they were like, if you take metric you will just not be able to cope up with IIT questions. It'll be so hard, it'll be so different. There, you'll have to mug [memorize] but in the JEE, you'll have to think, and you won't be able to do both. You can't mug in the morning and be applying concepts in the evening.
AS: So are you planning to also do the entrance exam for Anna University [the regional engineering university]?
STUDENT 5: No, at Anna University, you need your board marks and it's very hard to get into because state [board] students, they don't have much to read, they just mug up the book with questions and score 100 percent, whereas in CBSE we have hard problems.
AS: So Anna doesn't differentiate between state board and central board?
STUDENT 5: No, it's just marks, the percentage, which is why the metric students can get in.

This palpable sense of the difference in school boards and their correlation with kinds of training was also echoed by alumni. Here are
three alumni perspectives on this issue, the last one from a lower-caste
state board alumnus who echoes the sentiment about the different
training received at the state and central board schools:

> ALUMNUS 1: I was from the central board which is not so lenient—
> so we knew we were up against the wall. So we had to work rather
> hard. So, to be honest with you, at one point we thought that JEE or
> nothing else because our board scores usually never matched up to
> what the state board students got.
> ALUMNUS 2: This is just my perception, but most non-Brahmins
> would not send their kids to central board schools, and I think this
> was because they would think that scoring marks is tougher in cen-
> tral board.
> ALUMNUS 3 (FROM STATE BOARD): JEE was intense. So, unless you are
> really, really bright and don't need to apply yourself, getting in would
> require enormous application. So, if you take Padma Seshadri Bala
> Bhavan [central board school], there would be 20 guys coming into
> IIT per year. I was the only guy who joined from my [state board]
> school. That was an anomaly, because if you take five years after and
> five years before I entered, nobody went from my school.

For these coaching class students and IIT alumni, a CBSE education does not merely reference a kind of training; it also indexes a regional caste landscape where the school boards map onto upper caste
and lower caste and associated intellectual abilities. As with the JEE,
there is an interplay here between ascription and achievement. While
CBSE schooling formally extends a certificate of achievement, it also
tacitly certifies upper-caste culture.

The symbolic association of CBSE schooling with upper-caste conceptual rigor helps to explain why, in the face of the crisis produced
by the coaching industry, IIT Madras faculty proposed prioritizing the
school board examination as the principle basis of admission. Unlike
regional engineering colleges, however, the type of school board would
also factor into the evaluation. As with the reform efforts linking the
colonial ICS exam more closely with an Oxbridge education, the proposal to shift the relative weight of the JEE and the school boards in

the IIT admissions process was aimed at securing the link between the CBSE and the IITs. With more and more students from Kota and Hyderabad defying expectations of who properly belongs in the IITs, these attempts to elevate "the gifted" over "the coached" have resorted to older caste landscapes of education as a means to produce the intended outcomes of the JEE.

The Mental and the Manual . . . Redux

While across Chennai, the legacy of Non-Brahminism continues to structure practices of distinction and forms of collective affiliation around the JEE, within IIT Madras other forms of differentiation have also come into play. Campus life produces not only an equation between Tamil Brahmins and intellectual merit but schisms between upper-caste urban English speakers, who come from histories of education, and upper castes from other backgrounds, whose presence makes more tenuous the association between upper casteness, conceptual ability, and merit.

The most rapidly expanding group of students on campus are from the states of Andhra Pradesh and Telangana. Ever since their capital city of Hyderabad began to double as a JEE coaching capital in the early 2000s, the number of IIT aspirants from the state has risen sharply, with a majority of successful students opting for IIT Madras in neighboring Tamilnadu over more distant campuses.[55] The expanded scale of coaching has brought in students from small towns and rural parts of the state who belong to landed upper castes, such as the Kammas and the Reddys. These are families without the same histories of educational capital who now aspire to give their children opportunities on par with the urban intelligentsia. In producing differences among upper castes, their presence has troubled the easy distinction between upper and lower. Unlike in greater Chennai, where the coaching industry reinscribes the divide between Brahmin and non-Brahmin, the presence of students from Andhra Pradesh and Telangana within IIT Madras destabilizes the very notion of what it means to be upper caste.

I asked former IIT Madras director M. S. Ananth whether he thought the expansion of coaching had changed the kind of student who attends the IIT. "There has been a change," he acknowledged.

I would say a fraction of them are still the same, exactly as they were, the bright ones, motivated, who are a joy to teach, they still exist. But there is about 15–20 percent of students who are either burned out, or who have come through these coaching classes and think they have arrived already. They don't think they need to make an effort, they think they'll anyway get a degree and a job, simply because they are IITians. That fraction alarms me, because that is a sort of infection. It can spread. What you need is a collection of people who will reinforce each other's thinking in terms of values.[56]

While he acknowledged that this cavalier attitude toward an IIT education is not limited to students from Hyderabad or Kota, it was this subset that he singled out for comment. It was they who embodied a kind of intellectual inertia and premature sense of arrival that he feared would "infect" their peers, precipitating a downward spiral of declining standards.

The term "infection" is a striking metaphor indeed. It casts "the coached" as an alien intrusion in the corporate institutional body that threatens to weaken it from within. The ex-director was not alone in holding this opinion. Such sentiments and concerns about "the coached" are also echoed by alumni. Chatterjee, an alumnus from the 1980s who is now a professor at MIT, noted that IIT alumni currently doing their PhDs under him described peers who had come through four years of coaching as "just so intellectually tired that they didn't work very hard in IITs." This was not the fault of the institutions, Chatterjee quickly added, because "the IITs cannot provide a value system that society does not by and large have. . . . I mean, there were a few professors at IIT who did a very good job of teaching us, okay? There were a few of them that took personal interest in some of us and so forth and so on. But that's not why IIT was great at the time. It was because of students and their interaction with each other."

What do we make of this sense of an erosion of values and its threat to the collective enterprise of peer learning and exceptional ambition? What values are supposedly in decline because of the coaching industry and its "burned out" products?

The key value that alumni and administrators identify as under threat is that of engineering education as a process of holistic intellectual

formation. Many spoke of "coaching factory" students as overly instrumental in their approach to the IITs and attributed this to a fundamentally different orientation toward knowledge. Chatterjee recalled
that when he went back to receive the Distinguished Alumnus prize
at his alma mater, "the one thing the faculty complained about is that
the exam doesn't test intrinsic intelligence anymore as much as it
tests how much practice you've had." As we have seen many times
over, this is a well-worn contrast between knowledge as an expression
of innate conceptual intelligence and knowledge as a mechanistic,
embodied practice. The very notion of a "coaching factory" reinforces
this mind-body distinction: its students are likened to the mass-
produced commodities of the industrial shopfloor, which are defined
by their generic, unexceptional quality.

The mechanistic approach to knowledge bred by the coaching industry is associated with a narrowing of intellectual horizons. Shankar,
a professor in the Humanities Department at IIT Madras and a 1980s
alumnus, mentioned a debate competition for which he was one of
the judges. "We heard about 30 students do their 2-minute, 3-minute
speeches," he recalled, "and we were shocked by the quality of debate. . . .
Some of them were reading off their notes and just the body language
and the ability to communicate seemed too inadequate." I asked how
he squared this with the reigning assumption that IIT students are the
best of the best. "The best in some very structured, narrow way," he
responded. "They've been groomed for a particular exam. That's what a
lot of people are lamenting right now: the loss of the well-rounded
individual."[57]

Of course, "the well-rounded individual" is not just a victim of the
coaching industry. The compartmentalization of knowledge, as a result of which the humanities and social sciences are increasingly regarded as irrelevant to the making of the Indian engineer, has long been
in the making. Furthermore, the IIT system and its fetishized exam
have been key catalysts in this very process of severing the technical
sciences from other branches of study. Yet the narrowing of intellectual horizons that has been a steady trend in postindependence Indian
engineering is conveniently transposed onto its latest, non-elite entrants. This, then, seems less a lament about the compartmentaliza-

tion of knowledge as such than about the threat posed by the expansion of the IIT student body beyond a desired constituency.

Faculty and administrators bemoan the narrow horizons of "the coached" not just as evidenced in their approach to education but also in their attitude toward future employment. As one administrator who oversees the Alumni Office said ruefully, "Rote learning is the norm [for them] and the IIT merely represents a paycheck and a local job for life." He worried that this new breed of student would mean fewer diasporic success stories of the kind that have become so emblematic of IIT exceptionalism. "For cultural reasons, fewer of them go abroad," he elaborated, "and this will definitely mean a decline from those days when seventy percent of Silicon Valley companies had IITian names on the board."[58] This presumed parochialism of "the coached" is contrasted to the long-mobile upper-caste subject, with his pan-Indian and now global affiliation.

Finally, these narrow horizons are seen to threaten not only the career trajectories that have underpinned global brand value but the campus culture as well. Students and alumni from across the past fifteen years mentioned the parochial loyalties that students from Andhra Pradesh had brought with them. Sudipta, a 2004 alumnus, put it this way: "If you look for groupism in the campus, that is the only form you will find it in, on the basis of language. There is a huge number of people coming from Andhra Pradesh. You will find most of them staying together. Other than that, there is no distinction."[59] The regionalism of Andhra students—especially their tendency to speak in their native Telugu—came in for repeated mention as a violation of the IITs' national and global ethos. Of course, Brahmin Tamil and Hindi are also heard quite commonly on campus, and other forms of collectivity are key to what it means to be a "real" IITian. I heard numerous stories of male bonding over all-night debates on everything from obscure mathematical formulas to the evidence of science in Sanskrit texts. Such interactions take place in the dorm room and not the classroom and mark a form of upper-caste homosociality. But it is only the use of Telugu that is marked as an unacceptable form of parochialism that violates campus social norms and is better suited to students at other institutions.

Lurking behind all this commentary on the decline of values seen in the instrumentality and narrow horizons of "the coached" is an argument about the market. Despite the fact that all IITians pay money for coaching classes, it is only in relation to "coaching factory" students that the market is identified as an illegitimate mediator. Indeed, it is strange to hear IIT administrators bemoaning the instrumentality of "the coached" when one of the hallmark features of the IIT pedigree is its market value. After all, this is what is encapsulated in the term "brand IIT." But for them, the contrast between "the gifted" and "the coached" seems to hinge on a perceived relationship between nonmarket and market value. "The coached" are deemed illegitimate because they are seen as gaining admission to the IIT not through their innate knowledge but because they paid money for coaching classes. Their achievement is thus superficial and not emblematic of their true abilities. While they are pure creatures of the market, "the gifted" have "raw intelligence" that is recognized but not produced by the market. Through this shadow play between market and nonmarket value, the intimacy between achievement and ascription is reinstated and "true" merit denied to students from Andhra Pradesh.

In sum, Telugu students are seen as problematic because they are the wrong kind of upper caste. Their unfamiliarity with English and their open embrace of regionalism are at odds with the cosmopolitan intellectualism that is supposed to distinguish upper from lower. How did those designated as "the coached" experience the coaching industry? How did their time at IIT Madras affect their sense of self and standing? And to what extent did they internalize or contest pejorative assessments of their merit?

The Coached

In the 2000s, the number of students from Andhra Pradesh began to rise steadily. While a few had come from other coaching centers, the floodgates opened when the Sri Chaitanya and Narayana franchises took off. Begun in 1986, the Sri Chaitanya franchise has expanded to 250 institutions across nine states. The Narayana group started in 1980 and has grown steadily to its current scale, comprising over 200 schools, 400 junior colleges, 9 professional colleges, and 500 coaching centers spread over thirteen states. Not only have these franchises expanded geographically, but they've also moved lower and lower down the educational ladder. Now they offer students the option of beginning college examination training as early as the sixth grade.

Abbas, a 2016 IIT Madras alumnus from Andhra Pradesh, spoke to me about his time in the Sri Chaitanya coaching center and at IIT Madras. He also offered an account of why the two franchises have been able to monopolize the space of education in Andhra Pradesh and Telangana and what the ramifications have been for their students. Here, I use Abbas's experiences and insights as a window onto the "coaching factory" phenomenon.[60]

Abbas attended one of the Sri Chaitanya coaching centers from 2007 to 2009. He chose that particular center because of only one consideration: its track record of getting students into the IITs. His center happened to be the most coveted because of its phenomenal success rate; just over Abbas's two years there, approximately sixty students gained admission to IIT Madras. But even this pales in comparison to what followed. Abbas described his time at Sri Chaitanya as "a watershed," after which both coaching franchises expanded far more aggressively into secondary school education. The expansion was not just down the educational ladder; the franchises also ranged beyond cities into smaller towns. "I come from a small town," Abbas offered by way of example, "and we have our own Chaitanya/Narayana schools there. We don't have Chaitanya/Narayana colleges, but we have schools."

I asked Abbas what accounted for the timing of this expansion in mass coaching. It was the change in the format of the IIT exam. "The IIT entrance test was subjective before," he explained. "When it was subjective there were few pockets in Andhra Pradesh—like the Ramaiah coaching center in Hyderabad—which used to be popular, but Sri Chaitanya and Narayana were not that popular. They were not known to send so many students into the IITs. But once the exam became objective, it became easier for the sort of training they give to be very effective at getting students into IITs. What you do is practice so much that it becomes very easy to actually crack the exam. And that was what turned the wheel." The new format of the exam allowed coaching centers to chalk up more successes, which in turn attracted increasing numbers of people to them. Abbas narrated this shift as a sea change in aspiration. "The IITs were always famous, always had some kind of an aura," he acknowledged. "When students go to IIT, they settle well, they get good jobs and good life, and all that." But, he went on, "it was inaccessible. What people thought was, it was only for geniuses." The coaching industry changed that impression by making the IITs "not so distant anymore. They were now within reach." When people saw that there was a real chance of getting into one of these prestigious institutes, they "refused to settle for something local." And this, he underscored, made the IITs less of a purely urban, purely English-speaking phenomenon, with "more and more people attempting the exam from distant, remote areas." It also helped that the centers trained students with an eye to placing them in one of a range of institutions. While most did not end up at the IITs, their training qualified them for a number of other lower-tier institutions, such as the regional engineering colleges.

Who, I pressed, were these "people" for whom the IITs had recently become an imaginable ambition? Coaching is now "across the board," he explained, "as long as you have money to access it. With the change in the exam format and the expansion of coaching centers, Abbas continued, "all the land owning castes from Andhra—the Kammas and Reddys who had money and power but not education—they started coming in huge numbers. There are lots of Reddy and Kamma students now who come from Andhra into IITs."

In one sense, then, the coaching franchises have democratized access to the IITs, at least for rural landowners. By doing so, they have challenged the prevalence of upper castes with histories of educational capital. For Abbas, this was an important counter to the doom-and-gloom story prevalent among IIT faculty and administrators. "Yeah, in a sense, the culture of IIT is changing," he acknowledged. "This is something that IIT professors and administrators firmly believe. They say that when the exam was subjective, we used to get only people who were deserving, who really had merit. Once it became objective there was so much influx from these coaching factories that the standard of IIT decreased. They feel that these people didn't deserve to be here and they were not eager to study once they got to IIT because, after working so much in the two years before, they just let go." After rehearsing the string of criticisms typically leveled against "coaching factory" students, Abbas continued that "there is a hint of truth to this, but the place it is coming from . . . I'm not sure if that is what we should focus on." After all, he said, trying to be tactful, "before the exam was objective, IIT was mostly a . . . it was a lot of . . . there was a considerably larger number of Brahmins in IITs." To the extent that it forced a change in the social profile of the IITs, Abbas felt the coaching industry was a good thing. For him, the expansion of access mattered far more than the concern over diminishing standards, which, he felt, was more an alibi to keep the campuses socially exclusive.

But Abbas also pointed to the coaching franchises' own mechanisms of internal stratification:

> Earlier, when they were not so famous, you just had to pay money. Not now. Now you have to qualify for entry by taking an exam and there are different levels of coaching they give depending on your marks. It's not your choice anymore. They have the say. They will decide whether your child is suitable for IIT, whether he can go for IIT, or whether he doesn't have the required skills to do it. They will decide and place you in a section. So and so sections get this kind of training, so and so sections get this kind of training. They have it all worked out about what kind of training to give to which kind of student.

The intensely competitive environment has also generated hostilities within the big coaching centers between upper-caste students who aim for admission in the "general category" and lower-caste students who are eligible for quotas. At one level, it was understandable, Abbas acknowledged:

> General category students are so frustrated with what is happening—because it's not an easy thing to study for 12 hours and all that—that they look with envy at OBC and SC/ST students. They think, you know, these people can just chill out, even if they score less they will get a better branch than me or get a better IIT than me. And this feeling is carried into the IITs. They look at that person and think, he was in a section lower than me at the coaching center and now he is in a better branch than me.

Abbas summed up the larger structure of competitive ranking with this observation: "It's almost like a mini caste system, you know? The central board Brahmins look down on the Andhra bunch. Within the

Andhra bunch, higher castes look down on the quota students. You have hierarchies, one beneath the other."

Abbas did not contest criticisms of the coaching factory as a site for rote learning or as indicative of the intensified commodification of education. At the same time, his own concerns came from a distinctly different vantage point from those leveled by more socially elite IITians. For him, the problem with the coaching industry was not its effect on merit but its crippling intensity and regional monopoly of secondary education. Even while it has opened access to those who previously could not have conceived of trying for the IITs, it has imprisoned an entire generation of students in brutally exacting regimes of study.

Abbas spoke to me at length about how time is organized at Sri Chaitanya coaching centers. Classes started at 6:00 a.m. and went until noon, followed by individual study hours from 2:00 p.m. until 10:00 p.m. This routine went on for fourteen months, at which point the students would complete the syllabus for the eleventh and twelfth grades. In the remaining ten months, they had exclusive study hours from 6:00 a.m. to 11:00 p.m., with thirty- to sixty-minute lunch and snack breaks, and approximately twenty to twenty-five exams per week. Not only were they trapped in this monotonous routine, but they were physically enclosed within the campus and let out only once in two weeks for a day's "outing." The outing day was quite the spectacle. "You're let out and you just fall upon the city," Abbas recalled with horror. "The whole city is blocked, you know, the buses and everything. There are so many centers, and all of the students are let loose at the same time, and there are crazy lines in front of the movie theaters, in front of the restaurants." Abbas highlighted the contrast between the chaos of outing day and the strict discipline of coaching center life, where interaction with the opposite sex was virtually forbidden. "You actually weren't allowed to talk to women," Abbas explained. "If you talked, you would be penalized because it's supposedly the age people waver. So we are not supposed to have any interaction with women students, so that we don't get disturbed by . . . things. Yeah, those are the words we were told." In fact, the center was so "removed from social reality" that he "didn't know that 26 / 11 happened" till he left for home.[61] Reflecting on the experience, Abbas paused and said slowly, "It really was like a prison."

As with prisons, the relentless pressure with little outlet often led to mental health problems. In the middle of his second year at Sri Chaitanya, Abbas confided, "something went wrong, I broke. I was just feeling so suffocated, but no one understood, not my parents or the college. They just gave me a 5-day break. I was struggling but, you know, there was nothing much I could do. This seemed like the only option. This is what you've worked for all your life, and you don't want to throw it away. So I struggled in the last few months leading up to the exam." By the end of the second year, Abbas experienced a serious deterioration in his health. He became depressed and developed symptoms of obsessive compulsive disorder, although it wasn't diagnosed until after he'd left the center. In the end, after two years of endless work, he got into IIT Madras but was too preoccupied with his mental problems to experience any satisfaction, let alone elation. "There was a kind of indifference that I developed after two years," he said. "It didn't matter anymore what I was doing."

In a sense, the experience of the "coaching factory" has made its students impervious to the criticisms they face at IIT Madras about their lack of merit. Abbas acknowledged that there are constant distinctions drawn between "the Andhra way" and more "legitimate" ways of gaining admission. He even indicated that most of his peers from Andhra agreed with these assessments. "All of us were aware that what they're saying was true," Abbas told me. "We agreed that [the coaching centers] were factories, we agreed that there was rote learning. But what we felt was, that's what my life is, there's nothing I can do about it, it was that kind of emotion. The conversation didn't move beyond that. If we resented how we were perceived, then that would become a conflict—but there was no conflict as such."

Instead, students from Andhra found comfort in numbers. "There was no sense of isolation," Abbas said. "No feeling that this person is attacking me because, you know, you just turn to this side or that side, and everybody is the same as you. People who come from such factories, we are now the majority." Moreover, there was a strong sense of community among students from Andhra's coaching centers. "When it comes to coaching centers," he explained, "there was a sense of community despite caste tensions. This is a person from this place, this is someone from my turf, that kind of a thing."

I pointed out that this collective solidarity was a source of griev-
ance for other IITians I had interviewed, who equated it with a form of
regional parochialism unsuited to a national institute. In response,
Abbas acknowledged that most students from Andhra tended to speak
in Telugu and stick together. At first, he attributed this to the single-
minded focus on technical training inculcated in coaching centers.
"We who come from Andhra coaching centers, we have neglected all
other subjects," he bemoaned. "Because this was not a normal education we got. We were solely focusing on maths, physics and chemistry.
So we were not really being trained in anything else. There has never
really been an application of other subjects within our clique." From
this critique of narrowed intellectual horizons, Abbas then resorted to
a different argument. "We talk in Telugu," he proposed, "because there
are so many of us, there is not really a necessity to try to speak in any
other language." Besides, he pointed out, it was not a choice for those
who were not comfortable in English:

> If you come from a family which spoke English, if you had a circle of
> friends with whom you spoke English before coming to IIT—I mean,
> basically city people—those people had no problem mingling with
> other IITians. They could easily shift languages. Among other stu-
> dents who come from towns and villages, who didn't have any sub-
> stantial English language training, they would suffer a bit, they
> would have some discomfort. I mean the conversation could still
> happen, but it would not be as the other person expects it to be, it
> won't be as smooth. He will obviously spot grammar mistakes and
> all that.

We might think of Abbas's explanation of Telugu "groupism" as an account of regional solidarity. Even as he indicted the structural hierarchies of Indian education that subjected students like him to the extreme pressures of the coaching industry, Abbas valorized the forms
of collective identification and support that such experiences generated.
For students like himself, strength in numbers was what got them
through their IIT years and allowed them to disregard accusations of
intellectual inferiority. It also allowed them to transform campus
culture from its erstwhile grounding in upper-caste, cosmopolitan
nationalism. Now, Telugu students are a counterforce to contend with

in student body elections, where they vote as a bloc, and in campus events where they insist on their presence as a regionally defined constituency.

At the end of the interview, I asked Abbas if he thought mass coaching was in sum a good or a bad thing. "I still struggle to come to terms with it," he confessed, "because I am a first generation college student. My father was the first in his family to get a school education so this was something very prestigious for him, you know? His son going to a college—you know it was something that happens once in a blue moon in communities like ours." His family, Abbas elaborated, were Muslim jute bag weavers from rural Andhra Pradesh, who never benefited from formal education. Their social marginality was exacerbated by spatial marginality; his family lived in a Muslim majority town called Tulukabad, which translated as "village of Turks." When Abbas's father completed eighth grade, he refused to stop studying and join the trade. As a result, he was turned out of the house. He managed to educate himself and to instill in his son the value of education. "So education was something very big for him, for me, for everyone in the family," Abbas affirmed. "But this is not the way. Because we—all of us—the coaching centers were literally torture for all of us. And that is being normalized." I asked Abbas whether his father understands what he went through. "Yes," he replied. "He does. The thing is, many people see this as inhumane. But they feel helpless. They say, what else can one do? Because this is shown as the only way your kid can get to any of these colleges, any of these prestigious universities." Now that Abbas has been to an IIT, he is routinely approached for advice. "And this is a tension that I face," he admitted. "Someone in 10th standard from a lower-caste or Muslim background comes to us, comes to my father or to me for advice. I don't know what to tell that person. I know he'll go through a lot of torture if I say study there, but if he doesn't do that, he's just left nowhere." The coaching centers have so thoroughly monopolized the educational arena in Andhra Pradesh and Telangana that the only alternative, Abbas said, would be to study in "bad colleges which don't have much faculty or much infrastructure which is what economically weaker sections do." For the middle class, he concluded, this is the only alternative. Even though coaching sends most middle-class families into debt, the promise of a well-paying job makes it seem like a worthwhile investment, "a shortcut, you know, to settle well."

I asked Abbas if he ever took his criticisms of the coaching industry to IIT administrators, whose own concerns partially dovetailed with his. "They don't care but they should," he said, "because a lot of crimes are committed in their name, locking students in for two years, having a 16-hour study day. They created the myth of the IITs and others perfectly capitalized on that mythology through the coaching centers. Now, the image that was always there of IIT within the public, the image that they helped to cultivate, it was inaccessible for a long time, and now that it has become accessible, there's a huge storm and you can't stop it."

As we have seen throughout this chapter, the examination in India has always staged a dialectic between ascription and achievement. From the ICS exam to the IIT-JEE, the modern examination has functioned as a putatively democratizing measure for testing individual achievement to the exclusion of other, ascriptive criteria. When one looks more closely at the social effects of such exams, however, their role in gatekeeping, cultural certification, and ranking comes into view. As with efforts to maintain certain race and class criteria for the ICS, the IIT-JEE has also been subject to reform when people who do not fit the profile of the "gifted" IITian—urban, mobile, English educated, upper caste—gain admission to the IITs. Efforts to stabilize the boundary between "the gifted" and "the coached" occur at every point along the pathway into the IITs. As Bourdieu and Passeron point out, most poor and lower-caste students are eliminated from the very "possibilities of candidature."[62] Among those who can afford coaching classes, there are other mechanisms of distinction. "Boutiques" are distinguished from "factories." "Coaching factory" students are typecast as parochial, instrumental, and unmeritorious. In these ways, the examination produces merit not as the index of individual ability but as a modern expression of caste and class difference. As we have seen from Abbas's story, the examination is also an incorporative force—"a huge storm"—that, even while it expands access to elite institutional spaces like the IITs, eliminates other approaches to knowledge, value, and a life worth living. In the process, students like Abbas become victims of caste and class hierarchies of value and a profiteering industry that seduces with the promise of mobility while reinforcing older assumptions of social and intellectual inferiority.

We have seen how the coaching industry challenged the relationship of ascription and achievement through the market. In response, upper-caste IITians engaged in maneuvers of various kinds to distinguish themselves as "the gifted." This dialectic between new claims to access and efforts to retrench upper-caste meritocracy created distinctions between the "right" and the "wrong" upper castes. We will now turn to another challenge to upper-caste meritocracy advanced not through the market but through the law. Chapter 6 delves into the history of India's affirmative action system and its impact on the dialectics of caste and the meanings of meritocracy. How, we will ask, did the extension of quotas for lower castes redraw the lines of opposition? What did upper castes do in response? And how did Tamilnadu figure in this evolving set of dynamics? Let us now turn to the transformations of caste through the politics of affirmative action.

6

Contesting Reservation

IN SOME RESPECTS, affirmative action—or reservation, as it is known in India—was a more fundamental challenge than the coaching industry to the IITs' claim to meritocracy. The reservation system recognized how enduring forms of structural inequality shape differential access to education and the need for redistributive measures to level the playing field. It acknowledged caste discrimination as the basis of nonachievement. At the same time, it left unnamed caste inheritances as the basis of achievement. This imbalance between naming caste as a factor on one side and not naming it on the other has reinforced the representative status of upper castes as subjects whose merit is purely the result of talent, not history. In this sense, reservation policy, too, was only a partial critique of meritocracy.

What the law left unnamed, however, politics did not. The naming of caste capital as the basis of achievement was especially voluble in Tamilnadu and other regions with powerful movements for caste rights. As we saw in Chapter 3, Non-Brahminism and Dravidianism marked Brahmins in particular as beneficiaries of caste, leading to the early implementation of quotas in education and employment. These political challenges produced a more symmetrical analysis of caste by illuminating its relationship to both nonachievement and achievement. With the advent of independence, Tamil Brahmins adopted two strategies. First, as citizens of a liberal democracy, they made recourse to the Constitution's baseline of equality and nondiscrimination to challenge reservation. But they also argued that, as Brahmins, they were quintessentially meritocratic. This interplay between their civic unmarking as liberal democratic citizens and their cultural marking as caste subjects has given Tamil Brahmin claims to merit both a universalistic and an identitarian character. As we will see, what began as a Tamil Brahmin reaction to regional political transformation has now proliferated nationally. With the rise of Other Backward Class (OBC) politics in the northern "Hindi belt" and the implementation of OBC quotas in 1990 and 2006, claims to merit have not only proliferated but come to express newly consolidated forms of upper-caste affiliation.

In this chapter, we will look at how the structuring force of caste in education was addressed within the domains of postindependence law and policy. We will also see that Tamilnadu plays an important role as an outlier to liberal constitutionalism where the legacy of regional politics is evident in the approach to reservation. How, we will ask, did the shifting terrain of reservation policy shape the contours of Tamil Brahmin and upper-caste affiliation at IIT Madras?

Caste and Citizenship

Within Indian modernization theory of the 1940s, caste was antithetical to modern social life and had no place within a democratic polity. This was the promise of independence. At the stroke of the midnight hour, the equal citizen was to take the place of the unequal subject. At the same time, Indian statesmen acknowledged the persistence of social inequalities that needed redress by the state. B. R. Ambedkar, Dalit lawyer and key architect of the Indian Constitution, was the most strident in his rejection of presumptive equality. In November 1949, Ambedkar issued a warning to the Constituent Assembly: "On January 26, 1950, we will have equality in politics and inequality in social and economic life. We must remove this contradiction at the earliest moment, or else those who suffer from inequality will blow up the structure of political democracy which this Assembly has so laboriously built up." He further elaborated on the two forms of persistent inequality: "On the social plane, we have in India a society based on the principle of graded inequality which means elevation for some and degradation for others. On the economic plane, we have a society in which there are some who have immense wealth as against many who live in abject poverty."[1]

There was general agreement in the assembly that the graded inequality of caste and the disparities of class demanded substantive redress. However, consensus broke down when it came to mechanisms of redress. Two key points of debate emerged at the time, which have been remarkably resilient. The first concerned the relative weighting of the fundamental right to equality and nondiscrimination and the directive principle of redress for caste disabilities. The question of whether implementing forms of redress was itself discriminatory and a violation of the right to equality was and has remained hotly debated. Despite acknowledging caste capital as a persistent form of structural advantage requiring state intervention, statesmen and lawmakers treated reservation as a temporary departure from a liberal baseline of formal equality. Even Ambedkar, the most strident critic of the Indian caste system, ultimately upheld the ideal of a liberal norm. Arguing before the Constituent Assembly in November 1948, Ambedkar cautioned that the drafting committee had "to safeguard two things, namely, the principle of equality of opportunity and at the same time satisfy the demand of communities which have not had so far representation in the State."[2] The solution he offered was to clearly delimit the quota because "unless you use some such qualifying phrase as 'backward,' the exception made in favor of reservation will ultimately eat up the rule altogether. Nothing of the rule will remain."[3] By distinguishing rule from exception, Ambedkar reinforced formal equality as the necessary basis of constitutional law. The law still had to uphold the principle of "caste blind" equality even if society was far from achieving this standard. The demographic calculus is key here: regardless of the actual distribution of power and resources, Ambedkar maintained that only a minority could be covered by caste quotas. Otherwise, "nothing of the rule will remain." As we will see, in future judgments, the 50 percent ceiling on reservation was brought up repeatedly as the tipping point between (rational) law and (irrational) politics and became a key touchstone for antireservation activism.

The second point of debate was around the appropriate constitutional language of social differentiation—specifically, whether caste should be accorded legal recognition. While caste classification was deemed necessary for Scheduled Castes (SCs) suffering the stigma of untouchability, there was far less consensus on how to classify the intermediate castes. Even Kaka Kalelkar, chair of the first Backward Classes Commission established in 1953, advised the president to reject his own commission's recommendations because remedies on the basis of caste would not be in the interest of society and country. Instead, he proposed that the principle of caste be eschewed altogether in favor of other indices. The central government agreed with Kalelkar's objection and echoed his concern that recognizing "certain specified castes as backward may serve to maintain and perpetuate the existing distinctions on the basis of caste." A 1961 missive to regional state governments urged that "while the State Governments have the discretion to choose their own criteria for defining backwardness, in the view of the Government of India it would be better to apply economic tests than to go by caste."[4]

We see in these concerns the palpable discomfort around acknowledging the very forms of lived inequality that rendered equal citizenship more aspirational than real. There was even a perverse twist of logic whereby naming the problem itself became the problem. Three Supreme Court judgments encapsulate this enduring tension between the endorsement of formal equality and the recognition and redress of substantive inequality: the 1951 Champakam Dorairajan case, the 1992 Indra Sawhney case, and the 2008 Ashoka Kumar Thakur case. The first challenged the constitutionality of the Madras Presidency's 1921 Communal G.O. (Government Order) reserving seats in regional medical and engineering colleges on the basis of caste and religion. The second challenged the reservation of 27 percent of central government jobs for OBCs, as recommended by the government appointed Mandal Commission. The third challenged the other part of Mandal, the reservation of 27 percent of seats for OBCs in all centrally funded educational institutions, including the IITs.

Across these three cases, we see shifts and continuities in the legal landscape of reservation and in the framing of the debate. The courts moved definitively toward an embrace of reservation as a necessary mechanism of recompense and redistribution. At the same time, the focus on the appropriate criteria for determining "backwardness" left largely unaddressed the social bases of merit. Even as more and more ink was spilled in debating the caste versus class contours of historical disadvantage, the inheritances that underwrote merit slipped out of view. The effects of this asymmetry are evident in the popular politics around reservation whereby the claim to merit on the part of upper castes is taken largely at face value. While there were many other cases on reservation, these three are particularly significant because each addressed a key site of upper-caste capital accumulation: regional government education (1951), central government jobs (1992), and central government education (2008). The succession of cases also marks shifts in the geography of accumulation from the regional to national state and from the public to the private sector.

Across these cases, we see the consistent stance of the Tamilnadu government as a political outlier. In refusing to accord the individual citizen primacy over the caste collective, in opposing the coupling of caste with class criteria, and in exceeding the 50 percent ceiling on reservation, Tamilnadu disregarded the liberal norm of formal equality. This has made Tamilnadu a pivot of antireservation arguments and generated a unique antipathy between IIT Madras and the regional polity. This is all the more so because Tamilnadu's reservation system has prioritized the rights of OBCs—the Shudras of Periyar's Dravidian collective. The steady growth in OBC quotas has redistributed positions in education and employment from upper to intermediate castes. At the same time, it has had a more limited impact on those at the very bottom of the caste ladder, and even exacerbated status conflicts between intermediate castes and SCs. In this sense, Tamilnadu's reservation system has kept in place the work of caste as a system of graded inequality while enhancing opportunities for OBCs.

1951: The State of Madras v. Srimathi Champakam Dorairajan

In 1950, two Tamil Brahmin petitioners, Champakam Dorairajan and R. Srinivasan, appealed to the Madras High Court to protect their right to equality and nondiscrimination. Both Dorairajan and Srinivasan argued that their fundamental rights as guaranteed under Article 15(1) and Article 29(2) of the Constitution had been violated by the Communal G.O., which mandated quotas in regional medical and engineering colleges.[5] Dorairajan had not actually applied for admission in the Madras Medical College; however, she claimed that upon inquiry, she had come to know that, as a Brahmin, she would not be admitted. Srinivasan, on the other hand, had applied for and been denied admission to the College of Engineering, Guindy. In his affidavit, he claimed that his marks in the school examination and the college admissions test would have secured him admission "if selections had been made on merits alone."[6]

The timing of this case signaled the effort by Tamil Brahmins to take advantage of a new postindependence political configuration. In appealing to the Constitution, Dorairajan and Srinivasan sought the support of the judiciary in checking the redistributive measures of the Madras government and restoring their claim to regional education. In its judgment, the Madras High Court responded as they had hoped. It held that the Communal G.O. constituted a violation of the fundamental rights of citizenship guaranteed by the Constitution and shot down the contention of the Madras government that Article 29(2) needed to be read alongside Article 46, charging the state with promoting the educational and economic interests of "the weaker sections of the people."[7] Instead, the court held that Article 46, which falls under "Directive Principles" in Part IV of the Constitution, could not in any way override or abridge the fundamental rights guaranteed by Part III.

The language of the judgment both acknowledged and effaced inherited caste capital as the basis of citizenship rights. The judges argued that if selection had been made solely on the basis of "merit," Brahmins would have obtained 249 seats out of the roughly 400 seats in government engineering colleges instead of the 77 they were allotted under the quota. Rather than proof of stark structural inequalities, the court treated this calculus as evidence of injustice against Brahmins. Consider this quote from the judgement:

> It may be that through the fortuitous operation of a rule, which in itself is not discriminatory, a special advantage is enjoyed by some citizens belonging to a particular caste or community. This advantage is not taken away by Article 15(1). If, for instance, students belonging to a certain community or caste by reason of their caste discipline, habits and modes of life, satisfy the prescribed requirements in larger number than others, it is not permissible to shut them out

on that score. . . . It would be strange if, in this land of equality and
liberty, a class of citizens should be constrained to wear the badge of
inferiority because, forsooth, they have a greater aptitude for certain
types of education than other classes.

Here, we see how the "special advantage" enjoyed by Tamil Brahmins
is naturalized as caste culture and made consistent with the fundamental rights of citizenship. Even as caste is acknowledged, it is re-
made from a system of graded inequality into community life. By contrast, it is the quota as a mechanism of redistribution that is identified
as a source of discrimination denying Brahmins their "greater aptitude
for certain types of education" and stigmatizing them as "inferior."
The afterlife of this remarkable statement equating Tamil Brahmin
educational capital with the rights of citizenship and the quota system
with discrimination is still evident in upper-caste claims to merit. It
laid the groundwork for subsequent arguments about upper-caste rights
as consistent with democratic principles and lower-caste rights as a
violation of these principles.[8]

In April 1951, the Supreme Court upheld the verdict of the Madras
High Court. The unanimous verdict of both courts in striking down
the Communal G.O. met with a swift response from Ambedkar and
Nehru. In June 1951, the First Amendment to Article 15 of the Constitution was passed, stating that "nothing in this Article or in Clause (2)
of Article 29 shall prevent the State from making any special provision for the advancement of any socially and educationally backward
classes of citizens or for the Scheduled Castes and Scheduled Tribes."[9]

The first amendment signaled a standoff between the judiciary
and the national executive on the relationship between fundamental
rights and distributive justice. By the time of the next major reservation
battle in the 1990s, however, the courts had shifted toward a greater
recognition of quotas as a necessary precondition for equality. The intervening years also witnessed the consolidation of Dravidianist
rule in Tamilnadu and the increasing divergence between regional
and national stances on the caste question. Both trends were evident in the second landmark judgment on reservation: the 1992 Indra
Sawhney case.

1992: Indra Sawhney v. Union of India

Between 1951 and 1991, the Government of India set up two commissions to investigate "the condition of the socially and educationally backward classes." As noted earlier, the first Kaka Kalelkar Commission of 1953 was both ambivalent in its views and inconsequential in its effects. This was not the case for the second B. R. Mandal Commission set up in 1979. Not only were its recommendations implemented a decade later, but "Mandal" has become a hugely controversial household word in India.

The Mandal Commission picked up where the Kalelkar Commission left off. It developed a more comprehensive social scientific methodology for determining social and educational backwardness and, on that basis, recommended 27 percent reservation for OBCs in civil posts and services falling under the central government and in public sector enterprises and banks.[10] When added to the already existing 22.5 percent for SCs and Scheduled Tribes (STs), Mandal brought the total quota of reserved seats to 49.5 percent, just under the Supreme Court limit of 50 percent.

There are four noteworthy points in the Mandal Commission's report. The first relates to the social life of caste. The report cautions against any hasty conclusion about the weakening of caste as the basis of social organization. While it acknowledges the increased pace of social mobility and the weakening of some "traditional features of the caste system," it maintains that "what caste has lost on the ritual front, it has more than gained on the political front."[11] The report observes that the related shifts in the power equation between high and lower castes had exacerbated social tensions that could be contained if "the ruling upper castes handle the legitimate aspirations and demands of the historically suppressed and backward classes."[12]

The second point relates to the definition of merit. In a chapter titled "Social Justice, Merit, and Privilege," the report states that "merit in an elitist society is not something inherent but is the consequence of environmental privileges enjoyed by the members of higher castes." The report also takes on Kalelkar's opposition to caste classification with a decisive statement on the relationship between caste and class.

Referring to two prior judgments, it argues that "caste is also a class of citizens and if the class as a whole is socially and educationally backward, reservation can be made in favor of such a caste."[13] Finally, the report echoes previous judgments in emphasizing that OBC candidates recruited "on the basis of merit in open competition along with general candidates shall not be adjusted against the quota of 27 percent reserved for them." In other words, Mandal mandated that the "general category" not become a de facto quota for upper castes.[14]

Significantly, the Mandal Commission targeted the very niche that had been insulated from regional political demands: the central government jobs monopolized by groups with a long history of education, whose children populated central government schools and colleges, like the IITs. Unlike regional government jobs, which had been opened up to new aspirants through quotas for SCs, STs, and OBCs, this upper echelon had the 22.5 percent quota only for SCs and STs, which often remained unfilled. Moreover, as we have seen in the last two chapters, because of their insulation from regional politics, central government education and employment had become synonymous with upper-caste meritocracy.

The Mandal Commission's report was discussed twice in both houses of Parliament in 1982 and 1983 with no decisive outcome. It was only during the prime ministership of V. P. Singh (1989–1990) that Mandal came into effect. Singh's statement in Parliament in favor of implementing the commission's recommendations called into question the very notion of merit in a highly unequal society. "We talk about merit. What is the merit of the system itself?" he queried. "That the section which is 52 percent of the population gets 12.55 percent in Government employment? . . . That in Class I employees of the Government it gets only 4.69 percent? . . . I want to challenge first the merit of the system itself before we come to the question of merit."[15]

The uproar caused by the implementation of the Mandal Commission's recommendations on August 13, 1990, was responsible for the defeat of the V. P. Singh government in the 1991 general elections. Even so, the successor government of P. V. Narasimha Rao largely accepted Mandal while underscoring its class criteria and adding a 10 percent quota for economically backward groups.

The petitioners in the Indra Sawhney case issued several challenges to Mandal. First, they recycled older arguments from the 1951 Dorairajan case about reservation as a violation of equal rights. Second, they maintained that Mandal mandated the unconstitutional use of caste as the sole criterion for eligibility. Finally, they argued against the role of the executive in expanding the scope of reservation. In making the last argument against executive action, counsel K. K. Venugopal singled out Tamilnadu as a constitutional violator, remarking sardonically that "before every general election a few communities are added to the list of backward classes, only with a view to winning them over to the ruling party."[16] Tamilnadu was a clear case, he argued, of fundamental rights falling prey to politics.

The Sawhney judgment is exhaustive in its consideration of relevant cases both within and beyond India, most notably in the United States. In the majority opinion, Justice Jeevan Reddy largely upheld the government orders implementing the Mandal recommendations. First, he underscored the admissibility of caste as a criterion in determining backwardness with a reminder of Ambedkar's original intent in using the terms "class" and "backward." Going by his words, Reddy argued, "it cannot be concluded either that 'class' is antithetical to 'caste' or that a caste cannot be a class or that a caste as such can never be taken as a backward class of citizens. The word 'class' . . . in our opinion, is used in the sense of social class—and not in the sense it is understood in Marxist jargon." Second, he ordered the exclusion of the "creamy layer" from among the OBCs. This, he emphasized, was a matter of "proper and more appropriate identification of a class as a backward class. . . . If some of the members are far too advanced socially (which in the context, necessarily means economically and may also mean educationally), the connecting thread between them and the remaining class snaps. They would be misfits in the class. After excluding them alone would the class be a compact class. In fact, such exclusion benefits the truly backward." Third, Reddy struck down the 10 percent reservation for the poor as unconstitutional because there were no grounds for discriminating against those with economic means. Fourth, he limited the application of reservation to initial appointments and, invoking Ambedkar once more, recommended that the total reservation of seats remain under 50 percent so as not "to nullify the main Rule of equality." As we will see later in the chapter, those who opposed the OBC reservation system typically invoked these criteria in advancing their criticisms.

Significantly, the strongest arguments in support of the Mandal Commission came from states with powerful lower-caste movements: Bihar, Kerala, and Tamilnadu. Tamilnadu's political stance on reservation came through in two key arguments against the 1992 judgment. First, state counsel Siva Subramanium argued forcefully against the "creamy layer" exclusion, contending that it was "a mere ruse, a trick, to deprive the backward classes of the benefit of reservations." Second, he argued against the 50 percent ceiling as an arbitrary cap, especially in states like Tamilnadu, where the enumerated Backward Caste population was over 80 percent. Contra counsel Venugopal's indictment of Tamilnadu, Subramanium heralded the state as a model, with its long history of reservation dating back to 1921 and steady growth in the quota to the current level of 69 percent.

Before we move to the third judgment in 2008, let us take a moment to appreciate the significance of the judiciary's shift in perspective from 1951 to 1992. In 1951, the justices of the Supreme Court viewed reservation as a political corruption of the principle of formal equality. By 1992, their concern was no longer about upholding liberal principle but about finding the correct balance of merit and reservation as the means to substantive equality. Moreover, this form of substantive equality was now advanced in a language of technical measures. From the upholders of a liberal legalist vision pitted against the democratic calculations of the executive, the judges had themselves assumed the role of technocrats working to engineer the perfect balance of outcomes.[17] As we will see later in the chapter, upper-caste self-definition has similarly shifted from using only the language of formal equality to increasingly relying on the terms of reservation policy. Even as upper castes argued vociferously against reservation, they defined themselves more and more as members of the meritorious "general category." As with the JEE's categories of the "gifted" and the "coached," reservation provided them with a new language of hierarchical classification that has become the basis not only for caste distinction but increasingly for caste consolidation.

2008: Ashoka Kumar Thakur v. Union of India

The third consequential judgment on reservation was in response to what came to be known as Mandal II. This involved the second part of the Mandal Commission's recommendations: a 27 percent reservation for OBCs in centrally funded higher educational institutions, like the IITs. In 2005, the Government of India passed the 93rd Amendment to the Constitution, adding a fifth clause to Article 15 that allowed the state to make "special provisions" for socially and educationally backward classes in all educational institutions, whether public or private, state aided or non-state-aided. This was followed in 2006 with the Central Educational Institutions (Reservation in Admission) Act, which brought all central government educational institutions under the umbrella of the 27 percent OBC reservation. Together, the 93rd Amendment and the 2006 act opened the door to the implementation of Mandal II within the most elite echelon of public higher education.

Mandal I and Mandal II were implemented at very different moments. Unlike in 1992, when central government jobs were still highly coveted, Mandal II came well after the advent of economic liberalization and the explosion in private sector employment. It sought to democratize admission to the top echelon of public higher educational institutions like the IITs, which were proven stepping-stones to private sector opportunities.

The challenges to Mandal II came quickly. Altogether, there were twelve cases filed on various grounds. Most reprised older arguments about the fundamental right to equality and the need to exclude the "creamy layer." To these were added some new ones: (1) that while reservation for SCs/STs was justified, the economic advancement of OBCs and the severing of the "caste-occupation nexus" made them ineligible for reservation; (2) that the expansion of reservation policy to include OBCs was excessive and had resulted in "reverse discrimination" against the nonreserved; (3) that the 27 percent OBC quota was "not a genuine social engineering measure but vote bank politics"; (4) that the extension of reservation to government-aided, private educational institutions was an unconstitutional effort to nationalize them; and (5) that without a specified time limit, reservation was by definition unconstitutional. In these challenges, we see the sense of threat posed

to upper castes by OBCs in particular. Unlike SC/STs, OBCs are perceived as real competitors who, as in Tamilnadu, have the potential to
actually disrupt upper-caste entitlements. Indeed, we even see a rhetorical endorsement of the SC/ST quota as a counterpoint to the OBC
quota.[18]

But there were also those who felt that the government orders implementing Mandal II had compromised on social justice by incorpo-
rating class criteria. These petitioners maintained that caste as an autonomous and enduring system of stratification should be the sole
criterion. Once again, Tamilnadu represented this position most
clearly. The counsel for the Pattali Makkal Katchi, a Tamil political
party representing OBCs, argued that it was only the "creamy layer"
who could avail of such opportunities. "If the best from the lower caste
are deprived of these facilities and opportunities in the name of 'creamy
layer,'" he stated, "it will be counter-productive and frustrate the very
object of reservation, namely to achieve equality in status, facilities and
opportunities."[19]

Most of the challenges were shot down by the court. First, the justices maintained that a constitutional amendment "which moderately
abridges or alters the equality principle" cannot be said to violate the
basic structure of the Constitution. In striking contrast to the 1951
judgment, they argued for the crucial role of directive principles in a
democracy:

> It is the Directive Principles which nourish the roots of our democ-
> racy, provide strength and vigor to it and attempt to make it a real
> participatory democracy which does not remain merely a political de-
> mocracy with Fundamental Rights available to all irrespective of
> their power, position or wealth. The dynamic provisions of the Di-
> rective Principles fertilize the static provisions of the Fundamental
> Rights. The object of the Fundamental Rights is to protect individual
> liberty, but can individual liberty be considered in isolation from the
> socio-economic structure in which it is to operate? There is a real
> connection between individual liberty and the shape and form of the
> social and economic structure of the society.[20]

Second, they affirmed the constitutionality of quotas and pointed out
yet again that "the equality of citizens is the basic feature of the In-

dian Constitution but by 'equality' is meant not 'formal or technical equality' but 'real and substantial equality.'" Third, they referenced the 1992 *Indra Sawhney* judgment in reiterating that while caste was distinct from class, the correlation between the two made caste a legitimate basis for determining social and educational backwardness so long as it was not the sole criterion. In this, they also went against the Pattali Makkal Katchi's objection to the "creamy layer" exclusion while cautioning against applying "a strict income restriction" because this might mean that "those who are left in the particular caste may not be able to have a sufficient number of candidates for getting admission in the central institutions." To avoid this outcome, the justices authorized the central and state governments to "make a relaxation to some extent so that sufficient number of candidates may be available for the purpose of filling up the 27 percent reservation."[21]

Merit and the Nonreserved

The sequence of Supreme Court judgments from the 1950s through the 2000s illuminates changes in judicial opinion on reservation. From a more categorical stand in favor of formal equality, the court moved toward an embrace of compensatory measures to bridge the gap between formal and substantive equality. Nominally, the redress of caste inequality was an ambition shared by the judiciary and by lower-caste movements. However, they diverged when it came to the perception of upper castes. For the judiciary, the upper-caste subject remained the ideal citizen, defined more by individual merit than by caste history. Even as the courts ratified the redress of caste disability, they were unable and unwilling to fully acknowledge and address caste privilege. In all the wrangling over the precise parameters and criteria of backwardness, the assumptions behind what constituted merit were left largely unquestioned. Even as the quotas for OBCs, SCs, and STs expanded and reservation became an accepted mechanism of distributive justice, assumptions about the innate meritoriousness of the nonreserved stayed mostly in place. It was only the reserved who came to be marked by history and identity, while the nonreserved stood in simply for casteless, ahistorical excellence.

This is evident even in those instances where judicial statements directly addressed the question of merit. Take Justice Jeevan Reddy's statement in 1992 in response to the concern that "quota candidates" would necessarily mean a decline in the efficiency of administration. Reddy agreed that "the very idea of reservation implies selection of a less meritorious person" but went on to insist that "at the same time, we recognize that this much cost has to be paid if the constitutional promise of social justice is to be redeemed." Reddy further argued for a developmental approach to merit:

> Given an opportunity, members of these classes are bound to over-come their initial disadvantages and would compete with—and may, in some cases, excel above—open competitor candidates. It is unde-niable that nature has endowed merit upon members of backward classes as much as it has endowed upon members of other classes and that what is required is an opportunity to prove it. It may not, there-fore, be said that reservations are anti-meritian. Merit there is even among the reserved candidates and the small difference that may be allowed at the stage of initial recruitment is bound to disappear in course of time. These members too will compete with and improve their efficiency along with others.[22]

While Reddy insisted that the potential merit of the reserved only needed appropriate opportunities for expression, he stopped short of in-terrogating the social backgrounds of the nonreserved. Ultimately, his developmental logic about merit as the unfolding of natural ability led him to limit reservation to positions that were less prestigious. For higher levels of the state's educational, service, and administrative in-stitutions, he stated, "Merit . . . alone counts . . . and provision for res-ervation would not be advisable."[23]

These limits of judicial action maintained an upper-caste merito-cratic norm. Even as the directive principles were made actionable and arguments about formal equality challenged, the role of caste on the other side of the equation remained curiously invisible. This was es-pecially the case in the educational domain, with its correlation be-tween the "general category" and "merit-based" admissions. The se-mantic equivalence between the general and the meritorious reinforced the idea that those who fall within the general category do so not on the basis of accumulated caste privilege but by dint of their own merit. This categorical distinction between the meritorious / casteless and the reserved/caste-based has profoundly shaped the debate around educational equality in India. It has allowed those who fall within the general category to invoke what Bourdieu calls an "imaginary universe of perfect competition or perfect equality of opportunity, a world without inertia, without accumulation, without heredity or acquired properties," to argue that it is the system of reservation, and not the inheritances of caste, that undermines the modern republican ideal of equal citizenship.[24]

Satish Deshpande has argued that the unmarking of upper castes was built into the logic of constitutionalism from the outset. The new Constitution, he maintains, "constrained the victims of caste to demand justice as a caste-marked exception, while its beneficiaries were empowered to demand the perpetuation of their advantages as a casteless norm."[25] Deshpande dates this back to the 1951 verdict, which offered upper castes a form of agency "based on the universal-normative position of 'castelessness.' . . . Constitutionally and legally, caste was henceforth to be recognized only as a source of disadvantage or vulnerability, not as a source of privilege or advantage." For upper castes, Deshpande concludes, "caste-qua-caste has already yielded all that it can and represents a ladder that can now be safely kicked away. Having encashed its traditional caste-capital and converted it into modern forms of capital like property, higher educational credentials and strongholds in lucrative professions, this section believes itself to be 'casteless' today."[26]

Looking back at the three consequential judgments on reservations, Deshpande's argument holds, but only partly. It is true that in the logic of the legal judgments, the imagined future of castelessness was transposed onto the "general category." Even after the courts turned in favor of reservation, caste continued to be explicitly marked on one side of the equation. Judicial intervention reinforced the perception of upper castes as casteless moderns whose merit was attributed to accumulated talent, not privilege. However, there is another side to this process, which we see in the 1951 judgment: the marking of caste as culture, as natural aptitude, and as the very basis of merit. Contrary to Deshpande's argument, upper castes did not just come to think of themselves as casteless. Rather, there was a tension between marking and unmarking at the heart of claims to merit.

We see this first with Tamil Brahmins. The early marking of Tamil Brahmins *as Brahmins* by the Non-Brahmin and Dravidian movements catalyzed the interplay of self-marking and unmarking through which Tamil Brahmins made caste belonging consistent with merit. As we saw in Chapter 5 in relation to the JEE, they began to mark caste affiliation differently and in ways that aligned with democratic principles. In this chapter, we see even more clearly through Tamil Brahmin claims to merit that castelessness is less a fait accompli and more an aspect of upper-caste self-definition that has shifted according to circumstance. The commensurability of caste and merit within these claims shows that meritocracy is rarely just a universalistic politics of achievement. It is also always about particularistic ascription.

With the expansion in lower-caste rights politics across India from the 1990s, identitarian claims to merit have spread beyond Tamilnadu and become much more overt. Just as proponents of reservation have taken to the streets and the ballot box to make their demands known, so too have upper castes engaged in collective action to express their opposition to the expanding scope of reservation policy. And they have done so in the name of rational law and merit, and against executive authority that is susceptible to popular demands.

As we have seen, Tamilnadu's approach to reservation betrays a very different stance on caste that illuminates the enduring power of Non-Brahminism and Dravidianism, particularly its focus on status conflicts between upper and intermediate castes. First, the dominant perspective of the regional executive and public is of caste as a foundational social structure and politics as an expression of caste interest and conflict. The purpose of policy and politics, then, is not to move toward or shore up an ideal of casteless meritocracy; rather, it is to render caste a stronger and more dynamic basis for competition over resources and rights.

Second, reservation is understood more in continuity with the colonial era's approach to proportional representation than as provisional and temporary redress for historical disabilities. We see this in the Tamilnadu state counsel's stance on the Indra Sawhney case. By invoking a continuity with colonial policy, he explicitly folded postcolonial reservation policy into an earlier model of representation where ascriptive collectives are the basic units of political society. The model of proportional representation is evident in Tamilnadu's approach to the OBC quota, which was revised upward from 25 percent in 1951 to 31 percent in 1972 and 50 percent in 1980.

Finally, the steady expansion of quotas as part of Dravidian populism indicates the centrality of the political arena for the contestation of rights and resources. There has been strong political mobilization for advancing greater parity in caste representation in state employment and education, especially between OBCs and upper castes. Whenever the courts have pushed back, popular pressure has won the day. We see this in 1980, when the Anna Dravida Munnetra Kazhagam (ADMK) government instituted an annual income limit for reservation. The government order elicited widespread protests by the Dravida Munnetra Kazhagam (DMK) and other opposition parties, leading the ADMK to withdraw the income ceiling and increase the OBC quota to 50 percent, bringing the percentage of reserved seats to 68 percent. Both the government orders revoking the income ceiling and increasing the OBC quota were challenged in the Supreme Court. Upon direction from the Supreme Court, the Tamilnadu government constituted the Ambashankar Backward Classes Commission in 1982 to review the existing enumeration and classification of "socially and educationally backward" groups. On the basis of its finding that 87 percent of the state's population were eligible for reservation, the government further expanded the list of Backward Classes to include lower-caste converts to Christianity and Islam, bringing the total to 69 percent.

The remainder of this chapter considers the social life of the law. As we will see, the binaries of caste and class, law and politics, reason and populism, and liberal constitutionalism and illiberal vote bank appeasement have been consistent themes within anti-reservation discourse both within and beyond the IITs. Another common refrain, one that is particularly resonant in Tamil Brahmin narratives, identifies Tamilnadu as a constitutional violator because of its privileging of caste over class and its expansion of reservation beyond 50 percent. In all these arguments, we see efforts to rein in redistributive processes through recourse to a meritocratic status quo.

The Politics of Reservation

IIT Madras has become a key site for strengthening Tamil Brahmin and upper-caste affiliation in the context of an expanding reservation system. The place of Tamilnadu as an early adopter of reservation and the precedent set by Tamil Brahmins as the first "victims" of "anti-meritocratic populism" are both particularly salient to this process. While Tamil Brahmins were arguably one of the first upper-caste groups to articulate a more explicit, ascriptive claim to merit against reservation, such arguments have now become widespread. As we will see later in the chapter, these claims index new forms of political subjectivity that expand the parameters of caste affiliation. In a striking instance of the social life of governmental classification, "the general category" and "the reserved category" have become highly salient forms of collective affiliation with the latter standing in for the backward and the former for the non-backward.

Making Tamil Brahmin Merit

In Chapter 4, we saw the various ways that 1960s IITians approached the question of caste. While some acknowledged class differences on campus, most disavowed caste as a form of belonging or stratification within the institution. The one exception was Tamil Brahmins, who were more willing to acknowledge the salience of caste as group culture and as scapegoated identity. As the discursive target of Non-Brahminism, Tamil Brahmins came to be hypervisible and their claims to knowledge inextricably linked to caste privilege. This is expressed, for instance, in the sardonic name for IIT Madras in the Tamil vernacular press: Iyer Iyengar Technology.[27] At the same time, the caste marking of IIT Madras and of Tamil Brahmins did not preclude claims to merit. On the contrary, Tamil Brahmins understood the institution as meritocratic *because* of its association with them and its insulation from the pressures of regional lower-caste demands. Their marking as caste subjects has produced a heightened consciousness of their own collective affiliation. Sometimes, as we saw earlier, this sense of collectivity was expressed through their self-representation as an educationally oriented middle class with a unique knack for conceptual knowledge. Satish Deshpande's observation that the terminology of reservation policy evacuates caste markers from the general category is partially evident in this recourse to middle-class identity. However, in the context of Tamilnadu, a claim to castelessness on the part of Brahmins is implausible. Rather, caste ascription is part and parcel of their claim to merit. As we will see, this is even more the case when it comes to the issue of reservation, where caste becomes a far more explicit point of reference for merit.

For Tamil Brahmins who entered IIT Madras before the 1990s expansion of private engineering education, the founding of the institute was uniquely propitious. Affiliation to an "institution of national importance," where the only means to admission was the JEE, promised some measure of redress for what they perceived as their victimization by regional politics. Although it is only a small minority of Tamil Brahmins who actually attended IIT Madras, in the context of the Dravidianist transformation of regional society and politics, the institute acquired a symbolic significance well beyond its material ramifications. The association between caste and merit has underwritten the social formation of Tamil Brahmins more generally, in terms of both cross-class identification and disidentification with non-Brahmin Tamils. This is expressed most clearly through opposition to regional reservation policy, which they feel has denied them the only remaining form of social capital they have: education. The confluence of these factors has given IIT Madras outsized significance in the Tamil Brahmin cultural milieu.

Tamil Brahmin alumni from across the decades registered a sense of how their horizons had been narrowed in the region. Nagan, a 1970s alumnus, spoke of IIT Madras as a key destination for Tamil Brahmin boys. "A lot of Brahmins would go there," he said, "because if you were from Madras, and if you are a Brahmin, unless you're in the top one, two percent, you can't get into a professional college. Brahmins never got anywhere. So this was seen as a place that Brahmins could walk into if they made it through [the exam]."[28]

Similarly, Shankar, a 1980s alumnus, narrated his own path into IIT as part of a family and community pattern. "I graduated in 1983 and my sister had already done a PhD in IIT Madras in chemistry. One of my cousins was among the first batch of IIT Madras graduates, so it was very much the thing to do for upper middle class—not upper middle class—middle class Brahmin families, you know? This is what you do. You get into a profession, mostly engineering, mostly through IIT."[29]

Madhavan, the "star teacher" from Chapter 5 and a 1990s alumnus, also echoed this sentiment by framing the choice of the IITs as a non-choice. "Whether or not it's valid," he remarked, "there is definitely a very strong sense that the IIT is the only option for Tamil Brahmin boys which makes them try that much harder to get in. For Backward Caste boys, they know that not getting those extra marks will still mean that they can get into Anna [University] or some other engineering college." Madhavan spoke of how the aspiration to attend the IITs shaped schooling from much earlier. "It's instilled in Tamil Brahmin boys that IIT is the only institution they can reasonably aspire to because of reservations. Because of this, parents send kids to Central Board schools where the curriculum is more in line with the orientation of the JEE."[30]

Venkat, a 1980s alumnus, spoke in the strongest terms about Tamil Brahmins' sense of collective exclusion. He began by echoing many of the other comments we've heard about education as the principle form of middle-class capital:

> Education has always been highly cherished by the middle class in each society. It's a big deal. All Indian mothers want their kids to become doctors or engineers. Professional careers are seen as a status. So for kids like that it was the IITs that provided one outlet where it didn't matter who you knew, it didn't matter if you had money, you could get in on merit. And along with that came a lot of prestige because getting into IIT meant you had to pass this ridiculous entrance exam that was super competitive. So that basically created a concentration of alpha kids who wanted to make out and break out because they put the effort in, to crack the exam to get in, which is why you have the concentration of middle class kids.[31]

In Venkat's class imagination of Tamilnadu, there were the rich who "can always find their way out, say by going abroad or paying their way to college, or through influence," and the poor who "basically are in a situation where they need their kids to start working earlier to support the family finances." In the middle were people like him, "alpha

kids" whose families prized education and whose intellectual ambition drew them to the hypercompetitive JEE.

When I pushed him on who "kids like that" are, he expanded on his
class analysis to say that they were mostly "CBSE [Central Board of Secondary Education] kids," many of whose parents were themselves in the
central government services. He himself had attended the Vidya Mandir
school in Chennai, which he described as "a Brahmin school. It was
started by the Mylapore Brahmin Association, Ladies Association. . . .
So the kids that came to this school came from typically lower income
Brahmin families. There was a huge emphasis on mathematics, and lot
of pressure to do well at mathematics at the cost of everything else even
if you were talented in something different. That caused lot of kids, naturally or unnaturally, to get into IIT because the IIT entrance exam is
purely based on mathematics, physics, and chemistry."

Apart from class and caste, Venkat also used the language of genetics to signify Tamil Brahmin merit. He moved between describing
Tamil Brahmins as "a concentrated gene pool" and as "middle class"
achievers. This back and forth between genetics and class is perhaps
the starkest illustration of the interplay of ascription and achievement
through which Tamil Brahminness is constituted as a form of cultural
and intellectual inheritance.

Venkat's sense of being Tamil Brahmin was not just about culturally inscribed achievement; it was also about constraint. He characterized Tamil Brahminness as excellence in situations of "limited opportunity." We might think of this as the caste version of forging
character through hardship—a prevalent trope in modern narratives of
personal achievement. "Within Tamil Nadu," Venkat elaborated, "the
Brahmin community has been the one most affected by reservation
policies and the IIT was the one place you could get in purely on merit."
He then expanded his argument to include other populations whose
experiences he found resonant. "I think any community around the
world where you have put them in a box, they will fight back in some
form. The Jewish community has been successful for the same reason.
If you look at the Parsis—not that IIT is a community in that form,
but the concept is similar—the Parsis in my mind are the single most
successful community. There are only 55,000 of them globally, 40,000
of them live in Bombay and from there they control, not just business

but arts and sciences and politics, the armed forces." Success for Jews and Parsis, Venkat argued, was a by-product of having "their backs against the wall. They had to make it, which caused them to fight in a certain form, through an emphasis on education, with tremendous pressure from the family to overcome the odds and make it and work together as a community." It was "the same concept" at the IITs, "people who have not necessarily had normal opportunity doing what they had to do to make it." In equating reservation for lower castes with the historical constraints faced by Jews and Parsis, Venkat constituted Tamil Brahmins as an embattled minority within a region dominated by hostile lower castes. Their characterization as a middle class fighting with only one weapon in their arsenal—education—disregards the long and multifaceted history of Tamil Brahmin capital encompassing ritual authority, landownership, and state employment. Venkat substituted this longer history of various forms of capital accumulation with a more recent history of state intervention as a result of which, as he framed it, Tamil Brahmins' only recourse was to education. As we will see in Chapter 7, this idea of upper-caste IITians as a population stripped of other resources falling back on their intellect has acquired an added charge with diasporic mobility.

Tamil Brahmin affiliation with IIT Madras as a meritocratic refuge within the "caste-ridden" landscape of regional education was shaken with the extension of quotas to the IITs. This happened first in 1973 with the implementation of a 22.5 percent reservation for SCs/STs, and then again in 2006 with the 27 percent reservation for OBCs. I asked Venkat what he thought of the extension of reservation to the IITs. "I think it dilutes the gene pool," he told me. "The one thing about IIT was that it was purely on merit. It's not that just because you went through IIT you became such a kind of a person. Yes, it gives you [a] certain level of exposure but first was getting through the exam—that's important. So, if somebody who would have been 74,000 in that exam gets in because of some reservation policy, the definition would be you are diluting the gene pool. So I'm totally against it." Significantly, for Venkat, genetic predisposition was far more emblematic of who an IITian was than the training that person received at the institutes. While the training might offer "exposure," it was "genetics" that was the more definitive influence.

Many Tamil Brahmin alumni echoed Venkat's argument about reservation as an illegitimate tool used to deny the rights of the meritorious. But even those who acknowledged that reservation was a response to the historical advantages enjoyed by upper castes ultimately fell back on characterizing merit not as a by-product of those advantages but as an accumulated virtue that was attributable to a cultural propensity for knowledge. For instance, Swaminathan, a 1978 alumnus, dismissed the tendency to attribute Tamil Brahmin success in the JEE to innate talent. "It's historical," he offered by way of a corrective.[32] He then went on to elaborate on what he meant by history. "I mean, probably Brahmins have invested 2000, 3000 years in education as a fundamental thing, so you can deduce. . . . There are some controversial studies which have been suppressed, which have been about Brahmins and the rest, which are not being widely publicized. . . . You can't quote these in today's politically correct world, leave alone in your university. You're not allowed to say that there are actually differences in intelligence." When I pushed Swaminathan on how he understood the prevalence of Brahmins in institutions like the IITs, he paused and then said, "I think there are historical advantages. . . . Whether that translates into analytical intelligence as examined by tests, God knows, but I believe it is true because the results are like that. You have to have a good explanation for the exam results." Unlike Venkat's naturalization of merit as genetic, Swaminathan offered an explanation that made recourse to history but was cleansed of power and contingency. Rather, it was an origin story about the Brahmin propensity for education that has played out faithfully for "2000, 3000 years." Within it, there are Brahmins who have treated education as "fundamental," with the result of "actual differences in intelligence" evident in the JEE results. This is history as a stage for a predetermined drama where intellectual differences are rendered inevitable. It is history as cultural logic.

Swaminathan even acknowledged that Brahmins had been disproportionately represented in higher education and the professions but attributed this less to structural advantages than to a collective propensity to educational advancement. This propensity, he argued, led Brahmins to find opportunities in emerging educational fields. At first, it was in the literary humanities, then law, and finally the technical sciences. As with shifting professional tracks, one could also see this propensity to nose out the best opportunities in shifting institutional locations. Before the 1960s, Swaminathan elaborated, Brahmins had been the single biggest group in regional colleges. With reservation, lower-caste enrollment in government colleges expanded. Initially, this took Brahmins to the IITs. But by the 1990s, those who couldn't get into the IITs could also opt for private colleges. The embrace of private education, he emphasized, was a sea change in the Tamil Brahmin worldview. "Today it is not a stigma in a Brahmin family to go and study in Sri Venkateswara. It was in the late 1980s. You understand? It became an accepted thing."[33]

In one sense, Swaminathan's narrative of shifting Tamil Brahmin intellectual and institutional orientations was a history of change. But it was also the story of a caste mind-set. Swaminathan attributed to Tamil Brahmins a cultural trait of educational and professional achievement that allowed them to stay one step ahead of the curve. Ultimately, his "historical" account, too, came down on achievement as an expression of caste ascription. It is a story of Brahmins as uncannily resourceful and having a preternatural capacity for instrumental action. It speaks to faith in a form of collective agency in which, regardless of circumstances, they are able to make their own history.

These Tamil Brahmin narratives showcase the impact of reservation policy on caste identity. While most social analyses of reservation focus on its centrality to lower-caste identity and rights politics, here we see how profoundly reservation has molded upper-caste identity, rights claims, even notions of history. For Tamil Brahmins, the politics of Dravidianism and the policy of reservation shook a structure of settled expectations and catalyzed claims to both social and political victimhood as well as intellectual merit. In such claims we see the dialectic of ascription and achievement that makes it possible for Tamil Brahmins to characterize themselves both as a caste historically—even genetically—and as middle-class individuals whose membership in IIT Madras is testament to their merit. As an "institution of national importance" in the heart of "non-Brahmin" Tamilnadu, IIT Madras has helped to suture caste belonging and intellectual merit. Indeed, the institution's own claim to exceptionalism has been pivotal to the very production of Tamil Brahminness as the embodiment of middle-class meritocracy. This identitarian politics belies the commonsense assumption that upper castes have evacuated ascriptive markers and transcended a politics of caste in favor of more universalistic self-representation. What we see instead is the tacking back and forth between the particular and universal through culturally embedded expressions of meritocracy. Let us now look more closely at the impact of each set of reservation quotas on caste opposition and consolidation.

The 1973 Quota

Reservation was first extended to the IITs in 1973 through a 22.5 percent quota for SCs and STs. This central government quota was dwarfed by the existing regional quotas for SCs, STs, and OBCs, which stood at 49 percent. Still, the extension of reservation to the institute was seen as a capitulation to the politics of caste and a violation of meritocracy. For IITians, the 1973 reservation quotas blurred the distinction between IIT Madras and the wider world of regional engineering education, where caste and political connections were seen as the preferred currency.

One of the most vocal opponents was P. V. Indiresan, director of IIT Madras from 1979 to 1984. In his Director's Report of 1983, he indicted the 1973 reservation policy in a strong echo of the 1951 High Court verdict in favor of Brahmin petitioners Dorairajan and Srinivasan:

> Some members of the [Parliamentary Committee on Scheduled Castes] have gone so far as to say that what we need is an Indian standard and not an international standard of instruction. Whether we need or need not be aware of the latest developments in technology, it is necessary to debate the fundamental question whether, just because a group of people cannot cope with a certain level of education, they should have the veto power to deny such an education to the rest; whether social justice should imply that there shall be no institution at all in the country where merit shall be the criterion and also while the socially-deprived should have special privileges, the talented need have no rights of their own.[34]

The distinction drawn by Indiresan between "the socially-deprived" and "the talented" speaks volumes. By referring to the nonreserved simply as "the talented," his statement rendered the social bases of merit irrelevant. Furthermore, the distinction between "special privileges" and "rights" speaks to the recurrent theme of reservations as anti-thetical to democratic equality and meritocracy as consistent with it. Finally, by pointedly contrasting an "Indian" with an "international" standard, Indiresan assimilated the IITs into a global meritocratic norm that is inherently superior to the mediocrity of a nation willing to sacrifice excellence to social justice. In 2011, it was Indiresan who took the Indian government to court challenging the constitutional validity of the 2006 reservation policy. His pivotal role in the legal battle further underscores the significance of Tamilnadu as a precedent in a nationally proliferating politics of meritocracy.

Dynamics internal to the IITs make clear that Indiresan's distinc-tion between "the talented" and "the socially-deprived" had wide res-onance. SC and ST students started attending the IITs from the early 1980s, and from all accounts, their integration into the campuses was far from smooth.[35] Those who gained admission through reservation were routinely assumed to be intellectual and social inferiors who had stolen highly coveted seats from more deserving applicants. The cul-ture of the IITs rendered them intruders in a realm that was not right-fully theirs. That those who gained admission to the IITs through the 1973 quota suffered routine slights and indignities and were thoroughly alienated within their institutional settings was graphically revealed through a spate of suicides and attempted suicides across the various campuses.[36]

Conscription into Brahminness

Although the 1973 quota brought SC and ST students into IIT Madras, their small numbers and extreme marginality did not significantly shake up the cultural ethos of the institution. Their presence only con-tributed to the comfortable sense of a meritocratic norm that did not have to be defended. While upper-caste IITians did object to reserva-tion in principle, their response to the presence of these students was more paternalistic and pejorative than defensive.

When it came to Backward Caste students, there was a very dif-ferent dynamic at play. Unlike SC and ST students, around whom a speculative economy of evaluation, stigmatization, and masking flour-ished (more on this later), the Backward Caste students who gained admission through the "general category" were rendered illegible. The absence of a quota for them led to the unexamined assumption that they were upper caste. While this was the case more generally, it was especially so when it came to Tamils. The fraught regional tensions between Brahmin and non-Brahmin Tamils, and the need for Brahmin Tamils to claim caste exceptionalism via the IIT pedigree, translated into a process of conscription into Brahminness. Backward Caste Tamils were made into Brahmins simply by virtue of having gained admission through the general category.

The conscription of Tamil IITians into Brahminness was strikingly conveyed to me by Senthil, an alumnus from the 1990s. He was changing his clothes when his Tamil Brahmin roommate inquired into the whereabouts of his *poonal*, the sacred thread worn by male Brahmins. "When I told him that I don't wear one, he paused and then asked, 'Doesn't your mother get upset?' It never struck him that I was Backward Caste. In fact, I think he still assumes that I'm from a particularly liberal Brahmin family."[37] Siva, another Backward Caste alumnus from the 1980s, spoke of the discomfort of being party to antireservation debates among his peers. "As long as none of the SC/ST students were in the room, they felt free to say whatever they wanted about reservations, how they're unfair, that they bring down standards. A lot of them would also speak about the reservations in Tamilnadu as unconstitutional and say that this shows how corrupt the regional government is. It was a strange experience because my whole family are DMK supporters. But I didn't say anything so they had no idea that I'm not Forward Caste."[38]

We might think of these instances of caste misrecognition and conscription into Brahminness as "passing" in reverse: unlike the stories of passing in the United States, where blacks attempted to "pass" as white in order to avail themselves of the benefits of whiteness, here it is the upper-caste student who needs to assimilate his lower-caste peer.[39] This desire to erase difference is particularly telling in the context of Tamilnadu, where a long history of reservation has meant that increasing numbers of lower castes do in fact inhabit the same social spaces as upper castes. The blurring of boundaries through the dispersal of social capital has produced acute status anxiety among regional upper castes and the need to create new distinctions that once again differentiate high from low. IIT Madras has uniquely serviced this need: in response to the blurring of caste status boundaries in the wider region, within the walls of the institution it has become imperative to mark the Tamil IITian as Brahmin.

While Backward Caste Tamils were largely invisible to their Brahmin peers, the reverse was hardly the case. All the Backward Caste students I spoke with were acutely aware of the caste underpinnings of campus dynamics. They talked to me about how caste difference was channeled through the most mundane aspects of everyday life: clothes, vehicles, and language.

Senthil spoke to me about clothing. "The attitude was, I'm not going to dress up well," he explained. "Because you were an IITian, you could be eccentric. The whole thinking was about fundas, goals, concepts, and I really don't need to please you by fitting into what you think are social customs. So, if you invite me for a wedding, I'll make it a point to come in a torn T-shirt."[40] Senthil spoke of the upper-caste IITian scorn for social custom as something that he observed and even admired from a distance but never fully inhabited. "I was kind of an outsider," he told me, "because my house was five minutes from the campus. They would always see me as the kind of guy who would wear shoes outside. I was completely a part of the system but you wouldn't find me wearing torn slippers and patched jeans." Senthil then pointed to the crisp shirt, pants, and shoes he was wearing and said, "I'm more of a suit than the other guys but I didn't wear this outfit within IIT. In my four years I never once, you would never catch me in Dockers or something like that." I asked him if he meant he would consciously dress down. "Yeah," he responded. "The reason for that is I was moving in and out, and these guys used to make fun of me. So I would change my clothing on campus. If I dressed up there, I would be as much of a social outcast as I would be if I dressed down here."

In Senthil's sartorial code-switching, we see the negotiation between two worlds of caste. In the extra-campus world, Backward Caste pride was expressed through formal attire and social respectability. In the campus world, these very forms of status were denigrated as signs of crass materialism and intellectual inferiority. Instead, the campus norm was the performance of a kind of Brahminical austerity, where concern for anything but the cultivation of the mind was considered superficial and suspect. IITians were to embody "pure intellect" and eschew the trappings of the material world. As a result, Senthil, the Backward Caste student, felt social pressure to "dress down" or be ostracized as "a suit." Through these micro-evaluations of dress code, Backward Caste students worked to erase bodily signs of material aspiration for fear of appearing intellectually inadequate.

The active disdain for social custom and its associated forms of materialism extended to vehicles. Siva talked to me about the politics of transport. "Everybody in IIT had a cycle, but if you owned your own car, you'd be torn apart. I knew of classmates who would come by car to the gate and then walk. Nobody would know this guy came by car, and if they found out then the whole evening they will be like, this guy is so materialistic, he came by car." Like Senthil, Siva felt the need to perform austerity in order to be treated like a true IITian. Any sign of material wealth became outward evidence of intellectual paucity. For Backward Caste students like himself, he pointed out, this was more tricky than for wealthy upper castes. "Some of the wealthy upper caste kids from Chennai would come in cars and not care. But we already felt like we didn't really fit in, and if you then show up with a two-wheeler [motorcycle] or a car, it was even worse."

Finally, there was language. Here, too, there was a form of Brahminical common sense that made the campus feel culturally alien to Backward Caste Tamils. This is best illustrated through the words of Kartik, a Tamil Brahmin alumnus from 1995. He was from Mylapore, a predominantly Brahmin neighborhood in Chennai, and had grown up in a largely Brahmin world. As did his neighbors, Kartik spoke "Brahmin Tamil," a dialect that uses more Sanskrit derivatives.[41] He told me that he felt truly at home at IIT Madras. He talked about the comforting sense of homecoming he felt upon entering the campus gates, where the Brahmin dialect spoken by his family was ubiquitous.[42]

Part of this dialect was the resort to the familiar, something that was at odds with the more formal Tamil of many non-Brahmins. Nagan, another Tamil Brahmin alumnus, explained that at IIT Madras, "the way you converse, the way you address each other, it's all very Brahminical. The language, the culture of the school was very informal, as it was in my high school days, the way you deal with each other in high school, in a very back-slapping way." I asked Nagan if he thought that came out of a sense of commonality. "Yes," he agreed, "but it's also maybe a sense that we're different from the others. IITians had that feeling, we're different from the others. Most of them didn't say it, but it's there if you dig deep into their psyche."

For Backward Caste Tamils, however, this informality felt less like commonality and more like an insult. Pandiarajan, a 1970s alumnus, remembered that this tension was especially palpable in his day. He grew up in the southern Madurai district of Tamilnadu, where his father was in regional government service. Although he was Backward Caste, he studied at Madura College, which he characterized as an over- whelmingly Brahmin institution "from attendant to principal" that was jokingly referred to by non-Brahmins as "sambar college," in ref- erence to Brahmin vegetarianism.[43] It was because of his exposure to Brahmins, Pandiarajan told me, that he even thought to apply to IIT. Unlike non-Brahmins, he explained, "the information networking among Brahmins is far more efficient. Even at that time, there were national networks." As an example of the spatial reach of Brahmins, Pandiarajan pointed to cricket. "The caste community that really took up cricket first was the Brahmin community." He elaborated, "At that time, cricket was a sign of urbanization. And Brahmins were very ur- banized. If you read the jokes in *Kalki* and *Ananda Vikatan,* they had many about cricket that were only comprehensible to the Brahmin community. When there were cricket matches going on, the Brahmin boys would always hang on to the transistor radio. They had relatives in Chennai and would take a train to go watch matches. So the net- work was far more efficient among the Brahmins, and information flowed far more efficiently."[44] The existing social and spatial differences, Pandiarajan continued, were heightened by the spread of Dravidianism. "Nineteen sixty-seven was the year that DMK came to power," he re- called. "In 1968, Anna died, and it was Karunanidhi's period. Already, the Brahmins were complaining about reservations. As someone who straddled both worlds, I was acutely aware of the social disparities be- tween caste communities because I had been to the home of everybody in my school class and was treated differently by different groups."

Pandiarajan attended IIT Madras during the decade following the Dravidianist transformation of political life in the region. He experi- enced it as an upside-down world. In contrast to the growing power of Dravidianism across the state, Backward Caste Tamils were a tiny, illegible minority on campus. Most of the time, caste tensions were kept under wraps or addressed with humor. For instance, Pandiarajan and his Backward Caste friends would in private refer to Brahmin classmates from Chennai as "Mylos" or the "5Bs," referring to the Brahmin-dominated neighborhood of Mylapore and the 5B bus that terminated there. At other times, the tensions would come to the surface. Pandiarajan told me about one "cultural clash" in his first year between his friend Amudhan and a Brahmin classmate. "We had come from workshop, a bunch of people were washing their hands in the wash basin. A lot of people were standing next to each other and this guy, Kuppuswami, he wanted Amudhan to move a little bit. So he used the 'da' form. *En da, konja thalli nillenda.* [Dude, stand a little to the side]. And Amudhan got very wild because he is from Tirunelveli where the Tamil is very respectful."

These negotiations between Brahmins and non-Brahmins played out a different kind of caste drama from the tensions that emerged around the 1973 quota. Here, too, there was a working assumption of an upper-caste status quo and the need to locate oneself in relation to it. However, the same forms of stigma were not in operation because these Backward Castes had gained admission through the "general category." They had proven their intellectual worth by attaining JEE ranks that qualified them for "merit-based admissions" and were thus illegible as Backward Caste. Through the 1990s, campus dynamics were marked by an imbalance between the blithe ignorance of Backward Caste presence on the part of Brahmins and an acute awareness of caste differences on the part of lower castes.

Until the 1990s, the relatively small 1973 quota and the extreme marginalization of SC and ST students maintained the representative power of upper castes. As we saw from Indiresan's quote from 1983, the IITian defense of merit was still very much about an appeal to universalistic norms that came from a comfortable position of dominance. But changes beginning in the 1990s led to a more explicit and defensive politics of caste.

The 1990 and 2006 OBC quotas shifted the terms of engagement. Within IIT Madras, the opposition to reservation and claims to merit were still constitutive of Tamil Brahmin identity. However, the expansion of quotas to OBCs, first in central government jobs in the 1990s and then in central government educational institutions in the 2000s, produced a new structure of feeling. Merit came to be mapped onto an emergent form of upper-caste identity where what mattered was not caste affiliation based in understandings of endogamy and history but the governmental distinction between the "general" and the "reserved." The claim to merit as members of the "general category" was by no means a process contained within the IITs. Rather, the institutes were part of a much wider national shift toward upper-caste consolidation in reaction to the recommendations of the Mandal Commission.

The 1990 and 2006 Quotas

When Prime Minister V. P. Singh announced on August 7, 1990, that his government had accepted the Mandal Commission report and would move forward with implementing a 27 percent reservation policy for OBCs in public sector jobs, it ignited a firestorm in the northern Hindi-speaking belt. Upper-caste students took to the streets, staging sit-ins; setting up road blockades; and masquerading as vendors, sweepers, and shoe shiners in a graphic depiction of their future reduction to lower-caste labor. The starkest expression of opposition was self-immolation, with one Delhi University student, Rajeev Goswami, being the first to unsuccessfully attempt this tactic. Goswami's act sparked a series of self-immolations by other college students. In the weeks following his attempt, more than 150 students followed his example, with the death toll reaching 63. Those who immolated themselves were treated as martyrs who had sacrificed their lives for the country. In Delhi, agitating students even named one of the key traffic intersections that they commandeered Qurbani Chowk, or Sacrifice Square.[45]

Often, student ire was made explicit in suicide notes. Surinder Singh Chauhan, the first college student to die from self-immolation, left a note stating, "The responsibility for my death lies with those who consider reservation a vote bank, people like V. P., Paswan, Yadav, and so on."[46] Sushil Kumar, another college student from Haryana, consumed poison, leaving behind a note that said, "Only V. P. Singh is responsible for my death." In Pathankot, an eleventh-grade student, Narinder Kaur, hanged herself from a ceiling fan. Her suicide note requested that her eyes be donated to the prime minister "so that he can see better for himself the misery the report had brought upon the student community. There is no other reason but the Mandal Commission report which made me take such a step."[47]

Psychologists held forth in the news media, opining that it was usually the brightest students who resorted to such extreme measures. "Aspirations lead to greater frustration," explained the head of the psychology department at the All India Institute of Medical Sciences. "This in turn spurs you into action." Another added that suicide results "when you feel that the value of knowledge will take you nowhere. The pressure of being brilliant and not making it leads to intense psychic turmoil."[48]

That the spectacular courting of death was a political choice rationalized by media and clinical experts alike speaks volumes about the settled expectations of caste. Rather than a redistributive mechanism, reservation was widely regarded as political pandering to lower castes and a grave injustice to the meritorious. Characterizing reservation as "vote bank politics" not only gestured to an unseemly alliance between political elites and lower castes but also reinforced the sense that the beneficiaries of reservation were members of opportunistic caste groups devoid of educational qualifications. By contrast, the rhetoric about the frustrated aspirations and curbed brilliance of aggrieved students sidestepped their caste identities altogether in favor of foregrounding their intellectual abilities. On one side were politicized castes; on the other, meritorious students. One group was defined in purely ascriptive terms, the other in terms of frustrated achievement. It is only when we consider the opposition between "the meritorious" and "the reserved" that the presumed caste basis of merit comes into view.

Indeed, one of the accusations leveled against Mandal was that it was responsible for the spread of casteism, even of caste consciousness. As one political science research scholar lamented to a journalist, "We used to have Hindu College vs. St. Stephens or Miranda House vs. Lady Sriram College rivalries. Now they are forcing us to think on caste lines."[49] Rajeev Goswami's daughter, Simran, who moved to Michigan after her father's death in 2003, offered a perspective that sharply contrasted Indian and American social landscapes. "My father fought against the politics of reservation and for the recognition of merit," she stated proudly in a newspaper interview. Explaining her move to the United States, she added that she wanted "to get away from India's divisive politics" and was glad that her "new home has no reservation. . . . In the US, only merit is recognized."[50]

The idea that students who previously thought of themselves purely as individuals or as part of modern institutional formations were now compelled to enter into caste consciousness rendered Mandal not only unjust but regressively illiberal. Moreover, by granting quotas to lower castes, it purportedly violated the ideal of equality that was foundational to Indian liberal democracy. Much of the public discourse on Mandal rehearsed the virtues of castelessness as an ideal embodied by upper castes and disregarded the lived reality of caste discrimination and exclusion that reservation was intended to redress.

Significantly, most of the ferment around Mandal was limited to the north of India. The southern states, including Tamilnadu, experienced very little of it. Plus, the depiction of Mandal as a jolt into caste consciousness was a striking contrast to the more long-standing and pervasive caste hostilities in the south. The Mandal Commission quotas were part of a sea change in the northern Hindi-speaking belt, sparked by the political mobilization and consolidation of lower castes under the "OBC" banner from the early 1990s.[51] The political rise of Backward Castes in the north and the implementation of Mandal lent "OBC" the same charge in the north that it had in the south. What the Mandal Commission did, then, was to extend the southern dialectic of lower-caste claims to rights and upper-caste claims to merit to the north.

The 1990 OBC quotas catalyzed new lines of division and precipitated more defensive, upper-caste claims to merit as the nonreserved. The 2006 implementation of the second part of the Mandal Commission's recommendations—the reservation of 27 percent of seats for OBCs in all central educational institutions, including the IITs and IIMs—exacerbated this oppositional dynamic.[52] Mandal II further entrenched the distinction between "the general" and "the reserved" as a commonsensical and widely shared one through which the Indian public understood caste difference. The ubiquity of the reservation debate and the proliferation of its terms is evident in everyday discourse and on social media. While there are innumerable instances, I have selected just a few that showcase the rhetorical flourishes of the anti-reservation position.

One example is from 2009, just after the announcement of Mandal II. At the time, a joke circulated on the Internet. It went something like this: "India decides to send a space exploration team to the moon. Feverish negotiations begin immediately on the composition of the team, and after much haggling it is decided to include nine OBCs, six SCs, three STs, and, if there is any place left, two astronauts."[53] The point was to distinguish the caste-based from the meritorious. The OBCs, SCs, and STs, who are defined purely by their caste markers, are assumed to be utterly unqualified for professional positions and yet monopolize them because of political machinations. This leaves the upper castes, who are the only ones actually qualified for the professions, sharing the dregs of what remains. Caste and politics on one side, accomplished individuals on the other. What remains unstated but assumed are the upper-caste identities of the "astronauts."

Such assumptions about the undermining of standards through reservation are more commonly expressed through comments about "quota doctors." IIT Delhi alumnus and best-selling novelist Chetan Bhagat reprised this fear in a Facebook post where he played out a scenario ending with a rhetorical question: "Mr. A passed his medical examinations with more than 90 percentage marks in every subject. Soon he became a fully qualified doctor. Mr. B is Mr. A's classmate. He failed in every exam. But since he was from a backward (reserved) class the university awarded him with a degree and the medical council of India included him among the list of doctors. Now the question is, if you are feeling sick, or injured or not well in some other way, to get treated and cured will you fix an appointment for consultation with Mr. A or Mr. B?"[54] The post was "liked" by over 5,600 people and shared 1,500 times.

A second joke circulated after Prime Minister Modi's September 2015 visit to the United States. "Narendra Modi during his visit to America said to Obama, 'Yours is the strongest and most developed country in the world. What is the secret of your country's success?' Obama immediately said, 'Indians.' Modi was totally surprised by Obama's answer and asked, 'How?' Obama replied: 'You take Reserved Candidates whereas we take Deserved Candidates.'"[55] Here, the distinction between the "reserved" and the "general" cuts even deeper; the reserved are by definition undeserving. Moreover, according them primacy in education and employment has cost India its truly deserving citizens who have fled to the meritocratic West, where their virtue is recognized and accorded value. Left unconsidered is the irony of attributing this comment to America's first black president, who is himself a strong advocate of affirmative action.

There are also numerous comics that made the rounds in the late 2000s and 2010s. Three of them speak to the idea of reservation as an upper-caste handicap and a basis for exclusion. The first by a blogger named Indianskoolstudents on the blog *On the Road to Justice* is of a baby in the womb who, in a perverse twist on the stigma of being born lower caste or untouchable, wails, "Oh No!!! I belong to the general category," followed by a prayer, "Dear Lord!! Please!!! Make me born as SC/ST or to the max OBC."[56] The second is from a website titled Hyd-Masti and includes a set of reproduced antireservation comics. It replays the scene of Gandhi being kicked off a train, except here, the basis of his eviction is not race in South Africa but caste in India. "Reserved for OBCs," says the aggressor, who literally boots the bespectacled Father of the Nation, clad in a loincloth, out the train door. By implication, not only is reservation exclusionary, but it is also antinational. The antinationalism of reservation is further reinforced by the elite "Western"-suited and booted leg of the aggressor. A third replays the distinction between legitimate upper-caste votes and illegitimate lower-caste vote banks through the juxtaposition of two statues. The first statue with the words "Then" and "Vote" on the pedestal is of a beheaded B. R. Ambedkar holding a copy of the Constitution. The second with the words "Now" and "Vote Bank" is of an unspecified, prosperous OBC politician on whose shoulders Ambedkar's head has been transplanted. Through this juxtaposition, the comic appropriates Ambedkar for the antireservation cause while bemoaning the corruption of politics by lower castes.[57]

The final example is an online advertisement created by a group called India Resists in March 2016 that targeted beneficiaries of reservation. It features a girl who, accompanied by her father, goes to get a college admission form. When faced with the choice of two stacks, one marked "Quota" and the other marked "General," the girl hesitates and then picks up a "General" form. Her father is somewhat puzzled but ultimately proud of her choice. The message is clear: the "General" stack is for those lower castes who want to compete on their own merit, the "Quota" stack for those who want the stigma of the handout. The good lower-caste individual is one who opts out of reservation and instead chooses the "fairness" of open competition. This, the ad announces, is the "wind of new thought."[58]

Through the prism of antireservation rhetoric, we see an upside-down world where stigmatization and exclusion are the plight of upper castes and reservation is a corruption of preexisting norms of equality, fairness, and justice. But this is not simply about reestablishing a liberal baseline of equal opportunity and individual rights. What is unmistakable in these forms of antireservation discourse and practice is the outrage at the disruption of the natural order of upper-caste dominance. The self-immolations, the jokes, and the comics all express a deep sense of injustice in the face of thwarted expectations. In the process, they reinforce the notion that only upper castes are truly meritocratic subjects.

The consolidated categories of "general" and "reserved" also have a life beyond the campus. After the implementation of the 2006 quota, private sector job recruiters who were always keenly aware of the JEE exam ranking system became more vigilant about the cutoff for the general category. Several lower-caste students who got into IIT Madras through the 2006 quota recounted their chagrin at being pointedly asked for their JEE rank at the final stage of campus job recruitment; despite doing well up to that point, most never got the jobs. The more recent divergence in career opportunities for general and reserved category students is in contrast to the trajectories of lower-caste students who got in before the expansion of the quota. Unlike then, there is now a two-tier system of employment which ensures that the achievements indexed by the IIT pedigree are mitigated by caste ascription. Increasingly, only general category students are seen as legitimate holders of the pedigree.[59]

IITian Reactions

Within Tamilnadu, the one institutional site where opposition to Mandal was expressed publicly was IIT Madras. Still, IITians were not well represented in the 1990s anti-Mandal agitations because the

Mandal recommendations did not affect them directly. As early mi-grants to the United States and to the private sector, IITians did not experience the reservation of Indian public sector jobs as a significant threat. The 2006 reservation policy changes, however, were a different matter.

The 2006 quota brought the reserved category up to almost half of the total student population of IIT Madras. This increase has given the "general category" within the IITs a new charge. Now, from standing in for the unmarked norm, it is claimed as an upper-caste collective. This more openly articulated claim to merit as upper castes echoes the self-marking of Tamil Brahmins at an earlier moment. Now as then, the embrace of identitarianism is driven by a new sense of threat posed by lower castes. It has become more imperative to mark the "general category" as upper caste so that it is not devalued by association with the expanding reserved category. This is no longer a universalistic pol-itics of merit; it is an explicitly caste-based one.[60]

The more openly defensive posture as upper castes is evident in the remarks made by IITians about the 2006 reservation policy. We also see a recycling of some of the legal arguments against quotas that we considered in the first section of the chapter. In 2009, I spoke with a group of first- and second-year students who had gained admission to IIT Madras through the "general category." I offer here a curated set of their remarks:

STUDENT 1: I would be happier if they had reservations on economic grounds more than caste grounds. I know people who are from per-fectly normal families but they were not such good students. There is no reason for them to be given benefits. I don't think they were disadvantaged growing up in any way, and I don't see why they would be given preference. So I would think a more economic basis of screening people would be better.
STUDENT 2: See, there are many students who do not prepare for JEE seriously because of the feeling that they have reservation. In my plus-1 and plus-2 [eleventh and twelfth grades], I had many friends who didn't study and I asked them, "What are you doing all the time?" And they said, "Why should I study? I have reservation." It's very bad.
STUDENT 3: The bad thing about reservation is some good people who deserve to come to IIT, they lose their chances. Actually, 1,000 seats

are given to this reservation category and even though others are very good, they can't make it because they have to score 40 percent more than the reserved students.

STUDENT 4: It is at least better in IIT. In local engineering colleges, especially in Tamilnadu, if they have 122 seats, 100 are reserved for someone or the other. Only 22 are there for us out of 122. Upper castes are becoming backward castes now.

Unlike earlier statements about SC/ST students as marginal and inadequate that expressed the comfortable inhabitation of a campus mainstream, these express a sense of a more immediate threat. They are less about critical assessment from a secure vantage point than direct competition born of a sense of injustice and victimization. In them, it is lower castes who are entitled. Moreover, class functions to delegitimize OBC claims in particular. The overlap between caste and class inequality is far more apparent with SCs/STs than with OBCs, who are a more diverse constituency. By substituting caste with class, upper-caste IITians seek to deny the clearest form of privilege that they enjoy vis-à-vis OBCs.

While these interviews reveal the discursive contours of an upper-caste identity forged in opposition to the "reserved category," even more illuminating are the debates on social media. The Facebook site IIT Madras Confessions is intended to elicit anonymous posts from students who need to unload their hearts and minds for whatever reason. Started in February 2013, the site is open to any and all "confessions." However, the traffic on the reservation issue was so overwhelming that the site administrator made the executive decision to no longer post comments on this topic. "This page is not for any hatred or debates on one topic," he announced, "but for general emotional confessions."

In the posts that did make it onto the site, we see clearly how much the categories of "reserved" and "general" have been internalized as forms of collective self-definition. One thread offered a particularly illuminating window onto the contours of campus debate. It started with a post by a self-defined "reserved category student." This post is from February 23, 2013. I reproduce it here in full:

I am the first IITian in the history of my family (not that I have a great one, my father's a government employee and my grandfather was a daily wage laborer). When I got the seat my family celebrated, everybody was proud and I was treated like a hero. I was unaware of the repercussions I'll be facing once I cross the IIT gates. It all started when I told my rank to a senior for the first time, later on to my friends. I could see in their eyes that they've already judged me as incompetent and undeserving. Some of my batch mates debated zealously how they couldn't get a better branch but a reserved guy got it because of this unequal system. Some used to say "That fellow. He's so dumb. I guess he's a category student." I slogged my first sem and cleared all courses but I couldn't sustain this as the years passed. I flunked a few courses and my CG reached rock bottom. When I'll be sitting for [job] placements I am sure I'll not get placed before day 15 or may be before day 20. All the joy with which I came here has been sucked out of me and all I am left with is degradation of morale. This is the story of almost 90% of kids who enter this institute through reservation. This accompanied by social stigma, humiliation, excruciating pain and adverse psychological impact. Half the students either end up getting extensions or sem drops. . . . This is the shit we go through in this otherwise beautiful campus. . . . I tell you my dear friends from upper castes, I don't think you were ever reminded of your caste or had any need to know much about it, therefore consider yourself independent of all castes. But I, I am reminded of my caste every single day, every single moment. You might proudly/or not proudly say that you are a Mishra, Sharma, Varma, Reddy, Chowdary, Setty, Iyer, or some other caste. What would your reaction be when I come and tell you that I am a Dalit, Girijan or a BC? That's the reason I am writing this anonymously. To avoid being judged by my caste. You turn your faces when someone talks about caste, but fervently talk about reservations. Isn't this a new form of discrimination? Did we enter this college unlawfully? Did we do anything unconstitutional? Then why do you try to judge? Yes you could have got a better branch; your friend would have got into IIT, if there was no such thing as reservation. What crime did I do for you to blame me for that? Was it my choice to be born in a lower caste? Was it my choice to use reservation? Wouldn't you have done the same, had you been in my place? Isn't the whole point of reservation, me being treated equally? Saying caste system must be abolished, isn't going to help, my friend. Respecting every individual, irrespective of his caste, race, religion, competence, incompetence is what you need to do. Even I have been affected by my choice. I could not compete with geniuses like you so I fucked up. All I need is social acceptance. I too am an IITian, I too wrote JEE and probably there is some 30 or 40 marks difference between you and me. Should I be considered as shit because of that? What's the difference between your grandfathers who might have called my grandfather an untouchable? You have changed the name to reserved candidate. Please don't blame the system. If you have a better idea for bringing equality, get into the government, and change it. I am a human being and I have self-respect. Please keep that in mind before becoming Judgmental.

#Jai Hind

This post is remarkable both affectively and analytically. It is written as an appeal for empathy, recognition, and belonging. It is also an indictment of the caste culture of the institution. As it moves between abjection and indignation, the tension of inhabiting an institution where one is made to constantly feel the intruder is palpable. In his more critical moments, the confessor offers a systematic analysis of upper casteness as an affective disposition in which critiques of reservation stand in for open commentary on caste. This shift, he argues, is no shift at all but simply "a new form of discrimination." Far from giving up caste pride and superiority, upper-caste IITians have simply substituted "reserved candidate" for "untouchable." The confessor also challenges his upper-caste interlocutors to come up with a better solution for inequality than reservation and not resort to platitudes about the abolition of caste. What is particularly striking about the post is how clearly it maps upper casteness onto the general category and accords it social and ideological coherence. The notion of castelessness is summarily dismissed as a fiction that is belied by the treatment meted out to reserved category students.

The post elicited fifty-two comments and an equal number of shares. The range of reactions is very revealing. I showcase some representative examples here. One set of reactions was from lower-caste students who chose not to avail themselves of the quota and called into question the confessor's characterization of reservation as a non-choice. "'Was it my choice to use reservation?'" one post asked rhetorically, echoing the confessor. "Yes. I'm from a lower caste and I 'chose' to compete in the General Category. Just saying . . ." Another offered a similar remark supplemented with an argument in favor of caste-based reservation that echoes and inverts Indiresan's invocation of an "international standard": "Even I was eligible for reservation but I 'chose' to compete in the General Category so that I wouldn't block a seat for reserved category guys. Now, if I wasn't confident of my rank I would have definitely used this wonderful opportunity. When the MITs and the Stanfords have diversity clauses, it is sickening to see the pseudo-intellectuals argue that reservations should be based on economic factors alone." Another student who did take advantage of the quota gave the confessor a pep talk to not internalize the judgments of his or her peers about the reserved versus the general: "One obvious thing I want to put here. If you say there was hardly 30–40 marks difference between you and the ones who pass all the subjects here, then why are you flunking now? I would say, it would be better if you, as soon as possible, erase this thought of yours that you are a reserved candidate, and stop give a fuck to those who discuss about it. There are n reserved candidates in insti who do better than many stud JEE rankers. [personal experience ;)]. So wake up!"

Another set of posts called into question the veracity of caste discrimination. One post that got the highest number of "likes" cast doubt on whether ostracism was the real cause of the confessor's academic troubles. "Are you, in all your senses, telling that despite paying proper attention in the class, and despite studying regularly, you flunked?" After attributing failure to the confessor's own lack of hard work, the commentator reprised debates about caste versus class in order to debunk caste as a legitimate basis for reservation: "Please stop intertwining economic background with caste. For every person with reservation with non-ideal background, I can show you two with better-than-normal background and two who don't have reservation with a poor background."

A third set of commentators sought to rationalize the hostility of the confessor's peers through recourse to liberal arguments about the irrelevance of caste at the IITs. One did so by rejecting the confessor's equation between antireservation and caste sentiment: "Dude, some people discriminate u only bcoz u r a reserved candidate and got a seat in iit with relatively less score in jee but not that u belong to so and so caste." A second chose a more affective route to the same explanation: "For a change, consider yourself belonging to the general category, and your best friend/brother/sister couldn't get in, but a random dude who is well off and with a much lower rank gets in. Won't you feel indignant for your brother/sister/best friend? Won't you feel even a little bad?? It's only human! It's only natural!!" Another wrote a more emphatic defense of the institute as a casteless space: "All I can say is stop whining in such a self-absorbed way! I hardly see anyone (student or prof or staff) or anything (facility, syllabus, grades, opportunities, placements, et-fucking-cetera) discussing and/or discriminating based on caste! IIT has one of the most liberal crowd. So, please don't accuse and bad-mouth the institute and everyone in it, because you never know, the sensations-from-IIT-hungry media may publish that this is the true condition in IIT. And quote you for proof!"

We see in this range of comments the battle lines of the reservation debate. When they attempt to address the everyday casteism of campus life, "the reserved" are accused of intellectual inferiority, laziness, hypersensitivity, lack of empathy, lack of self-regard, lack of responsibility, and disloyalty. Across the diversity of positions, what comes through most strongly is the ubiquity of "general" and "reserved" as forms of collective self-definition and indices of evaluation. It is these terms that have come to stand in for the consolidated categories of upper and lower caste. Even the presence of lower castes who testify to gaining admission through the general category does little to disrupt these commonsense translations. In the standoff over expanded reservation, upper castes have constituted themselves as exclusive bearers of general category merit.

Caste Recognition, Misrecognition, and Stigma at IIT Madras

We saw in Chapter 5 how the distinction between "the gifted" and "the coached" operated as a defensive response to the expansion of coaching and the entry of students from Andhra Pradesh and Telangana, who did not fit the expected social profile of the "true" IITian. In this chapter, we have seen how the "general category" worked similarly to equate upper castes with the meritorious. When it came to "the coached," they were identified through their use of the vernacular and their supposed parochialism. But how were "the reserved" identified?

Before we come to the practices of distinction through which "the reserved" were set apart, let us consider the impact of reservation on the overall obsession with ranking. With the extension of reservation, the minuscule differences in rank were in some ways dwarfed by the power of the cutoff mark for the "general category" of admissions. The cutoff signified far more graphically the end of "merit"; it signaled the difference between the meritorious mainstream and its illegitimate outside. The outsized importance of this distinction puts into play a relentless diagnostics of caste to nose out those who were "the reserved." This, it turns out, was a very complicated issue.

I spoke with Udhay, a 1990s alumnus, about how people knew who the quota students were. Were there open questions about caste, I asked? No, he replied, "caste as such was not talked about. People wouldn't say, are you from this caste?" After further pressing, he revealed that it was from the JEE rank. "One of the first things you would ask when you met someone is, 'What did you get?' The first time everybody comes and enters the hostel, this rank thing is asked. So at that time you would know. Suppose I ask you, what is the rank you got? I know your branch. So, if you've got a low rank, and you're in a desirable branch, I know it is because of the quota."[61]

Madhavan, the "star teacher" who was a contemporary of Udhay's at IIT Madras, corroborated his recollections. "We all knew who the SC students were and they were definitely treated as intellectually inferior," he said. "We knew that in the JEE, the first 2000 get in, then you have the 1000s who don't, and then after all of them come the SCs. So there was a pretty clear sense that they shouldn't be there but managed to get in only because of the quota. Some professors would also treat them very badly."

The "outing" of quota students usually happened first through the circulation of information about JEE results. But there were all sorts of other ways in which, in the absence of such information, "general category" students still claimed to know who was admitted through the quota. This sense of knowing without having to ask hinged on all sorts of diagnostic practices through which the "truth" was revealed.

The first and foremost clue was academic performance. Udhay stated that there was "a huge difference between the students from the general category and this group. The reservation category would struggle a lot more in academics." But, he admitted, sometimes these assessments were not actually based on known "facts." "I think it was also that there was this impression that students like these would be able to do only certain kinds of things intellectually. Maybe not said openly but I think it was understood." Often, alumni stretched facts to fit their assumptions. Most alumni admitted to the difficulties of academic work at IIT Madras even while they singled out quota students as uniquely out of their depth. For example, Sharma, a 2000 alumnus, noted that "the kids who came in like that, the possibility of you having a lot of trouble is much higher if you were one of those kids. And I'm not saying that's true for . . . there are kids who came in through that route and they did fairly well, but if you see someone who is left behind, hasn't graduated in four years, there's a pretty good possibility they were not the regular students coming in because most of the regular students, I have trouble imagining they have difficulty passing, it's just not going to happen. But the special kids with . . . who come in through the other route . . . do have trouble."[62]

We see in these statements a foregone conclusion about academic performance. Quota students were by definition less able than general category students to perform well. Indeed, the same CGPA, or cumulative grade point average, was interpreted entirely differently depending on who earned it: "general category" students were assumed to get poor grades because they were too busy having fun, while quota students did so because they were not intellectually capable of performing up to standard.

Because the presumed intellectual difference between the general and the reserved acquired the status of uncontested truth, anything that disrupted it caused significant discomfort. This was the case with one person who was singled out by Madhavan. "The only SC boy I remember fitting in was Manikumar who was a Class 10 topper at DAV," he recalled. "He also got into IIT Madras through the SC quota but, because he was known to have been a topper, we had to treat him differently." Manikumar was a Dalit student who had excelled at DAV, a CBSE school in Chennai with an overwhelmingly Brahmin student body. Every year, a number of DAV students joined the IITs, giving it a reputation as one of the most conceptually challenging schools in the city. Manikumar had gotten a high JEE rank that put him comfortably

within the general category. However, he had chosen to avail himself
of the quota because it allowed him a better choice of branch. Besides,
as Manikumar himself put it to me, "it was my right." To his frustration, this became evidence that "I couldn't make the cut. Even when I
pointed out that if I hadn't taken a quota seat, one of them wouldn't
have gotten in, they still pretended that I didn't have the marks to get
in on merit."[63] Manikumar's own narrative of his IIT experience was
conflicted. On the one hand, he identified strongly with the Brahmin
peers with whom he had spent his school years. On the other, he was
continuously made aware of his own caste difference and admitted to
still being "rankled" by these memories. For Manikumar's IIT peers,
there was much about him that defied expectations. To explain him,
some resorted to nurture and not nature. "He grew up around Brahmins," Udhay offered, "and this meant that he set high standards for
himself. He wasn't a typical Dalit." In effect, Manikumar served as the
exception that proved the rule of Dalit intellectual inferiority. His presence did little to shake the reigning assumption that passing the JEE
without the quota was the purview of upper castes.

Another upper-caste diagnostic practice for identifying quota students was offered by Shekhar, a 1999 alumnus. At first he gave me a
more mystical explanation for how one could identify the SC/ST students. "You knew. I don't know how. You usually don't go up and ask
them obviously, but even in my first semester, I don't know how I knew
but I knew who were the quota students." When I pushed for clarifica-
tion, he followed up with a more concrete explanation. "Many of them
were from vernacular medium schools," he explained. "And I know
this because I have worked with many of them in English remedial
classes. They didn't even have a sense of basic grammar and construction. They couldn't read fluently and comprehending spoken English
was a far cry." I reminded Shekhar that he had mentioned the presence
of a number of vernacular medium students who got in through the
general category. Did they also face such difficulties in the classroom?
He paused and said, "No, that's a good point. I actually have a number
of friends who were from vernacular medium schools but they were
from . . . they were not from rich families but they were from educated
families."[64] With these twists and turns of logic, Shekhar managed to

hold on to his conviction that the need for English remedial coaching was evidence of reserved status.

One final example of a diagnostic method revolved around the roll number. Sagar, a 1990s alumnus, told me that one knew the SC/ST students from their roll numbers. "Each student had a number, an ID number. If a class had 60 students, there would be 60 ID numbers. In almost all cases the SC, STs were the block of numbers towards the very end because they got the lowest JEE ranks." I asked Sagar if this applied to every classroom, and he said, "Not always, but at least in my class, I think it was." Other students, however, called into question this correlation between roll numbers and quota students. "I don't think that was the case," Mahadevan told me. "I mean, the SC/STs definitely didn't mix with others but I don't think their roll numbers were also clustered together. Anyway, if this was the case, only the faculty would have this information, not the students."

In these instances of diagnostic work, we see the play of recognition and misrecognition through which caste difference is produced at IIT Madras. Upper-caste IITians latch on to certain "clues"—academic performance, English language ability, and the roll number, to name a few—which become overdetermined indices of one's admissions category and, by extension, of intellectual merit. Knowing that a student gained admission through reservation subjected that student not just to pejorative assessments of his or her intelligence but to other forms of suspicion. Udhay recalled that one of his friends who was "from the SC/ST category" was contesting the student body elections in the early 1990s. "I remember that he was actually discriminated against at that time, in the sense that his candidature alone was scrutinized unnecessarily, like, would he be trustworthy to handle funds, etc. These were questions that were brought up. These were not brought up with the other students, with the upper caste students. That was definitely one clear example of discrimination. I even remember that he alleged that he was being discriminated against because of his background." I asked Udhay how people responded to his allegations. "People of course denied that this was the case," he told me, "but it was an open secret. In fact, in our wing—he was one of our wing students—we felt that he was discriminated against, but the others were saying that it was not this reason, it was some other reason and all that, but this was in the air, during that election. I remember it clearly."

When asked directly about such forms of discrimination, many students reiterated that there was a baseline egalitarianism at IIT Madras underpinned by a culture of excellence. As Srikanth, a 1990s alumnus, put it, "One of the principles was egalitarianism, people were like, everybody is equal and the only way I'm going to assess you is your intellectual ability and nothing else matters. It doesn't matter where you come from."[65] This pairing of equality and excellence, and the bracketing out of quota students as an exception to both, harks back to eighteenth-century republicanism and its soaring rhetoric around birthing a new society based in an "aristocracy of talent." Now, as then, we see a naturalizing of hierarchy as the extension of legitimate differences in ability that are divorced from a broader social environment. In the process, excellence is rendered innate, as is its absence.

Dalit Experiences

Dalit students who gained admission through the quota system were only too aware of these relentless diagnostic practices. While a few like Manikumar chose to battle caste prejudice overtly, for others, trying to remain anonymous was the more viable option. This was made difficult by the explicit and overriding emphasis on the JEE rank as the marker of social and intellectual standing on campus. The effort to remain anonymous was even more challenging for students who scored below a certain mark in the examination. These students had to undergo a one-year preparatory course before being admitted to the institute, which made them conspicuously distinct from the rest of their cohort.

Satish, a Dalit alumnus from the 2000s, spoke to me about the agonizing contortions one would have to perform to avoid exposing oneself as a preparatory course student. "If you're part of the preparatory course," he explained, "it's very obvious that you come from a Dalit background, and that can get in the way of how you experience IIT."[66] This was even worse than qualifying directly for the quota based on your JEE results, he elaborated. For those students, "there is still a possibility to escape getting marked up to a certain point of time. And up to that time you'll have the opportunity to prove that you can actu-

ally do good in academics. But if people know you are in the preparatory course, I think that deal is kind of done."

Satish's experiences at IIT were an eye-opener. He told me that his
decision to take the JEE was almost unthinkable in his village. All the
children studied in vernacular medium schools, from where most went
on to local colleges or straight into low-paying government jobs. The
IITs just weren't part of the local universe of possibility. But when he
heard about the IITs from an ST friend who was studying for the JEE,
he decided to give it a shot. "I went and met him, and he gave me a list
of books that he thought were best to prepare for JEE. And because I
was living in this village, we did not have a big enough bookstore from
where I could buy these books. My father would go once in the month
to the district headquarters where his office was and I asked him to
get me these books."

Satish's JEE marks qualified him for the preparatory course, which
he initially experienced as a wonderful first exposure to the IIT campus
and to future friends. It was only once he entered his first year as an
IITian that he realized what a minefield the campus could be for a
Dalit. He learned very quickly to try to obscure his path into the
institute.

"I felt like an intruder at IIT," Satish confessed, but it was less about
an internalized sense of inadequacy than about the culture of the institution, where "most people were upper caste but knew nothing about
caste." Unlike more activist students, Satish chose to keep to himself
as a way of avoiding uncomfortable situations. "If you look at Rohith
or Kanhaiya," he elaborated, "they're trying to basically force . . . not
exactly force but claim their identity and basically go outright and say
that this is me, and I think that whatever is happening is not good. I
never did that. I kept to myself, avoided confrontations; if somebody
said something, I would just listen to it and not respond. I think that
became part of my personality."[67]

His quiet perseverance also garnered Satish a good job. However,
the placement process was also a very challenging experience where,
once again, the JEE rank loomed large. Satish was one of the candidates for a job with an Indian private outsourcing company. The two-
stage process consisted of a group discussion followed by an individual
interview. Satish fared very well in the group discussion on the place

of India within global outsourcing. Based on his performance in the discussion, he was invited for an individual interview with the CEO. This is where the trouble began. "Before the interview, we had to mention our JEE rank on a form and I wrote down that I belong to the reserved category." As a result, the entire focus of the individual interview was on this "confession." "They wanted to basically understand if I felt inferior maybe because I came from reserved category, if I had friends who came from general category, and generally how it has shaped my personality and my educational performance," Satish recounted. "After one point I think I became brutally honest. It became a question of standing up for myself; the job itself became kind of unimportant."

Satish did get the job offer and was asked to meet again with the CEO. "He told me that—he told me that you've done well in your academic experience within IIT and he saw a lot of potential—he basically showed confidence in me that I'll do great in his organization, but I have to start talking to people, networking with people. . . . He told me to come out of my shell and start interacting with people." I asked Satish if he thought the CEO would have said that to somebody who was not from the reserved category. "I don't think so," Satish replied. "It was very personal."

The JEE rank also followed Satish into his second job with an IT company. Soon after he joined the company, the manager invited Satish and his team out for drinks. "He asked me my JEE rank and I just told him the rank of a friend," he recalled. Soon after this incident, Satish was sent as his company's representative to a campus job placement fair at IIT Kanpur. There, he found himself among a number of other IITians, and the conversation turned to JEE preparation and ranks.

> We got into this room, three of us, and our managers, and the whole evening was spent on what their experiences were in coaching centers and what ranks they had. And I didn't know how to respond, because none of these people knew I come from the reserved category. They're looking for my reaction, they want to know where I basically prepared for JEE and so on. And I was deeply afraid, like, what do I do in this situation? There is a steep change in the way people perceive you once it's out in the open. But I'm working on it now. . . . I want to get to the point where I'm not afraid of it.

After Satish recounted these stories about the long shadow of the "reserved category," I responded by saying, "It's so unfair that you have to feel shame about this when the majority of people who get into the IITs come from histories of privilege and education. It's not because they're brilliant but because they've had advantages."

Satish paused and then gently corrected me. "It's not really about shame. It's more about how people's perceptions change and how it's going to impact your day to day life, you understand? We have to assess: does it risk our friendships, our working relationships? So I think a lot is at stake." Hiding the JEE rank, he insisted against my interpretation, was not about shame but about maneuver. It was about navigating a treacherous caste landscape where opportunities and empathies were unevenly distributed and prejudice was structural. It was a world in which achievement was seen as natural for some and impossible for others.

So, what was the takeaway for Satish about reservations? He told me that his relationship to reservations had shifted over time. First, he thought that "reservation as a policy is insufficient in the sense that it still does not make the learning environment very positive for students. It is hostile." But, he continued,

> I don't think that's actually the truth anymore. So many of my friends who are from the SC category, majority of them are from rural villages where they did not have access to coaching or tuition, nobody in their families was there to advise them how to prepare for interviews, they didn't speak English well—and still, they made it to the IITs. And in that sense, at times when I reflect, I feel really proud of myself, that I have made it to the big leagues. So in that sense, we have an incredible story. It became a source of inspiration for me to go out of my way and do even more brilliantly than when I was in IIT.

Reservation disrupted the tacit role of ascription by explicitly naming caste as a factor in the JEE outcome. In setting aside a percentage of seats for lower-caste groups, reservation policy sought to correct for historically sedimented disadvantages. At the same time, by marking only its beneficiaries as caste subjects, reservation policy underwrote the status of upper castes as emblematic of meritocracy. Initially, when only SC/ST quotas were implemented, the claim to meritocracy was expressed in universalistic terms that did not require an explicit defense of caste entitlement. At that time, only Tamil Brahmins, with their regional hostilities, equated merit explicitly with caste culture. However, this changed with the steady expansion of quotas in tandem with the growth in lower-caste rights politics. With the implementation of Mandal I and II, upper-caste claims to meritocracy were no longer simply universalistic; they became more defensive and explicitly identitarian in nature. The more strident identification with "the general category" against "the reserved" expressed a consolidated form of upper casteness irreducible to any one endogamous grouping.

Both universalistic and identitarian claims to merit were typically articulated against reservation. More recently, however, some upper-caste groups have demanded not the abrogation of reservation but its further expansion to include them. We see the demand for inclusion within the reservation umbrella, for instance, in the July 2015 claim by Gujarati Patidars.[68] Following the Patidar agitation in Gujarat, a number of other upper-caste groups began to agitate for inclusion in the reserved category: the Marathas in Maharashtra, the Jats of Haryana, and the Brahmins of Kerala. These demands for inclusion or reclassification within the reserved category rest on a key assumption: that the quota as a right to education and employment can be distinguished from the longer historical experience of social and cultural marginalization and stigmatization. Instead, such claims are leveled against the more recent history of redistribution, which they argue have disenfranchised upper castes of their rightful due. What we are witnessing is the appropriation of the language of injustice and redress by groups who have been the historical beneficiaries of caste. Much like the 1951 judgment by the Madras High Court, such claims transform reservation from an effort to redress inequality to its very source. By substituting a longer history of unequal material and symbolic capital with a focus on more recent efforts at redistribution, these upper-caste groups argue that they themselves are the victims of injustice who deserve redress from the inequities of reservation.

Let us now shift from these fraught dynamics within India to a different terrain of maneuver. In Chapter 7, we will look at how diasporic mobility to the United States has shaped the politics of merit. We touched upon this in Chapter 4 when considering the outward orientation of IITians as an expression of exceptionalism. In what follows, we will explore diasporic mobility in far more depth. How did IITians abroad engage with the expanding quota system in India? Did diasporic IITians feel the need to lay claim to meritocracy? And how were such claims shaped by a different national history of social stratification?

7

Brand IIT

Mass coaching and reservations brought new groups into the IITs and radically transformed the demographic makeup of these institutions. As a result, the social profile of the IITian as part of an urban, upper-caste middle class has given way to a more diverse student body. In reaction to these trends, upper-caste IITians have attempted to shore up their representative status by claiming the mantle of meritocracy. This has involved a robust politics of distinction through which the coached are distinguished from the gifted, and the reserved category from the general category. In the process, a consolidated form of upper casteness has emerged and, in the context of Indian higher education, acquired unique salience. We have also seen the role of Tamilnadu as an important precedent in the shift from a universalistic to a more identitarian expression of upper-caste identity. As targets of Non-Brahminism and Dravidianism, Tamil Brahmins were the earliest to frame merit as a caste claim. Their marking as Brahmins produced forms of self-marking as a tactic of meritocratic claim-making. With the spread of Other Backward Class (OBC) politics across India, this shift to a more explicit caste politics of meritocracy has also spread. At IIT Madras and beyond, the assumption now is that the general category is an upper-caste collective.

Through all these challenges to and defenses of upper-caste meritocracy, mobility has remained a key mechanism of caste consolidation and capital accumulation. We have seen in previous chapters how mobility within India under the purview of the central government contributed to the making of an upper-caste intelligentsia. It was precisely the caste capital provided by this mobility that was threatened by the Mandal Commission recommendations and produced such a strong backlash. But spatial mobility was by no means limited to national borders. Migration outside India has also been a long-standing source of upper-caste social and economic capital. This was certainly the case for IITians. As we saw in Chapter 4, IITians began to leave India from the late 1960s for what they perceived as greener pastures. In the very early years, these were brief forays for training in West Germany and other countries, after which they would return to work in Indian industry. But the pattern shifted once the United States came into view as the principal destination for IITians. The post-1960s waves of migration made up a more sizable, more permanent diaspora.

Migration from India predated independence. The late nineteenth century witnessed the first large wave of Indian migration to Burma, Ceylon, Malaya, Africa, the Caribbean, and the Pacific. The vast majority of these migrants were lower-caste indentured laborers. This was followed by a second wave of traders, clerks, bureaucrats, and professionals who went mostly to East and South Africa but also to the other British colonies where indentured laborers had preceded them. A third wave headed for the United States. There are clear differences between the experiences of lower-caste laborers and upper-caste professionals who began arriving in the United States from as early as the 1880s. But despite the fact that caste played a significant role in structuring migration and diasporic life, the scholarly literature on the Indian diaspora to the United States might lead one to conclude that caste largely vanishes as a social category beyond the boundaries of the Indian nation-state.[1] Instead, the most salient forms of self-definition appear to be class, gender, language, religion, and nation.

The story of the IIT diaspora suggests otherwise. The forms of accumulated caste capital detailed over the previous chapters were key factors in allowing for diasporic mobility. Moreover, the professional success of IITians in the United States has been hugely significant for reinforcing the link between meritocracy and caste. With geographical distance from India and from rising challenges to caste entitlement,

IITian achievement abroad once again appears as just that—self-made success. Diasporic mobility has helped to once again force caste into the shadows. However, the absence of caste as a public identity in the diaspora does not preclude its structural and affective workings. If anything, the institutional kinship within the overwhelmingly upper-caste IIT diaspora has become an even more potent form of capital. Diasporic IITians have been at the forefront of efforts to sustain and consolidate their affective ties and to make the IIT pedigree into a globally recognized brand.

Much of this work of branding has been driven by IITians in Silicon Valley, for whom entrepreneurial success has further reinforced their sense of being self-made individuals. Entrepreneurialism—and that, too, being nonwhite entrepreneurial successes in a new industry—has deepened their investment in a narrative of humble middle-class origins in which the brain is elevated as the sole form of capital and histories of caste are strikingly absent. U.S.-based IITians work to advance this narrative, not only in the United States but also in India, where they have been vocal advocates of market deregulation and privatization. Moving between U.S. and Indian contexts has entailed a balancing act between the marking and unmarking of caste as the basis of achievement. As we have seen, ongoing challenges to upper-caste dominance in India have disrupted settled expectations and produced a more strident defense of merit as caste property. The diaspora, too, is an important weapon in this fight. By showcasing diasporic success as the arrival of the global Indian, upper-caste IITians render the struggle for caste rights into a parochial—even regressive—endeavor.

Understanding the transnationalization of caste is particularly important in the current moment, when the rise to political power of middle and lower castes has partially obscured the workings of upper-caste capital. Indeed, it is particularly productive to think about how and in which contexts such capital is reconstituted. While in some ways formal political arenas and the broader cultural sphere have witnessed the entry of lower castes, elite education and the expanding private sector both within and beyond India have serviced the reconstitution of caste privilege by other means. In this sense, we might think of elite and private domestic and transnational arenas as spaces of upper-caste flight and retrenchment away from the pressures of lower-caste politics.

Political scientist Devesh Kapur has argued that the immigration of Indian professionals to the United States was one of the "safety valves" of Indian democracy.[2] Because they could immigrate, the fight over the distribution of political power and economic resources was less contentious than it might have otherwise been. Kapur argues further that the specific form of capital these elites possessed—advanced degrees as opposed to land—made for easy "exit," first from state employment to the private sector and then abroad. Since this was a transferable form of capital, "exit" also contributed to the further accumulation of capital.[3]

Kapur offers an illuminating and exhaustive account of the economy and politics of transnational migration that argues for the necessity of thinking nation and diaspora together. His work provides valuable statistical data on the social bases of migration, its economic effects on India, and the forms of politics it engendered both in India and the United States. What is less evident is how moving from one system of social stratification to another influenced the worldviews and practices of diasporic elites. Specifically, what did it mean for Indian professionals to move from a society where enduring caste stratification intersected with democratic change to a society where racial stratification operated similarly? How did they respond to their own racialization as U.S. minorities, and how did this experience shape their forms of identification and strategies of accumulation?

In this chapter, I will build on existing literature on the Indian diaspora in the United States to understand the impact of transnational mobility on IITians and of diasporic IITians on India. How, I will ask, was upper-caste identity forged in the United States, where IITians were positioned as both class elites and racial minorities? IITian diasporic experiences have to be understood in relation to the longer U.S. history of race and immigration. The 1965 U.S. Immigration and Nationality Act marked a key shift toward official multiculturalism and the representative power of Indian professionals.[4] This shift is key to the status of IITians as an influential subset of Indian professionals whose self-fashioning is keenly attentive to the market for identities. As we will see, their self-fashioning as ethnic entrepreneurs, helped by the catalytic impact of the Silicon Valley boom and enduring forms of transnational institutional kinship, has found fullest expression in the marketing of Brand IIT. Moreover, diasporic IITians have leveraged their status as financially successful global moderns to push for legal changes, market deregulation, and privatization in India.

The success of Brand IIT has also transformed the meaning of meritocracy by shifting the emphasis from intellectualism to entrepreneurialism. While upper-caste merit has always been about both intellectual prowess and capital accumulation, the emergence of entrepreneurial success as the clearest index of merit has produced new schisms among IITians. Now it is the diasporic entrepreneur who is heralded as the exemplar of meritocracy over and above the homeland IITian. Moreover, the elevation of entrepreneurialism as the most desirable form of meritocratic value has crystallized a new pecking order of IIT campuses, with IIT Bombay on top. Toward the end of the chapter, we will return to IIT Madras to gauge the impact of Brand IIT on students and alumni. How, we will ask, have Madras IITians responded to this most recent turn in the politics of meritocracy?

Mobility: Spatial and Economic

The IIT diaspora is an artifact of mobile capital. And as with coaching and reservation, the Tamil Brahmin story was an important precedent in the use of mobility as a strategy of upper-caste maneuver and accumulation. This earlier phenomenon anticipated later patterns of upper-caste flight, first from the public sector and then beyond India. Spatial mobility has allowed for economic mobility away from the democratizing pressures of class and caste politics.

As we saw in Chapter 3, colonial rule afforded Tamil Brahmins unique opportunities to move from the countryside to the city and outside the region for employment. The mass exodus of Tamil Brahmins to the city was facilitated by their unique relationship to land and labor. Brahmins long embodied "the cultural model of elite behavior and style among dominant peasants," where the mark of entitlement required "not putting one's hands in the mud."[5] This combination of a material reliance on and symbolic separation from the land was paralleled by Tamil Brahmins' physical separation from other agrarian castes in the space of the *agraharam*. Tamil Brahmin spatial exclusivity came in for harsh criticism by the Non-Brahmin movement, "which strongly objected to restrictions on public access and sought to 'de-sacralize *agraharam* space.'"[6] Their own relative detachment from the soil, colonial opportunities, and the pressures of Non-Brahminism propelled Tamil Brahmins out of the countryside and into the city, where they sought employment in the modern professions. The exodus was so rapid and large scale that by the 1930s, the author of a colonial report on Gangaikondan—a town in southern Tirunelveli district—could remark that "the Brahmin thrives best in towns and the rural soil is uncongenial to his genius."[7] Anthropologists Fuller and Narasimhan echo this conception of Tamil Brahmins in pointing out that urban Brahmins "do not go back to ancestral villages to absorb their food and water or hold family rituals—nor do they ever link their urban neighborhoods to rural ones." The reason, they argue, is that "for Brahmans, far more than for non-Brahmans, status and identity are independent of where they live.[8] In other words, Tamil Brahmins had come to contain spatial mobility as an ingredient of collective identity.

As we saw in Chapters 4 and 6, Tamil Brahmin IITians do foreground spatial mobility as the condition of possibility for self-fulfillment and professional advancement. In their narratives, the move from countryside to city, from the south to the north, and from the public to the private sector are strategies through which merit is preserved against the odds. Moreover, they characterize Tamil Brahmin mobility as a form of cultural genius that expresses a genetic predisposition to education and a preternatural capacity for instrumental action. As we also saw earlier, there is a palpable sense of victimization that accompanies mobility. In addition to being a theme in individual narratives, this comes through in the aggregate in a 1994 study of IIT Madras in which diasporic alumni indicated caste discrimination as a key push factor in their decision to migrate to the United States.[9]

Contra these culturalist assumptions that are at once claims to merit, these tactics are best seen in properly historical terms. The accommodation of new practices within preexisting caste identities was a by-product of colonial-era transformations in the meaning of caste from a question of lifestyle to one of birth and descent.[10] Tamil Brahmins took up this new model of caste by embracing professions opened up by the political economic transformations of the nineteenth and twentieth centuries, leading to their dominance of South Indian public life. The rise of the Non-Brahmin and Dravidian movements, and the education and employment quotas they generated, propelled a move out of the regional state bureaucracy to central government services and eventually beyond India. In addition, many exited the public sector altogether, a trend that was firmly established with the rise of the managerial sciences and the information technology sector, where they now occupy the upper echelons of managerial power.[11] While spatial mobility was certainly an important strategy, it was less an ingrained cultural disposition than a reactive maneuver in response to the economic and political transformations of the day. Moreover, some and not all Tamil Brahmins were able to avail themselves of these new opportunities.

Spatial mobility helped to shore up Tamil Brahmins' capacity for capital accumulation in the face of oppositional demands for the redistribution of power and resources. The Tamil Brahmin use of mobility as a strategy and form of self-representation is a key precedent to similar trends across India. In the postindependence period, diasporic mobility emerged as a key tool for a wide spectrum of upper castes looking to secure the conditions of capital accumulation in the face of increasing lower-caste demands for representation within public education and state employment. At the same time, the Tamil Brahmin emphasis on education and intellectualism as distinct upper-caste virtues has given way to entrepreneurialism as a new model of upper casteness. In the process, the Tamil Brahmin worldview now seems outmoded, a shift that is reflected in the rise of IIT Bombay within the pecking order of IITs.

There are several push-pull factors that catalyzed diasporic mobility among upper castes: Indian state developmentalism, the rise of lower-caste politics, and U.S. immigration policy. Indian independence in 1947 occasioned the building of a "mixed" economy weighted toward growing the public sector. By contrast, private sector growth was circumscribed and regulated by a system of quotas and permits pejoratively referred to as the "License Raj." Until well into the 1980s, state employment was the principal means of growing the middle class. Until the advent of economic liberalization in 1991, private sector jobs grew at a modest rate, while jobs in the public sector occupied a much larger share of employment.

The expanding public sector was paralleled by the growth in public institutions of higher education. Over the first fifty postindependence years, the number of colleges rose dramatically, as did the number of students enrolled in higher education. Until the 1990s, when education was opened up to private investment, the vast majority of these institutions came under the purview of either the state or the central government.

These two aspects of Indian developmentalism—the dominance of the public sector and the growth of higher education—were key factors in the formation of the upper-caste middle class, who constituted the bulk of the political and social elite in the early years after independence. As we have noted, unlike landed and commercial elites, their principal forms of caste capital—education and the white-collar professions—were highly mobile. And it was precisely these forms of capital that became targets of lower-caste rights politics. The aspirations of lower-caste groups found their most voluble expression in the demands for quotas in public institutions and the professional labor force, which were previously monopolized by upper castes. Increasing collective pressure from marginalized groups resulted in significant shifts in social representation within the bureaucracy and public sector enterprises.

In response to such challenges to their political and social hegemony, upper castes began to look to the private sector or outside the country. Among diasporic destinations, the United States emerged as the most desirable option after the mid-1960s because of changes in U.S. immigration policy. While the trickle of Indian migrants to the United States did increase in the 1940s and 1950s, the 1965 Immigration and Nationality Act opened the floodgates. The legal change was in large part due to Cold War hostilities. In 1957, the USSR launched Sputnik I and II into orbit, provoking panic in the United States over the technological prowess of its Cold War rival. In response, the U.S. government began a concerted effort to promote the study of science and technology, most directly through an enhanced National Science Foundation. Rather than training Americans, however, U.S. science came to rely on immigrants for its development. The Soviet cosmonaut

Yuri Gagarin's successful orbit of the earth in 1961 was a key catalyst in the decision to import technical labor. In 1965, on the heels of civil rights legislation, President Johnson approved new statutes that aimed specifically at increasing professional immigration—most importantly of scientists and engineers—to bolster the U.S. position in the space and nuclear races.[12]

The 1965 act precipitated the transnational migration of highly skilled professionals and students from India to the United States. The Indian-born population in the United States grew from approximately 13,000 in 1960 to nearly 1 million by 2000 and 1.5 million by 2007; with the inclusion of U.S.-born Indians, the numbers rose to 1.7 million in 2000 and 2.8 million in 2007. By 2007, the Indian-born population had become the fourth largest immigrant group in the United States, behind those born in Mexico, China, and the Philippines.[13]

It was also the most highly educated. Between 1994 and 2001, the U.S.-born population with a college degree or higher stood at 26.5 percent, compared with 70.8 percent of Indian-born migrants. By contrast, the percentage of college graduates in other foreign-born populations was similar to that for the U.S.-born. The percentage of the Indian-born with post–bachelor's degrees was 36.8 percent—far higher than the 8.5 and 8.6 percent for the U.S.-born and other foreign-born, respectively. As striking as these numbers are, far more so is the educational gap between Indian-born migrants and the Indian population as a whole: while 71 percent of U.S. Indian immigrants had some college education, just 3.42 percent of Indians did—a more than twenty-fold difference.[14]

This educational gap is even more stark when it comes to technical degrees. In 2000, one United Nations estimate put the total number of Indian expatriates in OECD (Organization for Economic Cooperation and Development) countries at 1.93 million, of which 51 percent were "highly skilled," with graduate degrees from the uppermost echelon of institutions. In comparison, the 2001 Indian census put the total number of graduates at 3.7 percent of the population, while the number with a technical degree or postgraduate degree was just 0.5 percent. In 1999, out of the estimated 1.5 million foreign-born U.S. residents with the highest degree in science and engineering, the largest group was from India, at 14 percent.[15]

The U.S. Indian population is also better off in terms of per capita income when compared to both homeland and host societies. By 2001, the total income of Indian-born Americans had grown to over $40 billion, or 10 percent of India's gross domestic product. This population has also gotten younger over time due to the large influx of H-1B visa holders from the late 1990s, all of whom are highly educated. After the information technology boom, their earning power also consolidated far more quickly than was the case with previous generations of migrants. While 33 percent of Indians who came during the 1990s were earning more than twice the native-born median for 2000, only 17 percent of those who came during the 1980s were earning more than twice the native-born median for 1990. These figures indicate a rapid process of economic consolidation for Indian migrants in the United States.[16]

The highly selective character of post-1965 migration has ensured that the Indian diaspora to the United States is a predominantly upper-caste formation. This is a key difference between the late nineteenth- and late twentieth-century migrations from India. Kapur puts it plainly: "While migrants in the nineteenth century came from poorer socioeconomic groups and from poorer parts of the country and went to (relatively poor) Southern countries, a century later virtually the opposite was true—they came from richer socioeconomic groups and from wealthier parts of the country and, with the significant exception of the large migration to the Middle East, went to industrialized countries."[17] Caste is a key factor underpinning this difference: upper castes predominate in the latter wave, with dominant castes as the second largest group, and Scheduled Castes and Scheduled Tribes making up at best 2 or 3 percent of Indian migrants to the United States.

In some ways, this pattern of migration has allowed for a less explicit defense of merit, because upper castes do not face the kinds of democratic challenges that are ongoing in India. The highly selective character of the diaspora and the illegibility of caste in the United States has made it easier to draw a seamless equation between being upper caste, being Indian, and having "merit." It certainly helps that the economic power of post-1965 migrants has eclipsed the lives and livelihoods of those who do not fit the image of the professional Indian.

Moreover, a subset of these iconic Indians—the IITians of Silicon Valley—have been at the forefront of professional networking and image-making to ensure that the Indian technical professional is immediately recognizable as a global commodity. Their networks of affiliation and accumulation work to reinforce the upper-caste underpinnings of Indian technical merit even while caste disappears from view.

Race and Indianness

Indians are currently one of the most affluent and educated populations in the United States, yet they are also a racial minority subject to American ideologies of white supremacy and black inferiority. As with other minorities, Indian Americans have had to navigate the landscape of American racism, where whiteness and blackness signify polar ends of a spectrum of opportunity and belonging.

The migration of Indians to the United States began in the late nineteenth century. By 1900, U.S. Census reports placed the "East Indian" or "Hindu" population—mostly upper-caste Hindu students, businesspeople, and professionals—at 2,050. Significantly, this number did not include Bengali Muslim peddlers, who arrived in the 1880s to sell their "exotic" wares and remained less legible to the law. From 1904 to 1924, Punjabi immigrants from rural peasant backgrounds arrived in Vancouver and were driven south to the Pacific Northwest by Canada's "whites only" policy. Here, too, they encountered hostilities. Following as they did in the footsteps of Chinese and Japanese immigration, Punjabi migrants were subject to the "yellow peril" racism sweeping the country. Dubbed the "turbaned tide," they were targeted by newly formed groups such as the Asian Exclusion League, which demanded the termination of Indian immigration. Despite these tensions, between 1907 and 1910 approximately 1,000 immigrants entered each year, and by 1910, there were up to 10,000 Indians in the country. During World War I, they were joined by Hindu and Muslim seamen on British steamers who jumped ship to remain in the United States. Legislation followed social hostilities: the California Alien Land Act of 1913 excluded Indians from landownership, and the "barred zone" Immigration Act of 1917 stopped all Asian immigration except from Japan.[18]

In spite of the racial targeting of Indians as a whole, caste and class proved to be important factors in determining what form of discrimination they faced and how they responded. While those who came to work the land, work in lumberyards, or work on the railroads bore the brunt of physical attacks, educated professionals who did not confront such direct hostility began crafting a racial politics that would distinguish them from their poorer compatriots, from other nonwhite immigrants, and from black Americans. As did Dravidianists in South India, educated Indians drew on the work of Max Mueller and other nineteenth-century ethnologists and linguists to argue in court battles that they, unlike those of African, Chinese, and Japanese origin, were entitled to naturalization as white people. Between 1907 and 1923, seventy Indian professionals gained citizenship on the grounds that they were members of the "Aryan race" and, as such, of white, or Caucasian, origin. These "advances" were reversed in the Bhagat Singh Thind case of 1923, in which the U.S. Supreme Court declared "Hindus" ineligible for citizenship on the basis that they were not "white persons." Although Thind identified himself as a "high caste Aryan of full Indian blood," the court ruled against him. The justices maintained that "while ['Caucasian'] and the words 'white persons' are treated as synonymous, they are not of identical meaning." In this instance, they determined that the "scientific" definitions must be subordinated to "common sense" understandings of whiteness. As a result, more than half of the seventy had their citizenship annulled by 1926.[19]

In contrast to Indian elites who sought to maintain their status by claiming whiteness, others found common cause with racial minority populations. Historian Vivek Bald's work illuminates what he calls "the lost histories of South Asian America." These are the stories of the Bengali Muslim peddlers, the Hindu and Muslim ship workers, and the Punjabi Sikh farmers who came to the United States, entered into interracial relationships with black and Hispanic women, and became part of multiracial communities across many sites in the United States, including New York, New Orleans, Baltimore, Detroit, and California's agricultural heartland. Their everyday lives are testament to a very different narrative of South Asian immigration, which showcases working-class solidarities across racial lines and the centrality of black neighborhoods within histories of U.S. immigration.[20]

Bald had difficulty unearthing these histories because they are at such variance to the more common story of elite Indian migration and endogamous social reproduction. Having found them, he argues convincingly that we should not reduce South Asian American history to the experiences of professionals. At the same time, Bald admits that the politics of representation has worked in favor of the professional elite, who have leveraged their power to challenge the mold of the "undesirable alien." Although the naturalization bill that President Truman signed into law in July 1946 made all Indians already resident in the country eligible for citizenship, Bald maintains that this was a mixed blessing. As he puts it, "these ideas—that U.S. Immigration policies toward India should favor scientists, engineers, and businesspeople and be driven by national considerations of trade and foreign policy—not only won out in 1946 but were eventually enshrined in the Hart-Celler Act, which opened the door to tens of thousands of skilled professionals from the subcontinent in 1965."[21]

In some ways, the 1964 Civil Rights Act and the 1965 Hart-Celler Act marked a break with a past of racially defined citizenship. But to what extent did the racial hierarchies of the late nineteenth and early twentieth centuries cease to structure American society and politics? Legal scholar Cheryl Harris questions the retreat from racial thinking that is presumed to have informed post–civil rights politics. Rather than marking an end to white privilege, she maintains that liberal discourses of formal equality have masked its continued operations. Harris points in particular to the landmark judgment in *Brown v. Board of Education* as a turning point for American racial politics because it marked the end of legal segregation and the reemergence of white privilege in a subtler form. "White privilege accorded as a legal right was rejected," she underscores, "but *de facto* white privilege not mandated by law remained unaddressed."[22] Harris goes on to argue that in failing to address the real inequities produced by segregation, "the status quo of substantive disadvantage was ratified as an accepted and acceptable base line—a neutral state operating to the disadvantage of Blacks long after *de jure* segregation had ceased to do so."[23] Other accounts buttress Harris's argument by showing how practices such as preferential lending, redlining, and attacking affirmative action have worked to secure "the possessive investment in whiteness."[24]

These analyses of race in the United States strongly echo those of caste in India. In both contexts, forms of caste and racial capital continue to stratify opportunity and status in the aftermath of legal equality. Furthermore, as with Indian discourses of castelessness, the language of race-blind equality has made it more difficult to track and tackle the work of whiteness as inherited privilege. How have IITians in the United States navigated these two forms of social stratification? What has become of caste in its twentieth-century encounter with U.S. racial stratification? Before turning to these questions, let us look more closely at a subset of Indian migration: the technical migrants who preceded IITians to the United States.

Indian Technical Migration: 1880s–1950s

We saw in Chapter 3 how, in the early twentieth century, Indian technical students sought to bypass the parameters of empire through transnational linkages to Germany and Japan. The United States was also a target of this extraimperial set of aspirations.

Until the 1940s, technical students went to the United States despite, not because of, the colonial state. In the face of meager colonial state support for technical training abroad, aspiring students fell back on family funds, financial support from nonstate organizations, or sponsorship by Indian native states. The importance of personal networks of kinship and patronage ensured that those who went abroad using these channels were from educated, upper-caste families. World War II occasioned a shift in this set of relationships between migrant engineers, American universities, and the colonial government. America's entry into the war enhanced its influence in India both militarily and in negotiations over Indian technical training. The result of these shifts was a new government plan announced in 1944 to send 500 Indians to Britain or the United States for advanced technical training. The plan elicited a flood of applications. Ultimately, the committee selected 600 students out of 9,000 applicants, more than half of whom opted for the United States over Britain.[25]

The more active part played by the colonial state in sponsoring Indian training abroad changed the social profile of students going to the United States. The students who had gone earlier were typically from commercial and industrial families with a background in business. With the growth in state sponsorship, the students who went to prestigious institutions like MIT were increasingly from families in the employ of the colonial state. Although both earlier and later sets of students were from upper-caste backgrounds, the World War II generation of migrants was positioned to have the kind of influence within the Indian state and its industries that their predecessors had lacked.

Historian Ross Bassett has written extensively about Indian technical migrants to the United States.[26] While he takes care to identify migrant engineers as class elites, caste figures less prominently in his account. When Bassett does address caste identity and sentiment, it is mostly limited to the early twentieth century and to upper-caste efforts to overcome an aversion to manual labor. One story involves the America booster Saranghadar Das, who exhorted Indians "to use America to re-create themselves and then to return and to create a stronger India." Bassett writes at length about Das's advocacy, which combined personal testimony with arguments about the beneficial effects of the American social milieu for the cause of Indian nationalism. Much like IIT alumnus John Abraham writing about his growing awareness of caste in the context of 1960s Germany, Das wrote about America as a place where he had to rethink caste sentiment. An "idler" who had learned to "hate every kind of manual labor," Das found his prejudices a liability in America. After being fired from jobs because he lacked basic manual skills, Das eventually "grew to accept and even revel in manual labor. He cleaned toilets and served as a day laborer in a sugar mill, bragging about his muscles as 'strong as iron bands.'"[27]

This fascination with his own musculature provides an important key to Das's relationship to body, labor, and nation. Unlike John Abraham, whose German experience provoked critical reflection on the social hierarchies of caste, Das's embrace of manual labor was a means to a reinvigorated Hindu nationalist masculinity. For him, the ultimate goal of such collective self-fashioning by upper castes was to end British colonialism, not transform Indian caste relations. In a piece titled "A Call of Duty to Young India," he called on Indians to immigrate to the United States "because we have been satiated with all kinds of servility and we long for manliness." It was only through diasporic experience, he argued, that Indians would be able "to develop the hidden resources of our continent," to make goods "right in India instead of importing them from foreign countries."[28] As Das saw it, a more robust Hindu masculinity would boost the productive capacities of the nation and become the basis of economic self-sufficiency. Left unstated in this call for a reinvigorated upper-caste self was its relationship to the lower-caste laborer.

As with aspiring engineers in India, elite diasporic Indians wanted to move away from classical and literary education and toward technical training while maintaining their social standing. The Massachusetts Institute of Technology's motto—*Mens et manus* (Mind and hand)—with the mind prevailing over the hand, was uniquely attractive to nationalistically minded Indians who sought a technical education befitting their own emerging role as India's future leaders. With the founding of the IITs in the 1950s and 1960s, the path hewn by these colonial migrants became much more established. Not only did MIT serve as an institutional model for the IITs (as we touched on in Chapter 4), but migration to the United States for study became an increasingly more common option for IIT graduates. Unlike their predecessors, most of these postcolonial migrants settled in the United States to form a permanent diaspora.

The IIT Diaspora

IITians were among the first technical students to leave independent India's shores to settle in the United States. As we saw in Chapter 4, training at the institutes had cultivated aspirations that they felt could not be fulfilled in India. The high rates of joblessness in the 1960s only enhanced their growing disillusionment with the state and the public sector. But unlike in the colonial period, IITians' extraterritorial ambitions were hardly the result of state neglect. In the 1960s, public expenditure at the IITs amounted to 16,400 rupees per student per year; by contrast, regional engineering colleges spent 7,000 rupees for their students. In addition, tuition at the IITs was a mere 200 rupees per year. In short, IITians were some of the greatest beneficiaries of the developmental state. At the time, the cost of sending a student to an IIT amounted to the per capita income of almost forty people. This was a significant state investment made with the expectation of a developmental payoff for the nation.[29] The patronage of the state also extended beyond this educational subsidy. As we have seen, the vast majority of IITians were the children of civil servants whose families had long derived their status and professional identities from a connection to the state.

Despite these factors, the social contract between IITians and the state implied in the educational subsidy was more honored in the breach. IIT alumni very quickly reoriented themselves toward the private sector as the only avenue of professional development and self-fulfillment. Unlike during the colonial era, when engineers typically remained within their familial and familiar groove, these children of middle-class civil servants realigned themselves and their expertise with private sector growth either within or outside the country. Even here, there was a difference between those alumni who stayed on in India and those who left. Alumni based in India approached the state pragmatically as a necessary partner without which little private business could get done. For diasporic engineers, however, it was a different story. Those IITians who sought their professional fortunes in the United States became more strident advocates of economic liberalization and private sector growth, and of limiting the developmental role of the state and public sector. Key to this reorientation has been their exposure to American antisocialism and their own entrepreneurial successes in the information technology industry. These experiences have fed an even more assertive claim to meritocracy, now at a global scale.

In Chapter 4, we considered the reactions of the 1960s generation of Madras IITians to the characterization of diasporic mobility as a "brain drain." While some agreed that the exodus of highly educated students was inimical for national development, others insisted that IITians' diasporic successes had been crucial in changing India's image abroad. Opinion, in other words, was divided. However, as diasporic IITians have consolidated their position overseas, the latter stance has strengthened, giving rise to the argument that the diaspora is in fact a "brain bank," a vital resource from which India can draw.[30]

This shift has been occasioned by a much larger number of alumni going to the United States. The majority from the 1960s cohorts remained in India, although only a few continued to go into the civil services and public sector industry. In the 1970s and 1980s, the pattern shifted. The emergent trend was for the top rankers of each cohort to try for higher study in the United States, and then to either stay on in academia or segue into industry. A 1988 study of IIT Bombay shows that 31 percent of graduates settled abroad as compared to 7.3 percent of engineers more generally. Moreover, the migration rate was much higher in those branches of engineering whose entrants were most highly ranked in the JEE and in their chosen courses of study. A 1994 study shows similar trends in IIT Madras: the percentage of alumni who migrated to the United States grew from 20 percent in 1968–1972 to 22 percent in 1973–1977, 27 percent in 1978–1982, and 35 percent in 1983–1987. As with IIT Bombay, there was considerable variation across branches of study, with the highest percentage of migrants coming from computer science, which was introduced in 1982 and rapidly became the most competitive branch. In 1986 and 1987, 58.5 percent of computer science B.Tech students went abroad.[31] Over the 1990s and 2000s, most diasporic alumni moved quickly from academia to private industry, where the combination of an IIT and a U.S.-university pedigree guaranteed high-paying options. The 2010s witnessed another shift, with the steady expansion of domestic and transnational private industry in India making the option of staying home more attractive. Those who did so typically did a stint in industry, earned an MBA at the Indian Institutes of Management, then landed in the higher echelons of industrial management.

How did successive waves of IITians negotiate the sociopolitical landscape of their new American home? How did their status as U.S. racial minorities shape the conditions for capital accumulation and their sense of themselves as meritocratic subjects? And what became of the forms of upper casteness forged at the IITs once these alumni came to the United States? It is to their stories and experiences and the ongoing transformations of upper casteness that we will now turn.

IITians and Racialization

In their study of the IITs, historians of science and technology Stuart Leslie and Robert Kargon quote a commonly used line: "When a student enrolls at an IIT, his spirit is said to ascend to America. After graduation, his body follows."[32] Another oft-told joke goes as follows: "When Nehru set up the IITs, he said it was to produce engineers and scientists who would help the country in its onward march . . . but he forgot to say which country."[33] Through the decades, diasporic IITians have continued to define themselves as members of an educated middle class whose migration was prompted by the corruptions of wealth and politics. As Chatterjee, a 1980s alumnus, succinctly put it: "If you had a family business, you stayed. If you were from a middle class family and your parents were educated but not wealthy, you went."[34]

In the early days, the process of getting to the United States was much more idiosyncratic. Unlike today, when the sequence of application, admission, and migration operates like a well-oiled machine, older alumni were far less aware and equipped with the resources to act on their diasporic ambitions. Well into the 1980s, they had only a vague sense of the United States before migrating there. What they did know was that it was the place to go for higher degrees suited to the caliber of training provided them in the IITs. Job prospects also seemed brighter than in India, although most never intended to stay on in the United States. When they arrived, depending on where they were, they experienced forms of isolation and discrimination that were utterly unfamiliar to Indian upper castes.

A typical story was that of Ganapathy, a 1980 Tamil Brahmin alumnus who migrated to the United States. Ganapathy drew a sharp contrast between the technologically connected, information-driven world of today and the early 1980s, when he attended Drexel University in Philadelphia. "Information, choices, students today know what they are getting into," he said. "I don't think we knew at all." He marveled at the memory of how little he and his classmates had to go on. "When I went to Drexel, I did not have any clue what Philadelphia was. I just knew I was going there, that's it. All the information I had was from a little prospectus that was sent to us. That was it." Once he arrived in the United States, contact with India was infrequent. "Every call cost in those days," he remembered. "I landed there and I called back from my friend's phone and the AT&T cost was $3.20 for the first minute and then $2.50 or something for the second and $2.20 for the third minute and so on. So I used to write a letter to my home and say, I'll call you on this Sunday at 10 a.m. your time, and then that would be a three minute call. I used to write down all the things I had to say and then, you know, it would be speed talking!" Even media about India was highly limited. "We used to pray for Indian news. Apart from a little newspaper called *India Abroad,* which used to be sporadic in nature, we used to get *The Hindu* International Edition where the information would be about three weeks late."[35]

Like many others of his generation of migrants, Ganapathy stayed on in academia. Unlike most, he returned to India in 2000 after sixteen years to teach at his alma mater, IIT Madras. I asked him whether returning had been a difficult decision. He had always wanted to return, he told me, "from the day I left." This was just part of "the inherently contradictory relationship" between Indians and the United States. "Honestly," he mused, "I believe that every Indian in the U.S.— at least most Indians in the U.S.—always in their heart feel like they should and want to come back. And probably every Indian in India in their heart feels they should go to the U.S." This "irony" was brought home to him when he and his wife finalized their plans to return. "When we decided to come back, we suddenly found that everybody was our friend. We got calls every day saying, 'Hey, how are you planning to go back? Even we want to go back.' And this was all before the dot.com bubble burst." What finally tipped the scales for Ganapathy and his wife was having a child and realizing that they wanted her to grow up around family. Despite the money, they decided that the social isolation and cultural alienation was not worth their while.

It didn't help that Ganapathy got a teaching job in Mississippi. At the time, "the only Indian thing you could get was a few packets of fairly ancient, outdated Indian spices at a Chinese shop. You had to travel to Memphis or to Birmingham, which was about a two and a half hour drive, to either get to an Indian restaurant or to see an Indian grocery shop." His Indian friends tried to dissuade him from taking the job because of the stories of racial violence. "I remember when I told my friends about the interview there, they thought I must have gone crazy. They said, we may not see you again, you may not come back." He even thought hard before purchasing a car. "I own a Honda," he said, "and I wondered, how will these people, you know, look at me if I own a Honda? Should it be a Honda or should I buy one of the American cars?"

Although Ganapathy offered a frank assessment of southern racism, he didn't let the North off the hook. "I saw the same thing in Philadelphia," he clarified. "I'd be denied homes because the wife would take one look at me, at the color of my skin, and say, she'll call the husband and husband will give an excuse not to rent me the house." It was different around the university, but renting a house "wasn't easy." Eventually, he and his wife did rent in the Philadelphia suburbs, but not before they looked in the city, where some friends had homes. "I went to some places on 69th street and beyond," he recalled. "We tried to rent a couple of places nearby. We couldn't do it. I mean, they were a very tight community. They didn't want any of us nearby. But all they had to do was go two blocks and the black community started . . . so there was no reason for them to feel so motivated, yet they were."

Significantly, the sharper distinction in Philadelphia between white and nonwhite, with Indians falling firmly on the nonwhite side of the boundary, contrasted with Ganapathy's experience in Mississippi. There, being a foreigner made all the difference. He told me a story featuring his wife. "In Mississippi, my wife had a tough time getting a job in the university. Finally, she found a job with a Fortune 200 company which was quite far away in a small town where there's only one big plant that made these things for tube lights, neon lamps. So she noticed that blacks were not allowed to park in the inner circle, even as late as 1992, '93." I asked Ganapathy if this was just understood or if there were written rules. "It wasn't written but they just wouldn't get a parking permit," he explained. "So she asked her boss, 'Where do you think I should park?' And he said, 'Of course, in the inner circle. You're not one of them. You guys are different.' So, that's Mississippi for you. But I don't think that's only in Mississippi."

Ganapathy's experience in Mississippi of being the exception that proved the rule of racism was echoed by John Cherian, an IIT Kharagpur alumnus who arrived in North Carolina before the 1964 Civil Rights Act. His brother-in-law, then a PhD student at the University of Iowa, urged Cherian to apply to its up-and-coming nuclear engineering program. It didn't take much persuasion, and in 1959, Cherian found himself a doctoral candidate in nuclear engineering in Ames, Iowa. Four years later, he arrived in North Carolina to take up his first job after completing his PhD. While there were already quite a few Indians in Iowa, Cherian found that at the time, there were hardly any in North

Carolina. In the university itself, he was one of two Indians, the other a professor of statistics who had arrived two years earlier. The year was 1963, and police crackdowns on civil rights demonstrators were rampant. Cherian found himself in a racially polarized society where he was a non-category. "My professor in Iowa warned me about the South," he recalled, "and I knew what he meant. He said North Carolina was the most progressive [state] but nevertheless the South." His first moments as a visitor in the state seemed to confirm that North Carolina was definitely southern and that in the South, Indians were definitely black: "When I came in April 1963 for an interview," he recalled, "the University folks reserved a room for me at the Velvet Cloak, a new hotel. When I got there at 11:30 p.m., lady behind the counter said, 'Would you mind waiting until the manager comes?' I think she had no clue what it was that had shown up! I could hear her making telephone calls, and I didn't want to be humiliated when the manager showed up. I probably would have had a room because the University made the reservation but I decided to leave anyway. I had seen a YMCA so I went there instead."[36]

When he arrived in North Carolina to stay, however, he encountered a different situation. "I had to find an apartment. I would call up and they would say, 'Yes, come and look,' and the lady would open the door and say 'I'm sorry, it's rented.' Then I decided to first say, 'I'm faculty at NCSU,' and then there was no problem at all." When I asked him if he thought his profession was key to this change in attitude, he hesitated, then replied, "Yes and no. Telling people I was Indian seemed to have the same effect. As soon as they figured out that I was a non-white foreigner, they treated me very well." In fact, Cherian stated strongly, it was as if white southerners were trying to prove a point. "I got the impression that the South was embarrassed to be mistreating foreign visitors," he explained. "They had no problem discriminating against U.S. blacks, but they went to lengths to ensure that we were fine. I think Southerners knew they weren't doing the right thing. Hudson Belk, for instance, had segregated bathrooms. I would go into the 'Whites Only,' maybe as protest, and never encountered any problem. There was a public swimming pool right outside the university. Of course, there were no blacks swimming. It had water fountains marked 'White' and 'Colored.' It was all very explicit but they didn't want someone from another country to think they did this with everyone." To drive his point home, Cherian told me about a friend of his, a fellow Indian graduate student, who had an experience similar to Ganapathy's when he moved from Iowa to Mississippi. "I had an Indian classmate in Iowa who moved to Mississippi which was supposed to be far worse than North Carolina and there too he encountered the same situation. They were treated fine, especially if his wife was wearing a sari because that was a clear sign that they weren't from here."

While wearing a sari was an everyday practice, a more deliberate politics of self-marking as foreign has been a long-standing form of Indian immigrant maneuver. Sometimes it was even promoted at an official level. A State Department memo cautioned Indians to prepare for "certain unfortunate experiences" they might have in America. By way of advice, the memo indicated that "many" Indians believed that "every Indian" coming to America should wear a turban initially, whether he had worn a turban in India or not, as a way of establishing that he was not African American.[37]

This education in American racism taught IITians how to navigate the pitfalls and promises of life in the United States. Of course, their experiences did vary depending on the socioeconomic landscape of their locality. Nonetheless, there was a common thread of understanding that emerged: the path to social and financial security was to avoid the taint of blackness. While professional Indians no longer did so through recourse to whiteness, as had earlier elite migrants, they now leveraged class, nationality, and, most importantly, educational achievement, to fashion themselves as members of a model minority.[38] They were helped in this effort by changes in the landscape of racial meanings in the United States after the 1960s and the information technology boom of the 1990s and 2000s. As we will see, IITians played an important role in associating Indianness with intellectual prowess and entrepreneurial success, in the process constituting themselves once again as uniquely meritorious.

Institutional Kinship

By the 1990s, the trend of going to the United States had become far more widespread and well established at the IITs. As several alumni from that decade told me, the only reasons to stay in India were to get a job right out of college, to do a management degree at the IIMs, or to enter a family business. There were also some who went into the Indian Administrative Service, although by this point, there were no more than a handful per cohort who took this option. Everyone else aimed for a higher degree in the United States. Udhay, a 1992 IIT Madras alumnus, explained to me how the application system functioned to ensure maximum success. I excerpt our interview here at length:[39]

AS: Did you have a pretty good sense of what universities you wanted to apply to?

U: Very good. It was all almost written down like a manual for us by our seniors. In fact, the entire application procedure itself was amazingly coordinated. That was one of the reasons why the IITs had a much higher percentage of students going abroad. It had nothing to do with the universities preferring IIT students. It was the network. It was the way the IIT students coordinated amongst themselves.

AS: How did the coordination work?

U: We had the concept of "safes," safe university, meaning if you're from this branch with this GPA, you would most likely get this university. Let's say I am the fifth rank in the department. If I apply to my safe, nobody above me is allowed to apply there.

AS: Because it wouldn't be safe for you anymore?

U: It wouldn't be safe for me. Plus, nobody so many ranks below me or with a higher GRE score than me should apply to the same university. Say I am the fifth rank, and the sixth rank guy applies, and the sixth rank guy has slightly better credentials elsewhere, maybe he will get through. But he doesn't even apply. So the university doesn't even get to know about him, right?

AS: And everybody subscribed to this system?

U: Everybody actually subscribed to it at that time. But even during our time, one or two violations of the system were there, like a student would apply to a university that he's not supposed to in a very secretive kind of way, and then he would be rebuked by all the students and he would be shunned. It's his will, of course, his wish. But the fear of being found out kept students from breaking the rules. Also because there was not too much information outside anyway available; the Internet was not popular at that point. So this network was the only thing that was working, and you wanted to use it.

AS: Were there tensions between departments over how this worked?

U: Yes, there were huge debates between one department and another in terms of allocation of universities. They would say you should not apply here. Or between the top-rankers and the other rankers. Often the top-rankers would want to apply to a lower university, but then the 10th rank guy, what will he do? So there would be heated debates in our department saying, look, you are not supposed to apply to this because you will get that. Now, that's a risk that a top-ranker has to take.

AS: Why do you think everyone cooperated? Was it a feeling that everyone from IIT should succeed?

U: In fact, we used to get a lot of help from our seniors, and we did this for our juniors also. For example, the IIT Madras student in a particular university personally wanted his juniors to come there. In fact, even I wanted some of my juniors to come, so when they wrote to me I would say, you know, write to this professor here, try to give them all the inside information that I had. I don't know why, maybe it's loyalty to this institution, maybe it's because we feel a bond with each other.

This form of institutional kinship was strong enough that even those who did not intend to go abroad participated in the collective ethos of U.S. orientation. Prakash, a 1993 alumnus, was one of only two students in his cohort who opted to stay in India. "When I graduated," he told me, "there were two different worlds: India and then the global world. I stayed in India for emotional rather than rational reasons." Only Prakash and one other student in his cohort did not write the GRE. "But I had a U.S. map," he said with a laugh. "Everybody was applying to universities so if I didn't know the U.S. map, I could not be in the conversation. So I learned, okay, University of Wisconsin–Madison is really good at this, University of Massachusetts–Amherst is a shitty school but you will definitely get aid. Stanford you will never get scholarship. Then there was Berkeley, MIT, state universities. So, you have this map: what are the universities, where do they excel, what does Cornell mean, what does CMU mean, what does UMCP mean, what is UMCP famous for." What *is* UMCP? I interrupted. "University of Maryland, College Park. CMU is Carnegie Mellon. There was a map in my room where I knew all the states, all the universities. I didn't apply but I knew who was applying where, how it was going, what's the game, how does it happen?"

It wasn't just the students who were part of the game. So, too, was the postman. "After having lunch," Prakash recounted with glee, "we would wait for the hostel postman. When he arrived, there would be fifty students cheering. And the postman, he'd been doing this for years, so he could tell from the weight of the envelope whether it was acceptance or rejection. And I've heard him talk to some of my classmates: what is your CGPA, what's your GRE score? Why don't you apply to this university? Have you done this? Have you done that? The postman knew more than any of us." I asked Prakash about those who didn't take the GRE. What did they do? "At that time CAT was there—the entrance exams for the Indian Institutes of Management—but it was just MBMs who took them . . . *Mera Bharat Mahan,* which means 'Indian son of the soil.' If you've decided to stay back, you're MBM. If you do CAT, you're MBM."[40]

Institutional kinship, lubricated by acronyms and based on ranking and compliance, extended into American university life and became stronger as the diasporic flow of IITians increased. Unlike earlier generations, who often found themselves to be one of few Indians on campus, alumni who arrived in the 1990s were usually in good company. Jayaram, a 1990 alumnus, characterized his entry into MIT as a seamless transition. He applied to do civil engineering because of advice from two seniors in the previous cohort who had gotten admission into the MIT program. "It was a well-trodden path," he said, "So I knew exactly what to do the first day I was there." It helped that the two seniors "were right there walking me through. It wasn't totally organized but it was more in these informal ways that the very powerful IIT alumni network worked."[41]

Initially, the IIT alumni network worked primarily as an information channel that facilitated entry into U.S. universities. As more and more IITians filled U.S. engineering departments and facilitated the entry of their juniors, the IIT system accrued name recognition. By the 1990s, it was no longer uncommon to arrive at Carnegie Mellon or MIT or Cal Tech and encounter several other IITians in one's program, even some from the same campus cohort. Udhay arrived at Carnegie Mellon in 1992 with three other classmates from his IIT Madras batch. It was the first year that so many people from IIT Madras had gotten in, he told me. "Many of us got placed way, way higher than what we were supposed to get. CMU was way higher than my safe, in terms of rankings." I asked Udhay if people at Carnegie Mellon know about the IITs. "Yeah," he said, "at Carnegie Mellon people were aware of IIT, my advisor was aware of IIT. He had been in Texas, Austin, and had come across other faculty who were IITians." I asked Udhay if there were students from other Indian colleges. "Among Indians, it was mostly IITians at Carnegie Mellon," he confirmed. Moreover, the institutional pecking order carried over from India and was replicated at a distance. "One good friend of mine was from Osmania University," he offered by way of example, "and she used to talk about how she was always looked upon as this odd creature in Carnegie Mellon. She was a senior to me, she has made it much bigger in her career, she is the CEO of a huge company and all that. So, obviously, once you're at Carnegie Mellon, nothing else matters. But she used to always talk then about how there was discrimination, that the IITians would think her somehow inferior." IITians' intellectual superiority, Udhay stressed, was very much about caste. "IITians think they're born intellectually superior, that other castes just don't have the ability to compete with us," he opined, "and that getting into the IIT proves it." Plus, he argued, this sense of caste superiority was even more pronounced among U.S.-based IITians. "I think some of the same biases that we carry in IIT are even more reinforced here because in the U.S. we don't even get to see other kinds of students. The only students you see from India are pretty much ninety-nine percent upper caste. IIT itself is a filtering mechanism. Migration to the U.S. is one more level of filtering."

It was not simply the caste filter of transnational mobility that allowed for IITians' claim to intellectual superiority. After all, other professional and student migrants to the United States were also typically upper caste. Elevating the IITs to prominence took active alumni advocacy. Once older IITians were established in faculty positions in the United States, they worked to shore up the reputational weight of the IITs relative to other Indian institutions. To give just one example, an IITian teaching at Duke University started a summer internship program exclusively targeting IIT undergraduates in hopes of luring some away from higher-ranked engineering and computer science PhD programs. When I asked whether other faculty in Duke's engineering school objected to the exclusivity of the program, he responded, "Why would they? They know that the IITs produce the best students and that all the engineering schools in the United States are competing for them."[42] And, indeed, this pattern is not limited to Duke; IITians that I have interviewed at Harvard, MIT, and Stanford are equally explicit about their goal of admitting and hiring their own. This is not to say that academic performance bears no weight for the success of IITians. Still, the power of institutional kinship has been hugely consequential in setting IITians apart, especially once increasing numbers of students from other Indian engineering colleges, as well as H-1B visa holders coming to work in the IT sector, began arriving in the United States.

Along with the enhanced reputation, the professional ambitions of diasporic IITians have also changed significantly. Through the 1980s, prestige was attached primarily to academic research and corporate employment. Jayaram recalled that the most common tales of diasporic success were of "a top professor somewhere" or "a top R&D guy in a place like Bell Labs." Unlike today, "there were fewer or no success stories related to entrepreneurship or even with respect to mainstream business. There was no Rajat Gupta, who is CEO of McKinsey, for example. People who went to the USA in, say, the '70s or '80s were not yet at the top of their game." Until the 1990s, the image of the successful IITian was still one that was largely in continuity with the late colonial and early postcolonial years: an upper-caste individual whose intellectual prowess allowed for lifetime employment in prestigious institutions.

The Silicon Valley boom gave rise to a new model. Moreover, by allowing for an unprecedented degree of spatial and economic consolidation, it transformed what was previously a more piecemeal effort at shoring up the meritocratic status of the IITs through networks of institutional kinship. But the rise of Silicon Valley also generated new hierarchies and tensions among IITians. Money-making diasporic entrepreneurs, most of whom came from the northern IITians, became the new emblems of meritocracy. In the process, the distinction between diaspora and homeland acquired new salience as a difference not just in space but in kind. However, the elevation of diasporic entrepreneurship as the new measure of merit did not go uncontested. Even as they appreciated the name recognition and enhanced global status promoted by their Silicon Valley counterparts, Madras IITians expressed ambivalence toward this new model of meritocracy. As we will see, as with the distinction between the gifted and the coached that we explored in Chapter 5, these tensions between diaspora and homeland have produced new cleavages among the "non-reserved."

The Silicon Valley Boom

Jayaram's insight into the gestation period needed for IITians to reach "the top of their game" is an important one. The IITians who emerged as the biggest Indian names in Silicon Valley got their B.Tech degrees no later than the early 1980s. Most did so in the late 1960s and 1970s. The country they left was pre-liberalization India, and the one they entered held out both the promise of economic success and the threat of racial minoritization. It was also the early days of the computer revolution. Many IITians who came to the United States for advanced degrees in other branches of engineering eventually switched to software, and almost all who did made their way from academia to industry.

It is clear from speaking to Silicon Valley's IITian entrepreneurs that they share a spatial imaginary of constraint and possibility. As do other IIT alumni, they echo the refrain that unlike the wealthy or the politically connected who could always find their way, they of the middle class were subjected to the limitations of a system that fostered mediocrity in the name of democracy. But there is an added emphasis that reflects their assimilation of American economic ideologies. Several characterized the India they left behind as one where the IITs were islands of possibility within a sea of socialist constraint. Compared to India, the United States for them is a capitalist land of opportunity where merit finds its due. Nevertheless, it, too, is not a uniform cartography. One key distinction recurred through the interviews: the contrast between the static, closed landscape of East Coast wealth and the dynamic, open frontier of West Coast capitalism. Silicon Valley, they told me, could only have happened in California.

The two narratives—one set in India, the other in the United States—dovetail nicely. In both, IITians are of "the middle," endowed with education but without other forms of capital. Taken together, the two work to reinforce the idea of the IITian as a uniquely talented individual who is able to leverage his brain to overcome structural limitations and rise to new heights. While this is like the other discourses of upper-caste intellectual merit we have considered, most importantly that of Tamil Brahmins, there is also something new. Entrepreneurialism has lent the claim to merit a different charge. In the full embrace of technological innovation, a deregulated private sector, and wealth accumulation as the basis of individual merit, IITians in Silicon Valley have become self-styled neoliberal capitalists. This is a significant departure from an older upper-caste orientation around higher education and lifelong professional employment, first in state bureaucracy and then in private enterprise. Like their counterparts in the IIT system, most Silicon Valley IITians are the children of civil servants and public sector engineers. In one generation, they have gone from being beneficiaries of the developmental state to being its most strident detractors. Moreover, they disparage not only the underdevelopment of the Indian public sector but the underachievement of their India-based counterparts. As they see it, Indian conditions have forced IITians who stayed behind to slip into mediocrity, with the result that only the entrepreneurial, diasporic IITian embodies true merit.

Naresh Bhosle was one of the earliest IITians to come to the United States and is one of the best-known Indian names in Silicon Valley. Bhosle graduated from IIT Kharagpur in 1965 and went to do graduate work at MIT. MIT's partnership with IIT Kanpur, along with the older colonial history of Indian engineers at MIT, made it a forerunner in admitting IITians. In his cohort alone, there were three IITians from Kharagpur, Bombay, and Kanpur. Bhosle went on to teach at MIT and then moved in 1975 to the University of Utah to head up its semiconductor laboratory. Although Utah "was a different America," it was already known as a center for computer science research, so he had an easy transition. After teaching there for five years, and upon the urging of the General Instrument Corporation, which had funded the university lab, he left academia to start a computer chip design automation company. Four years later, in 1984, he moved to Silicon Valley. By 1989, his company had gone public and Bhosle was a wealthy man who would become a major advocate of Indian entrepreneurialism.[43]

In our interview, I asked Bhosle if he came from a business background. No, he told me, his family was full of educators. The one exception was his father, who worked as an engineer for the Tata Iron and Steel Company (TISCO), an Indian multinational corporation founded in 1907 as a branch of the Tata Group of companies. Bhosle had grown up in the company town of Jamshedpur. It was inspiring to him. TISCO had overseen "the transformation of a jungle into a vibrant place in fifty years." He attributed his exposure to the Tatas as the first step in his turn to private enterprise. Still, this early experience was "vague." The more immediate catalyst was being a teaching assistant at MIT to Professor Bose, who started Bose Systems. "In one of the lectures designed for sharing experiences," Bhosle recalled, "[Bose] spoke about how he came to start the company, how he figured out that the market was ready, technology could be applied, and all that. I realized that companies can be started by faculty members. So the notion that, in America, people with no money but with unique ideas could start companies was established in my mind at MIT." I asked Bhosle if such a path was possible in India. "No," he asserted. "What I had in India was a Bachelors from IIT. When I came out, I was a true engineer. I had confidence that I could create things, but there was no money. In India, the notion was that you had to have your own family wealth to start a business. We came from the middle class. That's not wealth. But in America, bright ideas were funded by venture capitalists. Money came together with ideas. . . . This was all America, it was a new learning."

Kalyan, a 1982 IIT Bombay alumnus, echoed Bhosle's arguments about middle-class constraint in India. For him, the experience of IITians was emblematic of India's limitations on success. Kalyan had grown up in a largely Tamil Brahmin enclave of Bombay and came from a family of highly educated professionals: his father was a chemical engineer who worked for Unilever, India; his father-in-law was a physicist with the Atomic Energy Commission; his cousin had gotten his PhD from IIT Bombay. Despite this slew of credentials, Kalyan characterized himself and most of his IIT classmates as "solidly middle class." "We weren't the high class—these are not people who came to campuses in cars, right? I would say if you had a car, then you were upper class. And you'd be lower class if your parents didn't know English. And middle class would be, sort of classic middle of the road: you didn't have a car, you didn't have a phone at that time, but you were not struggling for two meals a day." Kalyan's categorical distinction between educational qualifications and tangible goods worked as a disclaimer of precisely the forms of caste capital held by most IITians. As we have seen, the disavowal of educational capital as capital through its contrast with other, supposedly more "concrete" forms is a common refrain that underwrites the upper-caste claim to merit.[44]

Right after graduating from IIT Bombay, Kalyan went to the University of Virginia to do a master's program in chemical engineering. His work in mathematical modeling soon took him to software engineering. This was 1984, what Kalyan called "the first innings of the software boom." Even after he shifted to software, he stayed on the East Coast, working as a product manager in Washington, DC, and Boston. Then in 1990, he quit his job and moved to California to join a start-up company. What induced him to move from an established company to a start-up? Kalyan acknowledged that this decision was in marked contrast to his father's life choices. "As opposed to going for the security of a large company, which my dad had to do for family reasons, I felt that I didn't have to fall for the same thing." Besides, he had a "taste" for "smaller, more nimble operations."

Both Kalyan and Bhosle characterized the move to Silicon Valley as the turning point in their professional lives. For them, America as the land of opportunity was crystallized in the idea that business could be the pursuit of the Everyman. But there was an added spatial dimension to their analysis. Bhosle qualified his rendition of American national mythology by drawing a contrast between Boston's Route 128 and Silicon Valley.[45] For him, Boston represented the America of racial exclusion and elite class entrenchment. By contrast, he told me, Silicon Valley was smaller, but it was "open." In part, this had to do with different institutional and funding ecosystems. "In the Boston area, you had Route 128 which was sponsored by Raytheon and government funded defense," Bhosle explained. "In Silicon Valley, the majority of funding came out of the semi-conductor industry, the computer industry, plus venture capital."

In addition to the funding ecosystem, there was also the physical space itself. Unlike other cities, Bhosle pointed out, Silicon Valley was "very concentrated and small. Around Stanford and Santa Clara, the number of people engaged in startups is much larger percentage-wise." This meant a different form of sociality. "You run into people when you're shopping, at school activities, they have shared experiences, they learn from each other. It's a very collaborative environment. Even the landlords know how startups work, and they work with you. People are willing to take risks with you: lawyers, accountants, everyone."

Kalyan offered a similar portrait of Silicon Valley but used it to draw a contrast between diasporic and homeland IITians. "There were certain people who were neither good academically nor had the skills," he told me. "And they worked in India. If you look at these IITians, very few of them have really done well technically. If you look at the Indian space satellite project or the nuclear energy project, or . . . look at anything of any significance in India, IITians have not really contributed much at all." By contrast, Kalyan continued, IITians in the United States had made their mark in the technology sector. This, he maintained, was due both to the caliber of diasporic migrants and the open nature of the sector, especially in Silicon Valley. I asked Kalyan if there were social barriers to racial minorities. "Maybe on the East Coast," he responded, "but even there, in the tech community, it's a lot more egalitarian. And California, it's definitely not there." As a final point, Kalyan echoed another of Bhosle's arguments. "Software is where you don't need any capital. If I need to set up a petroleum plant or a chemical plant, I better have a hundred million dollars, right? Whereas software, all I need is a $1,000 laptop and I'm in business."

One name that came up repeatedly in my interviews with Silicon Valley IITians was Vivek Bansal. Many pointed to him as a trailblazer, and Bansal himself was not shy about adopting this mantle. Like the others, Bansal represented California as a space of realization. He arrived there in 1971 and found it strikingly different from both Michigan and New Jersey, where he had been previously. Unlike those other places, which "were mostly white," in California "everybody was from someplace else. . . . There was no established local culture." Plus, high tech was upending the world of business. Bansal did very well in Silicon Valley. He cofounded a company and took it public in 1987, becoming the first Indian American founder and CEO to list a venture-backed company on the NASDAQ. Since then, he has been an angel investor in over thirty companies and become one of the most well-recognized faces of Indian entrepreneurship.[46]

These diasporic narratives are striking in what they say and don't say. Within them, the material constraints to capitalist success are overcome in the diaspora but only in the postracial landscape of Silicon Valley. California, where there is "no established local culture," is cast as a frontier where entrepreneurial risk is the name of the game and technical skill is valued on its own terms. As with other frontier myths of wild, unpopulated spaces that hold out the promise of unfettered accumulation, IITians play the role of settlers who usher in a futuristic capitalism by leaving behind the Old Worlds of India and New England.[47] Like in so many of the other accounts we've encountered, middle classness operates as a disavowal of caste inheritances, but here it also works to eclipse the racial contours of information technology. More broadly, as in the stories of IITians in the 1960s U.S. South and with other more recent deployments of the model minority trope, IITian success in California functions as an alibi of a regional political economy that is far from race neutral.[48]

Other Silicon Valley IITians had trajectories that were very similar to those of Bhosle, Kalyan, and Bansal. After coming to the United States to study, they switched from their chosen branch of engineering to software, segued from academia to the high-tech industry, started companies in other part of the United States, and then eventually relocated to Silicon Valley. Although Silicon Valley's Indians were not limited to IITians, IITians made up some of the early successes.[49] Moreover, many of them were from IIT Bombay. The compounded kinship of being IITians from the same campus gave them a strong bond to build on once they were in the same location. And they did so, not just by accumulating economic capital but by advancing a new image of the diasporic Indian as more than just technically savvy but as an entrepreneur. It is in the production of this image that we see the very deliberate race work done by IITians to crystallize a different form of upper-caste merit.

Race and Re-ascription

The information technology boom provided the grounds for the production of a new form of racial ascription: Indian entrepreneurial prowess. The beginnings of this project can be traced to the 1975 presidential address by Faqir Chand Kohli of the Tata Group to the Computer Society of India. A graduate of MIT who had returned to India in 1951 to work in different Tata enterprises, Kohli concluded his speech with the following statement:

> Many years ago there was an industrial revolution. We missed it for reasons beyond our control. Today there is a new revolution—a revolution in information technology, which requires neither mechanical bias nor mechanical temperament. Primarily, it requires the capability to think clearly. This we have in abundance. We have the opportunity to participate in this revolution on an equal basis—we have the opportunity, even, to assume leadership in this revolution.[50]

Here again we see the idea of information technology as the grand equalizer, where the brain is the only necessary form of capital. This time, however, it is yoked to an argument about resetting the terms of global capitalist history by upending existing forms of uneven development. While this argument about Indian revolutionary agency was floated earlier by people like Kohli, it was only fully leveraged in the 1990s in Silicon Valley. Between 1995 and 2005, 26 percent of U.S. tech start-ups founded by immigrants had Indian founders, CEOs, presidents, or head researchers. The Indian immigrant share of start-up companies outnumbered those of the United Kingdom, China, Taiwan, and Japan combined.[51] By the early 2000s, the image of the Indian had followed suit. In May 2000, technology magazine *Business 2.0* opined: "It's safe to say that without Indian immigrants, (Silicon) Valley wouldn't be what it is today."[52] In 2001, John Kenneth Galbraith, the former U.S. ambassador to India who had helped to set up IIT Kanpur, remarked that he had no idea that there would one day emerge "an Indian colony called Silicon Valley in the US." Within that larger category of Indian high tech, IITians were the most recognizable subgroup. Sandipan Deb depicts the aura around the IITian in characteristically superlative terms: "The story goes that in those heady years, you just had to mention in your resume that you were an IITian to have venture capitalists running after you."[53]

However, the notion of the entrepreneurial Indian as a sure investment was not one that emerged seamlessly from IIT alumni reaching "the top of their game" in Silicon Valley. It was consciously manufactured for popular consumption. Much of this effort was spearheaded by IITians and coalesced in the formation of the Indus Entrepreneurs (TIE), a networking group that began in Silicon Valley in 1992 and has now expanded to include sixty-one chapters in eighteen countries; India has the second largest number after the United States. In its organizational form, TIE was set up as a nonprofit organization that connected people—primarily South Asians but also others—engaged in the profitable business of high tech. Deep Parekh, a 1975 IIT Bombay alumnus and one of TIE's founders, pointed out that the founding of TIE proved to be valuable not just for those starting out in business but even for established entrepreneurs, like its founders. The very process of forming TIE clinched the working relationships of those who knew of each other's professional success only at a distance. It also clinched intergenerational ties as many of the older generation became angel investors in fledgling start-ups.[54]

Once some of these TIE-mediated start-ups succeeded, the industry began to take notice. But the organization's founders still wanted to establish the idea of Indian entrepreneurship in "the minds of mainstream America." As Bhosle put it, "We—particularly Indians—we were recognized for our engineering ability but there was always a doubt whether we could be good businessmen, whether we could start companies. Although many of us had succeeded by that point, there was always this notion in corporate America that 'these guys weren't anything but good technical people.' We wanted to change that. That was one of the very important goals of TIE which we managed to do by the end of 1990s." In an echo of anti-welfarist rhetoric, Bansal added that the result of TIE's efforts was that Indians in Silicon Valley were "seen differently, as people who engaged in self-help, not asking for handouts."

Bansal was the most categorical in his characterization of the new diasporic Indian. TIE, he emphasized, was part of "a new Indian image emerging." Previously, "everybody had assumptions about Indians, that we were Third World, third rate, even if individually some were different." In the mid- to late 1970s, he continued, American universities "became aware of a special breed of Indian who was doing very well in places like MIT, Michigan Tech, and Stanford." Still, it took until the 1980s for Americans to "become aware that there was a common thread behind these people: the IITs." Even so, "we were typecast as smart techies. We had genes which gave us mathematical prowess. But it wasn't clear that we had managerial talent, or sales and marketing talent, or financial talent." At the time, Indians were still seen by venture capitalists as a "huge risk." Plus, "there was a fear that senior whites would not want to work for Indians." Although some IITians had succeeded as entrepreneurs, "we were seen as outliers, as freaks, the lucky ones."

It was only in the mid-1990s that the "floodgates opened." With TIE's founding, the image of the Indian was expanded from techie to entrepreneur. "Now," Bansal concluded, "Indians have become a risk worth taking." Silicon Valley was key to clinching the image of the Indian entrepreneur. "This is where the best of the best all over the world compete," he crowed, "and Indians came out on top. Nobody was helping us but nobody was pulling us down either. So everyone says: wow, they know how to do this."

Brand IIT

This narrative timeline of Indian American self-fashioning sets up diasporic entrepreneurship as the realization of a promise that was in the making over several decades. Part of the story was the IITian's intellectual skill. Another part was Silicon Valley as the space of American innovation. The combination produced Indian entrepreneurship as a globally recognized value. But for Bansal and other IITians, the racial inscription of Indians as gifted entrepreneurs came at a risk: the overshadowing of the IITian as the epitome of Indian merit. Shoring up the value of the IIT pedigree became that much more important once other Indian engineers and entrepreneurs became commonplace in the United States.

The project of inscribing the Indian as entrepreneur was thus accompanied by a second project: branding the IITs. In their practice as company founders and angel investors, IITians already favored their own. Bansal admitted as much when he told me that he "was biased towards IITians." By the mid-1990s, he explained, "seven to eight people a day would come asking for investment." This volume of start-ups required discernment. Bansal's "standard answer was no" unless someone struck him as particularly innovative. Typically, these were IITians. However, it was not enough that networks of institutional kinship underwrote the flow of investment capital. IITians, especially those in Silicon Valley, took it upon themselves to make the IIT an immediately recognizable brand. This unfolded in multiple stages.

First, they had to ensure that IITians flagged their pedigrees more explicitly. "We looked at a number of people in very senior positions in a number of places in the U.S.," Parekh explained, "and noticed that their public resumes would not say that they graduated from IIT. Their U.S. credential would be prominent but for India, they would basically just indicate an undergraduate degree without an institution. So one of the first tangible steps we took was to individually go to a large number of people—at least 50–100 people—and encourage them to put down IIT in their bios. For example, Victor Menezes, who was at Citi Bank, was one of the persons. Raj Gupta, who was running Rohm and Hass, was another person. This was the first step in creating that branding."

The second step was creating an expansive sense of pan-IIT institutional kinship beyond the experiential bonds between members of the same cohort or institution. Several alumni characterized the forms of affinity linking IITians using the imagery of concentric circles. The innermost circle was made up of hostel mates, then moving outward were branch mates, batch mates, IITians from the same institution, and finally IITians across all institutions. But that last circle was not one that emerged organically out of the college experience. As a 1982 IIT Bombay alumnus, Kalyan noted that he felt the greatest affinity with his own cohort and campus mates. But, he qualified, "even from, say, the IIT Kharagpur 1998 batch, I probably know somebody who knows somebody and we get connected. So there are enough talking points, shared experiences, camaraderie. But this whole thing about being closer as IITians, that's a more recent phenomenon." This cross-campus affiliation was necessary, Parekh added, because the IITs didn't have instant name recognition in the United States. "We realized that if we continue to stay independent, with each campus having its own alumni association, we will not get the leverage that we would get if we combined them all together and created one common IIT brand."[55] It was only through branding that the IITs would be put symbolically on par with institutions like MIT, Stanford, and Harvard.

The third step was to give material form to this pan-IIT sentiment. In the early 2000s, Silicon Valley IITians created the Pan-IIT Alumni Association out of California. In 2004, it was registered as a nonprofit public benefit corporation.[56] With the forming of the corporation, Kalyan remarked with satisfaction, "the IIT network has become more powerful than the HBS [Harvard Business School] network. IITians help each other like I have never seen in any other network. My closest friends are IITians: I socialize with them, their families, I hike with them, we help each other's kids in their professional careers. My business partners in all my startups are IITians. If you belong to this network, there is instant credibility and trust. Pan-IIT has consolidated the brand." But what did it mean to make the IIT a brand, and why was it important to do so? When I pressed Parekh on why it was important to think of pan-IIT institutional kinship in terms of branding, he spoke of the investment payoff. "Now, when a VC looks at someone's resume and it has IIT on it, they pay more attention." Consolidating the brand by unifying all the campuses under a common organizational umbrella was intended to enhance the market value of an IIT pedigree.

The final step was media coverage. This was a conscious effort of the Pan-IIT Alumni Association's media team facilitated by preexisting relationships between Silicon Valley's IITian successes and the media industry. IITians typically point to one piece of media coverage as the tipping point, after which the IITs gained popular recognition in the United States: the 2003 CBS *60 Minutes* show that we encountered in the Introduction. Bansal explained the process that led to its filming. A producer at *CBS* had seen filmmaker Mira Nair's *Monsoon Wedding*, in which the groom, a U.S.-based IITian, returns to Delhi for an arranged marriage. "She and I met at some event," Bansal recalled, "and she asked me if I'd seen the movie. When I said yes, she said, 'What's IIT?' I said that I too was from IIT and could help if she wanted to do a story. That's how the *60 Minutes* story came about."

The *60 Minutes* piece, which aired on March 2, 2003, is an IITian's pipe dream. After lauding IITians' "brainpower," correspondent Leslie Stahl puts the IITs in perspective for an American audience by describing them as a combination of "Harvard, MIT and Princeton together . . . with a curriculum that may be the most rigorous in the world." As a final point of comparison, she says, "Imagine a kid from India using an Ivy League university as a safety school. That's how smart these guys are."

The piece features two IITians: for the diaspora, Vinod Khosla, co-founder of Sun Microsystems and Silicon Valley venture capitalist; for India, Narayana Murthy, founder of the software company Infosys, who is introduced as "the Bill Gates of India." Khosla testifies to the impact of the IIT diaspora on American business. Describing the IIT as "the hardest school in the world to get into," he emphasizes the value to U.S. business of an IIT education. "Microsoft, Intel, PCs, Sun Microsystems—you name it, I can't imagine a major area where Indian IIT engineers haven't played a leading role," he states. "And, of course, the American consumer and the American business in the end is the beneficiary of that." To drive the point home, Khosla asks and answers a question about job creation. "How many jobs have entrepreneurs, Indian entrepreneurs, in Silicon Valley created over the last 15, 20 years? Hundreds of thousands, I would guess. For America to be able to pick off this human capital, these well-trained engineers with great minds, it's a great deal." Khosla's final salvo on the piece is a masterful bit of image consolidation. "[IITians] are favored over almost anybody else," he argues. "If you're a WASP walking in for a job, you wouldn't have as much pre-assigned credibility as you do if you're an engineer from IIT." For his part, Narayana Murthy underscores the role of the IITs within India as a beacon of hope. "It's very easy to lose hope in this country," he says, "It's very easy to set your aspirations low in this country. But amidst all this, this competition among high-quality students, this institution of IIT, sets your aspirations much higher." Murthy also notes that there is another way in which the IITs are anomalous within the Indian context. "There is no corruption. It's a pure meritocracy."

The *60 Minutes* piece is a carefully curated bit of publicity that features choice quotes from prominent IITians and argues for diasporic success as a natural extension of an IIT education. Above all else, it is entrepreneurial success that is showcased as the inevitable outcome of the IIT experience. Stahl reinforces this angle by noting that "students act like entrepreneurs the whole time they're at IIT. They run everything in the dorms, which might be mistaken for cell blocks if not for all the Pentium 4 PCs. They organize the sports themselves. They even hire the chefs and pick the food in the mess halls." With this bit of exaggeration, the message is signed, sealed, and delivered: the IITs are islands of meritocracy in a socialist, low-achieving country whose best and brightest are naturally attracted to greener pastures abroad, where they are able to realize their full entrepreneurial potential.

The early 2000s were a critical moment for media exposure. In addition to the *60 Minutes* piece, various magazines featured articles on the IITs. *Forbes* did a story titled "Indians of Silicon Valley." *Business Week* came out with "India's Genius Factories." Together, all these media events put the institutions on the U.S. mental map and helped to consolidate Brand IIT. The final step was reaching out to the political class. Although most IITians speak with derision about "politics" and see themselves first and foremost as technical experts and entrepreneurs, they have not been shy about cultivating political recognition. Indeed, their successes on this front are proudly displayed on the website of Pan-IIT USA, the American branch of the Pan-IIT Alumni Association. The home page cites House Resolution 227 passed in the U.S. House of Representatives on April 26, 2005: "Graduates of the Indian Institutes of Technology (IIT) in the United States have made valuable and significant contributions to society in every profession and discipline. IIT graduates are highly committed and dedicated to research, innovation, and promotion of trade and international cooperation between India and the United States. The House of Representatives honors the economic innovation attributable to graduates of the Indian Institutes of Technology." The website also has laudatory quotes from Bill Clinton and Joe Biden and indicates that Mark Warner and Robert Ehrlich, the governors of Virginia and Maryland, declared May as IIT Graduate Month. Rounding out the praise-singing are prominent quotes from Bill Gates, founder of Microsoft; Jeff Bezos of Amazon; and, last but not least, Nobel laureate Amartya Sen.[57]

Through all these efforts, IITians have made Brand IIT synonymous with Indian genius and entrepreneurial success. That this work had as its target not just the U.S. media, public, and political class but IITians themselves is captured in a statement by Kalyan on the "synergy" between Silicon Valley culture and the culture of the IITs. "From very early on, there's both intense competition and enormous cooperation in IIT," he told me. Kalyan characterized this combination of competition and cooperation as unique to IIT. "There was a level of cooperation which I've never seen anywhere else," he said. "None of us would attend classes, but we'd get together and one person would study chapter 1, one chapter 2, one chapter 3, and we would all gather in four hours and teach each other." At the same time, "everyone was fully aware that they were competing for a limited number of 'A' grades. That's the sort of the enormous collegial plus competitive spirit I don't think I've seen anywhere else. Except in Silicon Valley where each company competes fiercely with the other one for talent and for technology, but at the same time they're partners. So, it's a very similar model."[58] By equating the ethos of the IITs with that of Silicon Valley, Kalyan and others cast entrepreneurialism as the natural instinct of the IITian, a disposition born of campus life and matured in diaspora.

Lost in this rhetorical echo chamber are the forms of inherited caste capital and state patronage that have gone into the making of the IITian. Instead, what we get is the image of the IITian as the product of natural selection who has an intuitive ability to ride the crest of contemporary capitalism. Absent as well is the changing meaning of merit within the IITs. The earlier emphases on civil engineering for state developmentalism in the 1950s and 1960s and on academic and private industrial research in the 1970s and 1980s have been eclipsed by a teleological account of entrepreneurialism as the realization of the IITian's true talent and transnational mobility as its necessary channel.

Transforming the Homeland

While building brand recognition in their host country has been a longer process, diasporic alumni have more recently begun forms of outreach to the homeland. Many have contributed handsomely to their alma maters as is evident in the array of IIT campus buildings bearing alumni names and in the awards they receive from their home institutions. More recently, these ongoing forms of individual outreach have been coupled by collective projects aimed at larger-scale structural transformation.

One such effort has been spearheaded by TIE. "Building bridges to the Indian subcontinent" was always one of TIE's goals, Bhosle noted, but it had to wait until they were well established in the United States. These bridges consisted of one ultimate goal: cultivating an entrepreneurial ethos in the homeland. In 1999, TIE leaders debuted their agenda in Delhi with a series of seminars on start-ups. Bhosle told me that while many of the details—"what's involved, how does it work, how options work, how do entrepreneurs make money, how do investors make money, how do employees participate"—were "new concepts to Indians," the most startling was "the fact that you can start companies without having your own money." The first seminar was held in New Delhi, where approximately three hundred people attended, including a sizable proportion of government employees. After this debut appearance, Bhosle and Bansal took the show on the road with the help of the National Association of Software and Services Companies. As part of the effort to encourage entrepreneurship and provide funding for startups, TIE launched chapters across India; there are currently seventeen chapters in India and two in Pakistan. At the opening of its first chapter in New Delhi, Bhosle gave a speech, which he paraphrased to me: "Freedom fighters in India earned political freedom for the country. This was very, very important. But political freedom is not enough. People need economic freedom as well. To attain economic freedom, you have to increase the total wealth in the country. It needs to be spread, but without creation of wealth you can't have economic freedom. The government cannot do it. It has to come from grassroots entrepreneurship. That's what we're here to encourage, teach, and help grow." These ideas caught on quickly, Bhosle continued, "but the legal structure was a key impediment to the formation of venture capital." He explained the process through which TIE collaborated with the Indian government to transform the legal landscape: "Indian partnership laws were old British ones where anyone who invested money was a general partner. In order to form a venture fund, the partnership laws needed to allow for limited partnership where partners can lose money without being liable for anything beyond that. Otherwise, nobody will give you money. We pointed that out and the government wanted more detail so we put them in touch with the best lawyers in Silicon Valley and they finally changed those laws."

Bhosle's narrative of homeland activism characterizes the diasporic IITian as a critical-change agent bringing India into the twenty-first century. Significantly, even homeland IITians are seen as not up to the task. Lost in this account is the centuries-long dynamism of Indian economic life captured in the work of historians and anthropologists alike.[59] Instead, in a faithful replay of imperial lore, we have a Third World economy trapped in the strictures of outmoded laws and habits of thought that needs an external catalyst to free up capital. But even Bhosle was measured in comparison with Bansal, whose rhetoric was a perfect echo of the free marketer's playbook. When I asked him about the goals of his own diasporic engagement, he said without hesitation, "to change Indian socialism and the leftist mindset by educating people, to promote free enterprise and entrepreneurship against top-down government policies and planning, and to foster liberty and self-reliance." His first step was to work at the ideological level. He collaborated with an economics professor at the University of Michigan to start a New Delhi think tank, which Bansal likened to the libertarian Cato Institute and the Ayn Rand–inspired Atlas Society.

Bansal's antipathy toward the Indian state finds various expressions. One is through his opposition to reservation, which he characterized as "socialist" and "anti-meritocracy." Parroting an oft-used argument that we encountered in Chapter 6, he asked, "If they were to reserve seats in medical school, would I choose a quota student to do my brain surgery?" He then added his own summary judgment: "Reservations take us back to socialism." His own solution to unequal opportunity was to start a second institution, Foundation for Excellence, with an IIT Kanpur alumnus. The foundation grants scholarships to help poor students pursue higher education in engineering, medicine, and computer science. Bansal made a point of emphasizing that unlike the undeserving quota students favored by the state, the foundation's students were meritorious candidates—"in the top percentile of their class"—who only needed financial help.

Bansal was not alone in his opposition to reservation. In 2006, as the Indian Parliament debated extending OBC quotas to the IITs, alumni in Silicon Valley organized under the banner of "Indians for Equality" started online petitions, street protests, and solidarity campaigns to make their opinions known and express their fear of "brand dilution." At one such protest, an IIT alumnus argued to an Indian reporter from *The Hindu* that the Indian government should "leave the IITs alone. . . . It is because of us that the West has recognized the worth of India. . . . Remember, brand India is brand IIT."[60] The notion that lower-caste entry threatens the IITs' institutional brand is a striking instance of the possessive investment in upper casteness. With the threat of lower-caste encroachment, IITians equate the market value of Brand IIT more explicitly with being upper caste. Moreover, with the invocation of the West as audience, IITians claim to be shoring up the value of "Brand India" itself through the protection of upper casteness.

The opposition to reservation feeds into diasporic IITians' impoverished view not only of the Indian state but of IITians who did not immigrate to the United States. While other diasporic alumni like Kalyan offered some version of this assessment, Bansal offered the clearest articulation of the hierarchy of diaspora and homeland. For him, the "socialist" conditions of India were corrosive, even of IITians. "The guys who stayed behind in India, what happened to them?" he asked rhetorically. "It's like day and night comparing them to us. In India, through '60s and '70s, there was nothing. IITians in India, after IIT they went into civil service, foreign service, or went to work for the Tatas. That's the way to power in India whereas here it was always through entrepreneurship." For Bansal, to stay in India was to be sucked into the state system in a downward spiral from excellence to irrelevance. As a parting salvo, he echoed Rajiv Gandhi's remark: "Brain drain is much better than brains in the drain."

Bansal's vitriol against the state only faltered when it came to the Hindu nationalist Bharatiya Janata Party (BJP). In fact, he dated his more active involvement in India to the first short-lived BJP government under Prime Minister Atal Behari Vajpayee. "Vajpayee was the best PM," he pronounced. "He opened up the economy. He sold public enterprises, liberalized airlines, finance, telecom. I was involved with some of this, especially in telecom. We had a company of experts set up at Stanford to advise the Government of India on privatizing the telecom sector which they accepted fully. Vajpayee was very receptive. I met with him four, five times at his office and when he came to DC." I pushed Bansal on why he was singling out the BJP when economic liberalization was initiated by the Congress Party. He responded that while changes might have begun with the Congress, the process stalled until the advent of BJP rule. For him, a key consideration was each party's attitude toward the United States. In his estimation, there was no daylight between being pro-liberalization and being pro-American. "BJP government was always more receptive," he restated. "[Narendra] Modi as well. Congress was by and large very anti-American. They're socialist, we're capitalist. Under Vajpayee, there was phenomenal warmth between U.S. and India. Under Sonia [Gandhi], it was a civil relationship. The warmth is back now with Modi." Bansal's embrace of Narendra Modi echoes the long-standing intimacy between India's domestic capitalist class and the BJP, which was an early critic of state developmentalism and a champion of the private sector. As with other majoritarian nationalisms, Hindu nationalism has long had a social base among the upper-caste middle class.[61] Most IITians are the perfect combination of both constituencies, having emerged out of the upper-caste middle class to become members of a capitalist class spanning homeland and diaspora.

Bansal's version of India's postindependence history and the place of the IITs within it offers some key insights into the diasporic IITian worldview. As his story goes, the IITs were a beacon of light within the darkness of Indian state socialism, but IITians had to migrate to the capitalist United States in order to avoid slipping into the mediocrity produced by socialist conditions. Once in the United States, their natural talents could find their best expression via entrepreneurial activity while IITians in India languished, producing a growing divergence between these nodes of alumni. Even as diasporic IITians flourished and their excellence was publicly recognized, homeland alumni devolved into anonymity within the steel frame of the state. Luckily, the shift to economic liberalization allowed for new bridges to be built between homeland and diaspora, links that were solidified with the rise of the Hindu nationalist, pro-capitalist BJP. In the process, diasporic

IITians were able to bring the spirit of entrepreneurship to India and cultivate a new generation of capitalists who could once and for all remove the nation's shackles of socialism. With the guiding light of diasporic entrepreneurship, Brand IIT becomes Brand India. This diasporic liberation theology places the nation's deliverance squarely in the hands of the U.S.-based IITian.

IIT Madras and Brand IIT

Brand IIT has certainly acquired an impressive reach, and its effect on perceptions of individual, institutional, and national value is undeniable. For one, the branding campaign has powerfully shaped student consciousness at IIT Madras. Students in the late 2000s liberally used the language of branding to define their own value. Sandeep, a 2009 alumnus, pointed out to me that as an IITian, "you are branded as intelligent." He went on to note that one's branch of engineering was hardly relevant to the value of the pedigree. "Once [job] placements begin in December," Sandeep explained, "you will see that everyone is going into finance and business and marketing, even though they haven't done any related courses. Still, companies believe these people are good enough. It is more about the brand name."[62]

It is clear that branding has shaped recruitment at the IITs. The annual event of the IITs' job-recruiting drive makes big news in India. In the last fifteen years, the number of private corporations that recruit on IIT campuses has increased exponentially. Now, IIT graduates join companies like Schlumberger, Shell Oil, Microsoft, McKinsey, Tata Consultancy Services, or Infosys for starting salaries that are considerably higher than what their parents earned at the end of a lifetime of work. This is intergenerational economic mobility at its most dramatic. Although most IITians are the children of professionals, within a single generation they have leapfrogged over their parents' modest incomes to earn hundred-thousand-dollar corporate salaries.

In India, the impressive salaries garnered by newly minted IIT graduates have been characterized as the realization of the brand—not just by IITians but also by the likes of Shashi Tharoor, former United Nations under-secretary-general for communications and public information. In a 2006 article, Tharoor commented, "'Brand IIT' has shown the way. In 2007, we must start to scale this up to the point where one day 'Brand India' becomes synonymous not with cheap products or services but with the highest standards of scientific and technological excellence."[63] This reference to an IIT education as a brand that has shored up India's comparative advantage in the global marketplace situates the IITs and IITians as the forerunners of a future Indian modernity free of the social and political encumbrances of the past. But Tharoor's comment does more. In equating India's developmental status with brand value, it reduces the social, political, and even ethical complexity of development to market price. In the process, the capacity to attract investment and accumulate wealth becomes the preeminent index of social value and intellectual merit.

Most homeland IITians also endorse the notion of Brand IIT as good for the institution. As one faculty member put it to me, "The brand is a kind of ISO mark, a mark of quality. You're assured of quality, like when you see a car 'made in Japan,' it immediately sells."[64] Another alumnus who is a managing director of a Chennai-based management and consulting firm echoed Tharoor's claim that "the biggest contribution of IIT (and largely by the IITians) is the brand that they have created at the global level. The IIT brand commands respect for capability and excellence of a very high order in most academic institutions, corporate circles across a wide range of industries, and even government. This success of the IIT brand . . . has increased the respect for India around the world. Of course, there have been other factors that have contributed to the 'India' brand, but IIT has a reasonable share in that success."[65]

Apart from the embrace of Brand IIT, the impact of Silicon Valley is also evident in forms of aspiration. When I asked students in 2008 and 2009 about their career goals, the role models whose stories came up most readily were Silicon Valley entrepreneurs. There are no longer professors or researchers, or even public servants, on these lists. But unlike the alumni they admire who made their mark in the U.S. technology sector, these students use branding to bypass careers in technology altogether. Ironically, the very deskilling that Kalyan disparaged as emblematic of homeland IITians has been precipitated by success stories such as his. For most students now, entrepreneurship is much more about the skill of making money.

The elevation of entrepreneurship is visible in the creation of a master's of science in entrepreneurship and the student-run Entrepreneurship Cell, or E-Cell, at IIT Madras. E-Cell's founders characterize themselves as "a group of students passionate about startups and the entrepreneurial journey" who aim "to make students and faculty 'entrepreneurial' in every work that they do." In a near perfect echo of Silicon Valley rhetoric, E-Cell proposes to "unlock students' latent inventive potential" and "bring together everyone interested in the startup world to help students best utilize resources to found or join startups." The group takes credit for "130+ Startups incubated, 150+ Ideas Bootstrapped, and 250+ Internships Offered." All in all, E-Cell strives to foster an "entrepreneurship culture" at IIT Madras.[66]

These resonances between diaspora and homeland might suggest that IITians in India have subscribed fully to the Silicon Valley model of upper-caste meritocracy. However, a closer look reveals differences hidden within avowals of institutional kinship. In 2008, the Pan-IIT Alumni Association held a conference at IIT Madras, the first in India after the inaugural event in San Jose, California, and a second in Washington, D.C. The conference was an ideal setting to see the status of the IITs on full display and, less obviously, to understand both the overlaps and the tensions between homeland and diasporic alumni. The overarching theme for this first India-based conference was nation-building, with sessions organized around six topics: research, entrepreneurship, rural transformation, infrastructure, education, and innovation. The tenor of press coverage spoke volumes about the standing of the IITs in India. A range of news articles covered the event with hyperbolic titles such as "IITians Have Brought Glory to the Country," "IITians Have Created a Global Brand," "Every IITian Has Created 100 Jobs," and "Bonding Back with the Best," the last starting with the line, "Some call it bonding, others call it networking but most call it family get-together."[67] The reportage foregrounded two issues: entrepreneurship and India's global image. Most articles held forth on the flourishing of entrepreneurship at the IITs as emblematic of India's global arrival, cementing the equation between Brand IIT and Brand India.

The intimacy between Brand IIT and Brand India was not only trumpeted by the press. Former prime minister Manmohan Singh also valorized the link between Brand IIT and Brand India as a way of marking the liberalizing Indian state's own disjuncture with a past of planned development. At his inaugural address to the conference, Singh stated, "I believe it is India's destiny to become a knowledge power and the IITs have contributed handsomely in the country's efforts to realize this destiny." Others offered other expressions of triumphalism. Raghuram Rajan, IIT Delhi alumnus and former chief economist of the International Monetary Fund, underscored the importance of free enterprise for India, even at a time of global financial crisis. Cautioning Indians not to rethink their commitment to economic liberalization, he noted that "world over, the middle class has lost huge wealth in the recent global financial crisis. Their attitude is now against free market economy. But market economies are prone to crisis. South Korea faced four crises since the '60s but it has weathered them." Rajan acknowledged the need for improving financial regulations but ended with a rallying cry for capitalism as the only system that values innovation. "Look at the alternative," he warned, "a government owned system— where the politician will be the patronizing personality. Recall where India was and where it has come now. It is time for the middle class to take along the lesser privileged sections so that the fruits of free economy are shared by all." After avowing his faith in the free market, Rajan ended with a crowd pleaser. When he was an IIT student, he recalled, it was impossible to get corporate sponsorship for their ventures. "We knew the reason later, because all the CEOs then were either from St. Stephen's or Loyola or Presidency; the IITians were still working their way up. I'm glad that there are at least 300 IITians who are CEOs of companies now," he concluded to thunderous applause from the audience.[68] With the invocation of the three institutions—one each in Delhi, Chennai, and Calcutta—Rajan drew a contrast between the elite graduates of colonial-era institutions and middle-class IITians for whom the free market was the best tool for success. Totally absent in this contrast were both the shared caste backgrounds of these student bodies and the massive state support for the IITs.

However, not all IITians echoed the commitments to branding, entrepreneurship, or the free market that reverberated across homeland and diaspora. Kalyanaraman, a 1966 IIT Madras alumnus based in Chennai and one of the organizers of the conference, offered one expression of dissent against the mainstreaming of the entrepreneurial model. In the midst of all the talk of Brand IIT, he saw his role as re-cuperating the less visible homeland IITian. When I asked him about how alumni activity in the United States and India compared, he said pointedly, "In USA, it's brand-building, here it's nation-building." As examples of nation-builders, he offered a diverse list of alumni: an ayurvedic doctor, a Reserve Bank of India governor, the chair of the Se-curities and Exchange Board of India, a school principal, a minister of environment, a petroleum secretary, some journalists, the head of an NGO working in primary education, and several others. "These are all IITians who have contributed to the development of the country," he underscored, "but all you hear about now is Silicon Valley." One reason it was easy to overlook the accomplishments of India-based IITians, Kalyanaraman contended, was because many of them still worked "with and within the system." He singled out the bureaucrat for men-tion. "You don't hear about such individuals but because these guys were there working, and despite all the corruptions and problems and the politicians, our country is still a good working democracy. Because twenty percent of our bureaucrats are dedicated people." Kalyanaraman acknowledged that an increasing number of diasporic IITians were now interested in "giving back," as evidenced in the theme of the confer-ence. But, he continued, none of this could happen without IITians based in India. "We are trying to be a link," he explained, "because, all said and done, we need to leverage the government to have any real impact and they [diasporic IITians] have forgotten how to navigate India."[69]

The divergence between diasporic and homeland attitudes toward state and nation was also evident in my conversations with past direc-tors of the IITs. In an echo of late colonial nationalism, one former di-rector of IIT Madras opined that while "global connectivity is impor-tant," national self-sufficiency must still be of paramount importance. "At the very least," he insisted, "it should be a system of give and take. What do we give? As Mahatma Gandhi said, we sell cotton and buy cloth. Even now, we sell raw materials and buy steel. This has to change." Another former director made the additional point that the IITs should remain public institutions. In the 1980s, he told me, IIT Madras was often forced to cut through red tape to get anything done. "Every so often," he recalled, "we had to go to Delhi, talk to people, cajole them and ask for money. And all the time, it was 'Why do you need this? Why do you need that?'" Even efforts to raise independent funds proved difficult. "When our faculty earned money through consultancies," he continued, "the Government of India said, 'We'll adjust it against your budget.' When alumni wanted to give us money from the U.S., the government said, 'We'll adjust it against your budget.'" Things reached a head in the early 2000s, when the OBC reservations were being debated in parliament. "The alumni got so fed up," he recalled, "that some of them contacted the Government of India and said, hand over the IITs to us. We will run it from the U.S. and we won't ask you for a single paise. They were going to form a consortium to take over the original five IITs. Immediately the Government of India panicked and said, no, no, no, the IITs are our property. Then the doors opened and they stopped asking so many questions." Despite all this—his frustrations as director, his strident opposition to Mandal, and his appreciation for diasporic alumni support—the director concluded that the IITs should nevertheless remain public. When I pressed for an explanation, he offered his view of state and market. "The private sector sometimes responds violently to market fluctuations," he said, "whereas the government has a sense of commitment. Last year when the American economy collapsed, Chidambaram was still the Finance Minister and he stated publicly that bank deposits were safe because of government regulations. We need that. We need that umbilical cord. We can't cut it fully." He then went on to depict a different structure of feeling binding state and citizenry in India. "I don't think the country is used to the American kind of system at all. We've always been governed by kings and now by the government. You know what the villagers in the north call the government? *Mai Baap*, our mother and father. So, so long as people have that attitude, the government cannot cut itself off."[70] With this combination of a populist and a cultural rationale, the director came down on the side of stable, secure, even paternalistic government as a necessary foundation for India and for the IITs. This was a far cry from the hypervaluing of risk, innovation, and rapid accumulation by Silicon Valley entrepreneurs, as well as from Raghuram Rajan's fidelity to the free market.

The "umbilical cord" also came up in the comments of other homeland alumni when talking about IITians' relationship to India. One of the showcase events of the conference was the release by Manmohan Singh of an Internet-based survey of alumni, *The IIT Alumni Impact Study, 2008.* The study's data on alumni career trajectories added up to a glowing success story. Significantly, a key emphasis was the impact of alumni in and on India, captured in information such as the following: among IIT alumni who are in "top leadership roles," almost 70 percent are based in India, with a third having returned after stints abroad; 54 percent of the top 500 Indian companies have at least one IIT alumnus on their board of directors; of the 17 percent in research and education, mostly in the technology sector, half are based in India; 9 percent are engaged in "social transformation work" in NGOs, government administration, or politics; and 9 percent are entrepreneurs, with 41 percent having founded more than one company, two thirds of which are in India.[71] These numbers were cited repeatedly in responses given by homeland alumni to the press, often to correct journalist assumptions about the "brain drain." In conversations with me, India-based alumni were quick to point to the study as vindication against the diasporic hijacking of the IIT story. Many also gestured to their own decisions to return to India as implicit criticism of diasporic acquisitiveness and evidence of their own stronger "cultural values."

Just as Brand IIT and attitudes toward the government produced differences of opinion among alumni, so too did entrepreneurship. Several IIT Madras faculty attributed a decline in students' research orientation and their interest in particular branches of study to the overemphasis on entrepreneurship. The "entrepreneurship craze," they told me, was both a threat to the intellectual standing of the institution and demoralizing for faculty whose students were far more interested in attracting the attention of venture capitalists than in learning the curriculum. One faculty member noted that entrepreneurial ambitions have produced an instrumentalism that has corroded the purpose of the IITs. Now, "instead of technology and engineering," he said in frustration, "all they want to understand is the business of business."[72] He also highlighted the growing sense among students that the classroom was no longer as valuable a space of training for the future as the E-Cell and other extracurricular spaces. In a striking instance of coming full circle, the laboratory had come to be valued above the classroom, although now the laboratory was a space associated with the "immaterial labor" of information technology. Faculty at U.S. universities also echoed this concern. Chatterjee, an IIT alumnus and MIT professor, pointed to the decline in research motivation and competence of his PhD students from the IITs. "The kids we get now, they still stand out dramatically in the classroom," he noted. "When they take exams, they're always the top in the class. But I don't see as many of them stand out in research."

Interestingly, these sentiments were echoed by a Silicon Valley IITian. Unlike his northern counterparts, who rejected the scaffolding of the large company as a barrier to entrepreneurial ambitions, Vishwanath, a Tamil Brahmin 1972 IIT Madras alumnus, was a "lifer" in IBM's research division. He expressed deep frustration with what he characterized as IITians' wholesale shift away from research. "Everybody thinks that either you should be an entrepreneur or you should have armies of people working for you," he groused. "When you give them the business card, they look and see, oh, does the word 'manager' appear there or not. Oh, it doesn't appear? Then you must be a loser. Or they ask you questions like—how many people report to you? what's the budget you control?—as if that proves that they are smarter than you." Vishwanath was not against branding per se; he just wanted the IIT brand to stand for research skill. He had become a practiced thorn in the side of highly visible promoters of the IITs, whom he would harass to "talk about scientists and technologists who have done very well in terms of their contributions to science, research, society, not just create this kind of hero worshipping of only the people who mumble stuff about innovation but have no credentials to back it."[73] His proselytizing didn't stop with the newsmakers. "I am trying to change peoples' attitudes," Vishwanath told me. "And not just the technical people. Also Appa, Amma, Thatha, Patti [Father, Mother, Grandfather, Grandmother], all these people that are part of the ecosystem, who play a significant role in shaping the thinking of kids."

At the 2008 conference, Vishwanath was in one of the sessions on research, where he gave a full-throated defense of academic and industrial research as the best way to realize the purpose of the IITs as emblems of meritocracy. But his increasing frustration with the direction of the IITs had also led him beyond the institutions. Vishwanath was appointed as IBM's India chief scientist from 2006 to 2009, during which time he traveled to what he called "no-name colleges" to spread his message about the excitement of research. "The idea," he told me, "was to brainwash these third- and fourth-tier undergraduate students into believing that a research career is a good thing, get them excited, not think the same old way that everybody thinks so they make decisions based on more than that one number: the salary." To his surprise, Vishwanath found these students far more receptive than IIT students, who "were all on the fast-track to money making." While rewarding, it was also evident that Vishwanath found it demoralizing to think of how few of these students were likely to find the support needed to pursue research careers.

Still other IIT Madras alumni offered a class critique of entrepreneurship. Madhavan, the "star teacher" from Chapter 5, called the lie to the idea of entrepreneurship as a natural expression of being an IITian. "Silicon Valley entrepreneurs come from more affluent families which allows them to take risks," he countered. "Most of us who came from middle class families would work hard to be toppers within the IIT and then go to a safe, well-paying job in the U.S. so we could send money home to our parents to buy their own home or get our sisters married. We weren't about to take a risk with our future and our families' future. This is the majority of IITans, not the Silicon Valley entrepreneurs."[74] Madhavan's pointed rejection of entrepreneurship as an institutional ethos and professional ambition spoke to differences within the ubiquitous claim to being middle class. In contrast to the claims to middle classness of Silicon Valley IITians, Madhavan identified entrepreneurial risk as itself an index of inherited capital. While he highlighted the forms of inherited capital required to be a Silicon Valley entrepreneur, others mapped the divergence between homeland and diasporic attitudes onto the significance of the region in shaping the cultures of the different IIT campuses. Some alumni pointedly opined that Mumbai's business culture may well have permeated the space of IIT Bombay to a greater degree than at other campuses and shaped the worldviews of its alumni.

In such expressions of dissent, we hear tensions between different imaginaries of upper casteness. Particularly noteworthy is the stance of some Tamil Brahmin alumni and faculty, who shared a distaste for the blatant embrace of accumulation, which they felt was more aligned with a mercantile sensibility. Some spoke of this as a departure from an older model of ascetic intellectualism, which was a trademark characteristic of IIT Madras. For them, the overt market orientation of Silicon Valley loyalists was unfitting for a meritocratic institution and threatened to blur the boundary between IIT Madras and its sociocultural environs. As with concerns around the impact of "the coached" on institutional culture, here, too, one hears anxieties around the "taint" of the market. Even as most also embrace the elevated standing of their brand, they reject what they see as an openly instrumental approach to the IIT pedigree. Vishwanath, the IBM scientist, put it most bluntly: "All these good Brahminical values that, at least in the minds of some people in the south used to mean that you should be good in academics and intellectual pursuits, that that should be the overriding ambition and you shouldn't be taken in by these material things, all that has vanished."

Vishwanath's invocation of Brahminical values speaks volumes about the continuing transformation of IITian understandings of meritocracy. As with the differences between urban cosmopolitan and rural upper-caste attitudes toward coaching, new tensions have arisen between intellectual and entrepreneurial models of upper casteness. Unlike "the coached," however, both homeland and diasporic alumni have laid claim to divergent understandings of upper-caste meritocracy. The model of upper casteness in which entrepreneurial wealth accumulation is elevated above all other pursuits and IIT Bombay tops the pecking order of campuses has not gone over well with all Madras IITians. To their surprise, those who were once emblematic of upper-caste meritocracy now find themselves resisting its most recent iteration.

In this chapter, we have tracked the decades-long sedimentation of the upper-caste, diasporic IITian as an entrepreneurial subject against the backdrop of a longer history of Indian migration. Indian diasporic life in the United States has always been a process of navigating the inheritances of caste with the pitfalls of racialization. The 1965 Immigration and Nationality Act allowed for an influx of Indian professionals who became representative of what was in actuality a more diverse diaspora. IITians were among this representative group of professionals. While they were less visible in the early years, a confluence of factors—the rise of information technology, the shift of many IITians to this sector, and the Silicon Valley boom—allowed for a newly coordinated effort to produce the image of the entrepreneurial Indian and Brand IIT. The project of forging and publicizing an entrepreneurial model of the IITian shored up the possessive investment in upper casteness dramatically. As they emerged as a risk worth taking, IITians have been catapulted into the ranks of the wealthy; the payoff of caste has never been as apparent. At the same time, the elevation of entrepreneurialism and of IIT Bombay as the ideal types of upper-caste meritocracy has generated new tensions. While some IITians oppose diasporic claims to meritocracy as expressions of First World superiority, others, such as Tamil Brahmins, seek to revalorize a model of the IITian as an intellectual and a nation-builder.

The rise of Narendra Modi has augured another shift in IITian projects of self-fashioning. In the United States, this has been seen most clearly in IITians' endorsement of the BJP's neoliberal capitalism. More recently, Modi's style of authoritarian populism has also garnered support in both the United States and India. In India, this is evident in an escalation of cultural nationalist politics on IIT campuses.[75] It is to this most recent expression of upper casteness within India, and its implications for the ongoing dialectic of upper-caste claims to merit and lower-caste claims to rights, that we turn in the Conclusion.

Conclusion

The Caste of Merit has tracked the role of engineering education in the transformation and consolidation of caste. As we have seen, the advent of political democracy reconstituted the terms of caste stratification and distinction. In particular, the ideology of meritocracy allowed upper castes new forms of maneuver through their remaking as meritocratic subjects. At the same time, Tamilnadu set a precedent for transforming the interplay between ascription and achievement. By throwing into relief the inheritances of caste, particularly in the spheres of higher education and white-collar employment, Non-Brahminism and Dravidianism forced upper castes into a reactive claim to merit on the basis of caste culture. From the 1990s, this dialectic of lower-caste claims to rights and upper-caste claims to merit expanded to national and even transnational scale. The scaling up of a reactive politics of meritocracy was catalyzed by the implementation of the 1990 and 2006 Other Backward Class (OBC) reservation quotas. Unlike the more universalistic claims to merit in previous decades, the threat posed by the entry of OBCs—first into central government jobs and then into centrally funded higher educational institutions—led to a sharp identitarian turn in upper-caste politics. This more explicit equation between caste and merit echoed the much earlier practice of Tamil Brahmin self-marking. Now, however, the self-marking of the meritorious indexed not discrete caste identities but a consolidated

315

grouping of upper castes arrayed in opposition to lower castes. Diasporic mobility was an important check on this oppositional dynamic.
In the United States, upper castes could claim a racialized version of
meritocracy in which caste served as a crucial basis of collective maneuver and capital accumulation even while it was discursively obscured. Unlike in India, where the expansion of lower-caste rights was
a partial challenge to the reproduction of caste privilege, the United
States allowed for the unfettered leveraging of upper casteness as a possessive investment, a process aided by assumptions about the innate
technical capacities of Indians within the knowledge economy.

In the 2010s, this ongoing dialectic of upper- and lower-caste claim-
making was complicated by a new factor: the election of the Hindu
nationalist BJP's Narendra Modi as prime minister in May 2014. Modi's
election has allowed for a retrenchment of caste power in ways that
mirror trends in the diaspora and undercut the gains of lower-caste politics. As a result of his election, IIT Madras and other central government campuses became more open battlegrounds of caste conflict. On
one side were OBC and Dalit groups, newly empowered by their enhanced numbers to challenge an upper-caste status quo. On several
campuses, lower-caste solidarity found expression in organization
building. At IIT Madras, OBC and Dalit students came together in 2014
to form the Ambedkar Periyar Study Circle (APSC). At the University
of Hyderabad, Dalit students had formed the Ambedkar Student Association (ASA) much earlier, in 1993, but it was reactivated in the new
political climate. As is evident in their invocation of Dalit icon B. R.
Ambedkar, both student groups were explicitly aligned with anticaste
politics and openly critical of the upper-caste culture of their campuses. On the other side, a long-standing politics of upper-caste meritocracy was yoked to a centrally orchestrated state project of Hindu
nationalism. The Modi government committed itself to a systematic
campaign of undercutting institutional autonomy by throwing its
weight behind groups allied to the Bharatiya Janata Party (BJP) and
criminalizing student opposition. For their part, the administrators of
central government institutions used the ascent of Modi to discipline
a more diverse and politicized student body and reinforce the upper-
caste culture of their campuses.

There is a pattern to this scapegoating that is visible across central government campuses. Following Modi's election, IIT Madras's APSC organized a range of events on political and social issues that were a striking echo of earlier Non-Brahmin and Dravidian causes. Some events responded to the Modi government's policy directives to central government institutions to hold a mandatory celebration of Sanskrit Week, establish separate dining halls for vegetarians and nonvegetarians, and adopt Sanskrit name boards for campus facilities. In response, the APSC organized a series of lectures. One was on the politics of language, in which the speaker challenged the notion of Sanskrit as the *Deva-basha,* or "mother of all languages," and illuminated its use historically to marginalize lower castes. Another addressed the history of bans on cow slaughter as part of the promotion of upper-caste norms of vegetarianism. Other APSC events addressed the ongoing impact of economic liberalization. At one, organizers screened Charlie Chaplin's *Modern Times* and discussed changing labor laws. At another, they staged a debate on genetically modified organisms and the plight of the Indian farmer.

In April 2015, the IIT Madras dean of students "de-recognized" the APSC on the grounds that the group had violated protocol in event programming. It was subsequently revealed that the dean had acted at the behest of the Ministry of Human Resource Development (MHRD), which was itself responding to an anonymous letter from a group of students accusing the APSC of "creating hatred among students in the name of caste . . . and against the prime minister and Hindus." The standoff between the APSC and the college administration quickly spiraled out from the campus as the de-recognition sparked protests in Chennai among Dravidianist, Dalit, and Left organizations. Demonstrations on other central government campuses followed, criticizing the overreach of the college administration and the Modi government. The issue became front-page news across media outlets and a touchstone for political opinion and mobilization, eventually leading to the APSC's reinstatement.

At the University of Hyderabad, events took a more tragic turn. There were two ASA events in particular that brought the group into a head-on collision with the BJP-affiliated student group the Akhil

Bharatiya Vidyarthi Parishad (ABVP) and eventually with the Modi government. The first was a protest against the hanging of Yakub Memon for his involvement in the 1993 Mumbai attack. The second was the screening of the film *Muzzafarnagar Baqi Hai*, on the 2013 communal riots that paved the way for Modi's victory in the 2014 general elections. In August 2015, BJP labor minister Bandaru Dattatreya wrote to the MHRD, charging the ASA of "casteist, extremist, and antinational politics" and with assaulting the ABVP president. Yielding to pressure from the MHRD, the university chancellor denied five Dalit members of the ASA entry into the dorms, cafeterias, and other social spaces on campus, and disqualified them from participating in student union elections. After experiencing twelve days of an administratively orchestrated social boycott that reeked of caste ostracism, one of the five, a student named Rohith Vemula, committed suicide. Vemula's death sparked outrage and led to a spreading politics of dissent across IIT campuses, seen in the mushrooming of groups allied with the APSC. Some, like IIT Delhi's APSC, kept the same name. Others, like IIT Bombay's Ambedkar Periyar Phule Study Circle, expressed their pan-IIT solidarity while indexing their own regional history of anticaste protest.[1]

A third confrontation occurred at New Delhi's Jawaharlal Nehru University (JNU) in early 2016. On February 9, 2016, the Democratic Students Union held a protest against the killings of Kashmiri separatist Maqbool Bhat and Afzal Guru, who was charged and convicted for the 2001 attack on the Indian Parliament. The university administration had withdrawn permission for the event shortly before it was due to begin because of protests by members of the ABVP. Four days after the event, Kanhaiya Kumar—the JNU student union president—was arrested by the Delhi police and charged with sedition. Two other student arrests followed. In response to the arrests, the campus came to a standstill, with thousands of students, faculty, and staff joining ongoing protests. The arrests also elicited criticism of the Modi government's heavy-handed approach to political dissent from across the country and from a large number of international scholars. Although investigations into the incident turned up nothing and led to all the arrested students being granted bail, an internal inquiry charged the students with procedural violations, and a range of sanctions were imposed on twenty-one students. In response, the students went on an indefinite hunger strike, and the Delhi High Court suspended the sanctions on the condition that the students end their strike.[2]

These confrontations highlight the conscription of central government campuses as one front in a war waged by the Modi government against those it deems enemies of the nation. To advance a Hindu nationalist vision of culture, history, and citizenship, and consolidate support for his regime, Modi has relied on the construction of an ever-expanding category of "anti-nationals." Cultural theorist Stuart Hall used the term "authoritarian populism" to point to a similar political strategy used during Margaret Thatcher's tenure in Britain.[3] Thatcherism, he argued, shifted British democratic politics toward authoritarianism by using a series of "moral panics" around race, law and order, and social liberalism to produce a populist groundswell of support for the increasing centralization of power.[4] Similarly, the Modi government's targeting of "anti-nationals" within central government institutions is part of a larger politics of authoritarian consolidation in the name of "the people" that includes violent attacks on Muslims and Dalits under the guise of cow protection, the policing of interreligious love and women's sexuality, the arrests of civil and human rights activists, and the killing of journalists.[5]

Under Modi, fomenting violence against "anti-nationals" has also been accompanied by the reversal of a rights agenda. A number of scholars have noted the paradoxical coupling in the 2000s of a neoliberal economic agenda promoting market-oriented accumulation strategies with social policy interventions aimed at protecting subaltern groups threatened by dispossession.[6] This was especially the case under the previous United Progressive Alliance (UPA) coalition government led by the Congress Party, which oversaw new rights-based legislation, including the Right to Information Act of 2005, the National Rural Employment Guarantee Act and the Forest Rights Act of 2006, the Right to Education Act of 2009, and the Right to Food Act and the Land Acquisition, Rehabilitation and Resettlement Act of 2013. The implementation of Mandal II—the 2006 OBC quotas—was part of this wave of legislation. Each of these laws was a response to social movement mobilization during the 1990s against economic liberalization.[7] Through

these new laws, the UPA government sought to secure popular legitimacy through an agenda of "inclusive neoliberalism" while furthering
predatory growth that opened up manufacturing, mining, retail, and
banking to private interests.[8]

With the election of Modi as the head of the coalition National
Democratic Alliance government, this strategy of subaltern legal recognition was supplanted by a model of the "strongman savior." This
model, which elevated Modi himself as the answer to social ills, was
promoted and received differently by various and often polarized constituencies. For lower castes and the poor, Modi's own life story as a
tea vendor who rose up the ranks to political stardom, his diatribes
against elites, and his promises to fight corruption and to bring *acche
din* (good days) to all Indians were peddled as the antidote to the widening disparities of the 2000s.[9] For upper castes and the wealthy, it was
a different story. As we saw in Chapter 7, despite the Congress Party's
promotion of economic liberalization, Silicon Valley IITians heralded
Modi as the leader who would unshackle growth. For them and other
Indian elites, the rights-based legislation under the UPA was nothing
more than "vote bank politics," which was bad for business. Their support for Modi rested on the expectation that he would curb the welfare and social expenditures of the 2000s and extend to the national
level policies he had championed as chief minister of Gujarat, such as
the courting of foreign investment, a rollback of state regulations, and
a weakening of organized labor.[10] And, indeed, under Modi, inequalities in wealth and income escalated to the point where, by 2017, the
richest 1 percent of the Indian population owned 73 percent of the
country's wealth and controlled 21.7 percent of national income.[11] Not
only did inequality increase, the turn away from a rights-based approach toward the leveraging of moral panics undercut lower-caste
claims and secured the position of upper castes in the most lucrative
private sectors of the Indian economy.

As with the spectral targets of moral panics, the ferocity of the
backlash against reservation thus obscures how favorable the conditions actually are for the upper-caste accumulation of wealth. What,
then, explains the shrill defense of meritocracy and ominous predic-
tions about the end of liberal democracy that are directed at lower-caste
political mobilization? The "elite revolt" against reservation, and sub-

altern rights more broadly, suggests a remarkably powerful and resilient sense of entitlement, where any measure of distributive justice is perceived as a threat to the natural order of things.[12] In the successive fault lines between the mental and the manual, the gifted and the coached, the general and the reserved, diaspora and homeland, and authoritarian populism and lower-caste rights politics, we see the dynamic and sustained forms of maneuver through which the possessive investment in upper casteness is expressed and secured.

It is not only in India that IITians and other Indian professionals have come out in support of authoritarian populism. Some in the U.S. diaspora have as well. Once again, the linchpin has been merit. On February 3, 2018, members of the Republican Hindu Coalition marched to the White House in support of U.S. president Donald Trump's proposal to implement a "merit-based" immigration system favoring skilled workers and ending both chain migration for family members and the diversity lottery. Shouting slogans such as "Indians love Trump," "Clear Green Card Backlog," and "Trump bringing Ram Rajya" (the just rule of the Hindu god-king Ram), group members endorsed both Trump's immigration proposal and his call for a wall on the southern border with Mexico to keep out "illegals." The contrast between legal and illegal migrants was underscored in another chant: "No DACA without DALCA." In a play on DACA—the acronym for the Deferred Action for Childhood Arrivals program, which benefits approximately 690,000 "Dreamers," children brought illegally into the country—the demonstrators referred to their own children as "DALCA," with the "L" standing for "legal." The Republican Hindu Coalition has demanded that the children of high-skilled workers awaiting green cards be granted legal permanent residency immediately, while those in the DACA program be forced to pay a $25,000 fine to stay.[13] Here, again, we see efforts to secure upper-caste capital through recourse to forms of self-racialization aimed at distinguishing the meritocratic Indian from other "problem minorities."[14]

What are the implications of these processes for Indian democracy? In seeking to secure the conditions for capital accumulation, upper castes have both leveraged notions of ascriptive merit and aligned themselves with Modi's brand of authoritarian populism. Through this combination of strategies, they have attempted to curtail lower-caste

challenges to the stark inequalities of Indian society that have been
further exacerbated by neoliberal economic restructuring. Their hope
is that the pincer effect of the market on one side and the strongman
savior on the other will choke off the possibilities for a genuinely
popular democracy.

Even as elites evacuate public arenas and make explicitly identitarian claims to private spheres of accumulation, it is subalterns who
increasingly express commitments to the common good and call on
the state to advance universal equality, well-being, and rights. This,
in part, explains the overriding focus of lower-caste politics on reservation as a vehicle of rights. We have seen how critical quotas have
been to increasing lower-caste representation in public arenas of higher
education and professional employment. At the same time, they fall
short of more far-reaching measures of distributive justice. It is telling
that regions such as Tamilnadu, Bihar, and Uttar Pradesh, which have
witnessed state capture by OBCs and Dalits and the expansion of reservation, have yet to experience significant challenges to the unequal
distribution of wealth.[15] Rather, expanded caste representation, especially in government employment, has existed alongside enduring socioeconomic inequality and the persistence of vigilante violence
against Dalits who experience some measure of social mobility.[16] Caste
is still very much the basis for the reproduction of inherited privileges
and disadvantages. Furthermore, a caste politics focused solely on reservation obscures the place of public education within a larger political
economy of rising inequality. At a time when India's top 10 percent
commands a greater share of national income than in the United States,
Canada, Russia, China, and Europe, only a small fraction of the population can even claim the opportunities afforded by higher education
or white-collar employment.[17] In this sense, Tamilnadu is a sobering
reminder of the limits of a politics aimed at expanding caste representation within the middle class that is not accompanied by efforts to
address the structural reproduction of poverty. The lower-caste ambition to enter the professions has kept in place the hierarchies of labor
that underpin the graded inequalities of caste.

Recent trends in lower-caste mobilization, however, point toward
a more egalitarian politics. From the claims of Tamilnadu's farmers to
higher support prices and loan waivers to Dalit land claims in Gujarat,

new forms of political ferment augur more effective challenges to structural inequality. It is also promising that student mobilizations on
elite campuses against upper-caste meritocracy have made common
cause with such struggles among the rural and urban poor.[18] These
emergent forms of solidarity, which cut across class and sectoral boundaries, could be the most effective challenge yet to the possessive investment in upper casteness.

By contrast to these movements against the inheritances of caste,
meritocracy rings hollow as a corrective to older hierarchies of status.
As we have seen throughout this book, by bracketing out historically
accumulated advantages and disadvantages, the notion of meritocracy,
like that of a color-blind society, has come to service the reproduction
of inequality. Although meritocracy as a principle continues to animate
calls for equalization, the divergence between its ideal meaning and
its social life should call into question the assumption that meritocracy is indeed a leveler of opportunity.

Notes

Introduction

1. "Imported from India: Best and Brightest Want to Work in U.S.," *60 Minutes*, June 19, 2003, https://www.cbsnews.com/news/imported-from-india/.
2. *Dilbert*, September 15, 2003, http://dilbert.com/strip/2003-09-15.
3. For a comparable argument on engineering education and racial formation in the United States, see Amy Slaton, *Race, Rigor, and Selectivity in U.S. Engineering: The History of an Occupational Color Line* (Cambridge, MA: Harvard University Press, 2010).
4. But see Sara Dickey, *Living Class in Urban India* (New Brunswick, NJ: Rutgers University Press, 2016); Raka Ray and Seemin Qayum, *Cultures of Servitude: Modernity, Domesticity, and Class in India* (Stanford, CA: Stanford University Press, 2009); Surinder Jodhka and K. Newman, "In the Name of Globalization: Meritocracy, Productivity, and the Hidden Language of Caste," *Economic and Political Weekly* 42, no. 41 (2007): 4125–4132; Carol Upadhya, "Employment, Exclusion and 'Merit' in the Indian IT Industry," *Economic and Political Weekly* 42, no. 20 (2007): 1863–1868; C. J. Fuller and Haripriya Narasimhan, "Information Technology Professionals and the New-Rich Middle Class in Chennai (Madras)," *Modern Asian Studies* 41 (2007): 121–150; C. J. Fuller and Haripriya Narasimhan, "From Landlords to Software Engineers: Migration and Urbanization among Tamil Brahmins," *Comparative Studies in Society and History* 50, no. 1 (2008): 170–196; C. J. Fuller and Haripriya Narasimhan, "Traditional Vocations and Modern Professions among Tamil Brahmans in Colonial and Post-Colonial South India," *Indian Economic and Social History Review* 47, no. 4 (2010): 473–496; C. J. Fuller and Haripriya Narasimhan, *Tamil Brahmans: The Making of a Middle-Class Caste* (Chicago: University of Chicago Press, 2014); Ramesh Bairy, *Being Brahmin, Being Modern: Exploring the Lives of Caste Today* (New Delhi: Routledge, 2010).

5. There are obvious parallels to the arguments for meritocracy in the United States. As with caste in India, the arguments for meritocracy in the United States usually rest on critiques of affirmative action as a mechanism for perpetuating racism and posit a postracial society where individual talent will be recognized on its own terms. Unlike in India, where caste quotas have expanded steadily, such critiques have made their mark in the United States, as seen in the rolling back of affirmative action and the recourse to diversity as the only permissible language for addressing unequal representation. For critiques of the culturalist framing of caste that argue for the salience of comparing caste and race, see Gerald Berreman, "Race, Caste, and Other Invidious Distinctions in Social Stratification," *Race* 13, no. 4 (1972), https://journals.sagepub.com/doi/10.1177/030639687201300401; Kamala Visweswaran, *Un/common Cultures: Racism and the Rearticulation of Cultural Difference* (Durham, NC: Duke University Press, 2010); C. J. Fuller, "Caste, Race, and Hierarchy in the American South," *Journal of the Royal Anthropological Institute* 17, no. 3 (2011): 604–621; Gyanendra Pandey, *A History of Prejudice: Race, Case, and Difference in India and the United States* (Cambridge: Cambridge University Press, 2013); Clarinda Still, "Comparing Race and Caste," *Anthropology of This Century* 12 (2015), http://aotcpress.com/articles/comparing-race-caste/.

6. Sumit Sarkar, *Modern India: 1885–1947* (Delhi: Macmillan, 1983); Manu Goswami, *Producing India: From Colonial Economy to National Space* (Chicago: University of Chicago Press, 2004); Benjamin Zachariah, *Developing India: An Intellectual and Social History* (Oxford: Oxford University Press, 2005).

7. Shiv Visvanathan, *Organizing for Science: The Making of an Industrial Research Laboratory* (Delhi: Oxford University Press, 1985); S. Ambirajan, "Science and Technology Education in South India," in *Technology and the Raj: Western Technology and Technical Transfers to India, 1700–1947*, ed. Roy MacLeod and Deepak Kumar (Delhi: Sage, 1995), 112–133; Aparna Basu, "The Indian Response to Scientific and Technical Education in the Colonial Era, 1820–1920," in *Science and Empire: Essays in Indian Context, 1700–1947*, ed. Deepak Kumar (Delhi: Anamika Prakashan, 1991), 126–138; Deepak Kumar, "Racial Discrimination and Science in Nineteenth-Century India," *Indian Economic and Social History Review* 19, no. 1 (1982): 63–82; Padmini Swaminathan, "Technical Education and Industrial Development in Madras Presidency: Illusions of a Policy in the Making," *Economic and Political Weekly* 25 (July 1992): 1611–1622; Kris Manjapra, *Age of Entanglement: German and Indian Intellectuals across Empire* (Cambridge, MA: Harvard University Press, 2014).

8. Satish Deshpande, "Caste and Castelessness: Towards a Biography of the 'General Category,'" *Economic and Political Weekly* 48, no. 15 (2013): 32–39.

9. For analyses of women students in IIT Madras in the 1980s, see Carol Mukhopadhyay, "Family Structure and Indian Women's Participation in Science and Engineering," in *Women, Education and Family Structure in India,*

ed. Carol Mukhopadhyay and Susan Seymour (Boulder, CO: Westview Press, 1994), 103–133.

10. See, for instance, Afsaneh Najmabadi, "Beyond the Americas: Are Gender and Sexuality Useful Categories of Historical Analysis?," *Journal of Women's History* 18, no. 1 (Spring 2006): 11–21.

11. Following Antonio Gramsci, Partha Chatterjee has argued that the elevation of technology and the role of elite experts within postcolonial developmentalism has been central to India's "passive revolution" and the sidelining of more radical visions of socioeconomic change.

12. Louis Dumont, *Homo Hierarchicus: The Caste System and Its Implications* (Chicago: University of Chicago Press, 1970).

13. There is a sizable literature critical of Dumont. See, for instance, Gerald D. Berreman, "The Brahmanical View of Caste," *Contributions to Indian Sociology* 5, no. 1 (1971): 16–23; Nicholas B. Dirks, "The Original Caste: Power, History and Hierarchy in South Asia," *Contributions to Indian Sociology* 23, no. 1 (1989): 59–77; Gloria Goodwin Raheja, *The Poison in the Gift: Ritual, Prestation, and the Dominant Caste in a North Indian Village* (Chicago: University of Chicago Press, 1988). For more recent critiques of the treatment of caste as a social or cultural sphere distinct from the political economic, see Sumit Guha, *Beyond Caste: Identity and Power in South Asia* (Leiden: Brill, 2013); Rupa Viswanath, *The Pariah Problem: Caste, Religion, and the Social in Modern India* (New York: Columbia University Press, 2014); Nathaniel Roberts, *To Be Cared For: The Power of Conversion and Foreignness of Belonging in an Indian Slum* (Berkeley: University of California Press, 2016); David Mosse, "Outside Caste? The Enclosure of Caste and Claims to Castelessness in India and the U.K." (M. N. Srinivas Memorial Lecture, King's College London, November 29, 2016); B. Natrajan, "From Jati to Samaj," *Seminar* 633 (2012): 54–57.

14. Richard G. Fox, "Resiliency and Change in the Indian Caste System: The Umar of U.P.," *Journal of Asian Studies* 26, no. 4 (1967): 585.

15. M. N. Srinivas, *Caste in Modern India, and Other Essays* (New York: Asia, 1962); M. N. Srinivas, *Social Change in Modern India* (Berkeley: University of California Press, 1967).

16. André Béteille, "Caste in Contemporary India," in *Caste Today*, ed. C. J. Fuller (Oxford: Oxford University Press, 1996), 162.

17. André Béteille, "The Reproduction of Inequality: Occupation, Caste and Family," *Contributions to Indian Sociology* 25, no. 1 (1991): 25.

18. Stuart Hall, "Race, Articulation, and Societies Structured in Dominance," in *Black British Cultural Studies: A Reader*, ed. H. Baker, M. Diawara, and R. Lindeborg (Chicago: University of Chicago Press, 1996), 16–60.

19. Fuller and Narasimhan, *Tamil Brahmans*.

20. Fuller and Narasimhan, *Tamil Brahmans*, 121–122.

21. Viswanath, *The Pariah Problem*; Pamela Price, "Ideology and Ethnicity under British Imperial Rule: 'Brahmans,' Lawyers and Kin-Caste Rules in Madras Presidency," *Modern Asian Studies* 23, no. 1 (1989): 151–177; David A. Washbrook, "The Maratha Brahmin Model in South India: An Afterword,"

Indian Economic and Social History Review 47, no. 4 (2010): 597–615; Rosalind O'Hanlon and Christopher Minkowski, "What Makes People Who They Are? Pandit Networks and the Problem of Livelihoods in Early Modern Western India," *Indian Economic and Social History Review* 45, no. 3 (2008): 381–416; Guha, *Beyond Caste*; Susan Bayly, *Saints, Goddesses and Kings: Muslims and Christians in South Indian Society, 1700–1900* (Cambridge: Cambridge University Press, 1989); Susan Bayly, *Caste, Society and Politics in India: From the Eighteenth Century to the Modern Age* (Cambridge: Cambridge University Press, 1999); Nicholas B. Dirks, *Castes of Mind: Colonialism and the Making of Modern India* (Princeton, NJ: Princeton University Press, 2001); Nicholas B. Dirks, *The Hollow Crown: Ethnohistory of an Indian Kingdom* (Cambridge: Cambridge University Press, 1987).

22. Bernard Cohn, *An Anthropologist among the Historians and Other Essays* (Delhi: Oxford University Press, 1987); Guha, *Beyond Caste*; Thomas Trautmann, *Languages and Nations: The Dravidian Proof in Colonial Madras* (Berkeley: University of California Press, 2006); Thomas Trautmann, *Aryans and British India* (Berkeley: University of California Press, 1997).

23. For the ongoing interaction between caste, class, and other structures of social stratification, see Surinder Jodhka, "Ascriptive Hierarchies: Caste and Its Reproduction in Contemporary India," *Current Sociology* 64, no. 2 (2016): 228–243; Upadhya, "Employment, Exclusion and 'Merit'"; G. Carswell, G. De Neve, and J. Heyer, "Caste Discrimination in Contemporary Tamil Nadu: Evidence from the Tiruppur Textile Region," in *Contested Hierarchies, Persisting Influence: Caste and Power in Twenty-First Century India*, ed. S. Jodhka and J. Manor (Hyderabad: Orient Black Swan, 2017), 172–206; Clarinda Still, ed., *Dalits in Neoliberal India: Mobility or Marginalization?* (New Delhi: Routledge, 2015); C. Jeffrey, "Caste, Class, and Clientelism: A Political Economy of Everyday Corruption in Rural North India," *Economic Geography* 78, no. 1 (2002): 21–41; Roberts, *To Be Cared For*; V. Iversen and P. S. Raghavendra, "What the Signboard Hides: Food, Caste, and Employability in Small South Indian Eating Places," *Contributions to Indian Sociology* 40, no. 3 (2006): 311–341; B. Singh, *Unseen: The Truth about India's Manual Scavengers* (New Delhi: Penguin Books India, 2014); B. Harriss-White, "Matter in Motion: Work and Livelihoods in India's Economy of Waste," in *Critical Perspectives on Work and Employment in Globalizing India*, ed. E. Noronha and P. D'Cruz (Singapore: Springer, 2017), 95–111; D. Mosse, "A Relational Approach to Durable Poverty, Inequality and Power," *Journal of Development Studies* 46, no. 7 (2010): 1156–1178; S. Corbridge, J. Harris, and C. Jeffrey, *India Today: Economy, Politics, and Society* (London: John Wiley and Sons, 2013); K. Munshi, "Caste Networks in the Modern Indian Economy," in *Development in India: Micro and Macro Perspectives*, ed. S. Mahindra Dev and P. Babu (New Delhi: Springer India, 2016), 13–37.

24. B. R. Ambedkar, *What Congress and Gandhi Have Done to the Untouchables* (Bombay: Thacker, 1946).

25. Bayly, *Saints, Goddesses and Kings*; Bayly, *Caste, Society and Politics*; Dirks, *Castes of Mind*; Guha, *Beyond Caste*; Robin Jeffrey, *The Decline of Nair Dominance: Society and Politics in Travancore, 1947–1908* (Delhi:

Vikas, 1976); Robert Hardgrave, *The Nadars of Tamilnadu: The Political Culture of a Community in Change* (Berkeley: University of California Press, 1969); Gauri Viswanathan, *Outside the Fold: Conversion, Modernity and Belief* (Princeton, NJ: Princeton University Press, 1998); Geoffrey Oddie, ed., *Social Protest in India: British Protestant Missionaries and Social Reforms, 1850–1900* (Delhi: Manohar, 1979); Gail Omvedt, *Dalits and the Democratic Revolution: Dr. Ambedkar and the Dalit Movement in Colonial India* (Delhi: Sage, 1994); Dipankar Gupta, *Interrogating Caste: Understanding Hierarchy and Difference in Indian Society* (Delhi: Penguin 2000); Roberts, *To Be Cared For.*

26. For analyses of enduring caste discrimination in the contemporary Indian economy, see Ashwini Deshpande, *The Grammar of Caste: Economic Discrimination in Contemporary India* (Oxford: Oxford University Press, 2017); Craig Jeffrey, Patricia Jeffery, and Roger Jeffery, *Degrees without Freedom? Education, Masculinities, and Unemployment in North India* (Stanford, CA: Stanford University Press, 2008); S. Madheswaran and P. Attewell, "Caste Discrimination in the Indian Urban Labor Market: Evidence from the National Sample Survey," *Economic and Political Weekly* 42, no. 41 (2007): 4146–4153; Jodhka and Newman, "In the Name of Globalization"; S. Thorat and P. Attewell, "The Legacy of Social Exclusion," *Economic and Political Weekly* 42, no. 41 (2007): 4141–4145; A. Banerjee, M. Bertrand, S. Datta, and S. Mullainathan, "Labor Market Discrimination in Delhi: Evidence from a Field Experiment," *Journal of Comparative Economics* 37, no. 1 (2009): 14–27; A. Deshpande and D. Spears, "Who Is the Identifiable Victim? Caste and Charitable Giving in Modern India," *Economic Development and Cultural Change* 64, no. 2 (2016): 299–321; K. Hoff and P. Pandey, "Discrimination, Social Identity, and Durable Inequalities," *American Economic Review* 96, no. 2 (2006): 206–211.

27. In his ongoing research, political scientist Narendra Subramanian addresses the parallels between caste labor and social stratification in Tamilnadu's Thanjavur delta and enslaved labor and social stratification in America's Mississippi delta.

28. Alf Gunvald Nilsen, "Adivasi Mobilization in Contemporary India: Democratizing the Local State?," *Critical Sociology* 39, no. 4 (2012): 615–633.

29. Hardgrave, *Nadars*; Bayly, *Caste, Society and Politics.* Hardgrave chronicles one particularly dramatic instance: the transformation in status of the agrarian lower caste of Shanars in southern Tamilnadu. Previously treated on par with the untouchable castes of the region, the Shanars experienced a dramatic shift in economic and social standing as a result of agricultural modernization and religious conversion. Not only did they change their caste name from Shanar to Nadar to symbolize their new status, but they also began to claim a past of noble birth and an occupation as merchants who had been reduced to bonded labor through a twist of fate.

30. Anupama Rao, *The Caste Question: Dalits and the Politics of Modern India* (Berkeley: University of California Press, 2009); Viswanath, *The Pariah Problem.*

31. Guha, *Beyond Caste*; Washbrook, "Maratha Brahmin Model."

32. Pierre Bourdieu, "The Forms of Capital," in *Handbook of Theory and Research for the Sociology of Education*, ed. J. Richardson (Westport, CT: Greenwood Press, 1986), 46.

33. Bourdieu, "The Forms of Capital," 49.

34. Bourdieu, "The Forms of Capital," 49.

35. Pierre Bourdieu, "The Forms of Capital," 241–258.

36. Ross Bassett, *The Technological Indian* (Cambridge, MA: Harvard University Press, 2016).

37. James Kloppenberg, "The Virtues of Liberalism: Christianity, Republicanism, and Ethics in Early American Political Discourse," *Journal of American History* 44, no. 1 (1987): 1–33; John Carson, "Differentiating a Republican Citizenry: Talents, Human Science, and Enlightenment Theories of Governance," *Osiris* 17, no. 1 (2002): 74–103; John Carson, *The Measure of Merit: Talents, Intelligence, and Inequality in the French and American Republics, 1750–1940* (Princeton, NJ: Princeton University Press, 2006).

38. Carson, "Differentiating a Republican Citizenry."

39. Deshpande, "Caste and Castelessness," 33.

40. For other work on the reconstitution of upper castes as casteless, meritocratic individuals, see Ashwini Deshpande and K. Newman, "Where the Path Leads: The Role of Caste in Post-University Employment Expectations," *Economic and Political Weekly* 42, no. 41 (2007): 4133–4140; Jodhka and Newman, "In the Name of Globalization"; Upadhya, "Employment, Exclusion and 'Merit'"; S. Deshpande and U. Zacharias, eds., *Beyond Inclusion: The Practice of Equal Access in Indian Higher Education* (New Delhi: Routledge, 2013).

41. For an exhaustive account of India's approach to affirmative action, see Marc Galanter, *Competing Equalities: Law and the Backward Classes in India* (New Delhi: Oxford University Press, 1984). For an in-depth analysis of economic discrimination on the basis of caste, see Deshpande, *Grammar of Caste*.

42. For work on the persistence of caste in shaping economic opportunities in India's post-liberalization private sector, see B. Harriss-White, K. Vidyarthee, and A. Dixit, *Dalits and Adivasis in India's Business Economy: Three Essays and an Atlas*, ed. B. Harriss-White et al. (Gurgaon: Three Essays Collective, 2014); L. Iyer, T. Khanna, and A. Varshney, "Caste and Entrepreneurship in India," *Economic and Political Weekly* 48, no. 6 (2013): 52–60; S. Thorat, D. Kundu, and N. Sadana, "Caste and Ownership of Private Enterprise: Consequences of Denial of Property Rights," in *Blocked by Caste: Economic Discrimination in Modern India*, ed. S. Thorat and K. S. Newman (New Delhi: Oxford University Press, 2010), 311–327; S. Jodhka, "Dalits in Business: Self-Employed Scheduled Castes in North-west India," *Economic and Political Weekly* 45, no. 11 (2010): 41–48; Jeffrey, Jeffery, and Jeffery, *Degrees without Freedom?* There is also a sizable historical literature on the role of caste in trade and manufacturing. See, for instance, David Rudner, *Caste and Capitalism in Colonial India: The Nattukottai Chettiars* (Berkeley: University of California Press, 1994); Sharad Chari, *Fraternal Capital: Peasant Workers, Self-Made Men, and Globalization in Provincial India* (Stanford, CA: Stanford University Press, 2004); Lakshmi Subrama-

nian, "Banias and the British: The Role of Indigenous Credit in the Process of Imperial Expansion in Western India," *Modern Asian Studies* 21, no. 3 (1987): 473–510; C. A. Bayly and Sanjay Subrahmanyam, "Portfolio Capitalists and the Political Economy of Early Modern India," in *Merchants, Markets and the State in Early Modern India,* ed. Sanjay Subrahmanyam (Delhi: Oxford University Press, 1990), 242–265; Ritu Birla, *Stages of Capital: Law, Culture, and Market Governance in Late Colonial India* (Durham, NC: Duke University Press, 2009).

43. Deshpande, "Caste and Castelessness," 32.
44. For work on the relationship between ascription and democracy, see Jodhka, "Ascriptive Hierarchies"; Charles Tilly, *Durable Inequality* (Berkeley: University of California Press, 1998).
45. John and Jean Comaroff, *Ethnicity, Inc.* (Chicago: University of Chicago Press, 2009); George Paul Meiu, *Ethno-erotic Economies: Sexuality, Money, and Belonging in Kenya* (Chicago: University of Chicago Press, 2017).
46. For work on the social life of colonial classification, see Cohn, *An Anthropologist among the Historians;* Thomas R. Metcalf, *Ideologies of the Raj* (Cambridge: Cambridge University Press, 1995); C. A. Bayly, *Empire and Information: Intelligence Gathering and Social Communication in India, 1780–1870* (Oxford: Oxford University Press, 1996); Gyanendra Pandey, *The Construction of Communalism in Colonial North India* (Delhi: Oxford University Press, 1990); Dirks, *Castes of Mind;* Anand Pandian, *Crooked Stalks: Cultivating Virtue in South India* (Durham, NC: Duke University Press, 2009); Nandini Sundar, *Subalterns and Sovereigns: An Anthropological History of Bastar, 1854–1996* (Delhi: Oxford University Press, 1997); Viswanath, *The Pariah Problem.* For work on postcolonial caste politics, see Christophe Jaffrelot, *India's Silent Revolution: The Rise of the Lower Castes in North India* (New York: Columbia University Press, 2003); Omvedt, *Dalits and the Democratic Revolution;* Narendra Subramanian, *Ethnicity and Populist Mobilization: Political Parties, Citizens and Democracy in South India* (Delhi: Oxford University Press, 1999).
47. Walter K. Andersen and Sridhar D. Damle, *The Brotherhood in Saffron: The Rashtriya Swayamsevak Sangh and Hindu Revivalism* (Boulder, CO: Westview Press, 1987); Peter Van der Veer, *Religious Nationalism: Hindus and Muslims in India* (Berkeley: University of California Press, 1994); Thomas Blom Hansen, *The Saffron Wave: Democracy and Hindu Nationalism in Modern India* (Princeton, NJ: Princeton University Press, 1999); Christophe Jaffrelot, *The Hindu Nationalist Movement in India* (New York: Columbia University Press, 1996); David Ludden, ed., *Making India Hindu: Religion, Community, and the Politics of Democracy in India* (Delhi: Oxford University Press, 1996).
48. Matthew Frye Jacobson, *Whiteness of a Different Color: European Immigrants and the Alchemy of Race* (Cambridge, MA: Harvard University Press, 1999); Matthew Frye Jacobson, *Roots Too: White Ethnic Revival in Post–Civil Rights America* (Cambridge, MA: Harvard University Press, 2005).
49. Patricia Williams, *The Alchemy of Race and Rights* (Cambridge, MA: Harvard University Press, 1991); David Roediger, *The Wages of Whiteness: Race and the Making of the American Working Class* (London: Verso, 1991);

George Lipsitz, *The Possessive Investment in Whiteness: How White People Profit from Identity Politics* (Philadelphia: Temple University Press, 1998); Cheryl I. Harris, "Whiteness as Property," *Harvard Law Review* 106, no. 8 (1993): 1709–1791.

50. Antonio Gramsci, *Selections from the Prison Notebooks* (New York: International Publishers, 1971).

CHAPTER I ◉ The Colonial Career of Technical Knowledge

1. Michael Adas, *Machines as the Measure of Men: Science, Technology, and Ideologies of Western Dominance* (Ithaca, NY: Cornell University Press, 1989); S. Ambirajan, "Science and Technology Education in South India," in *Technology and the Raj: Western Technology and Technical Transfers to India, 1700–1947*, ed. Roy MacLeod and Deepak Kumar (Delhi: Sage, 1995), 112–133; David Gilmartin, "Scientific Empire and Imperial Science: Colonialism and Irrigation Technology in the Indus Basin," *Journal of Asian Studies* 53, no. 4 (1994): 1127–1149; Daniel Headrick, *The Tentacles of Progress: Technology Transfer in the Age of Imperialism, 1850–1940* (Oxford: Oxford University Press, 1988); Daniel Klingensmith, *One Valley and a Thousand: Dams, Nationalism, and Development* (Delhi: Oxford University Press, 2007).

2. See, for instance, Clive Dewey, "The Education of a Ruling Caste: The Indian Civil Service in the Era of Competitive Examination," *English Historical Review* 88, no. 347 (1973): 262–285.

3. But see Padmini Swaminathan, "Technical Education and Industrial Development in Madras Presidency: Illusions of a Policy in the Making," *Economic and Political Weekly* 25 (July 1992): 1611–1622; C. J. Fuller and Haripriya Narasimhan, "Information Technology Professionals and the New-Rich Middle Class in Chennai (Madras)," *Modern Asian Studies* 41 (2007): 121–150; C. J. Fuller and Haripriya Narasimhan, "From Landlords to Software Engineers: Migration and Urbanization among Tamil Brahmins," *Comparative Studies in Society and History* 50, no. 1 (2008): 170–196, C. J. Fuller and Haripriya Narasimhan, "Traditional Vocations and Modern Professions among Tamil Brahmans in Colonial and Post-Colonial South India," *Indian Economic and Social History Review* 47, no. 4 (2010): 473–496; C. J. Fuller and Haripriya Narasimhan, *Tamil Brahmans: The Making of a Middle-Class Caste* (Chicago: University of Chicago Press, 2014).

4. Quoted in Suresh Chandra Ghosh, *History of Education in India* (Jaipur: Rawat Publications, 2007).

5. Quoted in Shiv Visvanathan, *Organizing for Science: The Making of an Industrial Research Laboratory* (Delhi: Oxford University Press, 1985), 15.

6. Quoted in Headrick, *The Tentacles of Progress*, 325.

7. Gilmartin, "Scientific Empire and Imperial Science," 79.

8. W. H. G. Armytage, *Four Hundred Years of English Education* (Cambridge: University Press, 1964), 161.

9. E. Buck, "Report on Practical and Technical Education, Home Education, December 1901," in *Selections from Educational Records of the Govern-*

ment of India, vol. 4, *Technical Education in India, 1886–1907*, ed. K. D. Bhargava (Delhi: National Archives of India, 1968), 148.

10. John Wallace, "Technical Education for the Workman," in *Papers Relating to the Industrial Conference Held at Ootacamund in September 1908* (Madras: Government of Madras, 1908), 136–141.

11. Quoted in Ambirajan, "Science and Technology Education," 121.

12. Quoted in Ambirajan, "Science and Technology Education," 121.

13. G. Chesney, in a note dated February 22, 1869, in connection with the establishment of the Royal Indian Engineering College in England.

14. "Memorandum on Technical Education in India prior to 1886, by Mr. (Now Sir) A.P. MacDonnell, Dated 23rd July 1886," in *Selections from Educational Records of the Government of India*, vol. 4, *Technical Education in India, 1886–1907*, ed. K. D. Bhargava (Delhi: National Archives of India, 1968), 11.

15. Quoted in Visvanathan, *Organizing for Science*, 48–50.

16. *Report of the Public Works Commissioners* (Madras: Church of Scotland Mission Press, 1853), par. 612.

17. Gilmartin, "Scientific Empire and Imperial Science," 81–82.

18. Gilmartin "Scientific Empire and Imperial Science," 82.

19. Ghosh, *History of Education*, 114.

20. Ghosh, *History of Education*, 108.

21. Deepak Kumar, "Racial Discrimination and Science in Nineteenth-Century India," *Indian Economic and Social History Review* 19, no. 1 (1982): 63–82; Headrick, *The Tentacles of Progress*; Aparajith Ramnath, "Engineers in India: Industrialisation, Indianisation, and the State, 1900–47" (PhD thesis, Imperial College London, 2012).

22. W.T. Thornton, "Further Papers Relating to the Indian Civil Engineering College, March 23, 1871," in Great Britain, Parliament, *Accounts and Papers of the House of Commons*, vol. 50 (London, 1871), 226.

23. Alfred Chatterton, *Industrial Evolution in India* (Madras: Hindu Office, 1912), 19.

24. Chatterton, *Industrial Evolution in India*, 358–359.

25. Quoted in Headrick, *The Tentacles of Progress*, 306.

26. Quoted in Headrick, *The Tentacles of Progress*, 308.

27. J. A. Richie, "Progress of Education in India, 1917–1922," in *Eighth Quinquennial Review*, vol. 1 (Calcutta, 1923), 90.

28. Indian Industrial Commission, *Minutes of Evidence, 1916–1918*, 6 vols. (Calcutta: Superintendent Government Printers, 1918), 6: 6–7.

29. Quoted in Ramnath, "Engineers in India," 121.

30. Quoted in Ramnath, "Engineers in India," 123.

31. Anthropologist Ann Laura Stoler has written eloquently about colonialism in the East Indies as a process of disciplining both the colonized and the colonizer. This was similarly the case in British India. See Stoler's "Rethinking Colonial Categories: European Communities and the Boundaries of Rule," *Comparative Studies in Society and History* 31, no. 1 (1989): 134–161, and *Carnal Knowledge and Imperial Power: Race and the Intimate in Colonial Rule* (Berkeley: University of California Press, 2010).

32. Chesney, "Civil Engineering College in India."

33. Circular no. 35 P.W., dated Simla, June 29, 1870, Resolution by the Government of India, Public Works Department, India Office Records, V/27/865/5.
34. Quoted in Ramnath, "Engineers in India," 115.
35. Ramnath, "Engineers in India."
36. Quoted in Headrick, *The Tentacles of Progress*, 307.
37. Quoted in Headrick, *The Tentacles of Progress*, 317.
38. Indian Industrial Commission, *Minutes of Evidence*, 3: 262.
39. Indian Industrial Commission, *Minutes of Evidence*, 3: 262.
40. Indian Industrial Commission, *Minutes of Evidence*, 2: 262.
41. Indian Industrial Commission, *Minutes of Evidence*, 2: 261.
42. Indian Industrial Commission, *Minutes of Evidence*, 3: 80.
43. Indian Industrial Commission, *Minutes of Evidence*, 3: 80.
44. Indian Industrial Commission, *Minutes of Evidence*, 3: 80.
45. Indian Industrial Commission, *Minutes of Evidence*, 2: 149.
46. Indian Industrial Commission, *Minutes of Evidence*, 3: 326.
47. Indian Industrial Commission, *Minutes of Evidence*, 3: 326.
48. Quoted in Clive Dewey, "The Government of India's 'New Industrial Policy,' 1900–1925: Formation and Failure," in *Economy and Society: Essays in Indian Economic and Social History*, ed. K. N. Chaudhuri and Clive Dewey (Delhi: Oxford University Press, 1979), 228.
49. Quoted in Dewey, "The 'New Industrial Policy,'" 230.
50. Quoted in Dewey, "The 'New Industrial Policy,'" 230.
51. Chatterton, *Industrial Evolution*, 114.
52. K. D. Bhargava, ed. *Selections from Educational Records of the Government of India*, vol. 4, *Technical Education in India, 1886–1907* (Delhi: National Archives of India, 1968).
53. K. D. Bhargava, *Selections from Educational Records*.
54. Swaminathan, "Technical Education," 1612.
55. Quoted in Swaminathan, "Technical Education," 1613.
56. K. D. Bhargava, *Selections from Educational Records*.
57. Indian Industrial Commission, *Minutes of Evidence*, 2: 230.
58. Swaminathan, "Technical Education," 1613.
59. Visvanathan, *Organizing for Science*, 40.
60. Dewey, "The 'New Industrial Policy,'" 222.
61. Dewey, "The 'New Industrial Policy,'" 225.
62. Dewey, "The 'New Industrial Policy,'" 225.

CHAPTER 2 ◎ Building the IITs

1. Quoted in Aparna Basu, "The Indian Response to Scientific and Technical Education in the Colonial Era, 1820–1920," in *Science and Empire: Essays in Indian Context, 1700–1947*, ed. Deepak Kumar (Delhi: Anamika Prakashan, 1991), 367.
2. Clive Dewey, "The Government of India's 'New Industrial Policy,' 1900–1925: Formation and Failure," in *Economy and Society: Essays in Indian Economic and Social History*, ed. K. N. Chaudhuri and Clive Dewey (Delhi: Oxford University Press, 1979), 215–257; Basu, "The Indian Response."
3. Dewey, "The 'New Industrial Policy.'"

4. Basu, "The Indian Response," 132.
5. Quoted in Aparajith Ramnath, "Engineers in India: Industrialisation, Indianisation, and the State, 1900–47" (PhD thesis, Imperial College London, 2012), 96.
6. M. Visvesvaraya, *Memoirs of My Working Life* (Delhi: Publication Division, Ministry of Information and Broadcasting, Government of India, 1960); *Prosperity through Industry: Move towards Rapid Industrialization* (Bombay: All-India Manufacturers' Organization, 1943).
7. Quoted in Dewey, "The 'New Industrial Policy,'" 236.
8. Shiv Visvanathan, *Organizing for Science: The Making of an Industrial Research Laboratory* (Delhi: Oxford University Press, 1985).
9. Visvanathan, *Organizing for Science*.
10. Indian Industrial Commission, *Minutes of Evidence, 1916–1918*, 6 vols. (Calcutta: Superintendent Government Printers, 1918), 3: 324.
11. Indian Industrial Commission, *Minutes of Evidence*, 3: 323.
12. Indian Industrial Commission, *Minutes of Evidence*, 3: 150.
13. Visvanathan, *Organizing for Science*, 45–48.
14. N. R. Sarkar, *An Interim Report of the Committee Appointed to Consider the Development of Higher Technical Institutions in India* (New Delhi: Government of India, 1948), 1.
15. Sarkar, *An Interim Report*, 2.
16. Sarkar, *An Interim Report*, 4.
17. These included Lt. General Sir Thomas Hutton, Secretary to the Planning and Development Department; A. W. H Dean, Chief Engineer of the Central Public Works Department; General Sir Clarence Bird, Master General of Ordnance; Lt. General K. M. Loch, Master General of Ordnance; Major General D. R. Duguid, Director of Military Engineering; Major General H. M. Roome, Engineer-in-Chief; and Brigadier R. D. T. Woolfe, Comptroller General of Inspection.
18. Sarkar, *An Interim Report*, 6.
19. Stuart Leslie and Robert Kargon, "Exporting MIT: Science, Technology, and Nation-Building in India and Iran," *Osiris* 21, no. 1 (2006): 110–130.
20. Sarkar, *An Interim Report*, 19.
21. Sarkar, *An Interim Report*, 19.
22. Sarkar, *An Interim Report*, 20.
23. Sarkar, *An Interim Report*, 13–14.
24. Sandipan Deb, *The IITians: The Story of a Remarkable Indian Institution and How Its Alumni Are Changing the World* (New Delhi: Viking, 2004), 38.
25. "Convocation Address by Shri Jawaharlal Nehru at the First Annual Convocation, Held on 21st April, 1956," in *The Scholars' Avenue* (IIT Kharagpur campus newspaper).
26. Quoted in Srirupa Roy, *Beyond Belief: India and the Politics of Postcolonial Nationalism* (Durham, NC: Duke University Press, 2007), 118–119.
27. Roy, *Beyond Belief*, 118.
28. Roy, *Beyond Belief*, 118–119.
29. Roy, *Beyond Belief*, 119.
30. Roy, *Beyond Belief*, 128.

31. Roy, *Beyond Belief,* 121.
32. Tee Square, "Life and Times of an Obsolete Engineer," *IIT Madras Alumni Magazine,* June 2015, 1.
33. Deb, *The IITians,* 335.
34. David Gilmartin, "Scientific Empire and Imperial Science: Colonialism and Irrigation Technology in the Indus Basin," *Journal of Asian Studies* 53, no. 4 (1994): 86.
35. Deb, *The IITians,* 27.
36. Deb, *The IITians,* 40.
37. Deb, *The IITians,* 42.
38. C. Rajagopalan and Jaspal Singh, "The Indian Institutes of Technology: Do They Contribute to Social Mobility?," *Economic and Political Weekly* 3, no. 14 (1968): 570.
39. S. P. Sukhatme and I. Mahadevan, "Brain Drain and the IIT Graduate," *Economic and Political Weekly* 23, no. 25 (1988): 1285–1293.
40. Mihir Desai, Devesh Kapur, and John McHale, "The Fiscal Impact of High Skilled Emigration: Flows of Indians to the U.S." (Working Paper, Harvard Business School, November 2002).
41. Deb, *The IITians,* 36.
42. Deb, *The IITians,* 36–37.
43. P. V. Indiresan and N. C. Nigam, "The Indian Institutes of Technology: Excellence in Peril," in *Higher Education Reform in India: Experience and Perspectives,* ed. Suma Chitnis and Philip G. Altbach (New Delhi: Sage, 1993), 334–363.

CHAPTER 3 ◎ Challenging Hierarchies of Value in Madras

1. G.O. No. 218, 23 May 1855, Public Works Department, National Archives of India.
2. Quoted in S. Ambirajan, "Science and Technology Education in South India," in *Technology and the Raj: Western Technology and Technical Transfers to India, 1700–1947,* ed. Roy MacLeod and Deepak Kumar (Delhi: Sage, 1995), 129.
3. Quoted in Ambirajan, "Science and Technology Education," 119–120.
4. Quoted in Ambirajan, "Science and Technology Education," 120.
5. Quoted in Ambirajan, "Science and Technology Education," 122.
6. Quoted in Ambirajan, "Science and Technology Education," 122.
7. Quoted in C. J. Fuller and Haripriya Narasimhan, "Traditional Vocations and Modern Professions among Tamil Brahmans in Colonial and Post-Colonial South India," *Indian Economic and Social History Review* 47, no. 4 (2010): 488.
8. Fuller and Narasimhan, "Traditional Vocations," 487.
9. Fuller and Narasimhan, "Traditional Vocations," 488.
10. Fuller and Narasimhan, "Traditional Vocations," 488.
11. C. J. Fuller and Haripriya Narasimhan, "From Landlords to Software Engineers: Migration and Urbanization among Tamil Brahmins," *Comparative Studies in Society and History* 50, no. 1 (2008): 180.

12. Quoted in Padmini Swaminathan, "Technical Education and Industrial Development in Madras Presidency: Illusions of a Policy in the Making," *Economic and Political Weekly* 25 (July 1992): 1619.

13. Alfred Chatterton, *Industrial Evolution in India* (Madras: Hindu Office, 1912), 22.

14. G.O. No 340, 20 May 1905, Education Department, Madras, Tamil Nadu Archives.

15. G.O. No. 292, 4 April 1912, Education Department, Madras, Tamil Nadu Archives.

16. G.O. No. 292, 4 April 1912, Education Department, Madras, Tamil Nadu Archives.

17. Robin Jeffrey, *The Decline of Nayar Dominance: Society and Politics in Travancore, 1847–1908* (New York: Holmes and Meier, 1976).

18. G.O. No. 273, 8 April 1908, Education Department, Madras, Tamil Nadu Archives.

19. G.O. No. 312, 28 April, 1908, Education Department, Madras, Tamil Nadu Archives.

20. G.O. No. 31, 18 January 1907, Education Department, Madras, Tamil Nadu Archives.

21. G.O. No. 733, 1 April 1907, Revenue Department, Madras, Tamil Nadu Archives.

22. G.O. No. 516, 1 July 1907, Education Department, Madras, Tamil Nadu Archives.

23. Chatterton, *Industrial Evolution in India*, 152.

24. Swaminathan, "Technical Education," 1617 (emphasis added).

25. The following three paragraphs are also drawn from these sources: Arjun Appadurai, *Worship and Conflict under Colonial Rule: A South Indian Case* (Cambridge: Cambridge University Press, 1981); Nicholas B. Dirks, *The Hollow Crown: Ethnohistory of an Indian Kingdom* (Cambridge: Cambridge University Press, 1987); Burton Stein, *Peasant, State, and Society in Medieval South India* (Oxford: Oxford University Press, 1980); David Ludden, *Peasant History in South India* (Princeton, NJ: Princeton University Press, 1985); Stephen Barnett, "Approaches to Changes in Caste Ideology in South India," in *Essays on South India*, ed. B. Stein (Honolulu: University Press of Hawaii, 1975), 149–180; Brenda Beck, *Peasant Society in Konku* (Vancouver: University of British Columbia, 1972); David Washbrook, "Caste, Class, and Dominance in Modern Tamil Nadu: Non-Brahminism, Dravidianism, and Tamil Nationalism," in *Dominance and State Power in Modern India*, vol. 1, *Decline of a Social Order*, ed. Francine R. Frankel and M. S. A. Rao (Delhi: Oxford University Press, 1989), 204–264.

26. Dharma Kumar, "South India," in *The Cambridge Economic History of India*, vol. 2, ed. D. Kumar (Cambridge: Cambridge University Press, 1983), 207–241; Christopher J. Baker, *An Indian Rural Economy, 1880–1955: The Tamil Nadu Countryside* (Delhi: Oxford University Press, 1984).

27. Christopher J. Baker, *The Politics of South India, 1920–1937* (Cambridge: Cambridge University Press, 1976); Eugene Irschick, *Politics and Social Conflict in South India: The Non-Brahman Movement and Tamil Separatism,*

1916–1929 (Berkeley: University of California Press, 1969); Rupa Viswanath, *The Pariah Problem: Caste, Religion, and the Social in Modern India* (New York: Columbia University Press, 2014).

28. Marguerite Barnett, *The Politics of Cultural Nationalism* (Princeton, NJ: Princeton University Press, 1976); Bernard Cohn, "The Census, Social Structure, and Objectification in South Asia," in *An Anthropologist among the Historians and Other Essays* (Delhi: Oxford University Press, 1987), 224–254.

29. Pamela Price, "Ideology and Ethnicity under British Imperial Rule: 'Brahmans,' Lawyers and Kin-Caste Rules in Madras Presidency," *Modern Asian Studies* 23, no. 1 (1989): 154; Sumit Guha, *Beyond Caste: Identity and Power in South Asia* (Leiden: Brill, 2013).

30. David A. Washbrook, "The Maratha Brahmin Model in South India: An Afterword," *Indian Economic and Social History Review* 47, no. 4 (2010): 597–615.

31. Fuller and Narasimhan, "From Landlords to Software Engineers"; Fuller and Narasimhan, "Traditional Vocations"; C. J. Fuller and Haripriya Narasimhan, *Tamil Brahmans: The Making of a Middle-Class Caste* (Chicago: University of Chicago Press, 2014).

32. M. S. S. Pandian, *Brahmin and Non-Brahmin: Genealogies of the Tamil Political Present* (Delhi: Permanent Black, 2007), 159.

33. Pandian, *Brahmin and Non-Brahmin*, 159.

34. Appadurai, *Worship and Conflict.*

35. Barnett, *The Politics of Cultural Nationalism*; Price, "Ideology and Ethnicity."

36. V. Geetha and S. V. Rajadurai, *Towards a Non-Brahmin Millennium: From Iyothee Thass to Periyar* (Calcutta: Book Review Literary Trust, 1991), 135.

37. Geetha and Rajadurai, *Towards a Non-Brahmin Millennium*, 135.

38. Geetha and Rajadurai, *Towards a Non-Brahmin Millennium*, 131.

39. Geetha and Rajadurai, *Towards a Non-Brahmin Millennium*, 131–132.

40. Geetha and Rajadurai, *Towards a Non-Brahmin Millennium*, 133.

41. Quoted in Pandian, *Brahmin and Non-Brahmin*, 164.

42. Geetha and Rajadurai, *Towards a Non-Brahmin Millennium*; Pandian, *Brahmin and Non-Brahmin.*

43. Pandian, *Brahmin and Non-Brahmin*, 165.

44. Pandian, *Brahmin and Non-Brahmin*, 166–169.

45. Barnett, *The Politics of Cultural Nationalism*; Robert Hardgrave, *The Dravidian Movement* (Bombay: Popular Prakashan, 1965); Irschick, *Politics and Social Conflict*; Sumathi Ramaswamy, *Passions of the Tongue: Language Devotion in Tamil India, 1891–1970* (Berkeley: University of California Press, 1997).

46. Narendra Subramanian, *Ethnicity and Populist Mobilization: Political Parties, Citizens and Democracy in South India* (Delhi: Oxford University Press, 1999); Pandian, *Brahmin and Non-Brahmin*; Geetha and Rajadurai, *Towards a Non-Brahmin Millennium.*

47. Kathleen Gough, *Rural Society in Southeast India* (Cambridge: Cambridge University Press, 1981); Subramanian, *Ethnicity and Populist Mobilization*,

91; Washbrook, "Caste, Class, and Dominance," 215; Hugo Gorringe, *Untouchable Citizens: Dalit Movements and Democratization in Tamil Nadu* (London: Sage, 2005); Nathaniel Roberts, *To Be Cared For: The Power of Conversion and Foreignness of Belonging in an Indian Slum* (Berkeley: University of California Press, 2015).

48. Barnett, *Cultural Nationalism;* Subramanian, *Ethnicity and Populist Mobilization,* 91.

49. Subramanian, *Ethnicity and Populist Mobilization,* 143; Washbrook, "Caste, Class, and Dominance," 216.

50. Barnett, *Cultural Nationalism;* Ramaswamy, *Passions of the Tongue.*

51. Theodore Baskaran, *The Message Bearers: Nationalist Politics and the Entertainment Media in South India, 1880–1945* (Chennai: Cre-A, 1981).

52. M. S. S. Pandian, *The Image Trap: M. G. Ramachandran in Film and Politics* (New Delhi: Sage, 1992); Sara Dickey, "The Nurturing Hero: Changing Images of MGR," in *Tamil Cinema: The Cultural Politics of India's Other Film Industry,* ed. Selvaraj Velayutham (London: Routledge, 2008), 77–94; Subramanian, *Ethnicity and Populist Mobilization.*

53. Geetha and Rajadurai, *Towards a Non-Brahmin Millennium.*

54. Subramanian, *Ethnicity and Populist Mobilization.*

55. Washbrook, "Caste, Class, and Dominance"; M. S. S. Pandian, "Crisis in DMK," *Economic and Political Weekly,* 29, no. 5 (1994).

56. C. Fuller, "The Brahmins and Brahminical Values in Modern Tamil Nadu," in *Institutions and Inequalities: Essays in Honour of Andre Beteille,* ed. R. Guha and J. Parry (Delhi: Oxford University Press, 1999), 30–55; John Harriss, "The Great Tradition Globalizes: Reflections on Two Studies of 'The Industrial Leaders' of Madras," *Modern Asian Studies* 37, no. 2 (2003): 327–362.

57. Pandian, *Brahmin and Non-Brahmin,* 71.

58. Corinna Unger, "Industrialization vs. Agrarian Reform: West German Modernization Policies in India in the 1950s and 1960s," *Journal of Modern European History* 8, no. 1 (2010): 47–65.

59. "Reunification of Germany, Talks at Bonn Reviewed, Offer of Technical Aid to India," *The Hindu* (Madras), July 17, 1958.

60. "Bonn Offers to Set up Tech College in India, 100 Scholarships Also Proposed," *Indian Express* (Madras), July 15, 1956.

61. Excerpts from messages received on the occasion of the unveiling of the tablet symbolizing Indo-German Cooperation on December 3, 1962, at IIT Madras and on display at the IIT Madras Heritage Center.

62. "Technical Studies: Institute Opened in City," *The Hindu* (Madras), August 1, 1959.

63. "Technical Studies: Institute Opened in City," *The Hindu* (Madras), August 1, 1959.

64. Manu Goswami, *Producing India: From Colonial Economy to National Space* (Chicago: University of Chicago Press, 2004).

65. Kris Manjapra, *Age of Entanglement: German and Indian Intellectuals across Empire* (Cambridge, MA: Harvard University Press, 2014), 96.

66. Quoted in Manjapra, *Age of Entanglement,* 128.

67. Quoted in Manjapra, *Age of Entanglement*, 129.
68. Manjapra, *Age of Entanglement*, 128–130.
69. Odd Arne Westad, *The Global Cold War: Third World Interventions and the Making of Our Times* (Cambridge: Cambridge University Press, 2007); Unger, "Industrialization vs. Agrarian Reform."
70. Unger, "Industrialization vs. Agrarian Reform," 62.
71. Unger, "Industrialization vs. Agrarian Reform."
72. Manjapra, *Age of Entanglement*, 134.
73. Manjapra, *Age of Entanglement*, 134–135.
74. "W. German President Hails Indo-German Co-operation," *The Hindu* (Madras), December 3, 1962.
75. Ross Bassett, "Aligning India in the Cold War Era: Indian Technical Elites, the Indian Institute of Technology at Kanpur, and Computing in India and the United States," *Technology and Culture* 50, no. 4 (October 2009): 797.
76. Bassett, "Aligning India in the Cold War Era," 797n30.
77. Unger, "Industrialization vs. Agrarian Reform," 52.
78. Unger, "Industrialization vs. Agrarian Reform," 52.
79. Unger, "Industrialization vs. Agrarian Reform," 52.
80. Unger, "Industrialization vs. Agrarian Reform," 53.

CHAPTER 4 ◎ IIT Madras's 1960s Generation

1. Throughout the book, the names of interviewees have been changed to preserve their anonymity.
2. Interview with John Abraham, August 26, 2008. All subsequent quotes by Abraham are from the same interview.
3. Interview with Balachandran, September 17, 2008. All subsequent quotes by Balachandram are from the same interview.
4. Ram Krishnaswamy, *Reflections by IITians: Alumni Share Their Journeys* (Chennai: Sterling Prints and Conversions, 2008), 292.
5. Interview with Rajesh Vedula, December 17, 2015. All subsequent quotes by Vedula are from the same interview.
6. Krishnaswamy, *Reflections by IITians*, 68.
7. Krishnaswamy, *Reflections by IITians*, 56.
8. Krishnaswamy, *Reflections by IITians*, 57.
9. Interview with Vijayaraj, September 16, 2008. All subsequent quotes by Vijayaraj are from the same interview.
10. Krishnaswamy, *Reflections by IITians*, 17–18.
11. Interview with Thyagarajan, December 22, 2015. All subsequent quotes by Thyagarajan are from the same interview.
12. Krishnaswamy, *Reflections by IITians*, 98.
13. Krishnaswamy, *Reflections by IITians*, 58.
14. Sandipan Deb, *The IITians: The Story of a Remarkable Indian Institution and How Its Alumni Are Changing the World* (New Delhi: Viking, 2004), 27.
15. Krishnaswamy, *Reflections by IITians*, 97.
16. Shantiniketan is a town in West Bengal where national poet and Nobel laureate Rabindranath Tagore started Patha Bhavana, the school of his ideals,

whose central premise was that learning in a natural environment would be more enjoyable and fruitful. He received the Nobel Prize in 1913, and the school was expanded into a university in 1921.

17. Krishnaswamy, *Reflections by IITians*, 98.
18. Kumaran Sathasivam, *Campaschimes: IITM through IITian Eyes* (Chennai: IIT Madras, 2011), 69.
19. Krishnaswamy, *Reflections by IITians*, 176–177.
20. Krishnaswamy, *Reflections by IITians*, 178.
21. Krishnaswamy, *Reflections by IITians*, 209.
22. Krishnaswamy, *Reflections by IITians*, 210.
23. Krishnaswamy, *Reflections by IITians*, 211.
24. Interview with Kalyanaraman, December 10, 2008. All subsequent quotes by Kalyanaraman are from the same interview.
25. C. J. Fuller and Haripriya Narasimhan, *Tamil Brahmans: The Making of a Middle-Class Caste* (Chicago: University of Chicago Press, 2014), 27.
26. Fuller and Narasimhan, *Tamil Brahmans*, 17.
27. Fuller and Narasimhan, *Tamil Brahmans*, 26.
28. Other work on the imbrication of caste and class include Carol Upadhya, "Employment, Exclusion and 'Merit' in the Indian IT Industry," *Economic and Political Weekly* 42, no. 20 (2007): 1863–1868.
29. Krishnaswamy, *Reflections by IITians*, 197.
30. Deb, *The IITians*, 33.
31. Deb, *The IITians*, 33.
32. Sathasivam, *Campaschimes*, 58.
33. Sathasivam, *Campaschimes*, 59.
34. Tee Square, "Life and Times of an Obsolete Engineer," *IIT Madras Alumni Magazine*, June 2015, 8.
35. Tee Square, "Life and Times of an Obsolete Engineer," 8.
36. Krishnaswamy, *Reflections by IITians*, 224.
37. Krishnaswamy, *Reflections by IITians*, 225.
38. Krishnaswamy, *Reflections by IITians*, 225.
39. Krishnaswamy, *Reflections by IITians*, 230.
40. See for example, Evelyn Richter, "Student Slang at IIT Madras: A Linguistic Field Study" (MA thesis, English and American Studies, Chemnitz University of Technology, 2006).
41. Krishnaswamy, *Reflections by IITians*, 290.
42. Krishnaswamy, *Reflections by IITians*, 18.
43. Krishnaswamy, *Reflections by IITians*, 69.
44. Indian Institute of Technology, Madras, *Annual Report, 1962–63* (Chennai: IIT Madras, 1963).
45. Prince Frederick, "IIT-Madras: A Trip to the Roots of Technology," *The Hindu*, July 31, 2015.
46. Prince Frederick, "IIT-Madras: A Trip to the Roots of Technology," *The Hindu*, July 31, 2015.
47. Krishnaswamy, *Reflections by IITians*, 241.
48. Krishnaswamy, *Reflections by IITians*, 179.
49. Krishnaswamy, *Reflections by IITians*, 227.

50. Krishnaswamy, *Reflections by IITians*, 179.
51. Krishnaswamy, *Reflections by IITians*, 104.
52. Krishnaswamy, *Reflections by IITians*, 60.
53. Krishnaswamy, *Reflections by IITians*, 20.
54. Krishnaswamy, *Reflections by IITians*, 156.
55. Krishnaswamy, *Reflections by IITians*, 220–221.
56. Krishnaswamy, *Reflections by IITians*, 219.
57. Krishnaswamy, *Reflections by IITians*, 214–215.
58. Krishnaswamy, *Reflections by IITians*, 99.
59. C. Rajagopalan and Jaspal Singh, "The Indian Institutes of Technology: Do They Contribute to Social Mobility?," *Economic and Political Weekly* 3, no. 14 (1968): 565–570.

CHAPTER 5 ◉ Testing Merit

1. Shreeharsh Kelkar, "The Elite's Last Stand: Negotiating Toughness and Fairness in the IIT-JEE, 1960–2005," *Engineering Studies* (under review), 7–8.
2. For an ethnographic comparison with China's competitive examinations, see Zachary Howlett, "Fateful Action: Hierarchy, Transformation, and Ideals of Merit in China's National College Entrance Examination" (PhD diss., Cornell University Department of Anthropology, 2016).
3. This section of the chapter is indebted to the work of sociologist Satish Deshpande, especially his essay "Pass, Fail, Distinction: The Examination as a Social Institution" (Third Marjorie Sykes Memorial Lecture, Regional Institute of Education, Ajmer, March 3, 2010).
4. Pierre Bourdieu and Jean-Claude Passeron, *Reproduction in Education, Society, and Culture* (London: Sage, 1977), 153.
5. Bourdieu and Passeron, *Reproduction in Education*, 153.
6. Deshpande, "Pass, Fail, Distinction," 8.
7. Bernard Cohn, "Recruitment and Training of British Civil Servants in India, 1600–1860," in *Asian Bureaucratic Systems Emergent from the British Imperial Tradition*, ed. Ralph Braibanti (Durham, NC: Duke University Commonwealth Studies Center, 1966), 111.
8. Clive Dewey, "The Education of a Ruling Caste: The Indian Civil Service in the Era of Competitive Examination," *English Historical Review* 88, no. 347 (1973): 263.
9. Quoted in Dewey, "The Education of a Ruling Caste," 265.
10. Dewey, "The Education of a Ruling Caste," 266.
11. Quoted in Dewey, "The Education of a Ruling Caste," 267.
12. Dewey, "The Education of a Ruling Caste," 272.
13. Ann Stoler provides a fascinating comparative instance of how colonial discipline was applied to the colonizers as well as the colonized in the Dutch East Indies in "Rethinking Colonial Categories: European Communities and the Boundaries of Rule," *Comparative Studies in Society and History* 31, no. 1 (1989): 134–161.
14. Dewey, "The Education of a Ruling Caste," 283.
15. Bourdieu and Passeron, *Reproduction in Education*, 153.

16. Ramnath, Aparajith, "Engineers in India: Industrialisation, Indianisation, and the State, 1900–47" (PhD thesis, Imperial College London, 2012), 50.
17. Ramnath, "Engineers in India," 52.
18. Krishna Kumar, "Reproduction or Change? Education and Elites in India," *Economic and Political Weekly*, July 27, 1985, 1280–1284.
19. Krishna Kumar, "Reproduction or Change?," 1282.
20. Deshpande, "Pass, Fail, Distinction," 33.
21. Deshpande, "Pass, Fail, Distinction," 33.
22. Deshpande, "Pass, Fail, Distinction," 19.
23. Deshpande, "Pass, Fail, Distinction," 19.
24. Deshpande, "Pass, Fail, Distinction," 34.
25. Deshpande, "Pass, Fail, Distinction," 34.
26. Deshpande, "Pass, Fail, Distinction," 19.
27. Interview with Udhay, June 30, 2011. All subsequent quotes by Udhay are from this interview.
28. Interview with Swaminathan, December 12, 2008. All subsequent quotes by Swaminathan are from this interview.
29. Interview with Subramanian, July 8, 2009. All subsequent quotes by Subramanian are from this interview.
30. Interview with Venkat, May 5, 2009. All subsequent quotes by Venkat are from this interview.
31. Interview with Madhavan, October 12, 2008. All subsequent quotes by Madhavan are from this interview.
32. Shreeharsh Kelkar, "The Elite's Last Stand: Negotiating Toughness and Fairness in the IIT-JEE, 1960–2005," *Engineering Studies* (under review), 17.
33. Sandipan Deb, *The IITians: The Story of a Remarkable Indian Institution and How Its Alumni Are Changing the World* (New Delhi: Viking, 2004), 26.
34. Deb, *The IITians*, 26.
35. In the United States, Asian Americans have been at the forefront of a similar defense of the test as the most fair and objective mechanism of admission and opposition to changing the basis of evaluation. See, for instance, Elizabeth A. Harris and Winnie Hu, "Asian Groups See Bias in Plan to Diversify New York's Elite Schools," *New York Times*, June 5, 2018.
36. Pierre Bourdieu, *Homo Academicus* (Stanford, CA: Stanford University Press, 1984).
37. Interview with Chatterjee, July 2, 2009. All subsequent quotes by Chatterjee are from this interview.
38. Bourdieu and Passeron, *Reproduction in Education*.
39. "IIT Coaching Classes a Rs. 10k cr Industry?," *Times of India*, July 2, 2008.
40. These were terms used in interviews with Madhavan on October 12, 2008, and with Udhay on June 30, 2011.
41. Hemali Chhapial, "Hyderabad Beats Kota in JEE Preparatory Race," *Times of India*, April 9, 2011.
42. Hemali Chhapial, "Hyderabad Beats Kota in JEE Preparatory Race."
43. Maroosha Muzaffar, "Inside Kota's IIT Factories," *India Today*, July 30, 2015.
44. Muzaffar, "Inside Kota's IIT Factories."
45. Muzaffar, "Inside Kota's IIT Factories."

46. A *gurukul* was a type of residential schooling system in ancient India, where students would live near or with the guru (teacher).
47. Muzaffar, "Inside Kota's IIT Factories."
48. Muzaffar, "Inside Kota's IIT Factories."
49. D. Suresh Kumar, "JEE Fails to Get the Best: IIT Dons," *Times of India,* July 31, 2008.
50. Deb, *The IITians,* 53.
51. Interview with Jayaram, March 3, 2008.
52. Interview with Pandiarajan, December 13, 2015.
53. In fact, the school on the IIT Madras campus is a Kendriya Vidyalaya school.
54. "Objectives of KVS," https://kvsangathan.nic.in/about-KVS/our-objective, last updated February 8, 2019.
55. Telangana was carved out of Andhra Pradesh as a separate state in 2014. They share the city of Hyderabad as a capital.
56. Interview with M.S. Ananth, June 17, 2011.
57. Interview with Shankar, March 5, 2009.
58. Interview with Ganapathy, October 17, 2008.
59. Interview with Sudipta, October 15, 2015.
60. Interview with Abbas, April 28, 2016. All subsequent quotes by Abbas are from this interview.
61. "26 / 11" is the term used to refer to the November 26, 2008, attacks on Mumbai by the Islamic militant organization Lashkar-e-Taiba, during which 164 people were killed and 308 wounded.
62. Bourdieu and Passeron, *Reproduction in Education.*

CHAPTER 6 ◉ Contesting Reservations

1. B. R. Ambedkar's last address to India's Constituent Assembly, November 25, 1949, reproduced in *The Wire,* April 14, 2017, https://thewire.in/featured /ambedkar-constitution-assembly-democracy.
2. Quoted in Supreme Court of India, Indra Sawhney etc. v. Union of India and Others, November 16, 1992.
3. Indra Sawhney etc. v. Union of India and Others.
4. Indra Sawhney etc. v. Union of India and Others.
5. Article 15(1) states that "The State shall not discriminate against any citizen on grounds only of religion, race, caste, sex, place of birth or any of them." Article 29(2) states that "No citizen shall be denied admission into any educational institution maintained by the State or receiving aid out of State funds on grounds only of religion, race, caste, language or any of them."
6. The Supreme Court of India, The State of Madras v. Srimathi Champakam Dorairajan, April 9, 1951.
7. Article 46 states that "The State shall promote with special care the educational and economic interests of the weaker sections of the people, and, in particular, of the Scheduled Castes and the Scheduled Tribes, and shall protect them from social injustice and all forms of exploitation."

8. I would like to thank Sandipto Dasgupta for pointing out to me that this is an instance of the tendency in analytical liberal jurisprudence to privilege the formal "equality of opportunity" over the substantive "equality of outcomes."

9. Government of India, Ministry of Law and Justice, The Constitution (First Amendment) Act, 1951, http://legislative.gov.in/constitution-first-amendment-act-1951.

10. The Mandal Commission evolved eleven indicators for determining social and educational backwardness. These were grouped under three broad headings—"Social," "Educational," and "Economic":

A. Social:
   (i) Castes/Classes considered as socially backward by others.
   (ii) Castes/Classes which mainly depend on manual labor for their livelihood.
   (iii) Castes/Classes where at least 25 percent females and 10 percent males above the state average get married at an age below 17 years in rural areas and at least 10 percent females and 5 percent males do so in urban areas.
   (iv) Castes/Classes where participation of females in work is at least 25 percent above the State average.

B. Educational:
   (v) Castes/Classes where the number of children in the age group of 5–15 years who never attended school is at least 25 percent above the State average.
   (vi) Castes/Classes where the rate of student drop-out in the age group of 5–15 years is at least 25 percent above the State average.
   (vii) Castes/Classes amongst whom the proportion of matriculates is at least 25 percent below the State average.

C. Economic:
   (viii) Castes/Classes where the average value of family assets is at least 25 percent below the State average.
   (ix) Castes/Classes where the number of families living in Kuccha houses is at least 25 percent above the State average.
   (x) Castes/Classes where the source of drinking water is beyond half a kilometer for more than 50 percent of the households.
   (xi) Castes/Classes where the number of households having taken consumption loan is at least 25 percent above the State average.

11. Indra Sawhney etc. v. Union of India and Others.

12. Indra Sawhney etc. v. Union of India and Others.

13. The two judgments are C. A. Rajendran v. Union of India, September 29, 1967, and A. Peeriakaruppan etc. v. State of Tamil Nadu, September 23, 1970.

14. Indra Sawhney etc. v. Union of India and Others.

15. Indra Sawhney etc. v. Union of India and Others.

16. Indra Sawhney etc. v. Union of India and Others.

17. I thank Sandipto Dasgupta for this insight into the significance of the shift from abstract to technocratic language.

18. Supreme Court of India, Ashoka Kumar Thakur v. Union of India and Others, April 10, 2008.
19. Ashoka Kumar Thakur v. Union of India and Others.
20. Ashoka Kumar Thakur v. Union of India and Others.
21. Ashoka Kumar Thakur v. Union of India and Others.
22. Indra Sawhney etc. v. Union of India and Others.
23. Indra Sawhney etc. v. Union of India and Others.
24. Pierre Bourdieu, "The Forms of Capital," in *Handbook of Theory and Research for the Sociology of Education,* ed. J. Richardson (Westport, CT: Greenwood Press, 1986), 246.
25. Satish Deshpande, "Caste and Castelessness: Towards a Biography of the 'General Category,'" *Economic and Political Weekly* 48, no. 15 (2013): 36.
26. Deshpande, "Caste and Castelessness," 32.
27. Iyer and Iyengar are the two main Tamil Brahmin subcastes.
28. Interview with Nagan, July 5, 2008. All subsequent quotes by Nagan are from this interview.
29. Interview with Shankar, March 5, 2009. All subsequent quotes by Shankar are from this interview.
30. Interview with Madhavan, October 12, 2008. All subsequent quotes by Madhavan are from this interview.
31. Interview with Venkat, May 5, 2009. All subsequent quotes by Venkat are from this interview.
32. Interview with Swaminathan, December 12, 2008. All subsequent quotes by Swaminathan are from this interview.
33. Sri Venkateswara College of Engineering in Chennai is one of many private engineering colleges that were started in the mid-1980s.
34. P. V. Indiresan and N. C. Nigam, "The Indian Institutes of Technology: Excellence in Peril," in *Higher Education Reform in India: Experience and Perspectives,* ed. Suma Chitnis and Philip G. Altbach (New Delhi: Sage, 1993), 352; emphasis added.
35. Viney Kirpal, Nalini Swamidasan, Amitabha Gupta, and Raj K. Gupta, "Scheduled Caste and Tribe Students in Higher Education: A Study of an IIT," *Economic and Political Weekly* 20, no. 29 (1985): 1238–1248; Rukmini Bhaya Nair, *Technobrat: Culture in a Cybernetic Classroom* (Delhi: HarperCollins, 1997).
36. For work on Dalit educational aspiration and experience of discrimination, see Manuela Ciotti, "In the Past We Were a Bit 'Chamar': Education as a Self- and Community Engineering Process in Northern India," *Journal of the Royal Anthropological Institute* 12, no. 4 (2006): 899–916; Clarinda Still, "'They Have It in Their Stomachs but They Can't Vomit It Up': Dalits, Reservations, and 'Caste Felling' in Rural Andhra Pradesh," *FOCAAL* 65 (2013): 68–79; G. B. Nambissan, "Exclusion and Discrimination in Schools: Experiences of Dalit Children," in *Blocked by Caste: Economic Discrimination in Modern India,* ed. S. Thorat and K. S. Newman (New Delhi: Oxford University Press, 2010), 253–286; S. Desai, C. Adams, and A. Dubey, "Segmented Schooling: Inequalities in Primary Education," in Thorat and Newman, *Blocked by Caste,* 230–252; S. Deshpande and U. Zacharias, eds., *Beyond*

Inclusion: The Practice of Equal Access in Indian Higher Education (New Delhi: Routledge, 2013); Gopal Guru, ed., *Humiliation: Claims and Context* (Oxford: Oxford University Press, 2009); S. Jadhav, D. Mosse, and N. Dostaler, "Minds of Caste: Discrimination and Its Affects," *Anthropology Today* 32, no. 1 (2016): 1–2; Vinoj Kumar, "Dalits Not Welcome in IIT Madras," *Tehelka*, June 16, 2007; Anahita Mukherji, "Degrees of Bias," *Times of India*, September 14, 2014; *The Death of Merit: A Documentary* (Insight Foundation, 2011).

37. Interview with Senthil, May 5, 2009. All subsequent quotes by Senthil are from this interview.

38. Interview with Siva, May 25, 2011. All subsequent quotes by Siva are from this interview.

39. The whiteness literature I build on includes Adrian Piper, "Passing for White, Passing for Black," *Transition* 58 (1992): 4–32; Cheryl I. Harris, "Whiteness as Property," *Harvard Law Review* 106, no. 8 (1993): 1709–1791; Matthew Frye Jacobson, *Whiteness of a Different Color: European Immigrants and the Alchemy of Race* (Cambridge, MA: Harvard University Press, 1999); Matthew Frye Jacobson, *Roots Too: White Ethnic Revival in Post–Civil Rights America* (Cambridge, MA: Harvard University Press, 2005); George Lipsitz, *The Possessive Investment in Whiteness: How White People Profit from Identity Politics* (Philadelphia: Temple University Press, 1998).

40. "Fundas" is IIT lingo for "fundamentals."

41. On the politics of Tamil language, see Sumathi Ramaswamy, *Passions of the Tongue: Language Devotion in Tamil India, 1891–1970* (Berkeley: University of California Press, 1997).

42. Interview with Kartik, June 29, 2011.

43. Interview with Pandiarajan, December 13, 2015. All subsequent quotes by Pandiarajan are from this interview. *Sambar* is a South Indian lentil-and-tamarind-based vegetable stew.

44. *Kalki* and *Ananda Vikatan* were popular Tamil magazines started in 1941 and 1926, respectively.

45. Pankaj Pachauri and Philip George, "Mandal Commission: A Tragic Price," *India Today*, October 15, 1990.

46. V. P. refers to Prime Minister V. P. Singh. Paswan refers to Ram Vilas Paswan, a Dalit politician from Bihar who served as the Union Minister of Labor and Welfare in the V. P. Singh government. Yadav refers to Laloo Prasad Yadav, an OBC politician from Bihar who served as Chief Minister of the state from 1990 to 1997.

47. Harinder Baweja, "Mandal Report Touches a Peculiar Chord among Youth," *India Today*, October 31, 1990.

48. Baweja, "Mandal Report."

49. Pankaj Pachauri and Philip George, "Mandal Commission."

50. Irena Akbar, "25 Years of Mandal Protests," *Indian Express*, October 6, 2015.

51. Christophe Jaffrelot, *India's Silent Revolution: The Rise of the Lower Castes in North India* (New York: Columbia University Press, 2003).

52. The Government of India sought to preclude opposition to Mandal II by creating eight new IITs and doubling the total number of seats. Still, the reservation policy sparked protests within the IITs and other affected institutions.

53. I take this paraphrasing from Deshpande, "Caste and Castelessness," 32.

54. https://www.facebook.com/iamchetanbhagat/posts/mr-modi-to-obama -how-do-you-manage-to-grow-your-country-so-nicely-obama-its-beca /626833767464811/.

55. There are many versions of this joke. One appeared on the same Facebook page of Chetan Bhagat (https://www.facebook.com/iamchetanbhagat/posts /mr-modi-to-obama-how-do-you-manage-to-grow-your-country-so-nicely -obama-its-beca/626833767464811/).

56. Cartoon, *On the Road to Justice* (blog), June 16, 2006, http://indianskoolkids -antireservations.blogspot.com/2006/06/funnyand-satirical.html.

57. "Fun: Good Cartoons on Reservation Issue," *Hyd-Masti*, April 4, 2008, http://www.hyd-masti.com/2008/04/fun-good-cartoons-on-reservation -issue.html.

58. https://www.afaqs.com/advertising/creative_showcase/index.html?id =56296&media=TV.

59. Odile Henry and Mathieu Ferry, "When Cracking the JEE Is Not Enough: Processes of Elimination and Differentiation, from Entry to Placement, in the Indian Institutes of Technology," *South Asia Multidisciplinary Academic Journal* 15 (2017), https://journals.openedition.org/samaj/4291.

60. The social composition of the "general category" is also a hotly debated issue. It is unclear whether OBC and SC/ST applicants who qualify for admission through the "general category" are now relegated to the quota simply because they are eligible. If this is indeed the case, it makes the "general category" a de facto quota for upper castes against the Indra Sawhney ruling.

61. Interview with Udhay, June 20, 2011. All subsequent quotes by Udhay are from this interview.

62. Interview with Sharma, July 14, 2011.

63. Interview with Manikumar, November 6, 2008.

64. Interview with Shekhar, December 20, 2008.

65. Interview with Srikanth, August 10, 2015.

66. Interview with Satish, June 30, 2015. All subsequent quotes by Satish are from this interview.

67. Rohith Vemula was a PhD student and student activist of the Ambedkar Student Association at the University of Hyderabad who committed suicide on January 17, 2016. I address his story at more length in the Conclusion. There were a number of thoughtful journalistic pieces about meritocracy written after Vemula's death. A representative one is Nissim Mannathuk-karen, "Being the Privileged," *The Hindu*, February 6, 2016. Kanhaiya Kumar is a former president of the Jawaharlal Nehru University Students' Union and leader of the All India Students Federation. In February 2016 he was arrested and charged with sedition by the Delhi police for alleg-edly "anti-national" activities. I address his story as more length in the Conclusion.

68. Ghanshyam Shah, "Caste in the Hindutva Lab," *Outlook India,* August 19, 2016; Ananya Vajpeyi, "Caste Conflict: Why the Patels Are Protesting," *Foreign Affairs,* September 29, 2015.

CHAPTER 7 ◉ Brand IIT

1. For exceptions, see Vivek Bald, *Bengali Harlem and the Lost Histories of South Asian America* (Cambridge, MA: Harvard University Press, 2015); Devesh Kapur, *Diaspora, Development, and Democracy: The Domestic Impact of International Migration from India* (Princeton, NJ: Princeton University Press, 2010). For nonscholarly material, see Thenmozhi Soundararajan, Maari Zwick-Maitreyi, and Natasha Dar, *Caste in the United States: A Survey of Caste among South Asian Americans* (New York: Equality Labs, 2018).
2. Kapur, *Diaspora, Development, and Democracy,* 181.
3. Kapur, *Diaspora, Development, and Democracy,* 20–21.
4. Vijay Prashad, *The Karma of Brown Folk* (Minneapolis: University of Minnesota Press, 2000); Bald, *Bengali Harlem;* Sucheta Mazumdar, "The Politics of Religion and National Origin: Rediscovering Hindu Indian Identity in the United States," in *Antinomies of Modernity: Essays on Race, Orient, Nation,* ed. Vasant Kaiwar and Sucheta Mazumdar (Durham, NC: Duke University Press, 2003), 223–257; Sucheta Mazumdar, "Racist Responses to Racism: The Aryan Myth and South Asians in the United States," *South Asia Bulletin* 9, no. 1 (1989): 47–55.
5. C. J. Fuller and Haripriya Narasimhan, *Tamil Brahmans: The Making of a Middle-Class Caste* (Chicago: University of Chicago Press, 2014), 50.
6. Fuller and Narasimhan, *Tamil Brahmans,* 31.
7. Quoted in Fuller and Narasimhan, *Tamil Brahmans,* 50.
8. Fuller and Narasimhan, *Tamil Brahmans,* 55.
9. R. Natarajan, K. Ganesh Babu, and M. S. Ananth, "The Nature and Scope of the Brain-Drain of Engineering Graduates," *International Journal of Engineering Education* 10, no. 1 (1994): 119.
10. David A. Washbrook, "The Maratha Brahmin Model in South India: An Afterword," *Indian Economic and Social History Review* 47, no. 4 (2010): 597–615; Sumit Guha, *Beyond Caste: Identity and Power in South Asia* (Leiden: Brill, 2013).
11. C. J. Fuller and Haripriya Narasimhan, "Information Technology Professionals and the New-Rich Middle Class in Chennai (Madras)," *Modern Asian Studies* 41 (2007): 121–150; C. J. Fuller and Haripriya Narasimhan, "From Landlords to Software Engineers: Migration and Urbanization among Tamil Brahmins," *Comparative Studies in Society and History* 50, no. 1 (2008): 170–196; C. J. Fuller and Haripriya Narasimhan, "Traditional Vocations and Modern Professions among Tamil Brahmans in Colonial and Post-Colonial South India," *Indian Economic and Social History Review* 47, no. 4 (2010): 473–496.
12. Prashad, *The Karma of Brown Folk;* Bald, *Bengali Harlem;* Sucheta Mazumdar, "The Politics of Religion."

13. Kapur, *Diaspora, Development, and Democracy,* 53.
14. Kapur, *Diaspora, Development, and Democracy,* 72.
15. Kapur, *Diaspora, Development, and Democracy,* 120.
16. Kapur, *Diaspora, Development, and Democracy,* 72.
17. Kapur, *Diaspora, Development, and Democracy,* 176.
18. Brett Melendy, *Asians in America: Filipinos, Koreans, and East Indians* (Boston: Twayne, 1977), 186; Bald, *Bengali Harlem;* Prashad, *The Karma of Brown Folk;* Mazumdar, "Racist Responses to Racism."
19. Quoted in Mazumdar, "Racist Responses to Racism," 50.
20. Bald, *Bengali Harlem.*
21. Bald, *Bengali Harlem,* 5.
22. Cheryl Harris, "Whiteness as Property," *Harvard Law Review* 106, no. 8 (1993): 1753.
23. Harris, "Whiteness as Property," 1753.
24. This term comes from George Lipsitz, *The Possessive Investment in Whiteness: How White People Profit from Identity Politics* (Philadelphia: Temple University Press, 1998). See also Walter Johnson, "What Do We Mean When We Say, 'Structural Racism'? A Walk Down Florissant Avenue, Ferguson, Missouri," *Kalfou* 3, no. 1 (Spring 2016): 36–62.
25. Ross Bassett, *The Technological Indian* (Cambridge, MA: Harvard University Press, 2016).
26. Ross Bassett, "Aligning India in the Cold War Era: Indian Technical Elites, the Indian Institute of Technology at Kanpur, and Computing in India and the United States," *Technology and Culture* 50, no. 4 (2009): 783–810; Bassett, "MIT-Trained Swadeshis: MIT and Indian Nationalism, 1880–1947," *Osiris* 24, no. 1 (2009): 212–230; Bassett, *The Technological Indian.*
27. Bassett, *The Technological Indian,* 70–71.
28. Bassett, *The Technological Indian,* 71.
29. Bassett, *The Technological Indian,* 276.
30. See, for instance, Ajay Agrawal, Devesh Kapur, and John McHale, "Brain Drain or Brain Bank? The Impact of Skilled Emigration on Poor-Country Innovation" (National Bureau of Economic Research Working Paper No. 14592, December 2008); Annalee Saxenian, *The New Argonauts: Regional Advantage in a Global Economy* (Cambridge, MA: Harvard University Press, 2007).
31. S. P. Sukhatme and L. Mahadevan, "Brain Drain and the IIT Graduate," *Economic and Political Weekly,* June 18, 1988; Natarajan, Babu, and Ananth, "The Nature and Scope of the Brain-Drain."
32. Stuart Leslie and Robert Kargon, "Exporting MIT: Science, Technology, and Nation-Building in India and Iran," *Osiris* 21, no. 1 (2006): 118.
33. I heard this joke in many of my conversations with IITians.
34. Interview with Chatterjee, July 2, 2009. All subsequent quotes by Chatterjee are from this interview.
35. Interview with Ganapathy, October 17, 2008.
36. Interview with John Cherian, May 20, 1999.
37. Bassett, *The Technological Indian,* 184–185.

38. The first instance of Asian Americans being framed as a successful minority in contrast to other "problem minorities" was William Petterson's "Success Story, Japanese-American Style," *New York Times*, January 9, 1966. Since then, a sizable literature endorsing or challenging this framing has been generated by sociologists, anthropologists, literary scholars, and others.

39. Interview with Udhay, June 30, 2011. All subsequent quotes by Udhay are from this interview.

40. Interview with Prakash, September 25, 2008.

41. Interview with Jayaram, June 21, 2011. All subsequent quotes by Jayaram are from this interview.

42. Interview with Bose, March 20, 2011.

43. Interview with Bhosle, July 16, 2016. All subsequent quotes by Bhosle are from this interview.

44. Interview with Kalyan, June 8, 2016. All subsequent quotes by Kalyan are from this interview.

45. For an academic analysis of the contrast between Silicon Valley and Route 128, see Annalee Saxenian, *Regional Advantage: Culture and Competition in Silicon Valley and Route 128* (Cambridge, MA: Harvard University Press, 1996).

46. Interview with Bansal, June 17, 2016. All subsequent quotes by Bansal are from this interview.

47. There is a vast literature on the myth of the frontier as a site of accumulation. For a recent, evocative instance, see Anna Tsing, "Inside the Economy of Appearances," *Public Culture* 12, no. 1 (Winter 2000): 115–144.

48. Ruth Wilson Gilmore, *Golden Gulag: Prisons, Surplus, Crisis, and Opposition in Globalizing California* (Berkeley: University of California Press, 2007); Mike Davis, *City of Quartz: Excavating the Future in Los Angeles* (New York: Verso, 2006).

49. For an overview of foreign-born entrepreneurs in Silicon Valley, see Annalee Saxenian, *Silicon Valley's New Immigrant Entrepreneurs* (San Francisco: Public Policy Institute of California, 1999); Saxenian, *The New Argonauts*.

50. Quoted in Bassett, *The Technological Indian*, 261–262.

51. Kapur, *Diaspora, Development, and Democracy*, 95.

52. Sandipan Deb, *The IITians: The Story of a Remarkable Indian Institution and How Its Alumni Are Changing the World* (New Delhi: Viking, 2004), 7.

53. Deb, *The IITians*, 7–8.

54. Interview with Parekh, February 25, 2016. All subsequent quotes by Parekh are from this interview.

55. Interview with Parekh, February 25, 2016.

56. "About Us," Pan-IIT USA, https://www.iit.org/page/about-paniit-usa (accessed April 5, 2019).

57. "About IIT," Pan-IIT USA, https://www.iit.org/page/about-iit (accessed April 5, 2019).

58. Interview with Kalyan, June 8, 2016.

59. See, for instance, Sanjay Subrahmanyam, *The Political Economy of Commerce: Southern India, 1500–1650* (Cambridge: Cambridge University Press,

1990); David Rudner, *Caste and Capitalism in Colonial India: The Nattukottai Chettiars* (Berkeley: University of California Press, 1994).

60. Ashish Chadha, "Battle for Brand IIT," *The Hindu*, June 25, 2006.

61. For the relationship between Hindu nationalism, the middle class, and economic liberalization, see Stuart Corbridge and John Harriss, *Reinventing India: Liberalization, Hindu Nationalism, and Popular Democracy* (Cambridge: Polity Press, 2000); Thomas Blom Hansen, *The Saffron Wave: Democracy and Hindu Nationalism in Modern India* (Princeton, NJ: Princeton University Press, 1999); Arvind Rajagopal, *Politics after Television: Religious Nationalism and the Reshaping of the Indian Public* (Cambridge: Cambridge University Press, 2001); Lloyd I. Rudolph and Susanne Hoeber Rudolph, *In Pursuit of Lakshmi: The Political Economy of the Indian State* (Delhi: Orient Longman, 1987); Nikita Sud, *Liberalization, Hindu Nationalism, and the State: A Biography of Gujarat* (New Delhi: Oxford University Press, 2012).

62. Interview with Sandeep, October 10, 2008.

63. Shashi Tharoor, "Looking to the Future with Brand IIT," *Times of India*, December 30, 2006.

64. Interview with Ganapathy, October 17, 2008.

65. "IIT-ians Have Created a Global Brand," *Rediff*, December 18, 2008.

66. Home page, Entrepreneurship Cell, http://www.ecell.iitm.ac.in/ (accessed April 5, 2019).

67. K. Sreedevi, "Pan IIT 2008: Bonding Back with the Best," *Sify*, December 19, 2008.

68. "Raghuram Rajan Warns against Going Back to 'Old System,'" *Hindu*, December 20, 2008.

69. Interview with Kalyanaraman, December 10, 2008.

70. Interview with former IIT directors, December 19, 2008.

71. Pan-IIT Alumni India, IIT *Alumni Impact Study* (Mumbai: IIT Bombay, 2008).

72. Interview with Venkatakrishnan, July 18, 2008.

73. Interview with Vishwanath, December 20, 2008.

74. Interview with Madhavan, August 5, 2015.

75. Shreeya Sinha, "Indian Leader Narendra Modi, Once Unwelcome in U.S., Gets Rock Star Reception," *New York Times*, September 27, 2014; Vivian Yee, "At Madison Square Garden, Chants, Cheers, and Roars for Modi," *New York Times*, September 28, 2014.

Conclusion

1. Jyotirao Govindrao Phule was a nineteenth-century writer and anticaste social reformer from Maharashtra. Ajantha Subramanian, "For This Aspiring Carl Sagan, Merit Wasn't Upper Caste Property," *Times of India*, January 24, 2016; Ajantha Subramanian, "An Anatomy of the Caste Culture at IIT Madras," *Open Magazine*, June 11, 2015; Ajantha Subramanian, "When Students Struggle, They Win: Caste at the Heart of Indian Engineering," *Counterpunch*, June 10, 2015.

2. Aftab Alam, "Growing Intolerance Is Threatening Free Inquiry and Open Debate in India's Universities," *The Wire*, April 10, 2017; G. Arunima, "The Ongoing Attack on JNU's Democratic Academic Structures," *The Wire*, January 1, 2017; Thomas Crowley, "Modi's Student Crackdown," *Jacobin Magazine*, March 2, 2016.

3. I thank Alf Gunvald Nilsen for pointing me to Stuart Hall's work on authoritarian populism and to his own use of Hall to analyze Modi's India. See Alf Gunvald Nilsen, "An Authoritarian India Is Beginning to Emerge," *The Wire*, August 31, 2018; Alf Gunvald Nilsen, "From Inclusive Neoliberalism to Authoritarian Populism: Trajectories of Change in the World's Largest Democracy," in *State of Democracy: Essays on the Life and Politics of Contemporary India*, ed. Manas Ray (Delhi: Primus Books, 2019).

4. Stuart Hall et al., *Policing the Crisis: Mugging, the State, and Law and Order* (London: Macmillan, 1978); Stuart Hall, "Popular-Democratic versus Authoritarian Populism," in *Marxism and Democracy*, ed. Alan Hunt (London: Lawrence and Wishart, 1980), 157–185; Stuart Hall, "Authoritarian Populism: A Reply to Jessop et al.," *New Left Review* 151 (May–June 1985): 115–124.

5. "Dalit Family Stripped, Beaten as 'Gau Raksha' Vigilantism Continues," *The Wire*, July 13, 2016; Delna Abraham and Ojaswi Rao, "86% Killed in Cow-Related Violence since 2010 Are Muslim, 97% Attacks after Modi Govt Came to Power," *Hindustan Times*, July 16, 2017; Rohan Venkataramakrishnan, "How Real Is the Threat of Love Jihad?," *Scroll.in*, August 14, 2014; Vidhi Doshi, "'How Can They Hate Us So Much?' Asks Father of Muslim Teen Brutally Killed in Attack on Train in India," *Washington Post*, June 24, 2017; Kavita Krishnan, "Who Creates a Conducive Climate for Assassinations?," *The Wire*, September 12, 2017.

6. Kevin Harris and Ben Scully, "A Hidden Counter-Movement? Precarity, Politics, and Social Protection before and beyond the Neoliberal Era," *Theory and Society* 44, no. 5 (2015): 415–444; Sanjay Ruparelia, "India's New Rights Agenda: Genesis, Promises, Risks," *Pacific Affairs* 86, no. 3 (2013): 569–590.

7. Aradhana Sharma, "State Transparency after the Neoliberal Turn: The Politics, Limits, and Paradoxes of India's Right to Information Law," *Political and Legal Anthropology Review* 36, no. 2 (2013): 308–325; Anand Vaidya, "The Origin of the Forest, Private Property, and the State: The Political Life of India's Forest Rights Act" (PhD diss., Harvard University, 2014); Alf Gunvald Nilsen, *Adivasis and the State: Subalternity and Citizenship in India's Bhil Heartland* (Delhi: Cambridge University Press, 2018); Alf Gunvald Nilsen and Kenneth Bo Nielsen, "Social Movements, State Formation and Democracy in India: An Introduction," in *Social Movements and the State in India: Deepening Democracy?*, ed. K. B. Nielsen and A. G. Nilsen (London: Palgrave, 2016), 1–24.

8. For more on this notion of inclusive neoliberalism, see Arne Ruckert, "The Poverty Reduction Strategy Paper of Honduras and the Transformations of Neoliberalism," *Canadian Journal of Latin American and Caribbean Studies* 35, no. 70 (2010): 113–139; Kenneth Bo Nielsen and Alf Gunvald Nilsen, eds., *Social Movements and the State in India: Deepening*

Democracy? (London: Palgrave, 2016); Nilsen, "Inclusive Neoliberalism." For more on predatory growth under the UPA regime, see Amit Bhaduri, "Predatory Growth," *Economic and Political Weekly* 43, no. 16 (2008): 10–14; Kathy Le Mons Walker, "Neoliberalism on the Ground in Rural India: Predatory Growth, Agrarian Crisis, Internal Colonization, and the Intensification of Class Struggle," *Journal of Peasant Studies* 35, no. 4 (2008): 557–620.

9. Manali Desai, "Rethinking Hegemony: Caste, Class, and Political Subjectivities among Informal Workers in Ahmedabad," in *New Subaltern Politics: Rethinking Hegemony and Resistance in Contemporary India*, ed. A. G. Nilsen and S. Roy (Delhi: Oxford University Press, 2015), 54–75; Achin Vanaik, *The Rise of Hindu Authoritarianism: Secular Claims, Communal Realities* (London: Verso Books, 2017); E. Sridharan, "Behind Modi's Victory," *Journal of Democracy* 25, no. 4 (2014): 20–33; Nitasha Kaul, "Rise of the Political Right in India: Hindutva-Development Mix, Modi Myth, and Dualities," *Journal of Labour and Society* 20, no. 4 (2017): 523–548; Christophe Jaffrelot, "The Modi-centric BJP 2014 Election Campaign: New Techniques and Old Tactics," *Contemporary South Asia* 23, no. 2 (2015): 151–166; Subir Sinha, "Fragile Hegemony: Modi, Social Media, and Competitive Electoral Populism in India," *International Journal of Communication* 11 (2017): 4158–4180.

10. Radhika Desai, "A Latter-Day Fascism?," *Economic and Political Weekly* 49, no. 35 (2014): 48–58; Vanaik, *The Rise of Hindu Authoritarianism.*

11. Lucas Chancel and Thomas Piketty, "Indian Income Inequality, 1922–2015: From British Raj to Billionaire Raj?" (WID.world working paper, World Inequality Lab, 2017), http://wid.world/wp-content/uploads/2017/12/Chancel Piketty2017WIDworld.pdf, cited in Nilsen, "Inclusive Neoliberalism."

12. I take the term "elite revolt" from Stuart Corbridge and John Harriss, who elaborate the dialectic between subaltern mobilization and elite backlash in their political history of modern India, *Reinventing India: Liberalization, Hindu Nationalism, and Popular Democracy* (Cambridge: Polity Press, 2000).

13. Antonio Olivo, "High-Skilled Indian Workers Rally for Trump's Merit-Based Immigration Plan," *Washington Post*, February 3, 2018.

14. William Petterson, "Success Story, Japanese-American Style," *New York Times*, January 9, 1966.

15. Santosh Mehrotra, "Well-Being and Caste in Uttar Pradesh: Why UP Is Not like Tamil Nadu," *Economic and Political Weekly* 41, no. 40 (2006): 4261–4271; Craig Jeffrey, Patricia Jeffery, and Robin Jeffery, "Dalit Revolution? New Politicians in Uttar Pradesh," *Journal of Asian Studies* 67, no. 4 (2008): 1365–1396; Nathaniel Roberts, *To Be Cared For: The Power of Conversion and Foreignness of Belonging in an Indian Slum* (Berkeley: University of California Press, 2016); Divya Bharathi, *Kakkoos* (Madurai, India: Left Side Media, 2017).

16. Anupama Rao, "Violence and Humanity; Or, Vulnerability as Political Subjectivity," *Social Research* 78, no. 2 (Summer 2011): 607–632; Anand Tel-

tumbde, *Republic of Caste: Thinking Equality in the Time of Neoliberal Hindutva* (Delhi: Navayana Press, 2018).

17. *World Inequality Report 2018*, Executive Summary (Paris: World Inequality Lab, 2018), https://wir2018.wid.world/files/download/wir2018-full-report -english.pdf.

18. Ashwini Kulkarni, "Modi Government's Skewed Farm Sector Priorities Continue to Cause Farmer Distress," *The Wire*, June 15, 2017; Sukanya Shantha, "Blisters on Feet but Hopes on Land Rights Writ Large on Faces, Protesting Farmers Leave Mumbai," *The Wire*, March 13, 2018; Damayantee Dhar, "Dalits in Gujarat Find New Voice as Yatra Wends Its Way to Una," *The Wire*, August 9, 2016; Damayantee Dhar, "As Azadi Kooch Comes to a Close, Dalits in Gujarat Claim Land They Were Allotted 50 Years Ago," *The Wire*, July 19, 2017; Sudha Pai, "The BJP Is Losing the Support of Dalits in the Hindi Heartland," *The Wire*, April 4, 2018; Kancha Ilaiah Shepherd, "A 'Dalit Spring' Is on the Horizon," *Al Jazeera*, April 8, 2018; Danish Raza, "From Dalit Activist to Gujarat MLA: Tracking Jignesh Mevani's Journey," *Hindustan Times*, January 20, 2018; Aditya Nigam, "Gujarat 2017: The Meaning of Jignesh Mevani," *The Wire*, December 18, 2017.

Acknowledgments

ARGUMENTS ABOUT INNATE intelligence are certainly not unique to India. The world over, we find the impulse to naturalize intellectual ability and locate it in certain bodies and not others. In India, as elsewhere, assumptions about academic success and failure acquire the weight of common sense, difficult to budge and reinforced over time and by habit. It is striking how easily we obscure material worlds of opportunity and disadvantage from view, in the process transforming prejudice into discernment, exclusion into selectivity, and history into nature. At elite institutions like Harvard, the drive to identify the exceptional student, to find the diamond in the rough, and to deploy the language of ranking are ubiquitous practices. We trade in the currency of brilliance and exceptionalism, honing our diagnostic powers to a fine art. Most of us are aware that our students come from wildly varied circumstances, yet we continue to judge them using utterly decontextualized measures of merit. When we are pushed, we acknowledge that institutional stratification and its associated hierarchies of value are better explained by uneven resources than by the concentration of brainpower. And yet institutional rationales make it almost impossible to act on that knowledge. To keep in view the structural shaping of educational trajectories, to fully acknowledge that our intellectual endowments are gifts of society and not nature, to recognize a glowing résumé as an accident of history, would undercut the very notion of excellence. Instead, we herald the test score, the institutional brand,

357

the prize-winning academic monograph as markers of distinction, intellectual worth, and market value that tell a story of individual achievement and intrinsic merit.

This book expresses my disquiet in the face of such impulses to naturalize merit by writing out histories of privilege. My own professional trajectory is a case in point. As the beneficiary of state, caste, and family, I can hardly chalk up my academic successes to mere talent. The same is true of this book. As the product of innumerable conversations and acts of generosity both within and outside the academy, and of the conceptual paths hewn by other scholars of caste, race, and democracy, it would be absurd to claim this monograph as individual intellectual property. I have many, many people to thank for making this book a reality. It gestated for far too long and accrued many debts along the way. In part, it was difficult to bring to a close because the battle over meritocracy is a live issue in India and the United States. The steady stream of news about caste and racial discrimination, and legal challenges to affirmative action, make the subject of this book an ongoing story. Happily, over the long course of this book's development, I have met a growing number of colleagues working on merit and caste in India and on the intersections of race and caste. It has been my privilege to exchange ideas with them about the everyday violence of caste in India and about the resonances and connections between histories of caste and race.

The research and writing for this book were supported by the National Humanities Center, Harvard's Weatherhead Center for International Affairs, and the Harvard Asia Center. The decade of work resulted in articles along the way. The Introduction and Chapters 1, 3, 5, and 7 build on ideas first discussed in "Making Merit: The Indian Institutes of Technology and the Social Life of Caste," *Comparative Studies in Society and History* 57, no. 2 (2015): 291–322. Chapter 6 builds on ideas first discussed in "Meritocracy and Democracy: Indian Reservations and the Politics of Caste," in "Interrogating 'Diversity,'" special issue, *Public Culture* (2019).

The historical research for this book was done in the Tamil Nadu Archives. I thank the archive staff for their help in locating the necessary documents. The ethnographic work depended on the generosity of the many faculty, students, and alumni of the IITs. Two directors of

IIT Madras, M. S. Ananth and Bhaskar Ramamurthy, granted me interviews and access to the institution's archives and facilities. The Alumni Office, the Placement Office, and a number of other faculty and administrators engaged my questions in interviews and more informally. The Alumni Office also let me attend all the sessions of the 2008 Pan-IIT alumni conference. Most of all, I am grateful to the many alumni and students who granted me interviews that often required more than one session. This book would not have been possible without their patience in the face of my endless questions.

Thanks to invitations from colleagues, I have benefited from sharing this research at a number of different venues, including the Affirmative Action conference hosted by the South Asia Research and Information Institute at Southern Methodist University; the American Institute of Indian Studies' fiftieth-year conference in New Delhi; Brandeis University's Center for Global Development and Sustainability; Brown University's Center for Contemporary South Asia; Columbia University's South Asia Center; the Democracy and Its Trajectories conference at the University of Bergen, Norway; Harvard's Center for History and Economics; Harvard's Weatherhead Center for International Affairs; the Indian Institute of Technology, Delhi; the Indian Institute of Technology, Madras; the Interrogating Diversity conference at the University of Michigan–Ann Arbor; Jawaharlal Nehru University's conference on Sociology of Elites in Contemporary India; the Massachusetts Institute of Technology's Department of Anthropology; the Nehru Memorial Museum and Library in New Delhi; the University of California–Davis's Department of Anthropology; the University of Michigan–Ann Arbor's South Asia Institute; the University of Pennsylvania's Department of Anthropology; and the University of Wisconsin–Madison's South Asia Center.

My thinking and writing were vastly improved by the productive and challenging feedback from friends and colleagues, including Aniket Aga, Lori Allen, Nikhil Anand, Anjali Arondekar, Senthil Babu, Bernard Bate, Susan Bayly, Naor Ben-Yehoyada, Milind Brahme, Vincent Brown, Julie Byrne, Glenda Carpio, Partha Chatterjee, Sandipto Dasgupta, Manali Desai, Ashwini Deshpande, Satish Deshpande, Namita Dharia, Jatin Dua, Mandakini Dubey, Anthony Farley, Elizabeth

Ferry, Kathinka Froystad, Chris Fuller, V. Geetha, David Gilmartin, Maria Grahn, Matthew Hull, Surinder Jodhka, Jeffrey Kahn, Kalpana Karunakaran, Sudipta Kaviraj, Dolly Kikon, Kavita Krishnan, Ekin Kurtic, Smita Lahiri, Michele Lamont, Amulya Mandava, Townsend Middleton, Lisa Mitchell, Balmurli Natrajan, Jules Naudet, Kenneth Bo Nielsen, Alf Gunvald Nilsen, Surajit Nundy, S. Palaniappan, Geeta Patel, Norbert Peabody, Sunil Purushotham, Lucinda Ramberg, Mahesh Rangarajan, Anupama Rao, Raka Ray, Srila Roy, Balaji Sampath, Rajesh Sampath, Andrew Shryock, Mrinalini Sinha, Subir Sinha, Ajay Skaria, Amy Slaton, Smriti Srinivas, Rachel St. John, Banu Subramaniam, Narendra Subramanian, Nandini Sundar, Abha Sur, Deborah Thomas, Anand Vaidya, Christine Walley, Kath Weston, David Wood, Dilan Yildirim, and Emrah Yildiz. I am especially indebted to my writing group partners—Vincent Brown, Glenda Carpio, and Rachel St. John—for being the perfect comrades-in-arms through the writing of the second book. Another group that I could not have done without is the Political Anthropology Working Group at Harvard, which has been a cornerstone of my Harvard experience. Our biweekly discussions of works in progress have been some of the most generous and stimulating instances of intellectual exchange I have ever encountered. As I was wrapping up the book in fall 2018, I taught an undergraduate seminar on race and caste. The students in that class and the teaching fellow, Amulya Mandava, were a real inspiration. They pushed me to work through the thickets of jargon that are a staple of academic argumentation and convey in clearer terms the significance of understanding social stratification in place and across time. I thank them for their commitment to a difficult course and for challenging me in turn.

This book straddled two stints at Harvard, the first before tenure and the second after. Over this stretch of time, Harvard Anthropology went through many changes. The departure of three dear friends, Asad Ahmed, Engseng Ho, and Smita Lahiri, makes me wistful for the department that could have been. It has also been devastating to lose Mary Steedly, who was my most trusted senior mentor. Despite these losses, my strengthening relationships with newer and older colleagues, the everyday support of our fantastic staff, and my incredible students have made the department an intellectual and professional home for me. Harvard can certainly be frustrating and alienating, which makes one cherish the niches of friendship and belonging that much more.

It was a pleasure to work with Sharmila Sen, Heather Hughes, and Stephanie Vyce at Harvard University Press. I am grateful to my editor, Sharmila, for her honesty and wise counsel. Pitching the book to her was an uncanny experience because of how intuitively she understood its arguments. It made the decision to go with Harvard remarkably easy.

It is difficult to know how to properly thank family. My in-laws, Manuelita and Willie Brown, have been wonderfully supportive and generous with their warm and welcoming California home. My husband, Vincent Brown, has been such a seamless part of my life that it is hard to even step back enough to write this. We are coming up on a quarter century together of school, travel, jobs, kids, and all the rest in between. He has been my intellectual sounding board, co-teacher, co-parent, fellow hater of the New England cold, and fellow dreamer of other worlds. I am so lucky to have a daily companion who both challenges and grounds me. Over the past decade of research and writing, our daughters, Zareen and Anisa, have grown into curious, funny, passionate girls, who ask difficult questions and don't accept easy answers. Their fierce sense of justice in the face of unfairness and inhumanity gives me great hope that the world they make will be far saner and more equitable than the one we bequeath them.

I dedicate this book to my parents, V. Vasanthi Devi and K. S. Subramanian. Throughout my life, they have offered me unconditional support. Now with children of my own, I marvel at their unwavering faith in my judgment, even when I embarked on adventures that were so far from their own experiences. I hope that as my daughters grow, I too will have the faith and trust to know when to let them go. My parents were also instrumental in the making of this book. The year spent in Chennai for research and all the shorter stints since would have been impossible without them. They helped with everything from apartment and school hunting to taking care of our daughters. My mother, a historian by training who spent most of her life as a university administrator and an activist for education reform, introduced me to invaluable contacts for my research and kept me informed about the inequities of Indian education. My father, an Indian civil servant who became an international development practitioner before retiring and taking on a third career as a translator, read the whole manuscript with his discerning eye and offered critical suggestions. I have lived oceans away for most of my adult life, but they have always been there when I needed them. This book is a tribute to their support and care.

Index